INSIDE THE CRIMINAL JUSTICE ORGANIZATION

AN ANTHOLOGY FOR PRACTITIONERS

First Edition

Edited by

MARY ELLEN MASTRORILLI

Boston University

cognella® | ACADEMIC PUBLISHING

Bassim Hamadeh, CEO and Publisher
Janny Li, Acquisitions Editor
Susana Christie, Project Editor
Jackie Bignotti, Production Artist
Danielle Gradisher, Licensing Associate
Natalie Piccotti, Director of Marketing
Kassie Graves, Vice President of Editorial
Jamie Giganti, Director of Academic Publishing

Cover image Copyright © 2016 iStockphoto LP/KatarzynaBialasiewicz

Printed in the United States of America

ISBN: 978-1-5165-2992-6 (pbk) / 978-1-5165-2993-3 (br)

cognella® | ACADEMIC PUBLISHING

INSIDE THE CRIMINAL JUSTICE ORGANIZATION

AN ANTHOLOGY FOR PRACTITIONERS

CONTENTS

SECTION VI ORGANIZATIONAL POWER, ORGANIZATIONAL CHANGE   256

INTRODUCTION TO ORGANIZATIONAL THEORY, ORGANIZATIONAL STRUCTURE

INTRODUCTION

The mere mention of the term *criminal justice* evokes passion, curiosity, and debate. As a result, those of us who study criminal justice do so either to enter the profession, to advance in it, or to understand its inner workings. We want to comprehend the criminal mind and find solutions to nagging crime problems. Some of us aspire to be change agents heeding a call for criminal justice reform. Whatever one's reason to study criminal justice, we cannot ignore the importance of the criminal justice organization.

Think for a moment about what a criminal justice organization does. For example, it houses prisoners, processes criminal proceedings, advocates for victims, deploys law enforcement officers, oversees the supervision of offenders, and keeps our airports and international borders secure. For the system to be effective, organizations need to operate efficiently and with integrity, be transparent to engender public trust, and use tax dollars wisely by implementing programs and policies based on evidence, not ideology or instinct.

With all of this in mind, the goal of this anthology is to introduce you to the inner workings of the criminal justice system. To understand the nature of criminal justice, one needs to appreciate the role organizations play in carrying out public safety, beyond the everyday tasks and responsibilities of police officers, correction officers, prosecutors, judges, and other criminal justice actors. Organizations bring structure, clarity, and unity of purpose to the pursuit of vital goals and objectives.

The first two readings in Section I address organizational theory and structure. Students of criminal justice sometimes chafe at the thought of learning theory. They might feel it has no role in their day-to-day tasks or that it is too abstract to have any relevancy in the field. However, theory is important quite simply because it explains how something works. If you aspire to lead or are currently leading a criminal justice organization, it behooves you to understand the theories of what makes an organization tick. Theory and practice are closely related. For example, let's do a thought experiment. Imagine you subscribe to Theory X, which states that workers are lazy and need constant supervision. How would your organization operate and be structured? Then flip your perspective to Theory Y, that employees are inherently motivated to be productive and dedicated to their work. Would your organization look, feel, and operate differently? It surely would. Theory matters.

ORGANIZING CRIMINAL JUSTICE

RICHARD KANIA

The "O" in LODESTAR and the first "O" in POSDCORB both stand for "organizing." Organizing the work force is one of the essential responsibilities of a criminal justice manager. In Chapter 1 we considered how the study of organization and management has been complicated by popular misunderstandings of the key terms. It is easy to limit the conceptualization of "organization" to only its corporate-entity meaning, a synonym for "agency" (e.g., the organization, as in the FBI), thereby ignoring its process meaning (e.g., organization is the process of arranging and structuring cooperative human effort). The study of "organization" is not the study of an "organization" but the science of how organizations are best organized, structured, and arranged.

Often people join organizations and function within them with the assumption that they always have been as they are—that their structure is "set in stone" and immutable. This is absolutely false. Agency managers have both the authority (subject to laws) and the responsibility to alter and modify organizational arrangements to respond to new demands and changes in the work environment.

BUREAUCRACIES

Most modern criminal justice agencies are bureaucracies. In the course of human history a criminal justice bureaucracy is a relatively new concept, not yet 400 years old. Until the time of Cardinal Richelieu in France (1585–1642), there were no governmental or criminal justice bureaucracies in Europe. The Roman Catholic

Church, a large and widely dispersed organization, did have a system of self-governance that approximated a bureaucracy, and Richelieu applied many of those concepts to French government. He selected government officials on the basis of objective merit, naming judges who were formally trained in law to replace some of the feudal nobles who had been judges by birthright. By the time of Emperor Napoleon Bonaparte (1769–1821), France possessed an advanced governmental bureaucracy that included the management of the courts, the police, and the prisons by trained, merit-selected officials. The occupying French forces replaced the governing institutions of conquered nations with bureaucrats trained by the French. The consequence was the rapid spread of bureaucracy across Europe in the first years of the nineteenth century. Even the final, total defeat of the French in 1815 did not set back the progress of bureaucracy as an institution of governance in Europe. In the German states it was especially successful in taking hold.

Bureaucracy therefore is an essential element to consider as we study organization in contemporary criminal justice organizations. German scholar Max Weber was the first to recognize and examine the key features of a modern **bureaucracy**. Nicely summarized by Sam Souryal (1995: 10–11), its features include:

- a system of fixed jurisdictions
- enumerated tasks and duties
- predetermined goals and objectives
- explicit rules and procedures
- integration of the labors of large numbers of people
- hierarchical system of authority (chain of command)
- delegation of authority with supervised span of control
- career officials (bureaucrats)
- probationary appointments
- fixed salaries and benefits
- in-service training
- code of discipline
- information systems of internal communication, written records, and files

Maximilian Carl Emil Weber: Max Weber (1864–1920) was a German social scientist credited with being one of the founders of both sociology and public administration. Although best known today as a scholar and professor, he was active in German politics after World War I and served on the commission that drafted the Weimar Constitution.

Weber was a prolific writer on a wide range of subjects. His last work was *Economy and Society* (1922), published posthumously. Among his most important theoretical contributions

en.wikipedia.com

Max Weber was a German social philosopher who approached the study of bureaucracy both historically and analytically, identifying within it the features that have given it its great strength in public service. He also studied the origins and exercise of noncoercive power as an aspect of leadership.

were his analysis of power and authority and his detailed explanation of bureaucracy. He employed the concept of the **ideal type** as an explanatory device, and his description of bureaucracy was an example of an ideal type. In his day the concept of bureaucracy was seen as a positive development, as a superior way of managing and conducting public affairs. Its dependence upon merit selection of public officials was a major improvement on earlier ways of appointing government officials from the petty nobility.

When Weber wrote about "bureaucracy," he introduced us to some of the key organizational principles of modern bureaucratic organizations:

1. fixed jurisdictional areas

2. hierarchal principle

3. documentation (the files)

4. trained office management

5. career commitment (official duties, a "vocation")

6. official, stable learnable rules.

Some of the elements of bureaucracy had their conceptual origins in earlier ideas. A system of fixed jurisdictions, enumerated tasks and duties, and predetermined goals and objectives are aspects of "the division of labor," attributed first to Adam Smith (1776) and a key feature of the scientific managerial principles of Henri Fayol.

Hierarchal arrangements have been part of human social structure since ancient times. The delegation of authority with supervised span of control also is quite ancient, being a feature of armies in the earliest historical records. But there were new features to be found in bureaucracy. The merit selection of career officials, chosen objectively for their educational preparations, talents, and skills; initially giving probationary appointments; and entitling them to fixed salaries and benefits all were original ideas. The keeping of comprehensive files, the establishment of rules and procedures for the conduct of the work, and the system of internal discipline required to follow them all were new as well. Bureaucratic work ceased to be the responsibility of an individual practitioner and became instead the responsibility of the office he or she occupied. In this way an incumbent in the office could share the duties, responsibilities, and records of the office with associates and subordinates, and pass them on to a successor.

In Weber's mind, bureaucracy was the solution to many problems of governance and human organization. Today, however, bureaucracy is seen by many as a problem. Bureaucracy has developed a reputation for being cumbersome, slow, inefficient, and officious.

Box 1 Asterix the Gaul versus Bureaucracy

The French, who did so much to spread bureaucracy across Europe, often ridicule their own bureaucrats. The popular French-Belgian cartoon character Asterix must deal with the entrenched and unresponsive bureaucracy as one of the most difficult of *Les Douze Travaux d'Astérix [The Twelve Labors of Asterix]*, a parody of the "Twelve Labors of Hercules." In his eighth labor Asterix must secure "Permit A-38," contending with a multitude of bureaucrats and offices in an almost hopeless effort to secure this document. He only does so by playing the bureaucratic game against the bureaucrats themselves, demanding from them an imaginary permit to which he claims an entitlement.

While bureaucracy has become tainted by its abuses, done right, it still works better than most means for managing a large organization. Elliott Jaques wrote "In Praise of Hierarchy" as a defense of this essential aspect of bureaucracy (1990), yet Jaques too identifies real problems in hierarchal arrangements:

1. There are too many layers and too much distance between managers and labor, poor communication, deflection of responsibility, stress and conflict.

2. Mid-level managers rarely add to the productivity of their line subordinates; and even can reduce its value.

3. Bureaucracies often play into the nasty aspects of human behavior, greed, insensitivity, selfish careerism, unhealthy competition.

Jaques finds that hierarchy, like bureaucracy, when done right, works well. Both responsibility and accountability must be defined unambiguously. Someone must be held accountable for each of the tasks assigned to the organization—both for doing them and for seeing that they are being done. The focus must be on getting the job done; exercising authority is a very distant secondary aspect. If getting the job done can be made easier by distributing authority, then that is the way to go; if centralization gets more done, then centralize. However, "group decisions" must still be the manager's decision. The manager is responsible for buying into the decision, or into the decision-making process. To make **hierarchy** (which arranges the performers of tasks in a ranked or graduated series) actually work, several powers must be vested in the leadership:

1. The manager needs to retain the right to veto the employment or placement of any person not up the standards of the organization or of the tasks to be performed.

2. The manager needs to have the right to make work assignments.

3. The manager needs the power to conduct performance appraisals and to allocate or withhold rewards based on them; not just to make inconsequential recommendations.

4. The manager needs the authority to initiate removal procedures for nonfunctional or low-productivity staff.

Organizational Principles and the Courts: There are organizations that do not fit the bureaucratic pattern well (for example, the courts). Court officials are elected in many of the states, both judges and clerks of court. The courts are a meeting place for multiple bureaucracies with competing goals and objectives. Here the court staff, the police, the prosecutor, the public defender, and representatives of the probation office meet to determine complex questions of law, innocence or guilt, and consequences of convictions. Each of these represented bureaucracies has a different interest in the case before the court. Nevertheless, leaders in the judiciary have made significant organizational improvements in the courts. Among the most noteworthy of these court reformers was Arthur Vanderbilt.

Arthur T. Vanderbilt: In the area of the courts, major organizational innovations were introduced by Arthur Vanderbilt (1888–1957). A New Jersey native and politically active community leader, Vanderbilt helped bring about major constitutional changes in the organization of the New Jersey court system, and thereafter became its Chief Justice (1948–1957). In that capacity he also served as the director of the newly created Administrative Office of the Courts, the first such entity in the United States. Previously Vanderbilt was the president of the American Bar Association (1937–1938). He had served as Dean of New York University Law School and founded the Institute of Judicial Administration at New York University in 1950. He was a strong advocate of states establishing court administration agencies in a period when judges expected virtual autonomy in running their courts (Vanderbilt II, 1976). He wrote *Minimum Standards of Judicial Administration* (1949) (standardizing court practices) and *The Challenge of Legal Reform* (1955). Today his ideas form the basis of modern court administration. State agencies assure that their courts are consistent and uniform in their documentation, record-keeping, and routine procedural matters. Judges get training on routine judicial administration upon entering office.

Organizational Principles and Law Enforcement: Introducing the concepts of organizational theory to law enforcement were Leonhard F. Fuld, August Vollmer, and Orlando W. Wilson. Fuld penned the first American book on police administration (1910), intended primarily for police executives. Vollmer and Wilson were mentor and protégé. Together these two men substantially altered the path of law enforcement in the United States in the first half of the twentieth century. Both were prolific writers on police organization and administration (Vollmer, 1936; Wilson, 1950). Raymond Fosdick (1920), Elmer Graper (1921), and Bruce P. Smith (1940) were other pioneers in the application of scientific management principles to law enforcement.

August Vollmer: The first law enforcement position held by August Vollmer (1876–1955) was as an elected town marshal in 1907. Vollmer had earned a national reputation as an innovator and publicist of new ideas while serving as police chief in Berkeley, California. He was an advocate of the selection of college-educated men for police work. In an age when many police departments still did not even require a high school diploma, the need for college-educated police was not immediately appreciated.

Often called the "father of modern law enforcement," Vollmer reorganized the Berkeley Police Department, created new units within it, and increased its capacities with motor vehicles outfitted with one-way radios that could monitor the police dispatchers (but could not at that time reply to them). Never feeling bound by the old ways of doing things, he was willing to experiment with organizational experiments. He wrote many articles about his innovations, and in 1936 published a compilation of his progressive ideas in *The Police and Modern Society*.

en.wikipedia.org

August Vollmer was a leading American law enforcement innovator and reformer. He introduced many ideas into policing we now take for granted: patrol cars, radio dispatch, MO files, and criminal profiling among them. He also recruited and hired the first college-educated police officers, and helped create criminal justice education in the United States.

Orlando W. Wilson: Orlando W. Wilson (1900–1972) was a police chief and educator who was instrumental in applying managerial concepts to police agencies. His book, *Police Administration*, is a classic in the application of scientific management concepts to police practices. Wilson was one of the first college-educated police officers (a street cop, not a college-educated police executive).

Wilson was hired by another great leader in law enforcement, August Vollmer, to be an officer in the Berkeley Police Department in 1921. He earned his bachelor's degree while a police officer and then took his first chief of police post in Fullerton, California, in 1925. In later years he directed police departments in Wichita, Kansas, and Chicago, Illinois, and was involved in public safety in Italy and Germany in the war-time occupations of those nations.

Wilson created the School of Criminology at U.C.-Berkeley in 1950 and served as its first dean. As a police manager and as an academic, he sought to apply the basic principles of good management to law enforcement and did much to create the emphasis on "professionalism" in policing that has characterized its development in the last half century (R.C. McLaren, 1977; in Wilson and McLaren, 1977).

Bruce P. Smith: Bruce Smith (1892–1955) was a leading advocate of **economies of scale**, arguing that the consolidation of smaller police forces into larger ones, replacing sheriffs with state police, and other centralizing efforts would provide for greater efficiency in law enforcement. He helped develop the Uniform Crime Reports (UCR) for the International Association of Chiefs of Police (IACP) and the FBI (Wilson, 1956: 235). His book, *Police Systems in the United States* (1940), was the peak expression of the reform ideal merging with the rising focus on better managerial practices.

Organizational Principles and Corrections: Leaders in correctional management began making contributions to the better organization of prisons and jails in the nineteenth century. Such early leaders as John Howard, Jeremy Bentham, Alexander Maconochie, Dorothea Lynde Dix, Elam Lynds, and Zebulon Reed Brockway already were mentioned in Chapter 3 on the historical antecedents to criminal justice management. In the twentieth century, new ideas were offered by reform-minded leaders seeking to further improve upon prison and jail organization. Three famous twentieth-century correctional reformers were Katharine Bement Davis, Mary Belle Harris, and George Beto.

Katharine Bement Davis: Katharine Bement Davis (1860–1935) was the first woman to be appointed New York City Correction Commissioner (1914), and her selection made news around the world. She was the first woman to run a major municipal agency in New York. She managed an agency with 650 uniformed and civilian employees; 5,500 inmates in nine city prisons and jails; and a $2 million annual budget. Between 1918 and 1928 she served as the head of the Bureau of Social Hygiene, funded by the Rockefeller Foundation. With her sponsorship, the Bureau published *Women Police* and Edith Spaulding's *Experimental Study of Psychopathic Delinquent Women.* Having earned a Ph.D. at the University of Chicago in 1900, she was a social reformer and activist for much of her life. She undertook a highly controversial sex study of 2,200 women, which began in 1920. Among her achievements was the recruiting of Mary Belle Harris, another prison reformer (McCarthy, 1997).

Mary Belle Harris: Mary Belle Harris (1874–1957) was appointed superintendent of the women's workhouse on Blackwell's Island, New York, by Katharine Davis. She revised institutional rules to transform the workhouse, which was badly overcrowded and one of the worst on Blackwell's Island, into a model institution, with a library, an exercise yard, and an inmate classification system. Harris later moved to New Jersey to head the State Reformatory for Women at Clinton. Harris later served in corrections posts in Pennsylvania and the U.S. Bureau of Prisons women's prison in Alderson, West Virginia, where she was the first woman to be a warden in the federal system. She also earned a Ph.D. at the University of Chicago. In a 1936 book about her career in penology, *I Knew Them in Prison*, Harris recounted her life, accomplishments, and penal reforms, and credited Davis with having a major influence on her correctional career (McCarthy, 1997; Rogers, 2000).

George John Beto: George John Beto (1916–1991) was appointed to the Texas Prison Board in 1953 (later renamed the Texas Board of Corrections), serving until 1959. Soon after that he served on the Illinois Parole and Pardon Board. In 1962 he returned to the Texas Department of Corrections. The prisoners called him "Walking George" because he unexpectedly visited the prisons to observe them. He helped secure legislative approval and funds for prison system reforms. Among the reforms he helped bring about were an eight-week prerelease program, giving prisoners counseling and education. In 1969 he helped institute a special work-release program, and also expanded college-education programs at prisons in cooperation with Sam Houston State University. He helped the university develop its criminology program, and the American Correctional Association elected him its president for 1969–1970. Though a reformer, Beto favored authoritarian disciplinary practices.

After he retired as director of the Texas Department of Corrections Beto was a professor of criminology and corrections at Sam Houston State University (1972–1991). He is described as being "one of the visionaries who brought about the building of the Criminal Justice Center" at Sam Houston State University (Roth, 1997: 46). He was member of the National Advisory Commission on Criminal Justice Standard and Goals, 1972–1973 (Horton and Nielsen, 2005; Lucko, 2007).

Each of these leaders and reformers—and many others—have found creative ways to reorganize and revitalize criminal justice agencies to better provide the services they were created to deliver. In various ways they each applied the principles of organization to achieve these innovations and improvements.

PRINCIPLES OF ORGANIZATION

In the fourth edition of *Police Administration*, by O.W. Wilson and Roy C. McLaren (1977: 73–74), the following principles were set down, with application to police work first in Wilson's mind. However, the principles have much more general application in all public service organizational contexts:

1. Tasks should be grouped together in one or more units under the control of one person. In order to facilitate their assignment, these tasks may be divided according to:

   a. similarity in purpose, process, method, or clientele (functional),
   b. the time (temporal),
   c. the place of their performance (spatial), and
   d. the level of authority needed in their accomplishment.

2. Specialized units should be created only when overall departmental capability is thus significantly increased; they should not be created at the expense of reduced control and decreased general interest.

3. Lines of demarcation between the responsibilities of units should be clearly drawn by a precise definition of the duties of each,

   a. duties of a unit should be made known to all members of the unit.
   b. responsibility within the unit and between units should be placed exactly.
   c. such definition should avoid duplication in execution and neglect resulting from the nonassignment of a duty.

4. Channels should be established through which information flows up and down and through which authority is delegated.
   a. These lines of control should correspond to the delegation of authority, the placement of responsibility, the supervision of work, and the coordination of effort.
   b. Lines of control should be clearly defined and well understood by all members so that all may know to whom they are responsible and who, in turn, is responsible to them.
   c. Exceptions to routine communication of information through channels should be provided for emergency and unusual situations.

5. Structure and terminology should facilitate the understanding of the purposes and responsibilities of the organization by all its members. Avoid exotic arrangements and obscure jargon.

6. Each individual, unit, and situation should be under the immediate control of one, and only one, person, thus achieving the principle of unity of command and avoiding the friction that results from duplication of direction and supervision.

7. The span of control of a supervisor should be large enough to provide economical supervision, but no more units or persons should be placed under the direct control of one person than he or she is able to manage.

8. Each task should be made the unmistakable duty of someone; responsibility for planning, execution, and control should be definitely placed on designated persons.

9. Supervision should be provided for every member of the organization and for every function or activity. (If the supervision is not immediately available at the actual level of execution, it should be obtainable through referral to a predesignated authority.)

10. Each assignment or duty should carry with it commensurate authority to fulfill the responsibility.

11. Persons to whom authority is delegated should be held accountable for the use made of it and for the failure to use it.

These principles of organization often are depicted in the form of the organizational chart. Known by such terms as a "block chart," "plumbing chart," or a "wiring diagram," the organizational chart is the embodiment of the ancient adage that a picture is worth 1,000 words. These box charts use rectangular boxes to represent offices, units, or important individual officers in an agency. One of the learning objectives of this unit is teaching each student how to read, use, and later how to draw a correct organization chart.

Police patrol units take messages from the 911-dispatch center and respond to them as if they were taking orders (e.g., "Unit B-57, respond to a disorder at 123 4th Avenue"). Such a communication sounds like an order being given by a dispatcher to a uniformed officer. In organizational practice it is not. The dispatcher is "sharing information" with the officer. If the officer feels he or she should not respond to the call, the officer can decline it or request direction from his or her direct supervisor (e.g., "Unit B-03, this is B-57. I am monitoring a suspicious activity at 8th and Market Street. Request that another until respond to the disorder on 4th Avenue"). The field supervisor, shown as the solid line on the organization chart, has the authority to reassign the officer to take the call or assign another patrol unit to respond to it.

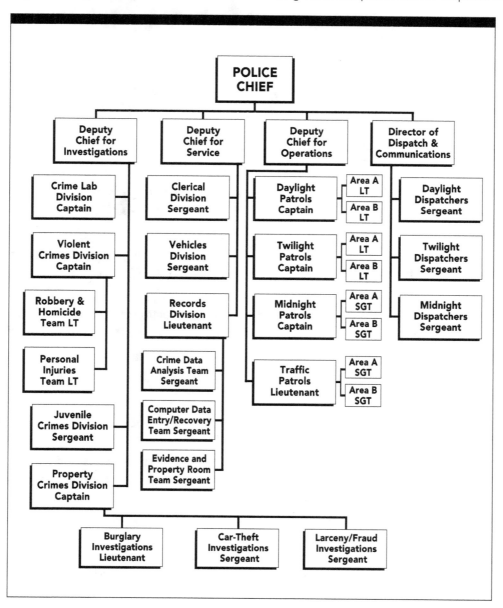

Figure 1

Sample Organization Chart

Box 2 Reading an Organization Chart

Solid lines represent command and supervisory relationships.

Dashed or dotted lines represent communications and coordination channels and interrelationships such as relationships as attachment, operational control (Op Con), liaison, and detail.

Boxes represent an "office," "department," or some other unit with a functional, temporal, or spatial division of labor.

Very similar units are often merged, by overlapping (stack) or "**comb**" **arrangements**, meaning that all such units are very similar in their organization/function.

The chart should show all elements supervised by a superior element/person with a single clear path from top to bottom.

A chart ought not create fictional relationships (yet some do, leading to people saying "I don't report to him!").

No box should be unconnected, but some will be in reality because of managerial or political compromises; e.g., the "independent" agency such as the office of the ombudsman, the "special prosecutor," or the "independent counsel."

No box should be connected to two or more supervisory boxes with a solid line, yet some can be linked by a dotted or dashed line, reflecting such relationships as attachment, operational control (Op Con), liaison, detail, or pre-authorized direct communication channels.

The way dotted-line, dual relationships can be handled includes concepts of *attached*, *operational control* (OPCON), *liaison*, and *detailed*.

Attached: When a unit (or an individual) is detached from its own agency and attached to a different organization, the receiving organization becomes responsible for that unit, providing its logistics, supervision, and duty assignments. A criminal justice example would be a judge, temporarily transferred from his or her home district to a different district to help reduce case backlogs in the receiving court district. For most purposes, that judge functions as if he or she had been transferred to the new district. Logistics support, such as office space, a courtroom, clerical support, and a wide range of other support activities, is provided by the receiving district. Eventually the attachment will end and the judge will return to his or her home district.

Operational Control (OPCON): When an entire unit from one organization takes its direction from another organization that is not normally part of its chain of command, it can be considered under operational control. Common examples in law enforcement are combined task forces of federal, state, and local law enforcement agencies that agree to protocols that place one of them in charge of the activities of the others. The Drug Enforcement Agency (DEA) often has operational control of drug investigations that have the full participation of state and local anti-drug agencies. The state and local units remain the "property" of their larger organizations, which provide most of their support and logistics, but their actual task assignments, direction, and supervision are transferred to the DEA agent in charge.

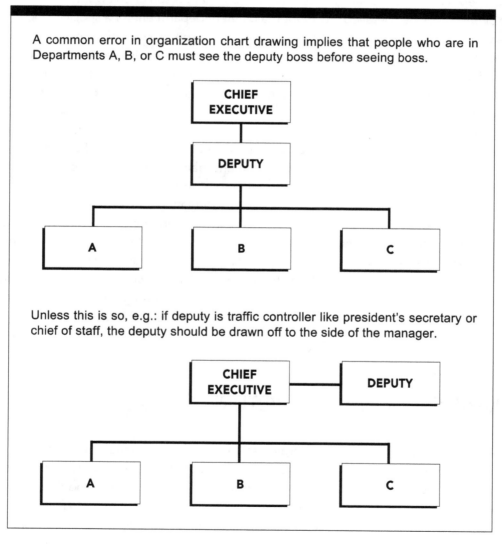

Figure 2

Common Organization Chart Error

Liaison: A liaison officer is an official of one agency who is assigned to work with a different agency as a means of facilitating coordination and communication between or among agencies. A common criminal justice example would be police, fire, rescue, and public health officials assigned to an emergency operations center established to respond to a major community crisis. They interact with each other and inform each other of what their home agency can contribute to the joint operation. Some liaison relationships are long-lasting; others very temporary. The long-lasting relationships take on the features of a detail.

Detailed: When a unit or an individual is detailed, that person or unit works for one department or agency but is "detailed" to support a different department for a specific function or a limited time. A common criminal justice example is an experienced police investigator being detailed to the prosecutor's office to conduct further investigation into a case being prepared for trial. Such an investigator remains an employee of the police department and will eventually return to the police department, but for the duration of the detail will work under the direct supervision of the prosecutor's office.

It might be worthwhile to clarify some of the terminology in common use in criminal justice agencies. An **officer** is an employee empowered to act on behalf of the agency or organization, and can be a part of the management team, having some supervisory duties. Formally speaking, a "police officer" would not be an "officer" within the police department in this sense, but a police sergeant or lieutenant with managerial duties would be. On the street, though, a police officer is authorized to act independently and takes on duties in his or her relationship to the public that imply being an "officer" of the police department. An "employee" need not be an officer. A clerk has a task to do but no supervisory or managerial powers to exercise in behalf of the agency. An agent will include a nonemployee engaged for specific acts (e.g., a lawyer hired to represent the agency or organization on a limited question or case). Agents who are not employees often do not appear on the organizational charts.

ORGANIZATIONAL STRUCTURE AND FUNCTION

Weber and Wilson both approached organization as a rational exercise, with an underlying assumption that workers are analogous to identical replacement parts in a working machine. This was also evident in Frederick Taylor's writings. However, the Hawthorne Studies invited questions about this assumption. Workers were "vital engines" even more than Robert Owen might have assumed. This gave rise to the human relations school and its model of human organizational behavior. In time other models have been proposed, so that now we can consider three major options that a leader may employ in organizing his or her agency:

1. **Bureaucratic-Scientific Management Model** (Gulick, 1937; Taylor, 1911; Weber, 1920; Wilson, 1950): Organizational principles are applied somewhat rigidly, with the hierarchy principle given very high priority. Authority is very precisely allocated, with those higher up in the hierarchy having more power. Rules are explicit, and organizational discipline is enforced. The agency's organizational chart clearly defines areas of jurisdiction and command-control relationships. Organizational communications, command, and control are expected to follow the chain of command. This approach dominated organization in criminal justice well into the middle of the twentieth century.

2. **Human Relations Model** (Herzberg, 1968; Maslow, 1970; Mayo, 1923; Roethlisberger 1941): Preceded by the ideas of Mary Parker Follett, and arising with the discoveries of the Hawthorne group (Mayo and Roethlisberger), older scientific management organizational principles were called into question. Hierarchy and command aspects were not abandoned, but their importance declined. Lines of command, control, and communication were often ignored in favor of work groups, operating as co-equals, even when they were comprised of different ranks. Rules were replaced by flexible guidelines. Rising in popularity in the 1960s, these ideas never fully replaced scientific management organization in criminal justice. They found expression in the 1970s as team policing, community policing, and empowerment of client populations in criminal justice priority-setting became popular.

3. **Situational and Contingency Models** (Fiedler, 1967; Luthans, 1976): these models promoted flexibility and situational management, and revived Mary Parker Follett's 1926 recommendation that leaders should take their orders from the situation. The application of CompStat in law enforcement and problem-oriented policing are both expressions of this approach. Criminal justice work-teams are created, reorganized, and disbanded as needed. There is more use of delegation and operational control practices than in scientific management, but less workplace democracy than was the case in human relations applications. The older scientific management-based principles reemerged as good practices, but not rigid formulae, for organizing criminal justice agencies.

APPLYING ORGANIZATIONAL PRINCIPLES

The **division of labor** in a criminal justice organization must reflect functional, temporal, and spatial demands placed upon it by its mission.

Functional Divisions of Labor: The tasks or functions a criminal justice agency has will be reflected by the internal divisions it adapts. Souryal (1985: 12–13) identified several factors to be considered, among them major purposes (missions), processes employed, subjects (specific services to be provided), and clientele.

A municipal police department needs to provide crime prevention, public safety, order maintenance, public service, and crime investigation services to the public. If the workload justifies it, there can be functional divisions to reflect each of these. Even a smaller police department will have patrol, services, and investigative units. The courts are called upon to hold bail and bond hearings, conduct civil and criminal trials, sentence people, collect fines, supervise probation conditions, hear appeals, and perform many other judicial functions. Court managers create units within the court system to provide these services. Corrections managers must classify, house, educate, medicate, treat, and release inmates. They will pay attention to classifications of inmates based upon their danger to correctional staffs and society at large, and thus correctional units will be developed that are maximum-security, medium-security, and minimum-security. There will be classification units. There will be medical, counseling, education and vocational training, parole-hearing, and other correctional units.

Clientele will include the aforementioned security grades in a prison population, youth offenders, victims, witnesses, the public at large, the staffs of the agencies, and many others. Specific units can be established to deal with the special requirements of various client groups. Police, court, and corrections units exist to meet the needs of juveniles. Prosecutors need to handle offenders, witnesses, and victims in different ways, and may choose to create divisions within their offices to provide those services.

The processes employed by modern criminal justice agencies often rely upon complex technologies the average agency employee simply will not possess. Police will reply upon crime scene investigation (CSI) experts and other advanced scientific elements to provide such technical support. Computers are very important in all the components of the criminal justice system, and having support staffs who can manipulate data efficiently on computer platforms is critical to all criminal justice agencies. Highly sophisticated communications equipment can be entrusted to centralized 911 dispatch and communications centers.

Henry Mintzberg identified five basic parts of an organization, and these are a modern reflection of the functional divisions of labor (1979):

1. **apex**—the top leadership and management team

2. **middle line**—mid-level managers and supervisors

3. **techno-structure**—specialists in the applications of complex technologies

4. **support staff**—clerical-administrative personnel who deal with internal matters

5. **operating core**—the actual workforce to do the labor of the organization

Temporal Divisions of Labor: Municipal police agencies, 911 centers, and correctional units operate 24 hours a day, seven days a week. In some larger cities magistrates also are available 24/7, and lower courts hold night sessions. Juvenile justice units have to respond to cases whenever they arise, not just between 9 A.M. and 5 P.M., Monday through Friday. On the other hand, state and federal investigative agencies and higher courts often can maintain "banker's hours" with 40-hour-a-week work schedules, so the organization of the criminal justice agency must reflect accurately the times when their services are needed.

Spatial Divisions of Labor: Many criminal justice agencies serve large geographical areas. Federal agencies need field offices across the entire nation. State agencies must be present state-wide. Police in large cities need to operate divisions or precincts to provide police services city-wide. Patrol operations must be provided over the entire jurisdiction being served. The courts have established districts so that every community has local or regional access to judicial services.

The **span of control** refers to the number of individuals routinely supervised by an officer of the agency. Tight control exists when a supervisor oversees only two or three subordinates. Loose control exists when a supervisor oversees a large number of subordinates. Therefore, span of control exists in inverse relation to intensity of supervision. When supervision does not need to be intense, the span may be increased without loss of manageability and productivity. This is often the ideal case in Theory Y scenarios. When supervision must be intense, span of control must be left small to achieve manageability and productivity. This is the case when Theory X is applied.

Span of control and the number of steps or layers in the command hierarchy exist in an inverse relation with affect on manageability and productivity. If an agency has each supervisor overseeing only a few subordinates, it will require many more layers of supervision. An increased span of control will produce a decrease in communication time and efficiency. This occurs because an increase in the hierarchy adds additional layers or links in the communication chain, and this produces delays and a decrease in communication transfer. The more extenuated the command-control chain, the more information is lost.

When does supervision need to be intense? Theory X-Scientific Management and Contingency models would recommend it with a work force that has low skills and little motivation.

When does communication "line-loss" need to be kept at a minimum? Theory Y-Human Relations and Contingent models would advise it when criticality, responsiveness, discipline, or control are critical to managerial situations.

There is an inherent paradox to all of this: an abbreviated chain of command can produce a greater span of control but also can enhance internal communication. However, this is not guaranteed. A greater span of control can reduce the communication line-loss in two ways:

1. more face-to-face communications will be necessary

2. fewer transmission links will be required from top down

A greater span of control also can reduce overall internal communications effectiveness by:

1. reducing the time a manager has with each subordinate

2. increasing the likelihood that the manager will miss someone

MANAGEMENT THEORISTS CONSIDER THE THREE MODELS

Philip Selznick (1948; 1992) sees an organization as a social entity existing to accomplish an "agreed purpose through the allocation of functions and responsibilities" (1992: 114). The maintenance of the system is an implicit agreed purpose; hence, his five "imperatives" (1992: 118–119):

1. The security of the organization as a whole in relation to the social forces in its environment.
2. The stability of lines of authority and communication.
3. The stability of informal relations within the organization.
4. The continuity of policy and of the sources of its determination.
5. A homogeneity of outlook with respect to the meaning and role of the organization.

The imperatives cross-cut the three models. However the criminal justice manager approaches the organization of his or her agency, these concerns must be met. It is the duty of the manager to select the appropriate organizational structure and the organizational model that will best enable the agency to meet its mission and responsibilities to the public.

•••

REFERENCES AND SUPPLEMENTAL SOURCES

Fiedler, Fred E. (1967). *A Theory of Leadership Effectiveness*. New York: McGraw-Hill.

Fosdick, Raymond B. (1920). *American Police Systems*. New York: Century.

Fuld, Leonard Felix (1910). *Police Administration: A Critical Study of Police Organizations in the United States and Abroad*. New York: Putnam.

Graper, Elmer Diedrich (1921). *American Police Administration*. New York: Macmillan.

Herzberg, Frederick (1968). "One More Time: How Do You Motivate Employees?" *Harvard Business Review*, 46(1): 53–62, reprinted in the *Harvard Business Review*, 65(5): 109–120.

Horton, David M., and George R. Nielsen (2005). *Walking George: The Life of George John Beto and the Rise of the Modern Texas Prison System*. Denton, TX: University of North Texas Press.

Jaques, Elliott (1990). "In Praise of Hierarchy," *Harvard Business Review*, 68(1): 127–134.

Lucko, Paul M. (2007). "Beto, George John," The Handbook of Texas on Line. Found at http://www.tsha.utexas.edu/handbook/online/articles/BB/fbenm.html

Luthans, Fred (1976). *Introduction to Management: A Contingency Approach*. New York: McGraw-Hill.

March, James G., and Herbert A. Simon (1958). *Organizations*. New York: John Wiley and Sons.

Maslow, Abraham H. (1970). *Motivation and Personality*, 2nd ed. New York: Harper and Row.

Mayo, Elton (1933). *The Human Problems of an Industrial Civilization*. Cambridge, MA: Harvard University Press.

McCarthy, Thomas C. (1997). "Correction's Katharine Bement Davis: New York City's Suffragist Commissioner." KBD Bio. New York City Department of Correction. Found at http://www.correctionhistory.org/html/chronicl/kbd/kbd_15.html

McGregor, Douglas (1960). *The Human Side of Enterprise.* New York: McGraw-Hill. Mintzberg, Henry (1979). *The Structure of Organizations.* Englewood Cliffs, NJ: Prentice Hall.

Roethlisberger, F.J. (1941). *Management and Morale.* Cambridge, MA: Harvard University Press.

Rogers, Joseph W. (2000). "Mary Belle Harris: Warden and Rehabilitation Pioneer," *Women and Criminal Justice*, 11(4): 5–28.

Roth, Mitchel (1997). *Fulfilling a Mandate: A History of the Criminal Justice Center at Sam Houston State University.* Huntsville, TX: Sam Houston Press.

Selznick, Philip (1948). "Foundations of the Theory of Organization," *American Sociological Review* 13(1): 25–35.

Selznick, Philip (1992). "Foundations of the Theory of Organization," pages 114–123 in *Classics of Organizational Theory*, 3rd ed., edited by Jay M. Shafritz and J. Steven Ott. Pacific Grove, CA: Brooks/Cole.

Smith, Adam (1776) [1937]. *The Wealth of Nations.* New York: Random House, Modern Library.

Smith, Bruce P. (1940). *Police Systems in the United States.* New York: Harper and Brothers.

Souryal, Sam S. (1995). *Police Organization and Administration*, 2nd ed. Cincinnati: Anderson.

Vanderbilt, Arthur T., editor (1949). *Minimum Standards of Judicial Administration.* New York: The Law Center of New York University.

Vanderbilt, Arthur T. (1955). *The Challenge of Legal Reform.* Princeton, NJ: Princeton University Press.

Vanderbilt, Arthur T., II. (1976). *Changing Law: A Biography of Arthur T. Vanderbilt.* New Brunswick, NJ: Rutgers University Press.

Vollmer, August (1936). *The Police and Modern Society.* Berkeley, CA: University of California Press.

Weber, Max (1922). *Economy and Society*, 2 volumes, edited by Guenther Roth and Claus Wittich. Berkeley, CA: University of California Press.

Wilson, Orlando W. (1950). *Police Administration.* New York: McGraw-Hill.

Wilson, Orlando W. (1956). "Bruce Smith," *Journal of Criminal Law, Criminology, and Police Science*, 47(2): 235–237.

Wilson, Orlando W., and Roy C. McLaren (1977). *Police Administration*, 4th ed. New York: McGraw-Hill.

DISCUSSION QUESTIONS

1   Elliot Jacques identified three problems associated with hierarchical bureaucracies: too many layers, reduced productivity, and unsavory human behavior. In your real or imagined bureaucracy, what three tactics would you implement to address those problems and why?

2   The reading author states that Selznick's five "imperatives" cut across the three models of organizational theory. In your opinion, which model(s) relates to each imperative?

ORGANIZATIONAL STRUCTURE AND THE IMPLEMENTATION OF STRATEGY

IRENE DUHAIME, LARRY STIMPERT, AND JULIE CHELSEY

[W]e have emphasized the importance of managerial thinking in the effective strategic management of firms, and noted the critical role managerial thinking plays in decisions about the formulation of organizational strategies and the implementation of those strategies. Earlier chapters addressing business definition, business strategy, and corporate strategy (the "what" of strategic management) noted that firms differ greatly in their ability to implement strategies effectively, and that managerial thinking about appropriate organizational structure for strategy implementation is an important potential source of competitive advantage.

The overall aims of any organizational structure are to implement the strategic initiatives that managers have formulated and to make organizations responsive to their managers, their shareholders or owners, and developments in their larger competitive environments. By developing especially effective structures, managers can give their organizations a significant competitive advantage.

CHAPTER OBJECTIVES

The specific objectives of this chapter are to:

- Define structure and describe its role in the implementation of strategy.

- Identify and describe the different components of organizational structure.

- Identify some of the problems associated with organizing and describe how the various components of organizational structure can be used to overcome these organizational problems that are common to nearly all firms and businesses.

- Discuss some of the emerging issues that are likely to have an impact on organizing and organizational structures in the future.

THE CHARACTERISTICS OF BUSINESS ORGANIZATIONS

In all organizations, managers have to think about the implementation of strategy, how to accomplish the plans and achieve the goals. In the smallest entrepreneurial businesses, we may see the entrepreneurs literally "doing it all"—working tirelessly to do every task themselves in the launch of their businesses or aided only by some immediate family—the classic "started in a garage" story of a business startup. But entrepreneurs who succeed in the startup stage soon pass the point where "doing it all" themselves is possible. They must rapidly expand the number of employees they have, and sometimes locations and other factors as well, and must delegate many tasks in order to meet demand for their product or service.

Organizing for effective implementation of organizational strategy, therefore, is critical for *all* firms beyond the entrepreneurial startup stage. It is obvious that the very large size and high level of complexity of firms like General Electric and Procter & Gamble, and the challenges of managing and coordinating such large organizations, force managers to focus on developing sophisticated structures. But it is important to recognize that the topics of this chapter apply to all firms beyond the entrepreneurial startup stage—the small and medium-size firms that make up the vast majority of business organizations worldwide as well as large firms like General Electric and Procter & Gamble. Indeed, failures of small and medium-size firms too often can be traced not to weaknesses in their strategies but rather to weaknesses in the implementation of their strategies.

How managers uniquely organize their firms can have enormous consequences for organizational effectiveness and performance, and organizational structure may be one of the most powerful—if not the most powerful—tools for achieving competitive advantage. Carol Bartz, CEO of Yahoo, summed up the importance of structure for innovation, "Organizations can get in the way of innovation, because people are all bound up," and don't know if they have the freedom to make decisions.[1] Similarly, here's how two respected organizational theorists assess the importance of organizational structure:

> most of the old, reliable sources of competitive advantage are drying up. No longer can companies located in a handful of money centers rely on exclusive access to capital, no longer can the Xeroxes and Polaroids of the world rely on the exclusive, proprietary technology that once assured them of a virtual monopoly. Markets that were once the exclusive domain of local producers are now fair game for competitors headquartered halfway around the globe. And highly skilled employees, their loyalty shaken by years of corporate cutbacks and downsizing, feel free to offer their services to the highest bidder …
>
> In this volatile environment where instability is the norm, we're convinced that the last remaining source of truly sustainable competitive advantage lies in what we've come to describe as "organizational capabilities"— *the unique ways in which each organization structures its work and motivates its people to achieve clearly articulated strategic objectives.*[2]

The growing size and complexity of firms and businesses thus requires the development of organizational processes and structures in order to implement their strategies. Today, all businesses will have the following characteristics:[3]

DIVISION OF LABOR

Employees in most companies generally do not perform a wide range of duties; instead, work is organized so that employees specialize in a particular task or set of related tasks. Organizations recruit or train specialists to perform these tasks, and such a division of labor allows these specialists to become increasingly adept at performing their job duties. For example, it would be very uncommon for a company to hire an individual to make some sales calls in the morning, do some manufacturing work in the early afternoon, and then perform some bookkeeping activities before leaving work at the end of the day. Instead, organizations hire marketing, manufacturing, and accounting specialists who then work within their respective areas of functional expertise.

HIERARCHY

Hierarchy is another characteristic of nearly all business organizations. Hierarchy is the "organization chart," or the arrangement of managers and employees into superior-subordinate relationships. The concept of *hierarchical levels* refers to the levels of managerial decision-making activity. A "tall" structure would have many (perhaps as many as eight) hierarchical levels from the CEO down to the lowest level of subordinates, while a "flat" structure would have fewer hierarchical levels (perhaps only two or three in companies that are just beyond the startup stage). Closely related to the concept of hierarchical levels is the concept of *span of control*. Span of control refers to the number of subordinates reporting to a manager. The greater a manager's span of control, the more subordinates that manager would have reporting to him or her.

DECISIONS ARE BASED ON RULES, POLICIES, AND STANDARD OPERATING PROCEDURES THAT SEEK TO PROMOTE EFFICIENCY

In most organizations, employees are not free to do whatever they want in any way they wish. Instead, their actions are guided by uniform rules, policies, and standard operating procedures that aim to promote standardization and efficiency. In most organizations, such policies and standard operating procedures are a very important component of structure, and, as we shall discuss later, such rules and standard operating procedures can have significant positive benefits and, at times, some negative consequences for organizational performance.

THE TENDENCY TO BECOME INFLEXIBLE AND RESIST CHANGE

One key characteristic of most organizations is their stability. Often, organizations rigidly adhere to their rules, policies, and standard operating procedures even when circumstances might suggest that exceptions or changes in policies might be warranted. Once set in motion, organizations can become quite resistant to change, preferring to "do things the way they've always been done." As a result, most organizations tend to resist leadership that initiates change. Mintzberg emphasizes this tendency, noting that all organizations are characterized by "bureaucratic momentum" and a desire for stability that can be quite pathological because businesses and firms must operate in dynamic environments.[4]

The remainder of this chapter is organized as follows: First, we define structure and take a closer look at the various components of organizational structure. We then consider some of the central issues and problems that are common to nearly all organizations and discuss how structures can be altered or modified to alleviate some of these problems. Finally, we describe several emerging issues that are likely to have an impact on how organizations structure their operations in the future.

A DEFINITION OF ORGANIZATIONAL STRUCTURE

Although hierarchy is the most obvious or visible component of structure, organizational structure includes much more than hierarchy or organization charts.

As already noted above, another important component of organizational structure is the written and unwritten rules, standard operating procedures, and systems that constitute organizations' marketing, production, personnel, and compensation policies as well as their accounting, financial control, and information systems. In addition, the lifeblood of any organization is the information and knowledge that resides in and is passed among organizational members and their departments. We have also come to realize that an organization's culture or its "informal structure" can be just as important as, if not more important than, its formal hierarchical structure, policies and systems, and flows of information. Thus, we will define structure broadly to include any mechanisms that facilitate the formulation and implementation of strategy and the overall coordination of the business enterprise. These mechanisms include:

- Hierarchical reporting relationships.
- Policies, standard operating procedures, and control systems.
- Information systems and flows of information moving through organizations.
- Culture.

The challenge confronting general managers is to combine these components into appropriate organizational structures that: 1) effectively implement chosen strategies, and 2) make their firms responsive to the leadership of owners and managers as well as to changes in the larger competitive environments in which firms operate. And as we will emphasize, this means much more than a re-organization or restructuring of lines and boxes on a chart. It needs to address critical issues such as the impact on information flow and business processes, effects on customers, and interrelationships among employees, to name a few.[5] In other words, these mechanisms need to *fit* together. When a change is made in one area, such as reporting relationships on the organization chart, managers need to consider the implications in the other areas. Policies may need to change, information systems may need to be adjusted, or even new norms created. As suggested by our model of strategic management, illustrated in Exhibit 1, these decisions about organizational structure will be influenced by managers' beliefs about how to organize and implement strategy. Finally, managers' beliefs and understandings are likely to be developed by their own trial-and-error learning, imitation of other firms' effective structures, and their own creativity and ingenuity.

THE COMPONENTS OF ORGANIZATIONAL STRUCTURE

HIERARCHY

Hierarchy is both the most visible and the most widely studied aspect of structure. This section focuses on three types of hierarchical structures—functional, multidivisional, and matrix—and examines the strengths and limitations of each type of structure. Later in the chapter, we examine some new types of hierarchical structures.

FUNCTIONAL STRUCTURES

Functional structures organize activities around functional activities or departments, such as manufacturing, marketing, research and development, and sales, as illustrated in Exhibit 2. The principal advantage of the functional structure is that its division of the organization into departments allows employees to specialize and become increasingly skilled at what they do. Because of its emphasis on specialization and efficiency, the functional structure has been described as the natural way for most firms, even fairly large firms, to organize their operations.[6] According to Naomi Stanford, a recognized expert in the field of organization design, the functional structure is well suited for firms operating with the following conditions:

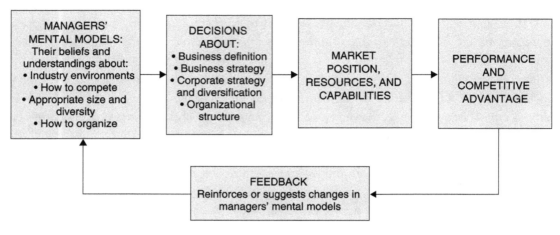

Exhibit 1

Managers' Beliefs, the Strategic Decisions Studied in This Book, and Their Influence on Performance and Competitive Advantage

- There are stable and undifferentiated markets.

- There is a successful, control-focused culture.

- There is a single product or service line.

- There is scale or expertise within each function.

- There are long product development lifecycles.

- The organization works to common standards.[7]

Yet many problems are associated with functional structures. First, communication and motivational difficulties can be particularly vexing in functional organizations. The various departments of a firm organized along functional lines must communicate with each other, but because of the structure's design, most information must flow up through functional "chimneys" before it can flow across to another functional department. Though it might seem reasonable that an employee in the manufacturing or production department who has a marketing question could simply telephone or e-mail a colleague in the marketing department, this is rarely done in practice, except in small, new organizations. Rather than simply telephoning a colleague in the marketing department, the manufacturing employee with a question would instead write a memorandum to his or her manager who might then relay the request to the vice president of manufacturing who would then forward the request to the vice president of marketing who would forward the memo to a marketing manager who would then deliver the memo to the employee he or she deems most qualified to answer the query.

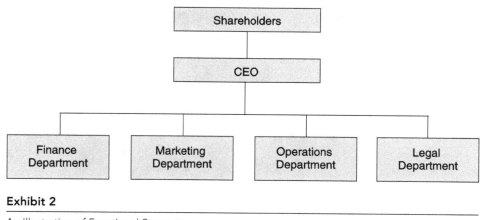

Exhibit 2

An Illustration of Functional Structure

Why this cumbersome process? Primarily because it keeps employees' supervisors informed and allows them to provide their input to policy questions.

Furthermore, the process leaves a "paper trail," allowing employees to show that they have kept supervisors informed. At the same time, however, the process increases the amount of time required to transmit data, slows decision making, and increases the likelihood that both the request for data as well as the reply will be distorted or altered as they move through the organization's hierarchy, all of which can undermine strategy implementation.

Also, in most functional organizations, some departments or divisions are designated *profit centers*—seen as responsible for generating the company's revenues, while other departments or divisions are designated *cost centers*—seen perhaps as important, but not responsible for generating revenues. Without responsibility for generating revenue, employees in cost centers can develop morale and motivation problems.

Finally, functional structures tend to overload top managers.[8] Because most information goes up before it goes across departments in functional organizations, much management time is spent just relaying information. Furthermore, top managers must referee disputes that inevitably arise between functional departments.

If these motivational and informational limitations become so severe that they prevent managers from noticing or responding to changes in their competitive environments, or if these problems limit the ability of their firms to effectively implement strategies, then changes in the hierarchy may be needed.

Most managers have found that as organizations grow and become increasingly diversified, they must make major changes to their firms' hierarchies. One response to these challenges was the development and adoption of multidivisional structures.

• • •

CROSS-FUNCTIONAL OR MATRIX STRUCTURES

Cross-functional or matrix structures represent a hybrid hierarchy in which a functional structure is overlaid or placed on top of a multidivisional (or geographical or product) structure. Exhibit 3 illustrates the types of matrix, or cross-functional team, structures that nearly all of the major automobile companies have adopted over the last two decades. The cross-functional structure illustrated in Exhibit 3 shows that the major automobile companies are organized along both product lines (e.g., small-car platform team, large-car platform team, truck platform team) as well as functional lines (e.g., engineering, production, marketing, and finance). Employees retain functional specialties, such as engineering, marketing, or production, but the company has placed employees in "cross-functional" product teams. As a result, engineers, marketing, and production people all work together on a "platform team" such as the small car team or the truck team. Other types of cross-functional structures are obviously possible; a firm pursuing a global strategy, for example, might be organized along both product and geographical lines.

Cross-functional structures are especially useful in a situation like that of the automobile companies when traditional functional or multidivisional structures would not be likely to distribute information adequately throughout the organization. In the past, the "chimney" problem (described earlier in the section on functional structure) has been particularly acute at U.S. automobile companies.

Engineers often designed cars that were difficult to build and/or that consumers didn't want. Ensuing discussions to correct problems and communicate across engineering, production, and marketing departments would take months or even years. Already the advantage of cross-functional product teams is seen in much shorter product development lead times and significantly lower product development costs at the major automobile companies.[14]

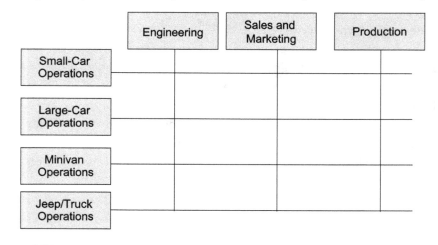

Exhibit 3

The Matrix or Cross-Functional Structure Adopted by Nearly All Major Automobile Companies

Some pharmaceutical companies are now making use of "drug discovery teams" to speed the development of new products. Like other types of cross-functional teams, these drug discovery teams consist of researchers who have different types of expertise but are focusing on a common problem. Working closely together, these discovery teams develop a common body of knowledge or team mental model that facilitates research.[15]

To summarize, a matrix or cross-functional structure is most appropriate when:

- The cost of labor is a primary driver.

- Projects require specialized skills and knowledge and these vary greatly.

- Major work is project based.[16]

Although the major advantage of the cross-functional structure is its ability to improve information flows, the matrix structure also has a number of drawbacks. One problem is often referred to as the "two-boss problem."

Employees working in a firm organized as a matrix will find that they often report to two bosses. In the automobile company example described earlier, an engineer working on the small car platform team is responsible to the head of the engineering department as well as to the head of the small car platform team.

Thus, if goals are not congruent throughout the firm or if the organization lacks an effective mechanism for settling conflicts and disagreements, the cross-functional structure can become unworkable. In fact, cross-functional structures have often produced either power struggles or outright anarchy as product managers struggle with functional managers.

Another problem that is sometimes encountered in cross-functional organizations has been referred to as "groupitis," or the tendency for cross-functional team members to believe that every decision needs to be made as a group.[17] Although group decision making offers many benefits, it can also slow progress if the group becomes bogged down in deciding too many details.

Another limitation of the cross-functional form that the major automobile companies and some high-technology companies have encountered is that specialists who are working on a product team often become so involved in working on the product that they lose touch with their specialty area. For example, some automobile companies have found a trade-off between the benefits of better information flow from having their engineers involved in product teams and the cost of having those engineers unaware of new developments in engineering technologies. Some companies have dealt with this challenge by having employees rotate into and out of product teams on fairly strict schedules.

We've already described how different hierarchies are more and less effective at moving information. For example, we noted that the automobile industry has embraced cross-functional structures and teams to better share information and overcome the limitations of moving information through or between functional silos or chimneys. Whenever the context demands the dissemination and application of information, we can expect more and more companies in different industries to adopt cross-functional structures as a way to improve decision making. Later in this chapter, we examine the *virtual* or *modular* structures and other new structural forms that many companies are adopting in order to more effectively manage information flows.

Many global companies have adopted cross-functional structures as a way to manage their international business activities and to improve coordination and information flows. Global companies have unique and significant organizational challenges. The structures that the managers of global companies adopt must assist them in their efforts to exploit opportunities to achieve economies of scale by centralizing their marketing and production activities whenever possible. At the same time, the structures of international companies must also accommodate differences in national cultures and variations in business practices. And, as in any organization, the structures of international companies must serve to coordinate business activities and to move information quickly and accurately across borders and around the world.

POLICIES, STANDARD OPERATING PROCEDURES, AND CONTROL SYSTEMS

Though organizational charts or hierarchies of supervisor-subordinate relationships are the most visible aspect of structures, much of the actual work of organizations and the implementation of strategies are accomplished through their policies, standard operating procedures, and control systems. Most organizational behavior is highly routinized; rather than "reinventing the wheel" every time a unit of work must be performed, organizations standardize most activities and functions in order to increase efficiency and reduce variability.

Thus, most large and even medium-size organizations have thick policy manuals describing routines and standard operating procedures for accomplishing an array of tasks, including everything from market research, engineering, and personnel recruitment to manufacturing, marketing, sales, and after-sales service activities. Furthermore, even strategic tasks, such as performance monitoring and the review of investment proposals, are routinized. As a result, accounting data from one period are comparable with data from other periods, and investment proposals are not considered uniquely but in light of uniform financial criteria.

The importance of this component of organizational structure should not be underestimated; indeed, it is probably fair to state that organizations' policies, standard operating procedures, and control systems play a critical role in influencing their successes in implementing their strategies as well as their failures. On the positive side, high performance is almost always associated with an effective set of policies, procedures, or systems. A low-cost, high-quality manufacturing operation is based on a set of policies and procedures that reflect a great deal of learning and prior experience. Firms make a series of successful acquisitions not because of luck or the intuition of their top managers, but because they have developed a set of procedures that helped them identify attractive acquisition candidates, execute the purchases, and successfully integrate the new units. Managers of many organizations believe that their firms' financial control systems are important sources of competitive advantage.

At the same time, organizations' procedures and systems can harm organizational effectiveness and even be pathological. Highly routinized policies and procedures can limit organizational flexibility and adaptability, and can make organizations very unresponsive to changes in their competitive environments. Managers' understandings of their firms' definitions tend to become tightly coupled with their firms' strategies, policies, and procedures. Because of this tight coupling and because firms' policies and procedures tend to be so highly routinized, managers can come to use their organizations' policies, procedures, and systems over and over again in an automatic, almost unthinking way. Although this automatic or reflexive use of policies, procedures, and systems minimizes ambiguity and promotes rapid decision making, it can become a serious liability if environmental conditions or competitive circumstances change.

Organizational policies and procedures can also unwittingly reward the wrong types of behaviors and, therefore, produce undesirable results. One example of how a company's systems can have an adverse effect on strategy and performance is provided by the Harvard Business School case study of the Dexter Corporation.[18] In this case, one of Dexter's businesses manufactures a key component for firms in the rapidly growing semiconductor industry. One Dexter executive summarizes the company's problem this way:

> We were doing very well but we were underinvesting in what turned out to be a very high-growth industry. We weren't putting in the marketing dollars and we weren't putting in the R&D dollars. We were growing ... at close to 20 percent, however, the semiconductor market was growing at 30 percent. So we were losing market share and didn't know it.[19]

And what role did Dexter's structure play in fostering this problem? First, until the time of the case, Dexter lacked some sort of monitoring system for gauging company performance against the competitive environment. The case also suggests a second factor, however. The casewriter again quotes the same Dexter executive:

> I would say going back one, two, or three years ago, that due to the constraints of the profit-sharing and the incentive program for the divisions, we probably underinvested in our two growth businesses.[20]

In other words, one of the company's control systems—its compensation system—which rewarded division executives on the basis of their division's bottom line return on investment—discouraged division executives from spending what was needed for marketing and R&D efforts in order to maximize the company's long-run performance outcomes.

Wal-Mart's attempts to enter the German market in the 1990s also show the negative effects of automatically or reflexively using certain organizational procedures and systems. Instead of being innovative and researching the local culture of the market it wanted to enter, Wal-Mart resorted to its general strategies that brought it success in the United States. The result of Wal-Mart's apparent ignorance of the local culture resulted in nothing short of a fiasco.

INFORMATION SYSTEMS AND INFORMATION FLOWS

Although a traditional aim of structure has been the organization of work—especially physical work or tasks—to implement or achieve strategic objectives, it now appears that the implementation of strategy is becoming increasingly dependent on the acquisition, storage, distribution, and application of information. Many companies have found that information and systems for managing the flow of information can be important sources of competitive advantage. The text has already noted how Wal-Mart has successfully exploited information and information technology to provide it with the most sophisticated logistics and inventory management systems of any retailing firm. Nearly all large retailing firms have come to realize that their ability to manage information about their costs, inventories, and customer preferences and shopping patterns can have a profound impact on their success in implementing their strategies.

One important factor behind the revolution in manufacturing is the incorporation of information technology to handle the flow of materials and labor through the manufacturing process. Computerized information systems allow companies to process vast amounts of marketing, production, and human resources data. Highly sophisticated information systems, such as MRP (materials requirement planning) and SAP, not only schedule production processes but they also automatically order raw materials, control inventories, and maintain general ledgers and other accounting records.

It is not enough to simply collect and manipulate information. The proliferation of computers and other information technology has vastly increased the ability of companies to collect, store, and distribute information. How that information is used and whether it is used in a way that offers companies a competitive advantage has quickly become the central question for the managers of firms in many industries.

Online businesses have the ability to collect vast amounts of information about their customers—when they enter the website, how often they enter, whether they come back, which pages they view, how long they spend on each page, whether they buy, how much they buy, what combinations of products they buy—but they frequently lack the ability to process this information. And, even if they could, they would still have to assess whether they are analyzing the right kinds of data and whether the insights they glean from their data processing efforts are worth the cost.

Even more challenging for online business firms "is to analyze and understand the behavior of the consumer and do it in real time, while the consumer is in the middle of the transaction."[21] While this is, indeed, a lofty goal, it's easy to see how an Amazon.com or other online business firm might be able to offer its customers a truly extraordinary level of personalized service if it can develop the information processing capabilities to offer its customers recommendations and shopping advice in a real-time fashion.

ORGANIZATIONAL CULTURE

If we think of organizations' hierarchical reporting relationships and their policies, procedures, systems, and information flows as more formal aspects of structure, then their cultures are a more informal, but no less important, aspect of structure. Anyone who has been involved for any length of time in businesses, schools, clubs, or religious institutions knows that nearly all organizations have cultures—widely shared norms and values—that have a powerful influence on their activities and operations. And, culture can have significant positive and negative impacts on performance. In fact, an organization's culture can be both an important source of sustained competitive advantage as well as a serious drag on its effectiveness.[22] As Edgar Schein, one of the preeminent writers on culture, has said: "Culture matters. It matters because decisions made without awareness of the operative cultural forces may have unanticipated and undesirable consequences."[23]

In many cases, an organization's culture reflects the myths and realities surrounding a founder or a key leader of the company. For example, the distinctiveness of the culture at Herman Miller can be traced to its founder D. J. DePree, and his son Max, who succeeded him as chief executive officer.[24] Both valued the importance of employee involvement and ownership in the business. The company's "Scanlon plan," in which employees are also owners of the business and enjoy profit sharing, not only follows from the company's culture, but also strongly complements it. Southwest Airlines also has a celebrated culture that reflects the influence of its legendary former chief executive, Herb Kelleher. Key features of Southwest's culture include an emphasis on decentralization of decision making, employee autonomy, and the importance of having fun at work.

An organization's culture can also be derived from or associated with its definition or identity so that those characteristics that make the organization distinctive in the eyes of customers or other external constituencies are also internalized as norms or values by the organization's employees. Again, under Kelleher's influence, Southwest almost certainly developed a distinctive culture early on, but as Southwest has grown and prospered in an industry that is characterized by stiff competition and very inconsistent profitability, Southwest's employees have almost certainly internalized their company's success and view themselves as "winners" who work for a "winning" organization. In this way, even strong cultures can be further reinforced and strengthened.

These examples also suggest how culture gets transmitted to employees. Quite often, new employees are socialized into an organization's culture as veteran employees pass along stories and myths. Stories about a dynamic leader, an employee's extraordinary efforts, a remarkable turnaround that saved the company from bankruptcy, or any other epic offer new employees a powerful model for their behavior.

The development and communication of effective cultures can be an important source of competitive advantage because they can provide employees with a sense of meaning and purposefulness. In his remarkable book, *Leadership Is an Art*, former Herman Miller CEO, Max DePree, writes,

> Every family, every college, every corporation, every institution needs tribal storytellers. The penalty for failing to listen is to lose one's history, one's historical context, one's binding values. ...
>
> As a culture or a corporation grows older and more complex, the communications naturally and inevitably become more sophisticated and crucial. An increasingly large part that communication plays in expanding cultures is to pass along values to new members and reaffirm those values to old hands.[25]

Effective cultures also motivate the types of behaviors that are important to organizational success in strategy implementation. For example, if culture helps to foster certain norms and behaviors that are desired by the organization or consistent with its goals and objectives, then culture can take the place of much supervisory activity.[26] In other words, organizations can establish formal supervisory and other structural controls to ensure employee compliance, and/or they can develop informal structural mechanisms, such as a strong culture, that can socialize employees into the organization's norms, goals, and objectives and encourage appropriate employee behaviors—a less expensive and usually far more effective alternative.

On the other hand, culture can also slow or retard organizational adaptation to change. If employees become so entrenched in their organization's way of doing things that they cannot objectively evaluate new developments in their firm's environment, then culture can have devastating consequences.[27] Donald Katz, in his analysis of the decline Sears, Roebuck experienced in retailing, found that the company's strong culture had prevented its managers from understanding the changes that were occurring in retailing:

> None of the consultants [hired by Sears] had ever encountered such awesome cultural and political impediments to altering an economic organization. They all sensed the richness and religiosity of the contrived family of Sears, and though they believed it continued to be the best of America in so many ways, they believed also that the Sears system was inimical to the survival of a great enterprise.[28]

Culture can also lead to fundamental problems in a company. Take for example a *Wall Street Journal* article, "Secretive Culture Led Toyota Astray," which highlights the impact Toyota's culture had on the company's early attempts to suppress the acceleration problems with many of its vehicles.[29] Or the critique of GM's corporate culture by a one-time GM executive, "GM's culture shows little tolerance for dissent, little appetite for making hard decisions and an insularity that has made it seem sometimes "tone-deaf" to broader societal concerns like the environment."[30] Similarly, many critics familiar with Enron believe that an arrogant culture was a major reason for the downfall of the company.

Thus, culture can be a double-edged sword, providing meaning, helping to socialize new employees, and motivating desired behaviors for implementing current organizational strategies, but culture can also be dangerous if it prevents managers and employees from being open to new ideas and new developments in their firms' competitive environments.

ISSUES AND PROBLEMS IN ORGANIZING

When an individual sits down to play a video game, his or her commands are executed immediately and precisely. General managers, in spite of impressive job titles, high-paying salaries, and willing subordinates, face a much different situation, however. In spite of their power and prestige, even the chief executive officers of the world's largest corporations find that the most carefully designed strategies often fail to get implemented because of a variety of organizational issues and problems. Here we will review some of these issues and describe how managers can use the various components of organizational structure to resolve these problems.

CENTRALIZATION VERSUS DECENTRALIZATION

Whether their firms are small or large, one important issue that all managers confront is the appropriate degree of centralization and decentralization. The more managers centralize decision making, the more control they can exercise over their firms. Centralized decision making can facilitate rapid implementation of strategies in some situations. It can also improve coordination, and a high degree of centralization may be required in vertically integrated organizations when different business units depend on each other for raw materials, components, and services. Effective management of related diversification strategies may also require a good deal of centralization in order to ensure that the related business units act on and realize the envisioned economies of scale and scope.

At the same time, decentralization can have a number of advantages. Decentralization gives lower-level employees and managers more opportunities to participate in organizational decision making. Decentralized decision making can enhance the esteem and morale of those employees and managers by making them feel as though they play important roles in their firms. Johnson & Johnson has already been mentioned as a company that excels with its decentralized structure, and its leadership development is well-respected by many people. Another decentralized company that has been a good breeding ground for leaders is the multinational conglomerate General Electric. Because lower-level employees are allowed to make important decisions, employees feel more responsible for their work.

Another example that highlights the advantages of decentralization is the contract that franchise owners of Great Harvest Bread Company Owners sign with the parent company owners. The first page of the contract emphasizes the company's desire for franchise owners to operate in a very decentralized way—"ANYTHING not expressly prohibited by the language of this Agreement IS ALLOWED"—and thereby encourages individual autonomy, initiative, creativity, and learning. Moreover, Great Harvest Bread Company provides individual franchise owners with many ways to share what they are learning at their franchise with other franchise owners. In such a way, the entire organization can get smarter and smarter.

Furthermore, because lower-level managers and employees in most organizations are more likely to be aware of unique or special circumstances surrounding various issues, decentralization of decision making is likely to lead to better decisions. And, because lower-level employees and managers are probably the first to become aware of changes or the potential for changes in the competitive environment, decentralized decision making can improve organizational flexibility and responsiveness to environmental change.

Centralization and decentralization thus have both advantages and disadvantages, and firms' unique missions and needs will determine the appropriate degree of centralization or decentralization. The various hierarchical structures that have been described here vary significantly in terms of their centralization and decentralization with functional structures being the most centralized and the cross-functional teams found in most matrix structures quite decentralized from top management. The degree of centralization can vary considerably inside any type of structure, however. For example, even in relatively decentralized multidivisional structures in which division managers are given a good deal of responsibility and control over their units' activities, accounting, finance, and treasury operations and decision making are almost always centralized in the corporation's headquarters.

Nor will managers agree on the appropriate degree of centralization or decentralization. Under its founder, Bernie Marcus, Home Depot was managed in a highly decentralized way in which each store manager was free to run his or her store in an almost completely autonomous fashion. When Bob Nardelli arrived from General Electric to take the reins as CEO, he insisted that many activities that were decentralized become much more centralized. In addition, he also required that the performance of individual stores be highly monitored by control systems in the corporate headquarters. The change in structure had a major impact on the company's formerly free-wheeling culture, and was not immediately embraced by most Home Depot employees.[31] When employee morale and firm performance declined, Nardelli was removed as CEO, and many activities were again decentralized.

COMMUNICATION AND LANGUAGE PROBLEMS

It is interesting to consider that an organization with eight hierarchical levels and a span of control of eight individuals per manager—not unreasonable assumptions—would have the theoretical capacity to employ over two million individuals! Yet, even the world's largest corporations rarely have more than a few hundred thousand employees. And, though it is certainly conceivable that organizations could have very tall hierarchies with a dozen or more levels of superior-subordinate reporting relationships, it is rare for even the largest business organizations to have more than eight hierarchical levels. What explains the difference between "theoretical capacity" and the actual size of today's largest corporations, and why do organizations rarely have more than eight hierarchical levels?

Although several factors limit the size of organizations, the most important limiting factor is communication. All modern organizations suffer language and other communication problems; research suggests that these problems intensify as organizational size and diversity increase. An excellent illustration of these organizational communication problems is provided by the children's game of telephone, in which one child in one corner of a room relays a message to the next child who relays the message to the next child and so on until a much-distorted message reaches the last child in the far corner of the room. In the children's game of telephone, the distortion of the original message will vary directly with the number of participants in the game. The same distortion occurs in organizations as information flows across hierarchical levels or from one department to another.

Researchers have long been aware of such communication problems. One organizational scholar writing in the late 1960s noted that

> a [manager] faces a world of vast scope, and therefore he must rely primarily on a formal information system to filter out "noise" and less important data and to provide an abstraction of the real world that preserves essential information about significant events.[32]

But he also acknowledged that data flowing through the organization could become so distorted that the resulting information "cannot convey what is going on in the world." As a result, managers work "in an analogue, abstract world."[33] Other researchers have made the same observation, noting that "almost all organizational structures tend to produce false images in the decision maker, and the larger ... the organization, the better the chance that its top decision-makers will be operating in purely imaginary worlds."[34]

Nor has information technology enabled firms to overcome these limitations. According to Martin S. Davis, former chairman and chief executive officer of Paramount,

> complexity has narrowed the capacity of managers. There are limits to the information they can absorb and the operating details they can monitor. Managers can be spread so thin that they overlook areas of true opportunity. The information age has not necessarily been accompanied by an ability to interpret and use the greater fund of information advantageously.[35]

In most organizations, however, the problem is even more complicated than is suggested by these concerns about information distortion and data overload because business firms are political organizations. Self-interested managers will often find it expedient to alter or otherwise intentionally distort a particular communication. Researchers have observed that information, and especially bad news, moves very slowly through organizations.[36] Managers who have unfavorable information to pass along have strong incentives either to alter or to slow down this information before passing it along. The result is a loss of management control, and strategy implementation inevitably suffers.

It is probably impossible to totally alleviate organizational communication problems. Certainly no hierarchical structure is free of communication problems. In fact, the various hierarchical structures that have been described in this chapter were all developed, at least in part, to alleviate communication problems and improve organizational responsiveness. The multidivisional structure aimed to reduce the problem of top management overload that often develops in functionally organized firms, yet it has failed to completely eliminate communication problems. As a consequence, many firms have adopted cross-functional structures to improve communication, coordination, and information flows. Future evolutions in organizational structure will almost certainly continue to address the communication problems that are inherent in all organizations. For example, some organizations have been able to develop highly effective intranets that link employees via email and the Internet to speed communication and facilitate the exchange of information. Yet even these sophisticated intranets must cope with the staggering growth of email, texting, and other forms of electronic communication, and the possibility that critical messages can be overlooked or not seen promptly.

CONFLICT

Because organizational life is political, conflict is an inevitable part of all organizations. Some conflict is almost unavoidable, as many business situations invite disagreements and animosities among individuals and departments. Some of these situations have already been noted. For example, the transfer pricing problem, found in any company in which one division produces a component or raw material or provides a service for another department, invites conflict. Functional rivalries are also often a source of conflict. Manufacturing managers often claim that engineers design products that are difficult to build or assemble, while engineers often feel as though manufacturing managers lack appreciation for the "elegance" of their product designs. Sales and marketing personnel will often conclude that accounting or finance departments prevent them from selling products or services by insisting that prices be kept high, while accounting and finance personnel often claim that sales and marketing departments are trying to "give away" their companies' products or services. Because of the way our thinking tends to become socialized or influenced by our surroundings, it is only natural that managers will come to hold the values associated with their respective departments.

An emphasis on "superordinate goals" (i.e., goals that are more important to all organizational members than their individual or group goals) can do much to reduce conflict among employees, departments, and business units. Superordinate goals can have powerful motivational impacts on employees.[37] Compensation systems can also be designed to motivate employees and managers to work to achieve overall organizational objectives rather than their own parochial interests. For example, bonus plans that reward managers based on the performance of their own division or unit *and* overall company performance are much more likely to get managers focused on overall company goals than compensation plans that reward managers solely on the basis of their own unit's performance.

At the same time, it's important to emphasize that conflict is not entirely negative. If conflict brings out different opinions and leads to a greater exploration of strategic options, it can be very beneficial for managerial thinking and for organizations. In fact, organizations without any conflict or disagreements are likely to be particularly vulnerable to groupthink. They are also more likely to be vulnerable to the forces of environmental change because they are unlikely to generate a variety of ideas for how their firms should anticipate or respond to the competitive dynamics in their industries.

A related problem is referred to as the "agency problem"—the tendency for the interests of principals (owners) and their agents (managers) to diverge.[38] The same agency problems exist within organizations between top managers and their subordinates, and no organizational structure, however carefully designed, can completely alleviate these agency and motivation problems.

In fact, problems of agency afflict all organizations at multiple levels: At the senior management level, for example, the objective of maximizing shareholder wealth will often take a back seat to other objectives that may be more aligned with the interests of managers and employees. At lower levels, many employees are extremely conscientious and often willing to do the work of several of their more average performing colleagues, but other employees are shirkers who will gladly let their more ambitious colleagues take up the slack. Furthermore, employees will naturally work harder on those initiatives to which they are more committed and on those that they see as serving their own best interests.

SUMMARY

As already noted, these issues and problems are an inevitable part of organizational life. We've already suggested some ways in which the various components of structure can be used to deal with these issues and problems. Multidivisional structures are necessarily more decentralized than functional structures, and we've already noted that one of the key advantages of the multidivisional structure is its ability to improve decision making in large and diversified companies. Cross-functional structures can further decentralize decision making to product teams and can also provide excellent forums for conflicting points of view to be heard and addressed in an effective manner. Similarly, effective organizational cultures can be highly motivational and can often minimize the need for more elaborate hierarchical structures.

Top managers' mental models—their beliefs and understandings about how to organize and implement strategy—determine how they combine the various structural components of hierarchy, standard operating procedures and policies, information systems, and culture into effective organizational structures. Unfortunately, many managers fail to give adequate attention to the structural issues and questions surrounding strategy implementation, preferring instead to focus their attention and energy on the formulation of strategy. Another common mistake is to fix one aspect of organization (e.g., the information system), and fail to consider the implications on policies or norms or reporting relationships. As a consequence, many very good strategies never live up to their potential but become "unrealized strategies" because of ineffective implementation.

EMERGING ISSUES AND NEW TYPES OF ORGANIZATIONAL STRUCTURE

This final section considers how the changing nature of work, demands for information, and emerging human resource management issues are encouraging the development of new organizational structures.

THE CHANGING NATURE OF WORK

The rapid rate of technological change, especially the rapid pace of developments in information technology, is having a profound impact on the nature of work in most industries. Products and services are becoming increasingly knowledge intensive. This shift toward more knowledge-intensive products and services has placed important new demands on workers. As a study prepared by the Hudson Institute suggests, these transformations in the economy will require a more educated and knowledgeable workforce.[39] Workers with four-year college or university degrees now earn, on average, more than 40 percent more than employees holding only a high school diploma, a premium that has grown considerably over the last 20 years and is likely to continue growing as our economy continues to transform the nature of work.[40]

Even more profound than these changing educational requirements, however, are the changes that are occurring in the nature of work itself. As noted earlier in the chapter, the traditional aim of structure has been to organize work—physical work—in order to implement strategies effectively. Employees were organized into functional departments so they could specialize and become increasingly proficient at their tasks. And, while Frederick Taylor aimed to remove "all possible brain work"[41] from employee's jobs, few jobs today depend solely on the physical labor or physical skills of workers. Now, workers are important for the knowledge and expertise they possess, and few tasks allow employees the luxury of working in isolation, unaware of what other employees in other parts of the organization know and are doing. Here's how one business manager described the ways this transformation in the nature of work is changing how his company views its workers:

> [W]e began to realize that when we looked at the social and technical changes that needed to take place in the work force and the workplace … that the real technology was in people's heads.
>
> The real cutting edge competitive piece to this was not the hardware that sat in front of them [the employees] or necessarily the social systems that were around them. It was the knowledge in workers' heads. That is the competitive edge.[42]

Organizational structure thus takes on added importance because of this changing nature of work. Even in manufacturing and other types of labor-intensive firms, employees are becoming less and less important for their physical labor. As in the service sector, nearly all manufacturing employees are now "knowledge workers," important not for their physical labor but for their expertise and know-how.

Further complicating the management of knowledge workers is that the knowledge employees carry around in their heads is relatively worthless unless they freely communicate and share it with others who need this information. Thus, structures that formerly sought to organize physical labor efficiently through specialization and into separate departments are almost certainly inappropriate and ineffective in encouraging employees to share their knowledge and communicate it with other employees. Companies have found information technologies such as email, the Internet, and intranets extremely helpful in disseminating the knowledge of individual employees.

At the same time, company cultures must often be altered to provide employees with incentives to share rather than hoard the knowledge and information that they possess.[43] For example, factory workers who hold a great deal of knowledge about their manufacturing processes are often reluctant to share that knowledge if their companies have a long tradition of labor-management conflict or animosity. Other workers can fear losing their jobs if they share specialized knowledge that they possess.[44]

Thomas Friedman has described how the changing nature of work and the importance of knowledge workers are requiring companies to rethink structural arrangements. In the following passage, he describes how the advertising firm, WPP, has rethought traditional modes of organization and structure:

> WPP adapted to get the most out of itself. It changed its office architecture and practices, just like those companies that adjusted their steam-run factories to the electric motor. But WPP not only got rid of its walls, it got rid of all its floors. It looked at all its employees from all its companies as a vast pool of individual specialists who could be assembled horizontally into collaborative teams, depending on the unique demands of any given project.[45]

These shifts imply that we will see major changes in human resource management and new types of organizational structures in the years ahead.

HUMAN RESOURCE MANAGEMENT ISSUES

As a consequence of the changing nature of work, companies need to focus more effort and energy on how jobs are designed, how work is organized, and how knowledge will be accumulated, stored, and shared with other employees as well as with customers and suppliers. In other words, companies will need to place a new emphasis on human resource management issues and policies—considerations that have frequently been downplayed.

The management of knowledge workers requires a radical rethinking of traditional organizational structures. At present, we know very little about the management of knowledge workers in any industry. The traditional, functional division of labor approach may enhance efficiency, but an unintended consequence of this approach is the "dumbing down" of work so that it becomes a repetitious, thoughtless, and mind-numbing exercise. One industry observer has argued that the problem with many traditional assembly line jobs is not the time lost as workers pass parts from one workstation to the next or the high incidence of costly repetitive stress injuries; instead, the problem is that employees "doing the same task repeatedly twenty-five hundred times a day cannot think, record data, study, teach, learn, maintain, improve, and otherwise perform as a world-class work force."[46]

A better approach is to organize work in such a way that employees become managers of their own processes, that they take responsibility for developing their knowledge and skills, and that they have opportunities for sharing their knowledge and skills with other employees, customers, and suppliers.[47] And, it is important that companies retain knowledge workers because they "become about three times more productive after ten years with the same employer than when they started work," and their "knowledge is key to keeping customers—whose longevity is the source of repeat sales and referrals."[48]

Finally, most companies are now realizing the value of adopting *high-performance work practices* that include all of the following components:

- Selective hiring.
- Extensive training.
- Decentralized decision making.
- Extensive sharing of information.
- Use of incentive compensation.[49]

Though researchers have long known the value of adopting such work practices, their widespread adoption has only begun to take on urgency with the changing nature of work and the growing importance of managing knowledge workers. Nearly all of the components of high impact work practices have a significant and strategic role for human resource managers and staff.

OUTSOURCING AND NEW TYPES OF HIERARCHICAL STRUCTURES

We are also seeing the emergence of new types of organizational structures that meet the information needs of the new work. Certainly we can expect that the trend toward the use of more cross-functional teams and matrix structures will continue. The managers of many firms have evaluated their value chains and concluded that many activities that their firms have traditionally performed have not contributed to competitive advantage, and they have now begun to contract with suppliers for these activities. It is conceivable, in fact, that many organizations could be radically restructured so that nearly all the activities they now perform could be supplied by outside vendors.

The resulting *virtual* or *networked* organizations focus on the one or few activities that are critical to their success while outsourcing nearly all other functional activities. Companies like Nike and Liz Claiborne operate in this way. Nike designs and markets footwear, but outsources all its production needs, leaving the company free to focus on those activities—marketing and product design—that provide it with its competitive advantage. Similarly, Liz Claiborne designs clothing lines, but, like Nike, Liz Claiborne contracts with other companies to produce its apparel products. Retail department and specialty stores sell the merchandise of both companies.

While Nike and Liz Claiborne are perhaps extreme examples, we see many organizations contracting out for services that have traditionally been handled in-house by functional departments. A large percentage of companies now outsource their payroll function, and some companies have even outsourced all of their data-processing operations. Advancements in information technology will only continue to push organizations toward greater outsourcing.

Organizational boundaries will become more fluid as firms rethink which activities and functions must be performed "inside the organization" and which activities can be outsourced to other firms.

Many observers have criticized organizations that have outsourced manufacturing and other activities, arguing that these firms are "hollowing" themselves and that they risk losing control of critical functions. Others have argued just the opposite, however. Dartmouth professor James Brian Quinn is one of the leading advocates of restructuring efforts that allow firms to focus attention on critical activities while outsourcing many less critical activities. In his defense of outsourcing, Quinn argues that:

- Intellectual and service activities now occupy the critical spots in most companies' value chains—regardless of whether the company is in the service or manufacturing sector— and if companies are not "best in world" at these critical intellectual and service activities, then they are sacrificing competitive advantage by performing those activities internally or with their existing levels of expertise.

- Each company should focus its strategic investments and management attention on those capabilities and processes—usually intellectual or service activities—where it can achieve and maintain "best in world" status.

- The specialized capabilities and efficiency of outside service suppliers have so changed industry boundaries and supplier capabilities that they have substantially diminished the desirability of much vertical integration, and, strategically approached, outsourcing does not "hollow out" a corporation, but it can decrease internal bureaucracies, flatten organizations, and give companies a heightened strategic focus, vastly improving their competitive responsiveness.[50]

In other words, companies must focus on those value-chain activities that are critical to their success, while the efficiency and quality of outside vendors allows companies to outsource their less central activities.

While much outsourcing has involved moving manufacturing jobs to low-income countries where it can be done much more inexpensively, more recent concerns over outsourcing have focused on the outsourcing of highly skilled and technical work. Many companies are now employing software developers in India and elsewhere. General Electric has opened a research and development center in India. At the same time, rapidly developing countries like India are now buying more products and services from the United States, which should help fuel U.S. domestic job growth, so economists are still struggling to reach an understanding of the full implications of this most recent wave of outsourcing for countries around the world. Clearly, different industries will be impacted differently by the opportunities and challenges posed by outsourcing.

Peter Drucker has concluded that the virtual corporation may well become the dominant form of organizational structure in the years ahead.[51] Drucker argues that it is not just because virtual organizations contract out less critical activities, allowing them to focus their attention and resources on those activities that are sources of competitive advantage. Drucker's more important observation is that contracting out these more peripheral activities may be a way to actually gain an additional advantage over competitors who keep these activities inside the organizational hierarchy. Drucker reasons that when employees are involved in an activity that is not central to the success of an organization (such as sorting the mail, janitorial work, manufacturing of components), they have only limited promotion opportunities and will therefore suffer from low morale and low job performance. By contracting out these peripheral activities, however, employees working for those contract organizations will have greater opportunities for advancement and will therefore have higher morale and be more effective in performing the duties and responsibilities of their jobs.

Another creative way of organizing to accommodate the changing nature of work is through an **ambidextrous organizational structure**. This structure addresses the need for both radical and incremental innovation. In this structure the new, exploratory, or innovative parts of the company are separated from traditional parts of the organization allowing for different processes, structures, and cultures. These new parts of the company aren't left totally by themselves; however, they are integrated into the traditional management structure so they can share important resources from the traditional units—for example talent, funds, and customers as illustrated in Exhibit 4. They are, however, enough outside the traditional structure that they aren't contaminated and their cultures are not overwhelmed by the forces of "business as usual."[52]

CONCLUSIONS: ORGANIZATIONAL STRUCTURE AND THE BOOK'S THREE KEY THEMES

THE IMPORTANCE OF MANAGERS AND MANAGERIAL THINKING

The optimal organizational structure for any firm involves balancing many different components of structure and dealing with a number of complex topics and issues, such as conflict, employee motivation, the appropriate degree of centralization and decentralization, and communication and language problems. In making important decisions about organizational structure, managers must weigh many considerations, but well-designed structures are essential if strategies are to be effectively implemented and if organizations are to be responsive to changes in the competitive environment. Managers' beliefs about how to organize are therefore a major influence on organizational effectiveness and performance.

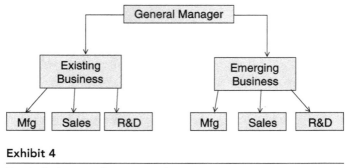

Exhibit 4

The Ambidextrous Organization Structure

At the same time, this chapter has underscored that structure in organizations is a much broader concept than the organizational chart or the formal hierarchy of an organization. While organizational theorists have long understood the importance of conceptualizing structure broadly, practicing managers all too frequently underestimate the power of the less visible aspects of organizational structure—communication and information flows, organizational routines, standard operating procedures, control systems, and above all, culture. Peter Senge captures the importance of these less visible aspects of organizational structure when he writes that "structure in human systems includes the 'operating policies' of the decision makers in the system," and that "redesigning … decision making redesigns the system structure." Structure, then, is "inextricably tied to how [managers] think."[53] Thus, managerial thinking not only plays an important role in designing organizational structures, but it is itself both a product of and a key component of organizational structure. This is a profound idea because it suggests how tightly coupled managers and managerial thinking are to the formulation and implementation of strategies in business organizations.

CHANGE AND THE NEED TO THINK DYNAMICALLY ABOUT STRATEGIC MANAGEMENT

As the intellectual or knowledge component of work continues to increase, managers will place ever greater pressure on their firms' structures to acquire and disseminate information and knowledge and to facilitate individual and organizational learning.[54] In addition, firms will continue to rethink their value chains. This will almost surely lead to more and more companies focusing on key value-adding activities that can be sources of competitive advantage, while contracting with other firms to perform less critical functions. Finally, because yesterday's source of competitive advantage—whether it be an effective business definition, a low-cost manufacturing capability, or a strong organizational culture—can quickly become tomorrow's competitive *disadvantage*, managers and their firms must become even more responsive to changes in their competitive environments.

THE IMPORTANCE OF ORGANIZATIONAL LEARNING

Organizing and organizations will continue because they provide the necessary context and continuity that knowledge workers require in order to function effectively. In short, organizational structures convert the creativity and expertise of knowledge workers into desired firm outcomes.[55] Yet, we know very little about how firms foster individual and organizational learning or what can be done to improve their ability to exploit this learning. One of the major automobile assembly companies recently undertook a study of its product development efforts and found that it had learned very little from its past mistakes and successes; every new vehicle development effort was essentially starting at zero, and the same mistakes were being committed over and over again with each new vehicle. On the other hand, a small coffee shop in Colorado Springs asks all employees, before punching out, to write comments in a running log about what went right or wrong during their shift; likewise, before they can begin working, arriving employees must read all comments that have been added since their last shift. These two examples are anecdotal, but the extremes they illustrate suggest the pressing need for thinking and research on organizational learning.

KEY POINTS

- Organizational structure includes *the mechanisms that facilitate the formulation and implementation of strategy and the overall coordination of the business enterprise.*

- The objectives of structure are to implement strategies and to make organizations responsive to their owners (shareholders), managers, and the competitive environment.

- Structure includes hierarchical reporting relationships, formal organizational control systems, flows of information, and organizational culture.

- Three traditional types of hierarchical structure are the functional, multidivisional, and matrix forms, each having some advantages as well as disadvantages and limitations for the effective implementation of organizational strategy.

- Though less visible than hierarchical structures, organizational control systems, flows of information, and organizational culture are other important components of organizational structure.

- Any structure will face a number of issues and problems, including communication and motivational problems, control loss, and the danger that owners' interests will be subordinated to managers' interests. Effective organizational structures can mitigate, but not completely eliminate, these problems.

- The competitive environment and the changing nature of work will lead companies to adopt new human resource management practices and to develop new structures, including virtual forms of organization.

KEY QUESTIONS FOR MANAGERS

- How effective is your organization's structure at allowing managers to implement strategies?

- How well does your organization respond to environmental changes? What aspects of your company's structure enhance the organization's responsiveness? What aspects of the structure inhibit responsiveness?

- How important is your organization's informal structure, i.e., its rules, processes, standard operating procedures, culture? In what ways are these informal elements effective? In what ways are they dysfunctional?

- What are some of the trade-offs your organization has made in the ways it deals with the central issues in organizing described toward the end of this chapter—centralization versus decentralization, conflict, and agency problems?

- How is the changing nature of work affecting your company? In what ways has your organization responded to the growing importance of knowledge work? What innovative structural components has your company embraced to enhance its effectiveness?

NOTES

1 A question of management: Carol Bartz on how Yahoo's organization structure got in the way of innovation. 2009. *The Wall Street Journal*, June 2: R4.

2 Nadler, D. A., & Tushman, M. L. 1997. *Competing by Design: The Power of Organizational Architecture*. New York: Oxford University Press: 5.

3 Weber, M. 1947. *The Theory of Social and Economic Organization*. New York: Free Press.

4 Mintzberg, H. 1978. Patterns in strategy formation. *Management Science*, 24: 934–948.

5 Stanford, N. 2007. *Guide to Organization Design*. London: Profile Books Ltd.

6 Williamson, O. E. 1975. *Markets and Hierarchies: Analysis and Antitrust Implications*. New York: Free Press.

7 Stanford, N. 2007. *Guide to Organization Design*. London: Profile Books Ltd. 49.

8 Williamson, O. E. 1975. *Markets and Hierarchies: Analysis and Antitrust Implications*. New York: Free Press.

9 Blumenstein, R. 1997. Tough driving: Struggle to remake the Malibu says a lot about remaking GM. *The Wall Street Journal*, March 27: A1, A8.

10 Wasserman, M. E. 1998. *Examining the Relationship between Research and Development Resource Flows and Knowledge-Based Capabilities: Integrating Resource-Based and Organizational Learning Theory*. Unpublished doctoral dissertation, Michigan State University.

11 Stanford, Naomi. 2007. *Guide to Organization Design*. London: Profile Books Ltd.: 57.

12 Davis, S. M., & Lawrence, P. R. 1978. Problems of matrix organizations. *Harvard Business Review* 56(3): 131–142.

13 White, R. 1979. *The Dexter Corporation*. Boston: HBS Case Services, Harvard Business School.

14 White, R. 1979. *The Dexter Corporation*. Boston: HBS Case Services, Harvard Business School: 11.

15 White, R. 1979. *The Dexter Corporation*. Boston: HBS Case Services, Harvard Business School: 12.

16 Bank, D. 1999. Know your customer: Companies have more data on their customers than ever. The trick is how to use it. *The Wall Street Journal*, June 21: R18. See also Clark, D. 1999. Managing the mountain. *The Wall Street Journal*, June 21: R4; Totty, M. 2002. So much information … *The Wall Street Journal*, December 9: R4.

17 Barney, J. B. 1986. Organizational culture: Can it be a source of sustained competitive advantage? *Academy of Management Review* 11: 656–665.

18 Schein, E. H. 1999. *The Corporate Culture Survival Guide*. San Francisco: Jossey-Bass.

19 DePree, M. 1989. *Leadership is an Art*. New York: Dell Publishing.

20 DePree, M. 1989. *Leadership is an Art*. New York: Dell Publishing: 82, 108.

21 Etzioni, A. 1965. Organizational control structure. In March, J. G. (Ed.), *Handbook of Organizations*. Chicago: Rand McNally.

22 See, for example, Terlep, S. 2010. GM's plodding culture vexes its impatient CEO. *The Wall Street Journal*, April 7: B1, B7.

23 Katz, D. R. 1987. *The Big Store: Inside the Crisis and Revolution at Sears*. New York: Viking: 41.

24 Linebaugh, K., Searcey, D., & Shirouzu, N. 2010. Secretive culture led Toyota astray. *The Wall Street Journal*, February 10: A1, A6.

25 GM culture: A problem that cash can't fix. 2009. *The Korea Herald*, March 3: 9.

26 Morse, D. 2003. A hardware chain struggles to adjust to a new blueprint. *The Wall Street Journal*, January 17: A1, A6.

27 Emery, J. C. 1969. *Organizational Planning and Control Systems: Theory and Technology*. New York: Macmillan.

28 Emery, J. C. 1969. *Organizational Planning and Control Systems: Theory and Technology*. New York: Macmillan: 114.

29 Boulding, K. R. 1966. The economics of knowledge and the knowledge of economics. *American Economic Review* 56(2): 8.

30 Davis, M. S. 1985. Two plus two doesn't equal five. *Fortune*, December 9: 177, 179, emphasis added.

31 Hamermesh, R. G. 1977. Responding to divisional profit crises. *Harvard Business Review* 55(2): 124–130; Milliken, F. J., Morrison, E. W., & Hewlin, P. F. 2003. An exploratory study of employee silence: Issues that employees don't communicate upward and why. *Journal of Management Studies*, 40: 1453–1477.

32 Kramer, R. M. 1991. Intergroup relations and organizational dilemmas: The role of categorization processes. In Staw, B., & Cummings, L. (Eds.), *Research in Organizational Behavior*, 13: 191–228. Greenwich, CT: JAI Press.

33 Berle, A. A., & Means, G. C. 1932. *The Modern Corporation and Private Property*. New York: Macmillan.

34 *Workforce 2000: Work and Workers for the Twenty-First Century*. 1987. Indianapolis: Hudson Institute: xxvii.

35 Wessel, D. 2004. The future of jobs: New ones arise, wage gap widens. *The Wall Street Journal*, April 2: A1, A5.

36 Quoted in Worthy, J. 1959. *Big Business and Free Men*. New York: Harper & Row: 67.

37 Kevin P. Boyle, quoted in U.S. Department of Commerce and U.S. Department of Labor. 1993. *The Work Place of the Future*. Washington, DC: U.S. Government Printing Office: 222.

38 Thurm, S. 1999. What do you know? *The Wall Street Journal*, June 21: R10, R19.

39 Aeppel, T. 2002. On factory floors, top workers hide secrets to success. *The Wall Street Journal*, July 1: A1, A10.

40 Friedman, T. L. 2005. *The World Is Flat: A Brief History of the Twenty-First Century*. New York: Farrar, Straus and Giroux: 209.

41 Schonberger, R. J. 1996. *World Class Manufacturing: The Next Decade*. New York: Free Press.

42 Senge, P. M. 1990. *The Fifth Discipline: The Art and Practice of the Learning Organization*. New York: Doubleday/Currency.

43 Senge, P. M. 1990. *The Fifth Discipline: The Art and Practice of the Learning Organization*. New York: Doubleday/Currency: 213.

44 See, for example, Becker, B., & Gerhart, B. 1996. The impact of human resource management on organizational performance: Progress and prospects. *Academy of Management Journal*, 39: 779–801; Pfeffer, J., & Velga. J. F. 1999. Putting people first for organizational success. *Academy of Management Executive*, 13(2): 37–48.

45 Quinn, J. B. 1992. *Intelligent Enterprise: A Knowledge and Service-Based Paradigm for Industry*. New York: Free Press: 32–33.

46 Drucker, P. F. 1989. Sell the mailroom. *The Wall Street Journal*, July 25: A16.

47 O'Reilly, III, C. A., & Tushman, M. L. 2004. The ambidextrous organization. *Harvard Business Review*, 82(2): 76.

48 Senge, P. M. 1990. *The Fifth Discipline: The Art and Practice of the Learning Organization*. New York: Doubleday/Currency: 53.

49 Senge, P. M. 1990. *The Fifth Discipline: The Art and Practice of the Learning Organization*. New York: Doubleday/Currency.

50 Drucker, P. F. 1994. The age of social transformation. *Atlantic Monthly*, November: 53–80.

DISCUSSION QUESTIONS

1   According to the reading, widely shared values and norms make up an organization's culture. Moreover, culture gets in the way of an organization making progressive change. What shared values and norms are commonly found in criminal justice organizations and how might they impede change? Provide real-life examples.

2   Superordinate goals, according to the reading, are goals that are more important to all organizational members than individual or group goals. Provide an example of an individual goal, a group goal, and a superordinate goal that might be found in a criminal justice organization. Would each individual goal promote conflict or teamwork?

SECTION I CONCLUSION

After reading the first two articles, you might be wondering why one was criminal justice-related and the other was not. This was not accidental. Public sector leaders can learn from our counterparts in the private sector, where innovation, creativity, and entrepreneurship are valued commodities. Those of us who lead criminal justice organizations sometimes believe that red tape (i.e., excessive bureaucratic rules) and mediocrity are part of the job. The phrase "good enough for government work" embodies this very idea. But those of us who aspire to be effective administrators who lead great organizations look to private business strategies for ideas about how to streamline operations, introduce cutting-edge practices, or increase flexibility within the confines of the law and regulations. The takeaway here is that ambitious administrators expand their thinking beyond day-to-day governmental routines and habits.

Focusing on organization structure might strike some as a rudimentary way to understand where employees fit in a pyramid. However, I challenge you to think in more strategic terms. Think of that pyramid serving as a lighthouse. At the very top, there is a glass dome known as the lantern room, where the lighthouse keeper can see what is on the horizon by day and assess weather-related information, like wind currents. By night, the lantern serves as a navigational aid to sailors. In other words, the keeper looks outward. This is much like the role of an executive. At the top of the organization, the executive looks outward at the landscape of politics, community stakeholders, national and local trends, and potential threats. Below the lantern room sits the spiral staircase leading to the watch room and the service room. Similarly, at the lower echelon of an organizational structure, mid-level managers gaze inward assessing daily operations, logistical and equipment needs, internal trends, and potential pitfalls. Organizational structure gives us a way to differentiate not only rank, power, and compensation, but also to distinguish between critical roles and responsibilities that make an entire organization operate at its highest caliber.

DECISION MAKING IN ORGANIZATIONS, ORGANIZATIONAL DEVIANCE

INTRODUCTION

March 20, 2018, was a bad day for the Massachusetts State Police. With a history of being an elite law enforcement organization the agency was deeply embarrassed when Boston newspaper head-lines and TV broadcast stations publicized that over twenty state troopers were being investigated in an overtime scandal. Overtime payments were paid to troopers for traffic patrols that were either partially or never conducted. A preliminary audit showed that the troopers in question never worked anywhere from 1 to 100 shifts. More disheartening, a local news station filed a public records request asking for overtime data. When the records when turned over, the agency commander decided to expand its investigation.

What can this story teach us about the concepts in Section II–Decision making and Deviance? First, it shows an agency chose to respond too slowly to troubling information revealed early in a scandal. It wasn't until the news media sought information on six named troopers that the agency decided to assertively investigate. This type of faulty decision making, believing that the problem was limited to one trooper and deciding not to look further, is an example of ignoring the age old maxim, "Where there is smoke there is fire."

Regarding organizational deviance, it is difficult to tell where this scandal fits until the findings of the investigation are released. Was it a systemic problem, a few rogue cops, or agency mismanagement?

With this in mind, Section II introduces two concepts that criminal justice administrators face every day: decision-making and organizational deviance. Despite the outsized role that decision-making plays in the functioning of a criminal justice organization, there is very little scholarly discourse on the subject. The Stohr and Collins article describes responses to eight obstacles that prevent effective decision-making and then goes on to propose six steps to improve decision-making. Both sets of recommendations are grounded in realities that affect managing criminal justice agencies today, such as politics, competing factions and stakeholders, and limited resources.

Organizational deviance, also known as bad workplace behavior, warrants informed attention and skillful management expertise. The article points out a critically important idea: organizational deviance is not always the result of one or a few wayward employees. Rather, the workplace environment itself can foster widespread unsavory, illegal, and unethical employee behavior. This is a powerful realization because it stresses that organizational leaders are ultimately responsible for promoting workplace quality, and toward that end, they can deal with deviance proactively, rather than reactively. Responses to organizational deviance often come in the form of employee discipline—such as firings, suspensions, and reprimands—all of which tend to create workplace martyrs or victims, which can entrench deviance instead of extinguish it.

DECISION MAKING AND PREDICTION

MARY K. STOHR AND PETER A. COLLINS

> To be, or not to be, that is the question: Whether 'tis nobler in the mind to suffer the slings and arrows of outrageous fortune, or to take arms against a sea of troubles, and by opposing end them?
>
> *Hamlet*, Act III, Scene I

> Ours is a time of uneasiness and indifference—not yet formulated in such ways as to permit the work of reason and the play of sensibility. Instead of troubles—defined in terms of values and threats—there is often the misery of vague uneasiness; instead of explicit issues there is often merely the beat feeling that all is somehow not right. Neither the values threatened nor whatever threatens them has been stated; in short, they have not been carried to the point of decision. Much less have they been formulated as problems of social science. ... The great sociologist C. Wright Mills comment[s] on the failure of social scientists to focus on core issues of "our times." Mills laments the jettisoning of reason and the failure to connect larger movements to individual existence.
>
> (Mills 1959: 11)

INTRODUCTION

One of the most representative titles of a criminal justice textbook, in terms of its content, is *Screwing the System and Making It Work* (Jacobs 1990). In essence, this not so well-known book is about a juvenile probation officer faced daily with no-win decisions regarding resources and his clients. Jacobs routinely had to decide how to reconcile his desire to help his clients with the fact that he had limited time, too many probationers to supervise, and too few programmatic options to refer them to. What to do? What to do? Or: Not whether to be or not to be a probation officer (as Hamlet might ponder), but how to be an effective one.

Ultimately, the probation officer's decision was to "screw the system to make it work," or to truly focus his time and talents on only the few clients he deemed most in need of his services, reluctantly ignoring the rest. By making this Solomonic choice, he believed that he might be "screwing" the system and perhaps his more neglected clients, but "making it work" for the youths he could focus attention on. He was not necessarily "happy" or "satisfied" with this decision, but he believed it was the best he could do with limited resources.

Such a scenario—scarce resources and too many clients—is emblematic of social service work for SLBs, as discussed earlier with reference to the work of Lipsky (1980). This reality fits the work of criminal justice practitioners today as much as it did more than twenty-five years ago, when Lipsky published his classic work. As Mills wrote almost fifty years ago, there is a tendency in human history to fail to make the logical connection between what happens globally and the individual experience; yet the phenomena are inextricably intertwined: "Neither the life of an individual nor the history of a society can be understood without understanding both" (Mills 1959: 3). One global truth that fits public sector work with few exceptions is that resources are always short and demand is always great; the SLB must make a determination, a decision, about how to reconcile these conditions.

So, given these constraints, how do criminal justice practitioners and managers make decisions? What sorts of influences are likely to affect how they make those decisions? Do they always act as our erstwhile juvenile probation officer did, focusing their resources on the most deserving and hard cases? What sorts of factors are likely to hamper effective decision making, and to improve it?

In this chapter we review the act of decision making: What it is, obstacles to effective decision making, and how that act might be improved. In addition, and relatedly, we will discuss decisions of one type, namely predictions, exploring how they are made and the typical errors associated with them. On this note we will touch on how brain cognition, and thus decision making, may be influenced by biology and environment and the implications of these connections for criminal justice actors and their work.

DECISIONS, DECISIONS, DECISIONS: WHAT THEY ARE AND WHO MAKES THEM (THE DECISION MAKERS)

A **decision** is simply a choice made by a person who is given the *discretionary power* to do so. There can be alternate options available to the decision maker, or it may be that no other choices are apparent. In our example, the juvenile probation officer made a decision to concentrate his time and resources on certain probationers, rather than spreading himself too thin. But what if he had not done this? What if he had tried to serve all his clients by rationing out limited time and resources to offer a little bit to everyone? In other words, what if he had maintained the status quo? Would this have been a decision? The answer is yes, it would. People in the criminal justice system, and in all other aspects of their lives, are forever making decisions to maintain the current operations even when they might be flawed.

EFFECTIVE DECISION MAKING

With little reservation, we can assume that the majority of criminal justice agency managers and actors are interested in making what we will define here as "effective" or "good" decisions, or those most likely to further the ends of justice. It is useful here to repeat the definition of *justice* given in the American Heritage Dictionary (1992: 456), as stated in Chapter 2: "[t]he quality of being fair; fairness. 2. The principle of moral rightness; equity. 3. The upholding of what is just, especially fair treatment and due reward in accordance with honor, standards, or law." Distinctions between formal and natural justice (law and morality) and how justice is precisely and fully defined are matters best left to philosophers. However, in this text, "justice" means that those who are guilty are caught, processed, and sanctioned, as befits community, professional, and moral standards, by system actors. We think that justice for our purposes also means that those who are innocent are given ample opportunity and the due process necessary to ensure that if they are caught up in the system, they do not remain there long and are not sanctioned. In terms of internal organizational operations, justice might also mean that employees are treated fairly and honestly by management and given the opportunity to develop and "give back" to their community. Effective or good decision making in criminal justice agencies, then, in our view, has to do with furthering the ends of justice for those processed by the system, and for the criminal justice actors who work in it.

TO ACT OR NOT TO ACT: THAT IS BUT ONE OF THE QUESTIONS!

The decision not to act is perhaps the most common decision of all. The police choose not to ticket or arrest, the prosecutor chooses not to prosecute, the community corrections officer or correctional officer in the jail or prison chooses not to pursue violations of rules. The truth is that we who study the behavior of criminal justice actors really have no idea how often such decisions *not to act* are made, since they usually do not come to official notice. Given the number of cases that flood the system each year and are sifted out, plus the official review that often accompanies decisions to act, it is likely there are more decisions not to act than otherwise (Bohm and Haley 2005). Judicial decisions made inside courtrooms or in front of legal actors, even concerning the least important of matters, are usually recorded for posterity. But so many other decisions by criminal justice actors, especially when they involve the decision not to act, are never reviewed or reviewable, simply because they are not known. For instance, police officers often do not file reports detailing why they did not write certain tickets for speeding. So the police organization, the public, and sometimes the alleged speeders, do not know why the decisions were made, or even that there were decisions; only the officers know.

Yet when a police officer does write a ticket, any number of people will know of that decision and some will review it, not the least of whom will be the alleged speeder! Such a decision to act then presents the greatest risk for the officer organizationally and therefore must be supported with ample evidence that a real violation occurred (through observation, but better yet because of unbiased evidence as provided, e.g., by a radar reading). Notice, however, that if the officer thinks, based on comparable evidence, that a speeding violation occurred but chooses not to act, there is usually no need to justify that decision, even though the dispatcher and perhaps a video recorder in the police car may document that the officer made the stop. But whatever way you look at it, it is just easier for an officer who witnesses a minor offense, absent organizational pressure to do otherwise, to decide not to act. This is the reason why criminal justice organizations, particularly police organizations that may stand to receive revenue from each traffic ticket, will pay careful attention to how many tickets are written by individual officers. In fact, they will often include that information in the officer's performance appraisal as a measure of how much work she is accomplishing on her shift, for example.

Such organizational surveillance or pressure regarding decision making may be both beneficial and detrimental to the ultimate goal of "good" decision making. Obviously, we want criminal justice actors to decide *to act* when there has been a violation of the law. But we also want them to have the discretion, as professionals, to determine when that is likely to have happened and to weigh the value of acting. So of course it is necessary for the criminal justice organization managers to watch and monitor how and why decisions are made, although an organization that applies too much pressure to make a decision one way or the other may thereby impose an obstacle to "good decision making."

OBSTACLES TO GOOD DECISION MAKING: LET US COUNT THE WAYS

Obstacles to "good" or effective decision making can come in many forms and from several sources. As we have seen, *the realities of the work of street-level bureaucrats* can force criminal justice actors to make less than optimal decisions. In essence, our juvenile probation officer was not "screwing" the system, but most of the clients, in order to "make it work" for those deemed most deserving or needy.

[G]roupthink has derailed many a decision-making process, and thus it constitutes a second and serious hindrance to effective decision making (Janis 1972). A prosecutor surrounded by only "yes people" who fail to challenge the status quo (or at least to question it) and who provide no alternative routes for action will often make decisions that do not achieve the best interests of justice for the community.

A third obstacle, as illustrated by police officers faced with ticket-writing decisions, indicates that *organizations can be both obstacles to, and facilitators of, effective decision making*. To repeat, because inertia or inaction is easier for officers in many cases of minor offenses—they do not have to do the paperwork and have it reviewed by others—organizational pressure to act may be inappropriate in some situations. Discretion with respect to minor offenses gives the officer the leeway she would not have with major offenses, where she would be compelled to act by law, practice, or conscience—or some combination of these. If the organization pressures her to act, to write the ticket when she otherwise would not, this can be an obstacle to good decision making only if the ticket was not warranted. … [O]rganizational pressure can also lead to decisions, which involves *organizational deviance* that violate the laws or professional practices one would expect from criminal justice actors and thus constitute poor decision making (Lee and Visano 1994; Walker 1993).

A fourth obstacle to good decision making is the *politics of organizational operation*. As we have discussed in several chapters, starting with Appleby's conception of the nature of public organizations early in the text through the later treatment of budgeting and planning, we have established that criminal justice agencies are centered in a political context. Laws and budgets that are formulated through give and take by political actors wrangling among themselves guide the actions of criminal justice organizations. What this means is that courtroom actors facing known time and resource constraints will tend to process cases more expeditiously than they might if there were more courtrooms, more judges, more prosecutors, more defense attorneys (Blumberg 1984). The numbers of those actors and those courtrooms are determined by political actors, presumably acting in the public interest, and they will allocate funding at the level that would allow more cases to be given more time, or not.

Of course, central to this discussion of politics is *money*, a fifth potential obstacle to good decision making, particularly when it is lacking. The example given of the courts and their processing of cases is really about both money and politics, or politics determining how much money will be allocated for criminal justice operation. An organization that is strapped for funds may decide, like our intrepid juvenile probation officer, to "screw the system" and focus on "making" only a part of it "work." Thus, courts might focus most resources on only the most serious cases, or systemwide policy may be to plead down even the most serious cases, to diminish prosecutorial or courtroom time expended on them.

Relatedly, space constraints in jails and prisons and *extremely heavy defense and prosecutorial caseloads and court dockets* represent a sixth obstacle to effective decision making for criminal justice actors. In Idaho, the lack of berths in treatment programs in the community has meant that judges sentence some offenders to prison, where they can in fact get treatment. Some might ask why this is a "poor" decision. The answer here is simple: Because it does not serve the ends of justice as we defined it. Judges in such cases will admit that some of the offenders did not *need* to go to prison for punishment, but they *desperately needed* substance abuse treatment. Why wasn't there substance abuse treatment available for indigent offenders in the community, one might ask? Because establishing and funding such programs is a political decision. So the state, courtesy of the taxpayers, ends up spending much more to incarcerate low-level offenders (about $20,000 annually for adult males) so that they can receive treatment. In turn, many offenders are more severely punished than their crimes warranted, according to the judges, and they are separated from their families and jobs, thus leading to a harder transition into the community once they parole.

This gets us to the point, and the seventh obstacle, that a *lack of available alternatives* or knowledge of such alternatives can also hinder good decision making. If judges have alternative sanctions or means of handling addicts—and in Idaho and other states, drug courts are providing such an alternative in large urban centers—then they might be able to improve their decision making and in turn better serve the ends of justice. Unfortunately, information about such alternatives, regardless of whether they "work," is sometimes sorely lacking in the criminal justice system. There are problems with getting up-to-date and applicable research on criminal justice practices, programming, and processes, and undoubtedly such a gap in knowledge impairs the criminal justice decision maker's ability to make good decisions (we will discuss the value of research a bit more in the following).

The eighth and final obstacle also relates to information as it affects decision making. The problem here is that there is *too much information* for the decision maker to sift through and use effectively. For example, there is now a plethora of information about the relative effectiveness of treatment programming. So the criminal justice planner reviewing that information for the first, or even the sixth, time could be overwhelmed by its complexity and depth. Yet somehow, people who make decisions about the content and duration of treatment programming will need to determine what information to pay the most attention to. A rule of thumb in terms of reviewing scientific research, as in this instance, is to look for studies that are well designed (Babbie 1992). That is, do they fit their subject, use multiple sources of both qualitative and quantitative data (also known as triangulation), and include enough subjects, and are they replicated?

However, when science cannot come to the rescue, so to speak, the decision maker will tend to evaluate the usefulness of information based on both logical and illogical factors. Illogical factors might include media presentations of infamous or non-representative cases, the order in which conflicting statements are received (what is seen or heard first or last will be given most credence), the mode of delivery (people will better remember information put to a tune or dramatically presented vs. spoken in a lecture), or who delivers it (famous or infamous persons, or those who have a dramatic flair, are more likely to be "heard" than others; Chiricos 2002; Dye and Zeigler 1989; Merlo and Benekos 2000). Other influential factors include who delivers the information (a trusted person or personality or someone with accepted expertise on a topic) and the mode of delivery (in a peer-reviewed academic journal vs. the popular press). It also makes a difference whether information fits the conventional wisdom or commonsensical notions about what is true and/or whether it is congruent with what has happened before.

People will also review information from the perspective of each individual's role as an organizational actor and make determinations about its truth and usefulness from that vantage point. Both the formal (training, official positions) and informal (subcultural and actual) practices of the organization will help people decipher the value of information. In other words, when faced with too much information, and absent any assurances about its validity from a scientific standpoint, the criminal justice manager and actor will try and sort through it using all sorts of filters; the danger arises when people are influenced by their own biases and predispositions, which may have been shaped by logical fallacies.

LOGICAL FALLACIES

One of the authors became acquainted with common logical fallacies in an undergraduate logic class. The professor was interested in preparing his students to "watch out for" and "beware" of failures in logic that frequently appear in public and private discourse and inevitably hamper the ability to make reasoned decisions. Classes on logic often include some discussion of logical fallacies or common errors in rhetorical arguments. Such fallacies are the refuge of the desperate and the deceitful, which is why we often see such tactics used in political discourse and over the airwaves. However, since criminal justice agencies and practices are guided mightily by the prevailing political winds, we often see such tactics used by those in or those critiquing criminal justice agencies or actors. The point of identifying common logical fallacies here is to prevent people from "falling" for them and thus making decisions that are influenced by the wrong conclusions they promote. Therefore, no discussion of decision making would be complete without touching on at least a few of the most common of these fallacies, including *ad hominem attacks, straw men, red herrings, begging the question* or *circular reasoning, the exception makes the rule,* and *appeals to patriotism/religion/emotion.* (Type "logical fallacies" into Google and you will be astounded at how many deceptive rhetorical tactics we humans have devised.)

Ad hominem attacks occur in arguments or discussions when the speaker or writer is attacked or slurred, without reference to the merits of what that person argued or stood for (Bassham *et al.* 2008). So for instance, if a police chief were to argue against the establishment of a certain crime control program, a person launching an ad hominem attack would make disparaging comments either directly or indirectly about the chief, perhaps accusing the person and his or staff of being "soft" on crime, rather than addressing the merits of the argument. Whether the research or current practice supports the development of such a program is irrelevant for people who launch an ad hominem attack in this instance, because their goal is to influence the decision making of stakeholders (not just the public, but also the mayor, the city council, and others), and they do not want the facts to get in the way.

The **straw man** logical fallacy is used by those who want to divert attention from the merits of the real argument or situation (Bassham *et al.* 2008). To do this they will construct an argument that is as easy to "push over" as a "straw man" would be. A person using this tactic will set up a false or weak (straw man) argument and, once it is shown to be false, will act as if the opponent's argument is false in its entirety. To cite Watters (2013: 5), a straw man argument can take this or many other forms, including the following:

1. Present the opponent's argument in weakened form, refute it, and pretend that the original has been refuted.

2. Present a misrepresentation of the opponent's position, refute it, and pretend that the opponent's actual position has been refuted.

3. Present someone who defends a position poorly as the defender, refute that person's arguments, and pretend that *every* upholder of that position, and thus the position itself, has been defeated.

4. Invent a fictitious persona with actions or beliefs that are criticized, and pretend that the person represents a group that the speaker is critical of.

Let's make our crime control program example more specific. Suppose a city council member who favored the establishment of a COMPSTAT program by the police department was to use a "straw man" argument. The council member might start by noting that failure to implement such a program will lead to greater crime in the streets. So an exchange between the police chief and the user of the straw man tactic might go something like this:

Police chief: We should not develop a COMPSTAT program in the city until the research indicates that it "works" to improve our ability to control crime.

City council member: Drug dealing on our streets should be stopped. COMPSTAT is a proactive solution that can solve our drug and larger crime problem.

Now of course by opposing the adoption of COMPSTAT now, the chief is not arguing that drug dealing on the streets should be allowed to go on. This is the straw man portion of the argument, because nobody wants drug dealing to continue. Thus, when the council member implies that to oppose COMPSTAT is to argue against a proactive crime control measure that will solve drug crimes, he deflates the chief's point about prudently waiting for research results and makes the chief appear to be reactive and perhaps "weak."

A **red herring** logical fallacy—the straw man fallacy could be a subgroup of the red herring—is also a diversionary tactic. As with all these tactics, it is used to divert attention from or mask the truth (Bassham *et al*. 2008). The difference is that the *red herring* tactic often entails an emotional twist, which is used to impair the listener's ability to make good decisions. Our police chief arguing against implementation of COMPSTAT now might have been educated at an elite Ivy League school, and his opponent might use this fact to argue that "the chief doesn't understand how things are done in this town." Now the police chief may in fact be well acquainted with how the department operates, having served in it for several years, but the person wielding this tactic is not interested in the truth. Rather, they are interested in making an argument in a fashion designed to convince members of a community in which reverse snobbism about education is widespread. The city councilman is also playing to the emotions of his audience, intimating that the chief is an outsider and not "one of us." Therefore group solidarity against those Ivy League outsiders requires that the community oppose what the chief wants to do in this matter. Where the police chief went to school of course has nothing to do with the merits of the COMPSTAT program.

Begging the question or circular reasoning involves restating in the conclusion the point on which the argument was based (Bassham *et al*. 2008). Thus the city council member might argue that "we know COMPSTAT is effective in reducing crime, because it is successful in reducing crime." The latter part of this statement "begs the question" about the program's effectiveness by stating that the program should be used precisely because it is (said to be) effective.

Another common logical fallacy used in public discourse about crime is **the exception makes the rule**, or "If it happens once or was true once, it must happen all the time or be true in every case" (Bassham *et al*. 2008). We often see this argument used by practitioners who will tell an anecdote and then apply the lessons from that story to all like circumstances and clients/suspects/offenders. Such an anecdote might begin: "You can't trust a such and such type of offender, because this one time I did and the person violated that trust," or "This treatment program should be adopted everywhere because we have seen fewer offenders return after they graduated from it." The point is that both statements may well describe what happened in the instances related, and they might even apply to all like instances, as these practitioners imply. But we do not know for sure that the statements apply to like circumstances or offenders, because each anecdote is only a single instance (the exception); there may be other explanations for what happened then, or comparable circumstances in which the same outcome would not occur (make the rule).

Thus a proponent of COMPSTAT might use this logical fallacy by arguing that "COMPSTAT 'worked' to reduce crime in New York City in a given decade and so it should be adopted in all cities." Again, it may be true that COMPSTAT "worked" to reduce crime in New York City in the given decade. Alternatively crime may have dropped in New York for the same reasons (e.g., changing demographics, decline in violent drug trade, increased social supports for some offenders, increased income of the poor in the latter part of the 1990s, displacement of the poor from urban corridors, etc.) that led to its decline nationally over the same period, none of which had anything to do with COMPSTAT (Bureau of Justice Statistics 2007). But the point is that one exception—the success of COMPSTAT in New York City even if true—would not be a valid basis for making the rule for all cities. Of course if scientific studies had empirically tested the relative worth of COMPSTAT programs and the evidence indicated that the programs were instrumental in helping reduce crime, then the success of the program in New York City would no longer constitute an exception.

Finally, a very popular set of logical fallacies comprises those that have to do with **appeals to emotions/patriotism and religion.** These tactics can take many forms, but essentially they use emotional events or scenes (e.g., this child was made homeless because of drug crimes, so we must implement COMPSTAT) and appeals to God and country (e.g., people who don't support COMPSTAT are godless commie-lovers—this might also be considered an ad hominem attack) to make their point. Again, and obviously, decision making is improved when it is based on valid information, not name calling of opponents, diversionary tactics, appeals to emotions, and/or nasty insinuations about opponents.

BIOLOGY AND COGNITION (SOCIAL INTELLIGENCE): A POSSIBLE UNDUE INFLUENCE

There is much emerging science that indicates our biology and environment are constantly interacting to shape our behavior (Walsh and Beaver 2009; Walsh and Ellis 2007; Walsh 2002). The reason a discussion of biology, as it affects cognition, fits in this chapter on decision making is obvious: Cognition, or thinking and understanding, is central to decision making. An important popular press book, *Social Intelligence: The New Science of Human Relationships*, describes how our reactions to each other and to our environment literally affect and are affected by our brain chemistry. As the author, Daniel Goleman (2006: 4), puts it:

> Neuroscience has discovered that our brain's very design makes it socia-ble, inexorably drawn into an intimate brain-to-brain linkup whenever we engage with another person. That neural bridge lets us affect the brain— and so the body—of everyone we interact with, just as they do us.

Clearly there is much we do not know about the brain and how it interacts with its environment, but the current science tells us that *spindle cells*, which guide social decisions, are much more prevalent in the human brain than in the brains of other animals (Goleman 2006). We also know that *mirror neurons* allow humans to anticipate the activity and emotions of others and to empathize with them, which probably explains why fallacious appeals to emotions are so persuasive for humans. According to Goleman (2006), we "catch" the emotions of others and they have an effect on our own chemistry and subsequently our behavior. When those around us display anger or are upset at us or others we tend to feel it in a bodily sense, and our own well-being and attitude are affected. Luckily the opposite is also true: those who exhibit a happy, contented, or hopeful outlook are more likely to inspire such feelings in others.

The knowledge that our brains can be affected in such a manner, needless to say, has major implications for all criminal justice agencies and their management. Our conception of how best to lead, communicate, motivate—you name it—are all likely to be affected by a greater understanding of how the brain operates in this social context.

Understanding that decisions are often affected by the emotional impact of others is important because it means that decision makers need to be aware of this impact and account for it in their decisions. A judge must think about whether his sentencing decision in a case is influenced by the actual crime committed or is being unduly affected by the community's and the victim's emotions. If the case involves a heinous crime where victim statements are taken into account in sentencing, are we not agreeing that the sentencing decision should reflect some emotional affect? What about police handling of a suspected "cop killer"? How might the emotions of all involved affect the decisions made in that context? What about parole boards or correctional officials who are overly swayed by emotional appeals of an unrepentant inmate, who has every intent of committing the same types of crimes once released? In each case the criminal justice actor must be aware that his own emotions and those of others are likely to have an effect on cognition, and that he may need to compensate for that effect.

PREDICTION

It is probably not an exaggeration to state that millions of decisions are made every day in the criminal justice system. One key type of decision making is "prediction," or making a decision about what will happen in the future. As defined by Vogt (2005: 244), **prediction** in a scientific context is "(a) using data to make a statement about the future ... (b) the more common use of the term ... refers to using data to "predict" outcomes that have already occurred." An example might be using data gathered on a cohort of offenders who were all released from prison during the same time period to investigate what variables or measures have an impact on recidivism. Later, these findings can influence the decision making of correctional program managers as they work to control or impact those measures that turned out to be key "predictive" factors.

As indicated by this definition and example, criminal justice decisions might be aided by the valid (true) and reliable (consistent) information that can be obtained through scientific investigation. Such investigations might be done qualitatively (e.g., using interviews or observations) or quantitatively (e.g., using surveys or agency data; Babbie 1992; Dillman 2000). Ideally such methods should fit the subject under study and be designed to best determine what is true about theory or well supported about the practice. Criminal justice managers and actors who fail to use scientifically obtained information to inform their decisions risk making predictions that do not fit reality and do not further the ends of justice.

Having said this, there are two types of errors common to prediction: false positives (or overpredicting the occurrence of phenomena; Type I error) and false negatives (or underpredicting the occurrence of phenomena; Type II error). It is likely because of real-world concerns about safety and security, not to mention political and media influence, that criminal justice actors, with the possible exception of defense attorneys, are more inclined to make false positive mistakes than false negative ones. Police officers, prosecutors, judges, and community and institutional correctional officers are more likely to predict future offending by persons who have been accused and convicted than the opposite. Because the vast majority of people who enter the criminal justice system do not in fact commit another crime, if indeed they are guilty of the one they were apprehended for, the overprediction of this outcome by criminal justice actors is likely.

Naturally, overprediction of reoffending or dangerousness leads to greater use of the whole criminal justice system, greatly enhances the monetary expenses of that system, and mars the ability to maintain a "just" system for those who are processed in it. On the other hand, if criminal justice actors were to commit the opposite error—that of false negatives or under-predicting reoffending or dangerousness—as sometimes also happens, the outcome would be a threat to the safety and security of the community, and impairment of justice likewise. The "solution" to this tendency to commit either type of error in prediction is to focus on developing a system and a series of processes and practices that improve decision making generally, which will have the collateral effect of improving predictions specifically.

WAYS TO IMPROVE DECISION MAKING

Based on what we have presented in this text and this chapter, we have come to believe that decision making in criminal justice agencies can be greatly improved by managers and other criminal justice actors. Generally speaking, the first step towards improvement is to *be aware of all the obstacles, errors, and rhetorical traps* (e.g., logical fallacies) that can impair effective decision making. Second, one must work to develop an atmosphere that *values organizational integrity* or one whose actors as a whole are honest, ethical, and can be trusted by the agency's members and by the community. An organization that has this reputation probably gained it by making effective decisions regarding its staff and the people they work with and for. Third, as much as is possible, one should work to *provide enough resources* so that staff can make the decision to devote the requisite time and effort to doing their jobs well. In addition to these more global ways to improve organizational decision making, the savvy criminal justice manager might also do the following:

- As much as is possible, insulate most criminal justice decision making, and decision makers, from political influence.
- Hire educated people, or support employees in educational endeavors that will prepare them for the complexity of their work (e.g., criminal justice or related classes that will give them the theoretical, historical, and research-based information they need to contextualize their decision making).
- Emphasize professional practices as a guide to effective decision making.
- Focus on the validity and reliability of information that informs decisions. In tandem, make efforts to encourage and enhance research done in and for the agency.
- Be aware of, and account for, the biological processes that are at play in decision making.
- Foster creative and open decision making processes, which encourage discussion and even dissent, and the consideration of alternative courses of action.

CONCLUSIONS

Criminal justice actors are constantly called upon to make decisions; yet often the information they have is incomplete or flawed in some way. Since at times that information is purposefully misleading, the criminal justice actor needs to be a wary consumer and a thoughtful reviewer of the source and validity of information. It is always best if solid research on a topic has been done, and then done again and again, so that the decision maker has a good basis for making a decision. But most of the time, considering criminal justice decisions on any number of topics, such research does not exist or is not developed enough to give real guidance to criminal justice practitioners and managers.

In such cases, which are most cases, decision makers need to fall back on professional practices, training, education, and known and legitimate actions or decisions that "worked" in the past for themselves or their colleagues. Awareness of the logical fallacies used to bend the truth by those trying to illegitimately persuade and distract decision makers is also critical. As one of our undergraduate professors, who shall remain unnamed here, cautioned: "When you hear such crap [in the popular press], your shit detectors should be going off." Thankfully, and as noted in this chapter, there are ways to improve the organizational environment so that decision makers are not floundering alone or, in some cases, relying on a personal "shit detector" to determine whether a given piece of information is true or worth listening to.

KEY TERMS

ad hominem attacks: occur in arguments or discussions when the speaker or writer is attacked or slurred, passing over the merits of what that person argued or stood for.

appeals to emotions, patriotism, and religion: these tactics can take many forms, but essentially they use emotional events or scenes and appeals to God and country to make a point that is not supported in logic.

begging the question or circular reasoning: restating as the conclusion a point in the argument.

decision: a choice made by a thinking being.

exception makes the rule: a logical fallacy that states that if it (i.e., the focus of the discourse) happens once or was true once, it must happen all the time or be true in every case.

prediction: in a scientific context, "(a) using data to make a statement about the future ... (b) the more common use of the term ... refers to using data to "predict" outcomes that have already occurred" (Vogt 2005: 244).

red herring: a logical fallacy—the straw man fallacy could be a subgroup of the red herring—and also a diversionary tactic since, like all these tactics, it is used to divert attention from the truth or mask it. The difference is that the red herring tactic often entails an emotional twist, which is used to impair listeners' or readers' ability to make good decisions.

straw man: a logical fallacy used by those who want to divert attention from the merits of the argument or the facts of the situation.

REFERENCES

American Heritage Dictionary (1992) *American heritage dictionary*, 3rd edn. New York, NY: Delta/ Houghton Mifflin.

Babbie, E. (1992) *The practice of social research*, 6th edn. Belmont, CA: Wadsworth.

Bassham, G., Irwin, W., Nardone, H. and Wallace, J. M. (2008) *Critical thinking: A student's introduction*, 3rd edn. Boston, MA: McGraw-Hill.

Blumberg, A. S. (1984) The practice of law as a confidence game: Organization cooptation of a profession. In G. F. Cole (ed.), *Criminal justice: Law and politics*. Monterey, CA: Brooks/Cole, pp. 191–209.

Bohm, R. and Haley, K. N. (2005) *Introduction to criminal justice*, 4th edn. New York: McGraw-Hill.

Bureau of Justice Statistics (2007) Crime characteristics. Office of Justice Programs, U.S. Department of Justice. Available at www.ojp.usdoj.gov/bjs/cvict (last accessed January 31, 2013).

Chiricos, T. (2002) The media, moral panics and the politics of crime control. In G. F. Cole, M. G. Gertz and A. Bunger (eds), *The criminal justice system: Politics and policies*. Belmont, CA: Wadsworth/Thomson Learning, pp. 59–79.

Dillman, D. (2000) *Mail and internet surveys: The tailored design method*, 2nd edn. New York, NY: John Wiley & Sons, Inc.

Dye, T. R. and Zeigler, H. (1989) *American politics in the media age*. Belmont, CA: Wadsworth.

Goleman, D. (2006) *Social intelligence: The new science of human relationships*. New York, NY: Bantam Books.

Jacobs, M. D. (1990) *Screwing the system and making it work: Juvenile justice in the no-fault society*. Chicago, IL: University of Chicago Press.

Janis, I. L. (1972) *Victims of groupthink: A psychological study of foreign-policy decisions and fiascoes*. Boston, MA: Houghton Mifflin.

Lee, J. A. and Visano, L. A. (1994) Official deviance in the legal system. In S. Stojokovic, J. Klofas and D. Kalinich (eds), *The administration and management of criminal justice organizations: A book of readings*. Prospect Heights, IL: Waveland Press, pp. 202–231.

Lipsky, M. (1980) *Street-level bureaucracy: Dilemmas of the individual in public services*. New York, NY: Russell Sage Foundation.

Merlo, A. V. and Benekos, P. J. (2000) *What's wrong with the criminal justice system*. Cincinnati, OH: Anderson Publishing.

Mills, C. W. (1959) *The sociological imagination*. London: Oxford University Press.

Vogt, W. P. (2005) *Dictionary of statistics and methodology: A nontechnical guide for the social sciences*, 3rd edn. Thousand Oaks, CA: Sage.

Walker, S. (1993) *Taming the system: The control of discretion in criminal justice, 1950–1990*. New York, NY: Oxford University Press.

Walsh, A. (2002) *Biosocial criminology: Introduction and integration*. Cincinnati, OH: Anderson Publishing.

Walsh, A. and Beaver, K. M. (eds). (2009) *Biosocial criminology: New directions in theory and research*. New York, NY: Routledge.

Walsh, A. and Ellis, L. (2007). *Criminology: An interdisciplinary approach*. Thousand Oaks, CA: Sage.

Watters, J. G. (2013) A very little guide to logical argument and fallacies. Available at: http://angellier. biblio.univ-lille3.fr/etudes_recherches/alittleguidetofallacies.pdf (last accessed January 31, 2013).

DISCUSSION QUESTIONS

1   Stohr and Collins assert that criminal justice decision makers who do not use sci-
    entific information risk making decisions that are both unrealistic and a hindrance
    to justice. Do you agree with this assessment? Must all decisions be made based
    on evidence? If not, on what other basis should criminal justice managers make
    decisions?

2   Some observers argue that criminal justice policy decisions are made based on
    emotions, such as a three strikes law borne out of anger and frustration toward
    repeat offenders, or a death penalty based on retribution for the taking of a life.
    What role should emotion play in criminal justice policy making?

MANAGING ORGANIZATIONAL DEVIANCE

FOCUSING ON CAUSES, NOT SYMPTOMS

MELISSA B. GUTWORTH, DANA M. MORTON, AND JASON J. DAHLING

Organizations experience staggering expenses when employees break rules, behaviors that are variously referred to as acts of organizational deviance, counterproductive work behavior, or organizational misbehavior.[1] For example, conservative estimates place the annual cost of internal theft at $6 billion in the U.S. (Wimbush & Dalton, 1997); computer-based loafing behavior, or cyberloafing, costs $600 million annually in the United Kingdom (Taylor, 2007) and upwards of $5.3 billion in the United States (Bennett & Robinson, 2003); and recovery from acts of anger and violence in the workplace cost over $4 billion per year (Bensimon, 1997). It is not surprising that managers are highly motivated to identify ways to control employee deviance given these statistics, and a large body of practical, "self-help" books for managers has sprung up to meet this demand in the last decade (e.g., Bruce, Hampel, & Lamont, 2011; Falcone, 2009; Grote, 2006; Scott, 2006; Shepard, 2005).

Despite the good intentions of these authors, there are two key problems that are typically evident in the books directed at practicing managers. First, employee deviance is usually interpreted as a function of person-level causes; deviance is oftentimes attributed to "bad employees" who must be controlled to prevent

Melissa B. Gutworth, Dana M. Morton, and Jason J. Dahling, "Managing Organizational Deviance: Focusing on Causes, Not Symptoms," *Received Wisdom, Kernels of Truth, and Boundary: Conditions in Organizational Studies*, pp. 153–180. Copyright © 2013 by Information Age Publishing. Reprinted with permission.

them from acting in undesirable ways. For example, Scott (2006) immediately describes problematic employees in terms of trait qualities that manifest in problematic behaviors (e.g., "the busybody and gossip, the backstabber, the incompetent" p. viii). While many of these books eventually arrive at the conclusion that deviant behavior is a result of interplay between individual differences *and* the work context, the emphasis is generally to seize upon the notion that deviant behavior is a function of bad apples rather than bad barrels (Kish-Gephart, Harrison, & Treviño, 2010). This orientation conflicts with the remarkable progress made in the scholarly literature in the past 20 years, which points to a wide set of workplace conditions that promote employee deviance (e.g., Aquino & O'Reilly, 2011; Bennett & Robinson, 2000; Griffin & O'Leary-Kelly, 2004; Lawrence & Robinson, 2007; Litzky, Eddleston, & Kidder, 2006; Vardi & Weitz, 2004).

The second problem with the practical literature is that most of the advice offered to managers is reactive and disciplinary rather than proactive and preventative. When managers focus on how to appropriately discipline employees (Grote, 2006), or how to have tough administrative conversations (Falcone, 2009), they miss the broader opportunity to consider their own behaviors and the workplace influences that may be prompting the deviant behavior to occur in the first place (Litzky et al., 2006). Managers may be able to suppress the symptoms of underlying problems by disciplining deviant employees, but deviance will continue to emerge if its causes remain unchecked. Proactively managing the work context, rather than reacting to employee deviance, offers the only true opportunity to free managers from the burden of regular disciplinary conversations.

Given these disconnects between the scholarly and practical literature on employee deviance, the central question we explore in this chapter is, "Why do managers focus on *what* rule-breakers do without considering *why* these employees deviate in the first place?" We contend that shifting the conversation to understand employees' motivations for engaging in deviance will enable managers to respond decisively and effectively to deviant behavior. Moreover, taking the focus away from deviant employees enables managers to recognize that they may be inadvertently contributing to the problem by allowing conditions that encourage deviance to persist (Litzky et al., 2006) or by making faulty assumptions about their subordinates' traits and qualities (McGregor, 1960).

To this end, we begin first by exploring the "kernel of truth" underlying the practical literature on the traits of deviant employees: there is a sizable literature linking individual differences to employee deviance, and a balanced assessment of the causes of deviance should certainly take this research into account (e.g., Berry, Ones, & Sackett, 2007). However, the broader body of research on deviance suggests that people have many different motivations for engaging in deviance, and that these motivations are typically driven to a greater extent by elements of the work context than by individual differences (Vardi & Weitz, 2004). Thus, we next offer a framework drawn from Vardi and Weitz (2004) to describe the different motivations for deviant behavior and review the recent literature on the contextual drivers of these motivations.

We structure this review around four main levels of analysis, namely (a) the organizational system, (b) the immediate team/workgroup, (c) the supervisor/subordinate dyad, and (d) the job characteristics experienced by individual employees. Third, given our motivational perspective on deviance, we consider a motivation for rule-breaking behavior that rarely appears in the practical literature – that people sometimes break rules with the intention of *bettering* the company. We explore the nascent literature on this topic given that these behaviors have the potential to actually improve workplace relationships and efficiency if managed appropriately. Last, we synthesize the literature that we review to distill a set of "must-do" recommendations for managers who are faced with a need to curtail and control employee deviance in the workplace.

THE KERNEL OF TRUTH: INDIVIDUAL DIFFERENCES AND EMPLOYEE DEVIANCE

The kernel of truth underlying the practical literature on employee deviance is that many individual differences are associated with organizational deviance (e.g., Berry et al., 2007). For example, research on the Big Five personality traits shows that conscientiousness, emotional stability, and agreeableness are all negatively related to counterproductive behaviors (Berry et al., 2007; Salgado, 2002). Other personality traits related to self-and emotion-regulation are also relevant to predicting employee deviance. For example, high negative affectivity, a general predisposition to feel negative emotions (Watson & Clark, 1984), predicts workplace aggression and other forms of counterproductive work behavior (Douglas & Martinko, 2001; Penney & Spector, 2005; Spector, 2011). With respect to self-regulation, people who possess high impulsivity (Henle, 2005), high reward sensitivity (Diefendorff & Mehta, 2007), and low self-control (Douglas & Martinko, 2001; Spector, 2011) are more likely to engage in workplace aggression and other deviant behaviors. Finally, the scholarly literature has suggested that a "dark triad" of personality traits consisting of Machiavellianism (Dahling, Kuyumcu, & Librizzi, 2012; Dahling, Whitaker, & Levy, 2009), trait anger (Douglas & Martinko, 2001; Spector, 2011), and narcissism (Spector, 2011) predict a wide spectrum of deviant work behaviors, including theft, lying, deceit, sabotage, and cheating.

Aside from personality traits, some research has shown that cognitive ability is also an important predictor of deviance. Although it is well-known that higher cognitive ability is associated with better job performance and greater success in job training (Gottfredson, 1997; Kuncel & Hezlett, 2010), cognitive ability is also negatively related to organizational deviance (Dilchert, Ones, Davis, & Rostow, 2007). People with low cognitive ability are theorized to be less likely to think about the harmful consequences of their actions before engaging in behaviors, which makes it more likely that they will commit acts of deviance with negative repercussions.

To summarize, many individual differences, such as personality and cognitive ability, correlate with organizational deviance. However, traits alone do not explain why employees engage in deviant behaviors (Tomlinson & Greenberg, 2005). Elements of the organizational context can greatly exacerbate or negate the effects of personality traits on employee deviance (e.g., Colbert, Mount, Harter, Witt, & Barrick, 2004); some employees never break rules despite having patterns of traits that are predictive of deviance, and other employees are driven to a wide range of deviant behaviors despite lacking any "red flag" dispositional markers. In the sections that follow, we focus on understanding the motivations that underlie employee deviance and the organizational experiences that shape them.

A MOTIVATIONAL FRAMEWORK FOR UNDERSTANDING DEVIANCE

To begin to understand the motivations underlying employee deviance, we introduce and elaborate upon Vardi and Weitz's (2004) framework for organizational misbehavior. Although past research offers a number of different frameworks to organize deviance research, Vardi and Weitz integrated many of these models while clarifying the motivational manifestations of intentional workplace misconduct. Their integrative approach suggests that neither the individual nor organizational/societal perspectives alone fully explain organizational misbehavior. What is also unique about their framework is that it does not assume that deviance is always harmful to the organization, a point that we explore in a section on constructive deviance later in the chapter.

Vardi and Weitz (2004) distinguished between three types of deviance based on the different motivations that drive them. These include misbehaviors intended to benefit the self (Type-S), misbehaviors intended to inflict damage and/or be destructive (Type-D), and misbehaviors intended to benefit the organization (Type-O). Type-S misbehaviors are actions that usually victimize the employing firm or its members for self-gain and are mostly internal to the organization. Employee theft committed with the intention of personal financial profit would be categorized as Type-S misbehavior. Type-D misbehaviors are vindictive and intended to hurt others or the organization, and its victims can be either internal or external. Examples of Type-D misbehaviors include sabotaging company-owned equipment out of anger or deliberately providing compromised service to a rude customer. On the other hand, Type-O misbehaviors, which are primarily intended to benefit the member's employing organization, are generally directed towards external victims. For example, a restaurant employee could choose to ignore a reservation made by an unknown customer to provide an immediate table for an important, repeat customer.

Critically, the motivational intention behind the misbehavior is what drives the classification of deviance. Vardi and Weitz (2004) clarified that these three motivations are shaped by a mixture of two categories of predictor variables: *normative forces* or *instrumental forces*. Normative forces are internalized organizational expectations and experiences, while instrumental forces reflect employees' beliefs about personal interests. According to their framework, Type-S misbehavior is shaped primarily by instrumental forces; Type-S misbehavior is self-serving and is therefore influenced entirely by a person's beliefs about securing favorable outcomes. Conversely, deviance committed to benefit the organization (Type-O) is driven by normative pressures. These behaviors are typically determined by the organization's subjective norms at the cost of possibly sacrificing self-interest for greater causes; the welfare of the organization is the motivating factor behind this type of deviance. Destructively-motivated deviance (Type-D) assumes that both normative and instrumental forces are simultaneously at play, or can vary depending upon the action taken and target victim.

Taking a motivational perspective allows managers to evaluate the underlying intentions that promote these different types of deviance. It is important to understand that Type-O, Type-S, and Type-D deviance are distinct and each is committed with different objectives in mind. In the next section, we explore the contextual predictors of employee deviance that can shape these various motivations. We primarily focus in this section on predictors of deviance that would be globally categorized as Type-D or Type-S, which are clearly detrimental to the organization. We review the nascent literature on the drivers of deviance intended to benefit the organization (Type-O misbehavior, or constructive deviance) separately.

CONTEXTUAL PREDICTORS OF DESTRUCTIVE AND SELF-INTERESTED DEVIANCE

Consistent with Vardi and Weitz's (2004) framework, an enormous variety of contextual variables in the work environment are predictive of organizational deviance. We review these variables in four categories, starting with macro-level, systematic influences and ending with immediate, micro-level job experiences that encourage deviance. Specifically, the contextual variables that predict deviance can be organized into those that reside at (a) the organizational level of analysis, (b) the team or workgroup level of analysis, (c) the supervisor-subordinate dyadic level of analysis, and (d) the individual job level of analysis. While many important contextual variables have effects that cut across these four levels, this framework enables managers to think systematically about an organization to identify where the primary drivers of deviance may lie. We summarize the body of research presented in these sections in Table 1, with a special emphasis on the psychological theories used to explain why these contextual variables are associated with greater organizational deviance.

TABLE 1 Summary of Contextual Predictors of Organizational Deviance

LEVEL OF ANALYSIS	PREDICTOR CONSTRUCTS	RELEVANT PSYCHOLOGICAL THEORIES OR MODELS	REPRESENTATIVE STUDIES
Organizational System	Ethical climate, Perceived corporate citizenship	Social exchange theory, Social learning theory, Social identity theory	Biron, 2010; Evans, et. al., 2011; Peterson, 2002
	Justice climate	Social exchange theory, Fairness theory	El Akremi et al. 2010; Aquino et al., 1999
	Reward, control, and punishment systems	Equity theory, Fairness theory, Goal setting theory	Horvoka-Mead et al., 2002; Litzy et al., 2006; Zoghbi-Manrique-de-Lara, 2011
Team/ Workgroup	Work group norms and pressures	Social learning theory, Bystander effect, Contagion effect	Ferguson & Barry, 2011; Robinson & O'Leary-Kelly, 1998; Tepper et al., 2008
	Organizational-based self esteem (OBSE)	Belongingness theory	Ferris et al., 2009
	Team autonomy	Job characteristics theory	Arthur, 2011
Supervisor/ Subordinate Dyad	Managerial oversight	Agency theory	Detert et al., 2007; Litsky et al., 2006
	Abusive supervision	Reactance theory, Fairness theory	Ashforth, 1997; Shao et al., 2011; Mitchell & Ambrose, 2007
	Psychological contract breach	Social exchange theory, Equity theory	Bordia et al., 2008; Morrison & Robinson, 1997
	Violation of Trust	Social exchange theory, Equity theory	Litsky et al., 2006; Morrison & Robinson, 1997
Individual Job Characteristics	Perceived job autonomy	Job characteristics theory; Job Demand Control Model	Hackman & Oldham, 1976; Baillien et al., 2011
	Role ambiguity, Role conflict (inc. work-family conflict)	Stressor-Emotion Model; Identity theory	Spector & Fox, 2005 Hauge et al., 2009; Darrat et al., 2010;

ORGANIZATIONAL SYSTEM

There are widespread, systemic influences on employee deviance that are formed on a broad, macrolevel within organizations, particularly with respect to shared organizational climates and reward systems. Social learning theory posits that individuals perceive the values of a social entity, such as an organization, as a guide to behavior that is learned through observation (Bandura, 1977). Therefore, an organization's climate can generate a strong influence over its members and dictate implicit or explicit organizational standards of conduct, acquired through modeling and direct conditioning (Biron, 2010). In particular, an organization's climates for ethics and justice have important implications for employee deviance.

Ethical climate. The ethical climate of a workplace refers to the shared perceptions among employees of what is considered ethically-appropriate behavior within the organization (Victor & Cullen, 1988). Many studies have found that ethical climate perceptions shape employee behavior, in particular the commission of organizational deviance (e.g., Biron, 2010; Evans, Goodman, & Davis, 2011; Peterson, 2002). For example, Biron (2010) found a negative association between perceptions of the organization's ethical values and employees' organizational deviance. She additionally identified several moderators of this relationship; abusive supervision weakened the negative relationship between ethical values and organizational deviance, while perceived organizational support (POS) strengthened it. POS refers to employees' beliefs about whether or not the organization values their contributions and cares about their well-being (Eisenberger, Huntington, Hutchison, & Sowa, 1986). The results of Biron's (2010) study showed that the lowest levels of organizational deviance were observed when there was low abusive supervision and high POS in a strong ethical climate. Conversely, the most deviance was committed under conditions of high abusive supervision and low POS in a weak ethical climate. These findings led Biron to suggest that the degree to which the employer's prescribed ethical values are consistent with its actions can have substantial implications for employee behavior. A negative reciprocity effect, the inclination to strike back in response to poor exchange relationships with organizational partners, may occur when the supervisor/employer acts in a way that is misaligned with the perceived organizational ethical values. These considerations are important when evaluating how an ethical climate as experienced by particular employees can influence organizational deviance.

In a related study, Evans et al. (2011) found that employee deviance can be influenced by the degree to which an employee considers his or her employer a good corporate citizen. This perceived corporate citizenship (PCC), an individual's evaluation of whether or not the employing organization fulfills the responsibilities of corporate citizenship, can greatly impact an employee's interpretation of his or her work environment. Results of their study indicate that employees who perceive their companies to be good corporate citizens are less likely to engage in costly and destructive behaviors. In addition to identifying this relationship, they discovered that organizational cynicism was positively related to deviance and mediated the relationship between PCC and deviance. This finding indicates that a cynical evaluation of corporate citizenship values can also play a role in whether or not employees will commit deviance.

Justice climate. A second type of organizational climate perception, the climate for justice, is also relevant to organizational deviance (Aquino, Lewis, & Bradfield, 1999; El Akremi,

Vandenberghe, & Camerman, 2010; Ménard, Brunet, & Savoie, 2011; Zoghbi-Manrique-de-Lara, 2011). The justice climate can be defined as the shared, group-level perceptions of justice that develop when people learn fairness information from others within their organization or team, leading to consistency in justice perceptions within the workplace (Roberson & Colquitt, 2005). Colquitt (2001) identified and described four types of justice evaluations that can be made at this collective level: distributive, procedural, informational, and interpersonal. Distributive justice relates to the belief that people receive fair amounts of valued work-related outcomes relative to their contributions. Procedural justice concerns perceptions of fairness about the process used to determine outcomes in the workplace, while informational justice is the perception of the accuracy and quality of explanations given about these procedures. Last, interpersonal justice addresses whether or not employees perceive that they receive fair interpersonal treatment (e.g., that they are treated with dignity and respect within the organization).

Injustice has been found to weaken the quality of social exchange relationships between employees and their supervisor and/or organization. El Akremi et al.'s (2010) study found that perceived organizational injustice resulted in low POS and leader-member exchange (LMX) ratings, evaluations of the relationship quality between supervisors and employees. These negative reactions to injustice could instill a negative reciprocity effect leading employees to respond with deviance. POS mediated the negative relationship between procedural justice and organization-directed deviance, indicating that employees directed their acts of retribution toward the organization that they felt had mistreated them. On the other hand, LMX mediated the negative relationships between informational and interpersonal justice and both supervisor-directed deviance and organization-directed deviance (El Akremi et al., 2010). Thus, when leaders can be held accountable for injustice, employees direct their deviance toward both that supervisor and the employing organization. Along similar lines, earlier studies found that distributive justice has a significant negative relationship with interpersonal deviance, and that interpersonal justice is related to both organizational and interpersonal deviance (Aquino et al., 1999). Thus, perceptions of injustice within the organization are likely to lead to evaluations of blame for this treatment, and employees will subsequently react with deviance toward the responsible leaders or organization in retaliation (Skarlicki & Folger, 1997).

Reward, control, and punishment systems. Organizational incentive and punishment systems can also contribute to employee deviance. For example, compensation that depends upon commissions or gratuities could create a financial motive for employees to commit deviance to achieve gains if deviance reflects the most straightforward way to profit (Dunn & Schweitzer, 2005; Kerr, 1995). Litzky et al. (2006) explained that many reward systems drive competition for rewards and may trigger deviant acts by promoting unscrupulous behaviors among coworkers looking to get ahead, or by allowing employees to rationalize deviance under the guise of meeting sales quotas.

With respect to control and punishment policies, Zoghbi-Manrique-de-Lara (2011) found that procedural justice fully mediated the effects of monitoring and punishment threats on employee deviance. The study examined how punishment and monitoring affect deviance, and results confirmed that punishment threats alone are hardly effective, but instead trigger deviance as a retaliatory behavior. Meanwhile, high levels of monitoring promote employee performance and ethical behavior. This is perhaps because employees perceive higher levels of monitoring as more fair. The author concluded that punishment, and to some extent monitoring, are more effective when used "in proper doses" to produce the greatest perceptions of procedural justice.

Control systems, especially those that are perceived as unfair, can also promote deviance among employees. For example, Sims (2010), using a case-study approach, examined the 2006 boardroom scandal at Hewlett-Packard to determine whether or not the observed workplace deviance from board members could be considered a retaliatory response to organizational power. Hewlett-Packard suffered from ongoing leaks of information by board members, despite the CEO's explicit expectation that she should be the one to communicate with the media about boardroom discussions. As Sims explained,

> The norms against such behavior were well established and often commu-
> nicated. The power, frustration, and deviance … suggests that this deviant
> behavior can be tied back to board frustrations experienced by [her] use
> of power to control board communication with the media. (p. 556)

Sims concluded that by firing the CEO, the board was displaying an act of personal aggression, a form of retaliatory deviance, in response to threats to social identity and frustrations with injustice.

To summarize, there are a variety of system-level constructs that can promote employee deviance in organizations. These include perceptual constructs such as the ethical and justice climates, along with formal organizational compensation and control systems. However, additional group-level drivers of deviance emerge in more immediate work groups and teams, and we turn next to this level of analysis.

WORK GROUPS AND TEAMS

Work groups and teams introduce additional motivators of deviance among employees. Some key influences that we review in this section include group norms and practices that are supportive of deviance, group pressures in the form of cohesiveness and desire to belong, and team autonomy.

Group norms and group pressures. Employees engage in more deviant behavior when they have direct or indirect knowledge of team or group members who have also committed deviant acts (e.g., Ferguson & Barry, 2011; Glomb & Liao, 2003; Robinson & O'Leary-Kelly,

1998). Additionally, work group cohesion compounds this effect; when groups are cohesive, direct observation of deviance is especially likely to result in bystanders committing subsequent deviance. One likely explanation for deviance contagion within work groups is that hearing or witnessing deviance leads to the acceptance of it, or perhaps the promotion of a deviant culture. A second explanation implicates social pressure. Specifically, employees report dissatisfaction with each other when one group member expresses less employee deviance than others, which creates additional pressures to conform to the deviant norm (Robinson & O'Leary-Kelly, 1998).

Group norms toward deviance also shape the way that employees react to abusive treatment from supervisors. For example, Tepper, Henle, Lambert, Giacalone, and Duffy (2008) found that abusive supervision has an indirect effect on organizational deviance via reduced commitment. This indirect effect was strengthened by group norms for deviance; in their first study, the effect was stronger when the focal employees perceived that their coworkers performed more acts of deviance, and the effect was stronger in their second study when coworkers actually reported more deviance in the workplace. Thus, employees look to their coworkers for cues as to whether organizational deviance is an appropriate response to supervisor mistreatment.

In another study, organizational-based self-esteem (OBSE) was found to mediate the relationship between organizational support and employee deviance (Ferris, Brown, & Heller, 2009). Organizational-based self-esteem is the degree to which an employee feels that he or she is a significant, capable, and worthy member of the organization (Pierce, Gardner, Cummings, & Dunham, 1989). Using a belongingness theory framework, Ferris et al. (2009) argued that when leaders and the organization do not provide support, lowered OBSE and increased deviance may result. Consequently, this need to belong motivates many employees' actions within work groups and teams in the office, and belongingness-related concerns should be taken into account when examining workplace deviance that unfolds at the team level of analysis.

Team autonomy. The organization and management of work groups can also promote deviant behavior. This may be particularly true with respect to team autonomy and self-management. For example, Arthur (2011) found that interpersonal deviance within teams was positively associated with the amount of autonomy given to the team. In highly-autonomous teams that supervise themselves, the absence of formal bureaucratic sanctions allows team members to act however they please without the fear of organizational consequences. Often, this freedom enables team members to apply informal sanctions that take on the flavor of interpersonal mistreatment, like bullying and incivility, to shape and punish the behaviors of non-conforming team members. Parallel findings were reported by Barker (1993), who found that self-managed teams developed and enforced strict normative standards for behavior that were oftentimes more stringent than the rules and norms set by the organization itself. However, Arthur (2011) cautioned that despite the positive association between team autonomy and interpersonal deviance, managers do not necessarily need to avoid job designs with autonomous teams. Instead, he argued that by increasing awareness and anticipating potential deviance, leaders can introduce training and other preventative measures prior to teamwork. This would allow both the employees and firms to harness the gains associated with autonomous teamwork while avoiding the likelihood of deviant behavior manifesting in the team.

Multiple theories offer explanations for the effects of group-level phenomena on deviance. Ferguson and Barry (2011) argued that social information processing theory plays a significant role in this process. Because social information is acquired via the social environment and personal interactions, an individual may use the knowledge of someone else's deviant acts to perpetuate or justify their own subsequent deviant interactions. Managers should be cautioned that the "proliferation of deviance can take a cyclical form … a kind of vicious cycle" (p. 89). Tepper et al.'s (2008) findings also offer the contagion effect as another possible explanation for coinciding deviance in workgroups. Drawing upon belongingness theory, Ferris et al. (2009) reiterated that the need to belong or form positive interpersonal relationships can significantly impact workplace deviance. When one's sense of belonging is thwarted (e.g. when those in the work group communicate, through actions or behaviors, that the focal individual is not valued), it can result in adverse reactions like deviant behavior. Although the explanations may vary, all of these studies demonstrate the extent to which work groups and teams can shape employee deviance.

SUPERVISOR/SUBORDINATE DYAD

Microlevel predictors that are experienced by specific employees, rather than large groups, have effects on deviance beyond those described at the system and team levels of analysis. One of these micro-level considerations is the nature of the relationship between the subordinate employee and his or her supervisor, which has been examined in terms of the *amount* of supervision that employees receive and the *quality* of the supervision that they receive.

Managerial oversight. One supervisor/subordinate dyad characteristic that correlates with deviance is managerial oversight. Managerial oversight is defined as the ratio of managers to employees who must be supervised (Detert, Treviño, Burris, & Andiappan, 2007), which generally speaks to the opportunities that managers have to observe and interact with their subordinates. Detert et al. (2007) found a negative relationship between the scope of managerial oversight and employee deviance, indicating that infrequent supervision can lead to more workplace deviance. Presumably, supervisors who are stretched too thin have insufficient opportunities to monitor their subordinates. Without providing a proper amount of supervision, supervisors create unstructured environments in which deviance can occur without consequence (Shultz, 1993).

Abusive supervision. While infrequent supervision has been shown to have negative consequences, the quality of supervision is typically of greater concern in recent research. Abusive supervision, a phenomenon that we noted at several points in the preceding sections, occurs when a manager uses his/her power and authority to mistreat particular subordinates (Ashforth, 1997). When subordinates experience this mistreatment by their supervisors, higher levels of workplace deviance occur (Detert et al., 2007; Shao, Resick, & Hargis, 2011). Abusive supervision has been found to lead to multiple types of workplace deviance: deviance directed toward others, deviance directed toward the organization, and deviance directed toward the supervisor (Mitchell & Ambrose, 2007). In addition to engaging in these harmful behaviors, employees who experience abusive supervision are also less likely to engage in citizenship behaviors that can benefit the organization (Zellars, Tepper, & Duffy, 2002). These findings are generally interpreted in terms of fairness theory or reactance theory, which take the perspective that employees are motivated to react to unreasonable treatment with hostile behaviors directed back toward the supervisor or toward other employees.

One specific study about abusive supervision exemplifies the impact that supervisory behaviors can have on deviance motivations. In a study of almost 500 employees in a variety of different jobs, the researchers focused on the consequences of abusive supervision toward employees who were high in social dominance orientation (SDO; Shao et al., 2011). SDO is an individual difference that entails a desire to maintain and enforce existing social hierarchies (Pratto, Sidanius, Stallworth, & Malle, 1994). While SDO itself has been linked to dominating behaviors toward others (Guimond, Dambrum, Michinov, & Duarte, 2003), Shao et al. (2011) found that the managerial behavior of abusive supervision activated this dominant tendency in high-SDO employees. Employees who were high in SDO, but who did *not* experience abusive supervision, exhibited overall lower levels of workplace deviance. Experiencing abusive supervision provided the necessary "trigger" for employees with high SDO to act out against their peers.

Violation of psychological contracts and subordinate trust. Psychological contract breach is another supervisory behavior that can influence deviance motivations. A psychological contract consists of a set of beliefs involving terms and agreements between the employee and his/her employing organization or particular coworkers (Rousseau, 1995). Importantly, these beliefs are one-sided; while employees believe that their understanding of the terms of employment is held by both parties, in actuality an employee's perspective may be quite different from the perspective held by his or her supervisor. Psychological contracts are breached when one party believes that the other has failed to fulfill his/ her promise or commitment; supervisors can very easily breach subordinates' psychological contracts because they may not fully perceive the way that subordinates have construed their work arrangements (Rousseau, 2004). When psychological contract breach occurs in organizations, employees feel betrayed and revenge cognitions are formed which provide the motivation for employees to commit workplace deviance (Bordia, Restubog, & Tang, 2008).

Along similar lines, supervisor behaviors that violate subordinate trust can motivate deviance (Litzky et al., 2006). When employees do not have trust in a supervisor or in the organization, they are more likely to anticipate broken promises and contracts (Morrison & Robinson, 1997) and respond accordingly. Some deviant acts that have been reported in response to distrust of management are stealing, sabotage, and verbal aggression (Litsky et al., 2006).

To summarize, the scope of managerial oversight, abusive supervision, psychological contract breach, and violation of trust are all supervisory conditions and behaviors that encourage employees to engage in workplace deviance. Additionally, employees who have certain individual differences (e.g., high SDO) have been found to vary in deviance intentions based on the presence of certain supervisory behaviors; the behaviors discussed in this section can act as deviance triggers in employees who would not otherwise act out.

INDIVIDUAL JOB CHARACTERISTICS

Our fourth and final category of contextual variables that promote employee deviance concerns the characteristics of individual employees' jobs. Here, we focus predominately on job autonomy and role difficulties, especially role ambiguity and role conflicts.

Job autonomy. Perceived job autonomy is positively related to job satisfaction and performance in a wide variety of research (e.g., Den Hartog & Belschak, 2012; Hackman & Oldham, 1976). Job autonomy exists when employees have freedom in their job to control how various aspects of the work are done (Den Hartog & Belschak, 2012). When employees perceive that they have control over their job, they are less likely to experience work strain and engage in deviant behaviors, such as workplace bullying (Baillien, De Cuyper, & De Witte, 2011). Consistent with job characteristics theory (Hackman & Oldham, 1976), employees believe that the organization trusts them with responsibility when they perceive high levels of job autonomy, and they are consequently likely to reciprocate with high performance and satisfaction. Conversely, low levels of autonomy suggest that employees are not trusted, which can promote acts of workplace deviance due to frustration or retaliation.

Role ambiguity and role conflict. Drawing on role theory (Sluss, van Dick, & Thompson, 2011), many studies have examined different role characteristics that promote employee deviance. For example, role ambiguity is experienced when an employee is uncertain about the expectations and responsibilities in his/her job (Katz & Kahn, 1978). One consequence of this uncertainty is that employees may remain ignorant of the expectations and the rules that govern their behavior in the workplace, making rule-breaking behavior more likely. Not surprisingly, researchers have found that ambiguity is positively related to a variety of negative work outcomes, including employee deviance, stress, and turnover (e.g., Litzky et al., 2006; Yang & Diefendorff, 2009).

Role conflict is another role characteristic that can influence employee behavior. Role conflict is experienced when employees are faced with conflicting or competing role expectations that are difficult or impossible to simultaneously achieve (Kahn, Wolfe, Quinn, Snoek, & Rosenthal, 1964). Like role ambiguity, this job characteristic has been shown to be related to deviant behaviors such as workplace bullying and aggressive behavior toward other organizational members (Hauge, Skogstad, & Einarsen, 2009; Spector & Fox, 2005). These effects are oftentimes explained in terms of stress models of deviance. For example, the stressor-emotion model of deviance states that work stressors, like role conflict, prompt negative emotions. These negative emotions, in turn, encourage strains that include deviant employee behaviors (Fox, Spector, & Miles, 2001; Spector, 2002). The stressor-emotion model also emphasizes that perceived control or autonomy should moderate these relationships, such that higher autonomy weakens the links between stressors, negative emotions, and deviance (Fox et al., 2001).

Conflict can also occur between work and nonwork roles. Some initial evidence suggests that this type of role conflict, called work-family conflict, can motivate organizational, interpersonal, and customer-directed deviance. Employees who may not normally engage in deviance report low job satisfaction when experiencing work-family conflict, and this negativity has been found to manifest as workplace deviance in a preliminary study (Darrat, Amyx, & Bennett, 2010).

SUMMARY

As evident by our review of the literature, contextual characteristics that reside at the organizational, team, supervisor-subordinate dyad, and individual job levels can all contribute to employees' motivations to engage in destructive and/or self-interested forms of deviance. By understanding how the organizational context can promote deviance, managers can take a more proactive approach to preventing this behavior. Although our discussion thus far has focused on the predictors of workplace deviance that Vardi and Weitz (2004) would categorize as Type-D or Type-S, we caution that some forms of deviance can be beneficial to an organization if managed carefully. We review these types of deviance, which are sometimes referred to as constructive deviance (e.g., Spreitzer & Sonenshein, 2004), in the next section.

SHOULD ALL DEVIANCE BE SUPPRESSED? CONSIDERING CONSTRUCTIVE DEVIANCE

Most deviance is automatically considered to be harmful in the work context and many organizations put forth great effort to punish and deter deviance in their employees. However, recent research has started to distinguish between two categories of deviance: constructive deviance and destructive deviance (e.g., Warren, 2003). Destructive deviance mostly results in damaging consequences and aligns with Vardi and Weitz's (2004) conceptualization of Type-D and Type-S forms of misbehavior. In contrast, constructive deviance can contribute positively to the work environment; this type of deviance in some respects aligns with Vardi and Weitz's

Type-O misbehavior. It is important for managers to recognize the difference between these two broad types of deviance and to understand the motivations behind them.

Recent literature has focused on empirically distinguishing destructive deviance from constructive deviance by studying the different outcomes associated with these behaviors (e.g., Dahling, Chau, Mayer, & Gregory, 2012; Galperin & Burke, 2006). In general, constructive deviance is distinguished from destructive deviance because it is conducted with *honorable* intentions to better the organization or its stakeholders (e.g., Spreitzer & Sonenshein, 2004; Morrison, 2006; Vardi & Weitz, 2004; Warren, 2003). Constructive deviance may be confused with destructive deviance by managers because, in both instances, the employee is overtly breaking a formal organizational rule or norm. Unlike destructive deviance, however, an employee engaging in constructive deviance is motivated by a desire to help the overall organization in some form.

Although research on constructive deviance is in its infancy, one of the more established examples of constructive deviance is prosocial rule breaking (PSRB; Morrison, 2006). PSRB has been defined as "the intentional violation of a formal organizational policy, regulation, or prohibition with the primary intention of promoting the welfare of the organization or one of its stakeholders" (Morrison, 2006, pp. 7–8). Employees engaging in constructive deviance believe that the act of breaking a formal rule or norm will ultimately lead to some benefit for the company. Some categories of constructive deviance/PSRB have been proposed that provide examples of behaviors that employees might engage in to help the overall organization. Constructive deviance, for example, may be committed in an attempt to improve efficiency, assist coworkers with work, and/or assist customers (Dahling et al., 2012).

Although two types of deviance have been established in the academic literature, the practical literature has focused largely on destructive deviance without acknowledging that deviance can also be constructive. This is an important oversight given that constructive deviance may be critical to prevent organizations from becoming inefficient and stagnant (Dehler & Welsh, 1998; Packer, 2011). Without employees who challenge the rules and norms of an organization in well-intentioned ways, organizations may miss opportunities to enhance employee flexibility, effectiveness, and adaptability (Dehler & Welsh, 1998).

Another way that constructive deviance has been said to be beneficial to an organization is by allowing employees to challenge organizational rules or norms that are harmful to the organization (Spreitzer & Sonenshein, 2003). Some rules may be outdated, ineffective, or immoral with respect to the objective that they were meant to accomplish. When employees act out against a rule in their daily working lives, it could mean that the rule is no longer benefiting the organization and needs to be reassessed. Without such constructive deviance, managers may be unable to identify and improve upon outdated or harmful norms that could ultimately lead to a business failure (Dehler & Welsh, 1998). Finally, an organization is unlikely to have creative problem solving without constructive deviance, which can also contribute to decreased organizational efficiency and growth (Galperin & Burke, 2006).

In summary, understanding the motivations behind deviance can help managers distinguish between the two types and address employee deviance accordingly. By understanding that some deviance is potentially beneficial to the organization, managers can avoid the myth that all deviance needs to be punished and question more carefully why deviance might be occurring. To this end, we conclude this chapter by drawing on the body of literature described previously to provide some recommendations for managers who are faced with a need to manage employee deviance.

RECOMMENDATIONS FOR MANAGERS

The theories and studies of employee deviance that we describe in this chapter offer a wealth of advice for practicing managers. In this section, we build on previous work (e.g., Litzky et al., 2006) to attempt to distill this advice down to a manageable body of recommendations that are summarized in Table 2.

TABLE 2 Recommendations for Managers to Reduce and Control Organizational Deviance Based on Our Research of Deviance Predictors

---

1. Set reward, control, and punishment systems with the potential for deviant behavior in mind.

- Explicitly reward ethical behavior; do not blindly reward results without consideration of how they were attained.
- Set performance goals carefully (with measurable and attainable criteria) and seek employee input.
- When control and punishment systems are necessary, compensate for their introduction with careful explanations and advanced warning to enhance fairness perceptions. Otherwise, these systems can actually promote rather than reduce deviance.

2. Set and reiterate clear performance expectations for subordinates to bypass role difficulties.

- Do not allow role ambiguity to persist; clarify what behaviors are expected and what behaviors are unacceptable for people who hold a particular role.
- Be mindful of role conflict for employees with extensive responsibilities. Help these employees resolve potentially-conflicting expectations by either arranging work reassignments or increasing coordination among the parties to which the employees must answer.
- Consider the extent to which work-family conflict may contribute to deviance, and refer people to Employee Assistance Programs (EAPs) if necessary.

3. Make every effort to understand subordinates' expectations and anticipated outcomes to avoid violating trust and psychological contracts.

- Talk openly with subordinates about how they construe the employment arrangement and what they feel that they have been promised in exchange for their work.
- Strive for mutually-held agreements about work exchanges that can reasonably be honored and that serve as the foundation for trusting relationships.

- Be careful not to overpromise outcomes for subordinates that cannot be delivered when the work is done.

4. **Model ethical behavior to serve as the foundation for a workgroup ethical climate.**

- Be aware that subordinates learn about desirable and rewarded behaviors by observing what their managers and coworkers do.
- Do not condone deviant behavior from individual subordinates; this tacit approval communicates to other employees in the workgroup that deviance is not a matter of concern.
- Managers should behave as they expect their subordinates to behave.

5. **Balance the provision of autonomy to employees with managerial accessibility and continued awareness of their activities.**

- Employees can and should be trusted with autonomy; this sense of responsibility is associated with many desirable workplace behaviors.
- Autonomy is only an asset when managers and subordinates trust each other, when roles and responsibilities are clear, and when managers remain accessible for feedback and clarification.
- Highly-autonomous, self-managed work teams should be carefully trained to avoid the development of coercive, unethical norms.

6. **Remain open-minded about the potential for constructively-deviant behavior and what deviance might suggest about obsolete or inefficient practices.**

- Recall that employees sometimes break rules with the well-being of the organization or its stakeholders in mind; the motivation behind an act of rule-breaking behavior should be identified before action is taken.
- Constructive deviance can be a valuable way in which employees identify ways to improve organizational effectiveness in a bottom-up fashion.
- If employees lack the perspective to understand that their well-intended deviance could potentially cause greater problems, provide careful explanations, set clear expectations for future behavior, and suggest other ways to advocate for changes.

7. **Strive to treat subordinates kindly and fairly; avoid expressions of abusive supervision.**

- Be mindful of employees' interpersonal justice perceptions, the extent to which they feel that they are treated with dignity and respect by decision makers.
- Strive to be scrupulously fair when making decisions about desirable outcomes; award these outcomes equitably using consistent, clear procedures.
- Do not express inappropriate hostile emotions or verbally abuse employees under any circumstances.

First, managers must set reward and control policies very carefully in light of research that shows (a) how reward systems can unintentionally encourage deviance and (b) that monitoring and control systems can be perceived as unfair in ways that elicit negative retaliatory behaviors. Ethical rule compliance can be motivated by reward systems that take into account employee behaviors rather than focusing exclusively on results and disregarding the context of how those results were attained (Aguinis, 2008). Performance goals should be set with attainable and specific criteria in mind, and ideally employees should be involved in setting those goals (e.g., Litzky et al., 2006). Although monitoring and control systems are sometimes also necessary to direct employee behavior, providing advance notice and careful explanations about why they are being used can greatly reduce employees' negative reactions toward the introduction of these systems in the workplace (Horvoka-Mead, Ross, Whipple, & Renchin, 2002).

Second, deviance can be greatly reduced if managers simply take the time to set and reiterate clear expectations for subordinates to resolve role challenges. Role ambiguity creates opportunities for employees to define for themselves what behaviors are acceptable and desirable (Yang & Diefendorff, 2008). Consequently, early and frequent clarification by managers is important when employees commit acts of deviance in order to prevent confusion about what constitutes acceptable behavior in the future. Clear expectations are likely to be particularly important when employees are struggling to reconcile many conflicting role demands and responsibilities (Spector & Fox, 2005); under these circumstances, it is especially likely that employees will "cut corners" and make choices that compromise the quality of their work. Some initial evidence also suggests that work-family conflict in particular can promote employee deviance (Darrat et al., 2010). Managers can refer their subordinates to appropriate employee assistance programs that may be able to help if problems experienced at home are negatively impacting an employee's behavior at work (Shumway, Wampler, Dersch, & Arredondo, 2004).

While setting clear expectations for subordinates is critical, promoting trust and avoiding psychological contract breaches requires managers to also listen to the goals and expectations that employees have for the employment relationship. Many contract breaches occur when managers act in ways that unknowingly violate important psychological contracts held by employees (Rousseau, 1995). Employees *believe* that their psychological contracts are mutually-held, so when their expectations are violated, they may blame supervisors and other representatives of the organization and engage in acts of retaliation that seem incomprehensible to observers. Given that psychological contracts are constantly works-in-progress, managers should make every effort to speak openly with subordinates about the outcomes that they expect to clarify any misconceptions before a contract breach occurs (Rousseau, 2004). Moreover, they should be careful not to "overpromise" outcomes that may be impossible to provide. As employees' psychological contracts are honored and respected over time, more trust will develop between employees and managers, making deviant behavior increasingly unlikely.

Fourth, consistent with many authors, we strongly emphasize the importance of managers in setting the foundation for an ethical workplace climate by modeling ethical behavior for their subordinates (e.g., Litzky et al., 2006). Employees learn about acceptable and desired behaviors by observing what their supervisors and coworkers do (e.g., Robinson & O'Leary-Kelly, 1998). Consequently, managers who behave unethically should not be surprised when their subordinates emulate this observed behavior. Similarly, given how easily unethical workplace norms can develop, managers cannot ignore any deviant behavior in work groups and teams. Letting this behavior perpetuate sends a tacit acknowledgement to other employees that such behavior is permissible, compounding the initial problem.

Fifth, managers need to strike a reasonable balance between giving teams and individuals autonomy without being too absent. Employees respond positively to autonomy and being empowered with responsibility, and these reactions make it unlikely that they will break rules with self-interested or destructive intentions. However, research on managerial oversight shows that managers who are removed from their subordinates and are inaccessible create too many opportunities for deviance to occur without consequence (Detert et al., 2007). Moreover, autonomous work is only possible when both employees and managers trust each other, and when role expectations have been made very clear so that employees know how to direct their own behavior. At the team level of analysis, highly-autonomous, self-managed teams should be trained and periodically observed to ensure that coercive norms that encourage deviance do not develop within the group.

Sixth, managers should think carefully about the possible motivations for employee deviance and identify if some acts of deviance may be constructively motivated. Constructive deviance has the potential to improve innovation within the organization and to challenge inefficient practices (Galperin & Burke, 2006). Therefore, engaging with constructively-deviant employees rather than simply suppressing this behavior can be beneficial. Managers must also recognize, however, that employees sometimes lack the perspective to understand why rules exist in the first place, and that their acts of well-intentioned deviance may have broader consequences than they understand (Dahling et al., 2012). In these circumstances, effective managers will provide this perspective by giving detailed explanations, setting clear expectations for what behaviors are permissible in the future, and suggesting other avenues through which employees might innovate or advocate for changes.

Last, while it may seem self-evident, managers must strive to be fair and to treat subordinates kindly. Abusive supervision has received extensive recent research attention, and it is abundantly clear that mistreatment at the hands of supervisors is a primary driver of retaliatory employee deviance (e.g., Detert et al., 2007; Shao et al., 2011). Abusive supervision most directly violates employees' sense of interpersonal justice, perceptions of the extent to which one is treated with dignity and respect by decision makers (Colquitt, 2001). However, abusive supervision can also entail violations of distributive justice through the unfair distribution of rewards, and violations of procedural justice through inconsistent or politically motivated decision making. Managers should make every attempt possible to be reasonable and respectful in their interactions with subordinates and to avoid expressions of abusive treatment at all times.

CONCLUSION

We hope this chapter provides some insight for managers about why deviance occurs and how best to manage these undesirable behaviors. Contrary to some of the practitioner literature that takes a simplistic, disciplinary view of deviance, the research we reviewed points to a wide variety of workplace characteristics that generate motivations for employees to act in self-interested or destructive ways. Understanding these motivations can help managers curtail these behaviors by proactively managing the organizational context and treating the causes of deviance rather than just its symptoms.

NOTE

1 An enormous number of terms have proliferated within the scholarly literature to refer to "bad behavior" in the workplace. To avoid unnecessarily confounding our discussion, we largely gloss over the fine distinctions between these behaviors and use the global term of "deviance" throughout this chapter. Griffin and Lopez (2005) provide a cogent review of the theoretical clarity of these competing terms for interested readers.

REFERENCES

Aguinis, H. (2008). *Performance management* (2nd ed.). Upper Saddle River, NJ: Prentice-Hall.

Aquino, K., Lewis, M. U., & Bradfield, M. (1999). Justice constructs, negative affectivity, and employee deviance: A proposed model and empirical test. *Journal of Organizational Behavior, 20*, 1073–1091.

Aquino, K., & O'Reilly, J. (2011). Antisocial behavior at work: The social psychological dynamics of workplace victimization and revenge. In D. DeCremer, R. van Dick, & J.K. Murnighan (Eds.), *Social psychology and organizations* (pp. 273–296). New York, NY: Routledge.

Arthur, J. B. (2011). Do HR system characteristics affect the frequency of interpersonal deviance in organizations? The role of team autonomy and internal labor market practices. *Industrial Relations: A Journal of Economy & Society, 50*, 30–56.

Ashforth, B. (1997). Petty tyranny in organizations: A preliminary examination of antecedents and consequences. *Canadian Journal of Administrative Sciences, 14*, 126–140.

Baillien, E., De Cuyper, N., & De Witte, H. (2011). Job autonomy and workload as antecedents of workplace bullying: A two-wave test of Karasek's Job Demand Control Model for targets and perpetrators. *Journal of Occupational and Organizational Psychology, 84*, 191–208.

Bandura, A. (1977) *Social learning theory*. Englewood Cliffs, NJ: Prentice-Hall.

Barker, J.R. (1993). Tightening the iron cage: Concertive control in self-managing teams. *Administrative Science Quarterly, 38*, 408–437.

Bennett, R. J., & Robinson, S. L. (2000). Development of a measure of workplace deviance. *Journal of Applied Psychology, 85*, 349–360.

Bennett, R.J., & Robinson, S.L. (2003). The past, present, and future of workplace deviance research. In J. Greenberg (Ed.), *Organizational behavior: The state of the science* (pp. 247–281). Mahwah, NJ: LEA.

Bensimon, H. (1997). What to do about anger in the workplace. *Training and Development, 51*, 28–32.

Berry, C. M., Ones, D. S., & Sackett, P. R. (2007). Interpersonal deviance, organizational deviance, and their common correlates: A review and meta-analysis. *Journal of Applied Psychology, 92*, 410–424.

Biron, M. (2010). Negative reciprocity and the association between perceived organizational ethical values and organizational deviance. *Human Relations, 63*, 875–897.

Bordia, P., Restubog, S. D., & Tang, R. L. (2008). When employees strike back: Investigating mediating mechanisms between psychological contract breach and workplace deviance. *Journal of Applied Psychology, 93*, 1104–1117.

Bruce, A., Hampel, B., & Lamont, E. (2011). *Solving employee performance problems: How to spot problems early, take appropriate action, and bring out the best in everyone.* New York, NY: McGraw-Hill.

Colbert, A. E., Mount, M. K., Harter, J. K., Witt, L. A., & Barrick, M. R. (2004). Interactive effects of personality and perceptions of the work situation on employee deviance. *Journal of Applied Psychology, 89,* 599–609.

Colquitt, J. A. (2001). On the dimensionality of organizational justice: A construct validation of a measure. *Journal of Applied Psychology, 86,* 386–400.

Dahling, J. J., Chau, S. L., Mayer, D. M., & Gregory, J. B. (2012). Breaking rules for the right reasons? An investigation of pro?social rule breaking. *Journal of Organizational Behavior, 33,* 21–42.

Dahling, J.J., Kuyumcu, D., & Librizzi, E. (2012). Machiavellianism, unethical behavior, and well-being in organizational life. In R. A. Giacalone & M. D. Promislo (Eds.), *Handbook of unethical workplace behavior: Implications for well-being* (pp. 183–194). Armonk, NY: M.E. Sharpe.

Dahling, J. J., Whitaker, B. G., & Levy, P. E. (2009). The development and validation of a new Machiavellianism Scale. *Journal of Management, 35,* 219–257.

Darrat, M., Amyx, D., & Bennett, R. (2010). An investigation into the effects of work-family conflict and job satisfaction on salesperson deviance. *Journal of Personal Selling & Sales Management, 30,* 239–251.

Dehler, G. E. & Welsh, M. A. (1998). Problematizing deviance in contemporary organizations: A critical perspective. In R. W. Griffin, A. O'Leary-Kelly & J. M. Collins (Eds.), *Dysfunctional behavior in organizations: Nonviolent behaviors in organizations* (Part A, pp. 241–269). Stamford, CT: JAI Press.

Den Hartog, D. N., & Belschak, F. D. (2012). When does transformational leadership enhance employee proactive behavior? The role of autonomy and role breadth self-efficacy. *Journal of Applied Psychology, 97,* 194–202.

Detert, J. R., Treviño, L. K., Burris, E. R., & Andiappan, M. (2007). Managerial modes of influence and counterproductivity in organizations: A longitudinal business-unit-level investigation. *Journal of Applied Psychology, 92,* 993–1005.

Diefendorff, J. M., & Mehta, K. (2007). The relations of motivational traits with workplace deviance. *Journal of Applied Psychology, 92,* 967–977.

Dilchert, S., Ones, D. S., Davis, R. D., & Rostow, C. D. (2007). Cognitive ability predicts objectively measured counterproductive work behaviors. *Journal of Applied Psychology, 92,* 616–627.

Douglas, S. C., & Martinko, M. J. (2001). Exploring the role of individual differences in the prediction of workplace aggression. *Journal of Applied Psychology, 86,* 547–559.

Dunn, J., & Schweitzer, M. E. (2005). Why good employees make unethical decisions: The role of reward systems, organizational culture, and managerial oversight. In R. E. Kidwell, Jr. & C. L. Martin (Eds.), *Managing organizational deviance* (pp. 39–60). Thousand Oaks, CA: SAGE.

Eisenberger, R., Huntington, R., Hutchison, S., & Sowa, D. (1986). Perceived organizational support. *Journal of Applied Psychology, 71,* 500–507.

El Akremi, A., Vandenberghe, C., & Camerman, J. (2010). The role of justice and social exchange relationships in workplace deviance: Test of a mediated model. *Human Relations, 63,* 1687–1717.

Evans, W., Goodman, J. M., & Davis, W. D. (2011). The impact of perceived corporate citizenship on organizational cynicism, OCB, and employee deviance. *Human Performance, 24,* 79–97.

Falcone, P. (2009). *101 tough conversations to have with employees: A manager's guide to addressing performance, conduct, and discipline challenges.* New York, NY: AMACOM.

Ferguson, M., & Barry, B. (2011). I know what you did: The effects of interpersonal deviance on bystanders. *Journal of Occupational Health Psychology, 16,* 80–94.

Ferris, D., Brown, D. J., & Heller, D. (2009). Organizational supports and organizational deviance: The mediating role of organization-based self–esteem. *Organizational Behavior and Human Decision Processes, 108,* 279–286.

Fox, S., Spector, P. E., & Miles, D. (2001). Counterproductive work behavior (CWB) in response to job stressors and organizational justice: Some mediator and moderator tests for autonomy and emotions. *Journal of Vocational Behavior, 59,* 291–309.

Galperin, B. L., & Burke, R. J. (2006). Uncovering the relationship between workaholism and workplace destructive and constructive deviance: An exploratory study. *The International Journal of Human Resource Management, 17*, 331–347.

Glomb, T. M., & Liao, H. (2003). Interpersonal aggression in work groups: Social influence, reciprocal, and individual effects. *Academy of Management Journal, 46*, 486–496.

Gottfredson, L. S. (1997). Why g matters: The complexity of everyday life. *Intelligence, 24*, 79–132.

Griffin, R. W., & Lopez, Y. P. (2005). "Bad behavior" in organizations: A review and typology for future research. *Journal of Management, 31*, 988–1005.

Griffin, R. W., & O'Leary-Kelly, A. M. (2004). An introduction to the dark side. In R.W. Griffin & A.M. O'Leary-Kelly (Eds.), *The dark side of organizational behavior* (pp. 1–19). San Francisco, CA: Jossey-Bass.

Grote, D. (2006). *Discipline without punishment: The proven strategy that turns problem employees into superior performers.* New York, NY: AMACOM.

Guimond, S., Dambrun, M. D., Michinov, N., & Duarte, S. (2003). Does social dominance generate prejudice? Integrating individual and contextual determinants of intergroup cognitions. *Journal of Personality and Social Psychology, 84*, 697–721.

Hackman, J., & Oldham, G. R. (1976). Motivation through the design of work: Test of a theory. *Organizational Behavior & Human Performance, 16*, 250–279.

Hauge, L., Skogstad, A., & Einarsen, S. (2009). Individual and situational predictors of workplace bullying: Why do perpetrators engage in the bullying of others? *Work & Stress, 23*, 349–358.

Henle, C. A. (2005). Predicting workplace deviance from the interaction between organizational justice and personality. *Journal of Managerial Issues, 17*, 247–263.

Horvoka-Mead, A. D., Ross Jr., W. H., Whipple, T., & Renchin, M. B. (2002). Watching the detectives: Seasonal student employee reactions to electronic monitoring with and without advance notification. *Personnel Psychology, 55*, 329–362.

Kahn, R. L., Wolfe, P. M., Quinni, R. P., Snoek, J. E., & Rosenthal, R. A. (1964). *Organizational stress: Studies in role conflict and role ambiguity.* New York, NY: Wiley.

Katz, D., & Kahn, R. L. (1978). *The social psychology of organizations* (2nd ed.). New York: John Wiley.

Kerr, S. (1995). On the follow of rewarding A, while hoping for B. *Academy of Management Executive, 9*, 7–14.

Kish-Gephart, J. J., Harrison, D. A., & Treviño, L. K. (2010). Bad apples, bad cases, and bad barrels: Meta-analytic evidence about sources of unethical decisions at work. *Journal of Applied Psychology, 95*, 1–31.

Kuncel, N. R., & Hezlett, S. A. (2010). Fact and fiction in cognitive ability testing for admissions and hiring decisions. *Current Directions in Psychological Science, 19*, 339–345.

Lawrence, T. B., & Robinson, S. L. (2007). Ain't misbehavin': Workplace deviance as organizational resistance. *Journal of Management, 33*, 378–394.

Litzky, B. E., Eddleston, K. A., & Kidder, D. L. (2006). The good, the bad, and the misguided: How managers inadvertently encourage deviant behaviors. *Academy of Management Perspectives, 20*, 91–103.

McGregor, D. (1960). *The human side of enterprise.* New York, NY: McGraw-Hill.

Ménard, J., Brunet, L., & Savoie, A. (2011). Interpersonal workplace deviance: Why do offenders act out? A comparative look on personality and organisational variables. *Canadian Journal of Behavioural Science/Revue Canadienne Des Sciences Du Comportement, 43*, 309–317.

Mitchell, M. S., & Ambrose, M. L. (2007). Abusive supervision and workplace deviance and the moderating effects of negative reciprocity beliefs. *Journal of Applied Psychology, 92*, 1159–1168.

Morrison, E., & Robinson, S. L. (1997). When employees feel betrayed: A model of how psychological contract violation develops. *Academy of Management Review, 22*, 226–256.

Morrison, E. (2006). Doing the job well: An investigation of pro-social rule breaking. *Journal of Management, 32*, 5–28.

Packer, D. (2011). The dissenter's dilemma and a social identity solution. In J. Jetten & M. J. Hornsey (Eds.), *Rebels in groups: Dissent, deviance, difference, and defiance.* Malden, MA: Wiley-Blackwell.

Penney, L. M., & Spector, P. E. (2005). Job stress, incivility, and counterproductive work behavior (CWB): The moderating role of negative affectivity. *Journal of Organizational Behavior, 26*, 777–796.

Peterson, D. K. (2002). Deviant workplace behavior and the organization's ethical climate. *Journal of Business & Psychology, 17,* 47–61.

Pierce, J. L., Gardner, D. G., Cummings, L. L., & Dunham, R. B. (1989). Organization-based self-esteem: Construct definition measurement and validation. *Academy of Management Journal, 32,* 622–648.

Pratto, F., Sidanius, J., Stallworth, L. M., & Malle, B. F. (1994). Social dominance orientation: A personality variable predicting social and political attitudes. *Journal of Personality and Social Psychology, 67,* 741–763.

Roberson, Q. M., & Colquitt, J. A. 2005. Shared and configural justice: A social network model of justice in teams. *Academy of Management Review, 30,* 595–607.

Robinson, S. L., & O'Leary-Kelly, A. M. (1998). Monkey see, monkey do: The influence of work groups on the antisocial behavior of employees. *Academy of Management Journal, 41,* 658–672.

Rousseau, D. M. (1995). *Psychological contracts in organizations: Understanding written and unwritten agreements.* Thousand Oaks, CA: SAGE.

Rousseau, D. M. (2004). Psychological contracts in the workplace: Understanding the ties that motivate. *Academy of Management Executive, 18,* 120–127.

Salgado, J. (2002). The Big Five personality dimensions and counterproductive behaviors. *International Journal of Selection and Assessment, 10,* 117–125.

Scott, G. G. (2006). *A survival guide to managing employees from hell: Handling idiots, whiners, slackers, and other workplace demons.* New York, NY: AMACOM.

Shao, P., Resick, C. J., & Hargis, M. B. (2011). Helping and harming others in the workplace: The roles of personal values and abusive supervision. *Human Relations, 64,* 1051–1078.

Shepard, G. (2005*). How to manage problem employees: A step-by-step guide for turning difficult employees into high performers.* Hoboken, NJ: John Wiley.

Shultz, C. J. (1993). Situational and dispositional predictors of performance: A test of the hypothesized Machiavellianism structure interaction among sales persons. *Journal of Applied Social Psychology, 23,* 478–498.

Shumway, S. T., Wampler, R. S., Dersch, C., & Arredondo, R. (2004). A place for marriage and family services in employee assistance programs (EAPs): A survey of EAP client problems and needs. *Journal of Marital and Family Therapy, 30,* 71–79.

Sims, R. L. (2010). A study of deviance as a retaliatory response to organizational power. *Journal of Business Ethics, 92,* 553–563.

Skarlicki, D. P., & Folger, R. (1997). Retaliation in the workplace: The roles of distributive, procedural, and interactional justice. *Journal of Applied Psychology, 82,* 434–443.

Sluss, D. M., van Dick, R., & Thompson, B. S. (2011). Role theory in organizations: A relational perspective. In S. Zedeck (Ed.), *APA handbook of industrial and organizational psychology* (Vol. 1, pp. 505–534). Washington, D.C.: APA.

Spector, P.E. (2002). Employee control and occupational stress. *Current Directions in Psychological Science, 11,* 133–136.

Spector, P. E. (2011). The relationship of personality to counterproductive work behavior (CWB): An integration of perspectives. *Human Resource Management Review, 21,* 342–352.

Spector, P. E., & Fox, S. (2005). The Stressor-Emotion Model of Counterproductive Work Behavior. In S. Fox & P. E. Spector (Eds.), *Counterproductive work behavior: Investigations of actors and targets* (pp. 151–174). Washington, DC: American Psychological Association.

Spreitzer, G. M., & Sonenshein, S. (2003). Positive deviance and extraordinary organizing. In K. Cameron, J. Dutton, & R. Quinn (Eds.), *Positive organizational scholarship* (pp. 207–224). San Francisco, CA: Berrett-Koehler.

Spreitzer, G. M., & Sonenshein, S. (2004). Toward the construct definition of positive deviance. *American Behavioral Scientist, 47,* 828–847.

Taylor, A. (2007, January 15). Gambling at work "costs employers £300M a year." *Financial Times,* p. 4.

Tepper, B. J., Henle, C. A., Lambert, L., Giacalone, R. A., & Duffy, M. K. (2008). Abusive supervision and subordinates' organization deviance. *Journal of Applied Psychology, 93,* 721–732.

Tomlinson, E.C., & Greenberg, J. (2005). Discouraging employee theft by managing social norms and promoting organizational justice. In R. E. Kidwell Jr. & C. L. Martin (Eds.), *Managing organizational deviance* (pp. 211–232). Thousand Oaks, CA: SAGE.

Vardi, Y., & Weitz, E. (2004). *Misbehavior in organizations: Theory, research, and management.* Mahwah, NJ: LEA.

Victor, B., & Cullen, J. B. (1988). The organizational bases of ethical work climates. *Administrative Sciences Quarterly, 33,* 101–125.

Warren, D. (2003). Constructive and destructive deviance in organizations. *Academy of Management Review, 28,* 622–632.

Watson, D., & Clark, L. A. (1984). Negative affectivity: The disposition to experience aversive emotional states. *Psychological Bulletin, 96,* 465–490.

Wimbush, J. C., & Dalton, D. R. (1997). Base rate for employee theft: Convergence of multiple methods. *Journal of Applied Psychology, 82,* 756–763.

Yang, J., & Diefendorff, J. M. (2009). The relations of daily counterproductive workplace behavior with emotions, situational antecedents, and personality moderators: A diary study in Hong Kong. *Personnel Psychology, 62,* 259–295.

Zellars, K. L., Tepper, B. J., & Duffy, M. K. (2002). Abusive supervision and subordinates' organizational citizenship behavior. *Journal of Applied Psychology, 87,* 1068–1076.

Zoghbi-Manrique-de-Lara, P. (2011). Predicting nonlinear effects of monitoring and punishment on employee deviance: The role of procedural justice. *European Management Journal, 29,* 272–282.

DISCUSSION QUESTIONS

1   According to the author, POS (perceived organizational support) "refers to the employee's beliefs about whether or not the organization values their contributions and cares about their well-being." In your opinion, why would POS serve to reduce organizational deviance? Do you think POS would be an effective approach against ethical lapses by employees who lack certain personality traits, such as conscientiousness, emotional stability, and agreeableness? If not, how would you deal with such individuals?

2   Criminal justice organizations, especially police departments and correctional facilities, are noted as having a code of silence, or an unwritten rule that officers will not report on each other's errors or ethical failures. How much do you think this phenomenon is driven by organizational factors rather than individual deviance?

SECTION II CONCLUSION

After having read the Stohr and Collins article on decision making, take a few minutes to reflect on your decision-making skills. What recommendations can you put into immediate practice? What skills do you possess that need to be nurtured and honed? If you are already a talented decision maker and manage people who are not, will the article help you mentor, supervise, or train your subordinates so that you can confidently delegate decision making to others? Some decisions have the potential to be impactful, while others might cause just minor ripples in the operations of an organization. However, all decisions require identifying choices, weighing the pros and cons of each one, and coming to a rational judgment that advances an organization's mission. Decisions, big or small, made within the context of a public safety agency, should never be rushed, minimized, or inexecutable.

No organization is without deviance, pathology, and wrongdoing. However, managers can reduce the incidence of deviance by skillfully managing and preparing for crises, putting qualified individuals into responsible positions to reduce administrative errors, and debriefing after a crisis to identify and fix shortcomings in policy, practice, and training. What makes the criminal justice organization unique when it comes to deviance are the cultural norms that standardize irregular behavior, such as the blue code of silence and noble cause corruption, where the ends justify the means. While some might feel that organizational deviance in criminal justice comes with the territory, an ethical leader should never settle for such pessimistic thinking.

Organizational deviance is particularly harmful in a criminal justice agency because it eats away at its sense of legitimacy. According to *Oxford Bibliographies in Criminology*, legitimacy is the idea that citizens consider something as valid or proper (Forst, 2014). It contributes to social cohesion and allows the state to carry out its potent responsibilities, up to and including the deadly use of force (Forst, 2014). Deviance occurs in every organization so the best a manager can do is work to reduce it, not eliminate it. And when deviance rears its ugly head, the most effective response is transparency (i.e., be open with the public no matter how bad it makes your agency look) and accountability (i.e., making individuals answer for their wrongdoings). Without transparency and accountability there is no trust. And without trust there is no legitimacy.

INTRA- AND INTERAGENCY COLLABORATIONS, STRATEGIC PLANNING

INTRODUCTION

Section III introduces two approaches that can, if implemented correctly, enhance the effectiveness of an organization: collaboration and strategic planning. In the public sector, where agency leaders compete with each other for their fair share of the public budget and wrangle with legislatures over funding priorities, cost saving measures can make or break an executive's wish list. Collaborating with other agencies is a way to share resources instead of competing for them. Collaboration in criminal justice can serve the profession well, since each sector (law enforcement, the courts, and corrections) strives to reach the lofty goal of protecting the public. However, the divergence begins in the methods used to achieve this goal. Law enforcement seeks to take bad guys off the street; the courts have the same goal, but they go to great lengths to ensure that the rights of the bad guys are protected; and corrections professionals strive to reform the bad guys, since most of them will be released one day. Even though each entity is working toward the same goal, role conflict can inhibit collaboration. Fortunately, collaborations do happen and many times they are successful. In the Hammond article, we learn how one county sheriff's department dealt with a severe crowding problem—specifically the facility was built for 422 prisoners yet housed 554. Collaborating is not easy, nor is it a luxury. It is a necessity. Criminal justice leaders need to learn how to work with other agencies and political bodies to carry out the mission the community entrusts to them.

In the Stohr and Collins article, we learn how strategic planning and budgeting are central to what a manager does. The quote at the beginning of the article is compelling; there is a connection between planning and doing. In the course of our work days, we do many different things and we need to take stock. Are we responding to crises in a prepared manner? Are we implementing well-thought-out proposals? Or are we merely reacting to chaos? Think through these questions as you read the Stohr and Collins article and determine how you can improve your agency's efficacy.

COLLABORATION, PARTNERSHIP, AND EDUCATION

ESSENTIALS FOR THE MANAGEMENT OF MENTALLY ILL OFFENDERS

W. DIANE WOOD, THOMAS FULKS, AND NICOLE TAYLOR

One of the current popular concepts in business today is the concept of "working in silos." This concept means that corrections professionals are unaware of what is going on outside of their respective areas; they are contained unto themselves. It is very difficult to produce positive outcomes in a correctional environment when using the silo approach. In corrections, there are so many different entities with differing goals and resources that simply trying to operate day-to-day requires absolute cooperation between staff. The notion of independent functioning has to be replaced with an interdependent philosophy. Recognition that corrections professionals need each other is essential to building collaborative relationships and to promoting positive outcomes.

One of the best examples of the need for an interdependent relationship is seen in the interface between health care staff and correctional staff. Correctional mental health, medical and custody staff strive to formulate case management strategies to manage and treat the mentally ill, including inmates who are identified as nonsuicidal self-injurers. Correctional staff are confronted daily with many challenges in the management and treatment of mentally ill offenders. Though there are many challenging aspects to working within the field of corrections, one that is common to most correctional facilities continues to confound correctional staff and is commonly misunderstood is the management of the mentally ill and self-injurious behaviors. Empirical research suggests that there is a trend toward an increasing prevalence of self-injury in the community, especially among adolescents and young adults.[1] Approximately 15 percent of teens report some form of self-injury and there is an even higher risk among college students.[2]

In 2010, the U.S. Department of Justice, Bureau of Justice Statistics estimated that more than half of the inmates in prisons and jails self-report that they suffer from mental health problems.[3] In 2013, the Office of Justice Programs reported that a national sample of women show high rates of mental health problems, with the majority meeting diagnostic criteria for a serious mental illness, lifetime post-traumatic stress disorder and/or a substance use disorder.[4]

Finding safe, humane and nonpunitive methods for handling inmates who are experiencing symptoms of a mental illness is an ongoing challenge for correctional staff, and an even greater challenge for correctional staff working in silos. The ongoing education of all correctional staff—breaking them out of the silo mentality—is an integral part of functioning successfully in the field. Working as an integrated, interdependent and multidisciplinary team is the first step to establishing the ground work for effective behavior management strategies and tearing down the silos that keep professionals from achieving goals.

When implementing and developing behavior management strategies, it is imperative that corrections professionals take a multidisciplinary and integrated approach that includes a philosophical mindset of interdependence. As many of the key players as possible should be involved, such as security, unit supervisors or managers, health care providers, and counselors or case managers. Collaboration, communication and consistency will turn these efforts into successes. Each stage in the process builds on the next and serves to draw the team closer together in both understanding and partnership. A main reason that behavior management strategies fail in prisons and jails is due to poor communication between disciplines and shifts. Even though one shift follows through, the next may be unaware and might not. Initially, the recommended process may seem to have a lot of needless steps, but in the long run, it will give staff the strategies they need to exact change in problem behaviors. Once staff become familiar with a facility's processes, they will begin to automatically respond in a prescribed manner to specific challenges. They will become comfortable with how to respond, which is often the bigger challenge. The only way for this process to occur is for the team to work together to learn how each other works, and to value those interrelated functions.

COLLABORATING THROUGH EDUCATION

An integrated multidisciplinary team approach is the recommended method for managing the complexities of the mentally ill offender and other difficult behaviors that confront the correctional employee. Having the support of a team is essential for successful outcomes, as well as helping to prevent staff burnout.[5] Most facilities have a behavioral health department to educate nonbehavioral health team members. They also help to make solid, consistent recommendations, in regard not only to treatment and clinical management of the typical mentally ill inmate, but also strategies to manage the most difficult inmates. An approach that encompasses security, custody and control parameters requires that each member cooperates and facilitates plans that will help manage the "unmanageable."[6] This fosters accountability and responsibility for all parties within the facility.[7]

As emphasized above, the ongoing education of all correctional staff is an integral part of functioning successfully in the field. A good example of this is the collaboration that began in 2013 between author Nicole Taylor, Ph.D., J.D., CCHP, mental health monitor with the Arizona Department of Corrections (ADC), and Corizon's corporate behavioral health team. The team is working in partnership to choose training activities that will help correctional officers manage the day-to-day challenges and prevent an escalation of disruptive behaviors. Author Thomas Fulks, Psy.D., Corizon's corporate assistant manager for behavioral health, partnered with ADC to present training to correctional staff at all levels, including wardens, correctional officer counselors and front-line correctional officers.

Through this partnership, Corizon and ADC were able to deliver essential training regarding the hallmark signs and symptoms of mental illnesses, and how to approach inmates with mental illnesses. Also covered was an overview of motivational interviewing techniques and targeted training for inmates most at risk, those on suicide observation. The training consisted of an in-depth overview of mental illness, and some of the common signs and symptoms associated with the most commonly seen diagnoses in corrections. The audience was encouraged to utilize those techniques in order to motivate their inmates toward more pro-social behaviors. De-escalation techniques were discussed in terms of how to take a highly emotional or potentially violent situation and calm it down. This collaborative approach resulted in client satisfaction for correctional staff. The initial collaboration was so successful that additional trainings are currently being developed by Corizon and ADC on the dynamics of groups and group facilitation techniques.

FORGING SUCCESSFUL PARTNERSHIPS BETWEEN CLIENTS AND VENDORS

It is becoming more common in corrections for medical and mental health services to be contracted out to a private vendor. Numerous state and county correctional institutions have adopted this practice as their health care service delivery system. As this trend grows, it is imperative that the two agencies work collaboratively in order to provide the necessary care to the inmate population. Two important elements must be in place for success to be assured— good communication and leadership teams.

Communication. State and county agencies and private vendors have many common goals, but inevitably have different approaches to reaching those goals. While the agency is invested in the outcomes, they become reliant on their private vendors to carry out the necessary actions to meet the health care needs of the inmate population. The very nature of the client/vendor relationship is that it is interdependent—each depends upon the other for success. Poor or no communication between partners rarely leads to positive outcomes. Also, agencies need to feel confident that the vendors address any deficiencies that may arise during the course of business. The vendor, on the other hand, needs to feel that the client is supportive of its efforts. As in all relationships, there must be a mutual understanding of one's role in the relationship and how that role impacts one another. The only way that this understanding is going to exist is if each of the parties communicate openly, honestly and often.

Additionally, both the client and the vendor need to provide quick and accurate responses when issues do arise. ADC and Corizon have been working on building local and regional teams in order to ensure that issues are addressed almost immediately. Often, site-level communication includes the wardens and deputy wardens to provide that ever-important triad needed to respond to the broad needs of an inmate population. Transparency in communication is essential. Even if a team member's functions are different, the goals are the same. Drawing anyone into the conversation who might be helpful—such as a correctional administrator like a warden, a front-line staff member or corporate representative—is beneficial. The bottom line is that you want to communicate with anyone who can help to provide solutions that work for everyone.

No individual can have all the answers all the time, but together, a team can find ways to sort out even the most challenging problems. Being at odds with a client is never a good practice, but it is important that both parties dedicate themselves to working in partnership; both recognizing how important it is to be on the same page and working out differing opinions until a mutual solution is reached. It can be a very rewarding relationship when all parties are working together for the good of the contract, and when looking out for what's best for the inmate population. Expectations can be misconstrued, misunderstood or simply overlooked if there isn't a solid dialogue between the client and vendor. Building a collaborative relationship with the client is a top priority in providing good patient care, proper documentation and ethical practices.

Leadership teams. ADC and Corizon mental health leaders recognized the importance of collaboration, and developed a leadership team approach to mental health care, which includes the mental health monitors and the Corizon regional behavioral health team. When asked about this leadership team approach, Mark Fleming, Ph.D., CCHP-MH, director of operations, behavioral health for Corizon in Arizona, said, "The foundation of success in the mental health program in Arizona stems from a collaborative and open-ended communication stream that begins with the ADC monitors and regional leadership, and ends with site-level leaders and staff. Further, the strong support from the Corizon corporate behavioral health team allows for additional expertise to ensure the highest level of patient care possible." Working together, this team often finds solutions to problems that they would struggle to solve individually. This combined team meets weekly to discuss any issues that arise, supporting a united front when discussing topics with the field staff. A united front is paramount in order to reduce staff splitting and to help the field staff feel supported by the entire leadership team. Such an approach allows for comprehensive feedback to be received by the field staff and ensures a more collaborative approach at all levels. When avoiding silos, everyone works better together.

A combined team approach also provides positive feedback and incentives as a group. This helps to foster better working relationships among those providing the care and those auditing the care. On-site training by the auditing team is also helpful in this collaborative approach. There is no reason to be seen as the enemy or take an adversarial position as an auditor. Auditors want to make sure that the provided mental health care meets expectations and contract requirements. The ADC monitors conduct audits to provide feedback, not to place blame. It should be seen as a "lessons learned" process.

Pulling together as a team will ease the burden for all in an effort to make the unmanageable more manageable and ensure the safety of staff and inmates. The goal of such an approach is to find ways to help staff feel supported, decrease the effects of burnout, and increase motivation to face another day that is filled with the inherent unknowns that will always be a part of working in the correctional environment. Ongoing educational activities will help strengthen the necessary collaborative partnership, reduce risk and increase positive outcomes. The authors feel that the best chance for success lies in the ability to create partnerships and foster those relationships. Through open communication and the utilization of leadership teams, a collaborative environment—where ideas are brought together to find creative solutions to difficult problems so often faced in corrections—can be nurtured.

CONCLUSION

Establishing a strong working relationship between partners and maintaining that relationship isn't an easy task. It takes a level of dedication and understanding from each participant to be successful. As partners, everyone has something to contribute, and everyone has something they need to learn. No one has all the answers, so teams need to work together to find them. Correctional systems and vendors dedicated to the use of interdependent multidisciplinary teams that communicate well together and have a shared philosophy are much better positioned to have success than those that do not. Through the collaborative use of educational and training opportunities with security and administrative staff, vendors hope to bridge the knowledge gap that sometimes exists when it comes to mental health care delivery. Likewise, when mental health care staff attend correctional training, they are better equipped to deal with an undoubtedly challenging population. The trick is having dedicated leaders from both parties of the partnership who understand and appreciate the need for these types of opportunities to occur. They must support one another, they must understand one another and they must work with each other as though they are part of the same organization—because they are.

ENDNOTES

1 Whitlock, J., J. Eckenrode and D. Silverman. 2006. Self-injurious behaviors in a college population. *Pediatrics*, 117(6):1,939–1,948.

2 Kerr, P. L., J. J. Muehlenkamp and J. M. Turner. 2010. Non-suicidal self-injury: A review of the current research for family medicine and primary care physicians. *Journal of the American Board of Family Medicine*, 23(2):240–259.

3 James, D. and L. Glaze. 2006. *Mental health problems of prisons and jail inmates*. Washington, D.C.: U.S. Department of Justice, Bureau of Justice Statistics.

4 Lynch, S. M., D. DeHart, J. Belknap and B. L. Green. 2012. *Women's pathways to jail: The roles and intersections of serious mental illness and trauma*. Washington, D.C.: U.S. Department of Justice, Bureau of Justice Assistance.

5 Lambert, E. G., N. L. Hogan, K. Cheeseman Dial, S. Jiang and M. I. Khondaker. 2012. Is the job burning me out? An exploratory test of the job characteristics model on the emotional burnout of prison staff. *The Prison Journal*, 92(l):3–23.

6 Boudoukha, A. H., E. Altintas, S. Rusinek, C. Fantini-Hauwel and M. Hautekeete. 2013. Inmates-to-staff assaults, PTSD and burnout: Profiles of risk and vulnerability. *Journal of Interpersonal Violence*, 28(11):2,332–2,350.

7 Salley, S. 2009. Positive reinforcement: Improving correctional environments. *Corrections Today*, 71(1):19.

W. Diane Wood, M.Ed., LPC, NCC, CCHP-MH, is corporate director of behavioral health for Corizon. Thomas Fulks, Psy.D., is corporate assistant manager of behavioral health for Corizon. Nicole Taylor, Ph.D., J.D., CCHP, is mental health contract monitor for the Arizona Department of Corrections.

DEALING WITH OVERCROWDING:

A City–County Collaboration

JACK HAMMOND

Ohio's Lorain County Sheriff's Office Jail Division has a rated inmate capacity of 422. When it first opened in 1977, it had a rated capacity of 166 inmates. When the 1980s arrived, so did overcrowding, and like many other facilities, we found ourselves involved in Federal litigation.

A GROWING PROBLEM

In 1998, a 208-bed addition opened and our rated capacity rose to 374. By the year 2000, the jail was once again full to capacity. With the permission of the Bureau of Adult Detention, we were granted clearance to add double-bunking in select dormitories. This raised capacity to its present level of 422.

ALL AVAILABLE ALTERNATIVES OTHER THAN CONSTRUCTION HAD BEEN EXHAUSTED

Our jail population continued to grow at dangerous levels through the mid 2000s, reaching a peak of 554 inmates in 2006. With help from other criminal justice agencies, we were able to decrease our population to a manageable level. Unfortunately, this created a side effect that still plagues our communities today. Our jail has fewer beds available for people who should be in jail. Ultimately, many of the crimes committed may go without the consequence of jail time.

A national firm undertook an assessment of the jail's future needs. Constructing additional bed space to solve this problem was still a consideration—until the recession arrived and additional bed space was no longer an option.

> With a population of just over 300,000, Lorain County is the 9th largest in the State of Ohio. The two largest cities within the county are Lorain, with a population of 64,097 and Elyria, with a population of 54,553. Elyria is the county seat. Situated on Lake Erie, Lorain County is located directly west of Cuyahoga County, the largest county in Ohio with a population of more than 1.2 million. Cleveland is its county seat.

In previous times, when faced with the recurring need for jail space, solutions were found. However, this time was different. All available alternatives other than construction had been exhausted. With an unstable economy, constructing additional bed space was not a consideration. Another result of the economic downturn was a rise in criminal activity. Then, to our dismay, the State passed a new Sentencing Bill in the spring of 2011 that has the potential to place more individuals in local jails as opposed to the State prison system.

The issue of overcrowding under any circumstances is never easy to overcome, but with this set of circumstances, the overcrowding problem seemed insurmountable.

AN UNEXPECTED OPPORTUNITY

Then, in the early summer of 2011, the City of Elyria, which is located in our county and the key holder to a relativity new jail, called. Chief of Police Duane Whitely asked our sheriff, Phil Stammitti, "Do you want our new jail?"

Because of the recession, the City of Elyria was forced to shut down its 56-bed jail operation. The city's efficient new jail had turned into one big storage closet.

Our initial excitement was short lived as we quickly realized the problems associated with integrating this new facility, which was only three miles from our sheriff's office. There was no extra money to expand, and without funds, how could it be staffed? Which inmates would be sent there? How would we book, release, and provide medical and mental health care for inmates? What about utility costs and approval from Elyria's City Council and the County Board of Commissioners?

Sheriff Stammitti and Chief Whitely then reminded us of our goal. Wasn't this exactly what our community needed? New means, more efficiency, and collaboration? The answer was a resounding yes! We left that meeting ready and willing to tackle these issues.

A CHALLENGE TO BE MET

At the beginning of our collaboration with the City of Elyria, key members of our jail staff toured the Elyria facility. They were asked for their opinions on how to integrate it into our system without increasing the budget. It was understood that the Elyria jail would be operated as an annex to the county sheriff's facility and that only the staff and resources currently available to us could be used.

The first—and perhaps easiest—question to answer was whom to house in the new jail. The unanimous response was the female population, which would create an additional 56 male beds at the main site. Over the course of the next few months, collaboration with the City of Elyria and the Lorain County Sheriff's Office continued. Eventually the Elyria City Council and the Lorain County Board of Commissioners entered into an agreement for the county to lease the city jail at no cost.

In the agreement, the City of Elyria would maintain the structure and utilities. In return, the sheriff's office would provide cost-free housing of inmates arrested by the Elyria police and charged with ordnance violations in addition to providing the State-mandated DNA collection of inmates arrested by the city's police.

A BRIGHTER FUTURE

Although there is still much to accomplish and many challenges lie ahead, a future that once looked bleak now has a ray of sunlight shining through. A tremendous amount of work has been and will continue to be put into this effort. The jail staff of the Lorain County Sheriff's Office is currently reinventing how it conducts daily operations that enable staffing of the Elyria Jail site. This is no small undertaking. When a jail operation of any size changes its long-term core operating procedures, the task can seem overwhelming at times, but certainly not unattainable. The new methods and procedures went into effect at the main jail last November.

In addition, a team was assembled to develop procedures for the Elyria annex. The move-in date for this facility was scheduled for this past January.

The collaboration between Lorain County's Sheriff Phil Stammitti and Elyria's Chief of Police Duane Whitely is to be commended. Their leadership and determination to provide the best services to those they serve were the driving forces behind this endeavor. In addition, the understanding and cooperation of the City Council of Elyria and the Board of Lorain County Commissioners must be recognized. Their willingness to approve this agreement and allow the two entities to collaborate was significant.

A new standard has been established for other communities in Lorain County to follow and aspire. With collaboration and a willingness to work together for the greater good, what once seemed impossible is now within reach.

Lt. Jack Hammond joined the Lorain County Sheriff's Office in December 1979 as a member of the Maintenance Department. In the summer of 1985, he was transferred into the Corrections Division to work as a line officer. He was promoted to sergeant in 1989 and then to lieutenant in 1999. In 2001, he was designated as the Operations Lieutenant overseeing all day-to-day operations of the Corrections Division. Designated Jail Administrator in 2006, he assumed the role of Corrections Division Commander in 2010. He may be contacted at *jhammond@ loraincountysheriff.com*. For more information about the Lorain County Sheriff's Office, visit *loraincountvsheriff.com*.

DISCUSSION QUESTIONS

1   Is it possible to have a shared philosophy among custodial, mental health, and medical staff within a correctional facility? If so, what would that philosophy be and how would you, as an agency leader, articulate it to employees?

2   After carefully reading the Hammond article, enumerate the number of collaborations that occurred in Lorain County. What do you think drove each collaboration: education, attitude, budget (pick one or more for each collaboration)?

STRATEGIC PLANNING AND BUDGETING

MARY K. STOHR AND PETER A. COLLINS

There is a connection between planning and doing ...

(Hrebiniak 2005: 65)

Zero-based budgeting sounds great in theory. But theory is not reality.

(Roger Simmons, County Commissioner of Ada County, Idaho 2001)

Public budgeting involves making and carrying out decisions regarding acquisition, allocation, and the use of resources, particularly money, by government. Although public and private budgeting are similar in many respects, public budgeting is often more controversial, more open to multiple influences, and more heavily regulated than private budgeting.

(Nice 2002)

INTRODUCTION: STRATEGIC PLANNING AND BUDGETING ARE AT THE VERY CENTER OF ALL THINGS ORGANIZATIONAL

People tend to think of strategic planning, but particularly budgeting, as very dry topics. Many students hem, they haw, they yawn, when these topics come up. As hard as we try, it is difficult to raise the enthusiasm for budgeting or strategic planning to the level elicited by, say, selection! People who have not worked in criminal justice agencies before, or have not paid attention to organizational management and politics, often just do not see the relevance to themselves of strategic planning or of a budgeting discussion. That many should find planning and budgeting boring is not necessarily surprising; these can be much neglected areas of study and comment that have not been presented creatively. A scholarly lament on the "arid landscape" of the literature on budgeting (Key 1940) remains applicable over a half-century later.

Of course, attitudes of boredom and nonchalance about strategic planning and budgeting are completely out of step with what these disciplines represent for public (and private) sector criminal justice organizations. For such organizations, and the people who work in and supervise in them, strategic planning and budgeting are at the *very center of the organizational universe*. This is true, regardless of whether it is recognized, because strategic plans spur and justify budgets. The budget, in turn, controls just about everything done by the organization as a whole, and by individual actors. Budgets determine pay, wage raises (or not), whether programs are funded, buildings built, computers and furniture purchased; budgets determine staffing levels, availability of promotions, training amounts, research, and on and on. Concomitantly, budgets and strategic plans affect stress levels, satisfaction with the job, and turnover of employees. In low-budget years or when budgets do not fit the strategic plan, even criminal justice agencies, with burgeoning numbers of clients, can be cut or—almost as bad—not funded at a level that allows them to continue operating as previously (Bryson 1995; Campbell 2003; Gaines *et al.* 2003; Hrebiniak 2005; Hudzik and Cordner 1983; Royce 2003; Smith 1997; Swanson *et al.* 1998; Wallace *et al.* 1995).

In short, for those who work in public and private criminal justice organizations, for those who have pursued such careers or want to, and for those who study such organizations, understanding strategic planning and budgeting is of paramount importance. Every topic that has been touched upon in this book is affected by how, or whether, an organization plans and budgets. In a very real sense, then, plans and budgets will influence who we are in any criminal justice organization and what we can become.

In this chapter, and keeping the proper recognition of the importance of planning and budgeting in mind, we explore some recent history on the following topics: Methods of planning, effects of planning, types of budgeting, and innovations in budgeting. We will first define strategic planning and budgeting and then, with politics ever on our minds, we will begin our discussion of budgeting with "some things to remember about public sector budgets" that are derived from the literature on this topic.

STRATEGIC PLANNING: DEFINITION, BENEFITS, AND THE DIFFICULTIES OF IMPLEMENTATION

According to Bryson (1995: 4–5) strategic planning is "[a] disciplined effort to produce fundamental decisions and actions that shape and guide what an organization is, what it does, and why it does it." To plan well, managers of an organization must have valid and reliable information, be aware of viable alternatives, and consider the future implications of all planning decisions. Should the organization be in a position to engage in strategic planning, Bryson (1995: 7) identifies the following benefits:

- the promotion of strategic thought and action;
- improved decision making;
- enhanced organizational responsiveness and improved performance;
- benefit the organization's people [as policymakers and key decision makers can better fulfill their roles and meet their responsibilities, and teamwork and expertise are likely to be strengthened among organizational members].

In sum, the organization that engages in strategic planning consciously develops a map for organizational operation. (Figure 1 is a simplified flowchart for the strategic plan of a criminal justice system in Anytown, USA.) Most strategic plans will reflect the organization's overall goals and mission, which are influenced by environmental, external, and internal processes, inputs, outputs, and feedback. So again, the strategic plan as Bryson defined it explicates what the organization is and does, and the reasons for its actions.

In most locations, for instance, the public defender's office can rationally choose to allocate its resources to certain types of cases while de-emphasizing others based on a plan. Bryson (1995) cautions, however, that there is no guarantee that a strategic plan will yield the benefits he lists, since for that to happen there must be leadership, the will to carry out the plan among organizational members, and the budget to implement the plan (Hrebiniak 2005). Hrebiniak argues, in fact, that the planning, as arduous as it can be in some organizations, is actually the easy part. Execution or implementation is really the most difficult part of strategic planning, and it is where most managers fail (Pressman and Wildavsky 1973; Rothman 1980). Therefore, that public defender's office may suffer politically (and potentially budgetarily) when it shifts resources to one type of case over others if the managers of the organization do not first persuade interested stakeholders (e.g., the police, courts, prosecutor's office, and community members) to buy into the plan.

IMPLEMENTING THE PLAN

The execution of a strategic plan follows the layout of Figure 1 (also keep in mind how this planning process relates to the systems theory presented in Chapter 4). Notice that the "Crucial Stage" label is applied to the implementation section. It is here that all the plans are put into action. However, some very important steps must precede implementation if organizational goals are to be met. First, during the initial planning stage, representatives from the organization, key stakeholders, and all other individuals involved should come together and pose questions that feed into objectives, which (in theory) reflect the general goals of the organization (Welsh and Harris 1999). This is done for several reasons; one is to flush out possible problems with planning design, and another is to explain why one particular design may be better than another. For example, if a state Department of Correction's ultimate goal is to increase funding for all treatment services available, the agency must gather information from several sources, both to help in the acquisition of more state or federal funding and to provide empirical evidence to guide and support decision making and policy planning. During the initial stage, then, the state agency might bring together professionals in the field for advice in the form of technical assistance (TA), for research support, and to field and answer the all-important questions that will direct the plan's objectives.

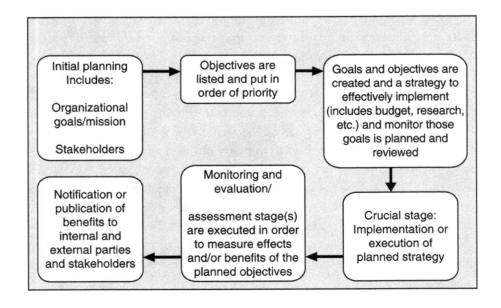

Figure 1

Example of a strategic planning flow chart

During that initial meeting or thereafter, the managers and stakeholders responsible for overseeing all stages of the strategic plan will position objectives in order of importance or priority (Welsh and Harris 1999). For example, in building a case for increased use of community policing, a planning group may prioritize a list of research objectives, and the most important will address or reflect the substantive question(s) posed in the planning stage (e.g., Does community policing increase positive interactions between the police and the public?).

Once the list of objectives, priorities, and goals has been completed, a strategy to effectively implement and monitor those goals is planned and reviewed. The proper planning of this stage (which includes budget, research, etc.) is critical to the actual implementation stage for several reasons. Organizations often are faced with limited resources, and their proper management may make or break the whole planning process. Therefore, budgeting the right amount of resources is paramount to success. The budget must cover all stages of a program's existence, and it must be understood that these resources will provide a continuum of support throughout the process. We shall return to this topic shortly.

We can also see that it is at this juncture that we map out how to effectively monitor and evaluate our plan. The evaluation may cover several key points in the plan at a variety of times (e.g., pre and post; multiple points during the progression of the plan), and it may include a strategy to effectively monitor and assess the proposed time line for implementation, contracts and contracted employee oversight, communication, budgeting, information gathering/data analysis/packaging and presentation, post assessment, and criteria for success (Welsh and Harris 1999).

It is during the final decisive stage, implementing the plan, that all previous measures are put into action and must be effectively managed. Here monitoring and evaluation/assessment stage(s) are executed to measure effects and/or benefits of the planned objectives and notification or publication of benefits to internal and external parties and stakeholders. It is here, too, that the organization planning committee, stakeholders, and all relevant parties assess whether the objectives are being met.

FAILURE OF EXECUTION

The reasons for failure of execution are multifaceted (Hrebiniak 2005). For one thing, managers are often trained on how to plan, but not on how to implement. Therefore, they may neglect to build support for programs and initiatives and to restructure the culture to support the plan; they may not understand how power will shape and influence implementation; and they may continue to emphasize the importance of plan execution without having constructed control and feedback mechanisms to monitor implementation (Hrebiniak 2005).

The very best of intentions by policymakers will not guarantee that a plan will be faithfully funded and implemented (Rothman 1980). In fact, at times, as with the implementation of juvenile courts in the first half of the twentieth century, just the opposite of the "best interests of the child" can play out when there is little oversight of powerful actors such as judges (Rothman 1980).

But even assuming that the money is there and there is widespread support for the strategic plan, "the best laid plans of mice and men," as John Steinbeck said, "often go awry." Pressman and Wildavsky (1973), in a classic study of the failure to implement a well-funded and agreed-upon anti-poverty program—economic development to increase minority employment in Oakland, California—found that it was the little things, the devil in the details, that stymied program implementation. Specifically, it was the lack of follow-through that kept this program from being adequately implemented. Agreements made for work should have been maintained, approvals and clearances from all interested parties were needed. These are the small and ordinary, but important, matters that should have been attended to but were not. And these are the types of things, according to Pressman and Wildavsky (1973), that are often neglected in implementation. "Failure to recognize that these perfectly ordinary circumstances present serious obstacles to implementation inhibits learning. If one is always looking for unusual circumstances and dramatic events, he cannot appreciate how difficult it is to make the ordinary happen" (Pressman and Wildavsky 1973: xviii). Thirty-plus years later, Hrebiniak (2005) makes a similar point: That achieving effective execution and change in organizations requires not just a plan and a budget, but sustained effort on the part of organizational members.

WHAT IS A BUDGET?

The implementation of a strategic plan is dependent on the development and execution of a budget; that is, a summary of expenses for a given program or organization. If as a student you were to devise a budget for your college education, you would likely list tuition and fees, books, rent, and food (or room and board), clothing, recreation, and miscellaneous items. Similarly, a transitional program for juvenile boys would budget for staff, housing, food, utilities, clothing, programming, school costs, recreation, maintenance, and miscellaneous. As with a personal budget, under each of these major headings for the transitional program would be subsidiary cost breakdowns, as in different salaries for the full-time and part-time staff positions, pay that varies by role (e.g., the director vs. the counselors), and health care and retirement benefits.

Table 1 gives a sample governmental budget. The proper planning (budgeting), implementation, and evaluation of an organization's goals and objectives takes fundamental, and in some cases advanced, mathematical and analytical skills, along with foresight and other

TABLE 1 Highlights of recent budget for the US Department of Justice (millions of dollars)

SPENDING	2010 ACTUAL	2011 ESTIMATE	2012 ESTIMATE
Discretionary Budget Authority			
Federal Bureau of Investigation	7,749		8,076
Drug Enforcement Administration	2,050		2,012
Federal prison system	6,185		6,791
US Marshals Service	1,151		1,253
Bureau of Alcohol, Tobacco, Firearms and Explosives	1,121		1,147
Detention trustee	1,439		1,595
United States attorneys	1,935		1,995
General Legal Activities	877		955
National Security Division	88		88
Office of Justice Programs, COPS, Office of Violence Against Women	3,552		2,964
Organized Crime and Drug Enforcement Task Force	527		
All Other	925	541	
Subtotal: Discretionary budget authority	27,599	30,351	754
Less Crime Victims' Fund discretionary offset	—	−5,820	28,171
Less Assets Forfeiture Fund cancellation	—	−387	−6,641
			−620
Total: Discretionary budget authority	27,599	24,144	20,910
Memorandum:			
Budget authority from supplements	206	—	—
FBI Overseas Contingency Operation	101	—	—
Total Discretionary outlays	27,736	26,731	24,074
Mandatory Outlays	1,828	6,770	
Existing Laws	—	—	8,977
Legislative proposal	1,828	6,770	100
Total Mandatory outlays		33,501	9,077
Total Outlays		29,564	33,151

Source: Adapted from Department of Justice Budget, April 8, 2013. Available at http://www.whitehouse.gov/sites/default/files/omb/budget/fy2012/assets/justice.pdf (last accessed January 31, 2013).

managerial know-how. In the formation of fiscal policy and yearly budgets, most criminal justice organizations employ computer spreadsheets and other statistical software. A strong working knowledge of various computer programs (e.g., Microsoft Excel, Microsoft Access, and SPSS [the Statistical Package for the Social Sciences]) is a must at the managerial level and, in some instances, for the day-to-day operations of the whole organization. Technological tools such as these provide the manager and the organization with the ability to both plan and implement objectives, goals, services, and research within the organization and then interpret and benefit from the use of that information.

THE FOUR STAGES OF THE BUDGET PROCESS

There are at least four stages in the budget process for organizations (Graham and Hays 1986; see Figure 2 for a chart of the budget process and Box 1 for an example). Before embarking on the development of a budget, however, a criminal justice agency must first consider the fiscal environment that affects their funding entity (Padovani and Young 2012). If tax revenues are up and the political actors (members of the legislative and executive branches at their level of government) are supportive, the agency will be able to develop a more generous budget than if the opposite is true. With this fiscal environment in view, the first stage of the budgeting process, which involves the preparation of the budget, may be begun. Often budgets are

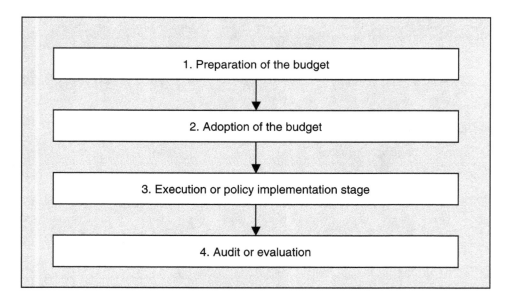

Figure 2

The four stages of the budget process.

prepared with several objectives in mind, and they are not created out of whole cloth every year. Typically, the starting point for staff preparing the budget is previous years' budgets. Staff will examine these budgets and allocate a similar amount of money to each item, while accounting for inflation. Briefly, the US Department of Labor defines inflation as "the overall general upward price movement of goods and services in an economy." If new monies are likely to be available, they will be budgeted to account for the likely increase in expenses and/or used to fund new initiatives. The more discretionary parts of the budgets are then often examined to determine whether they fit, and further, the plan for the program or organization. In other words, for our juvenile transition program, housing, food, the cost of running the building, and even staffing remain somewhat fixed, if not requiring moderate increases from year to year. On the other hand, programming, recreation, and other special project costs vary from year to year—that is, are discretionary—depending on the budget priorities set in a given year, the availability of funding, the approval of the transitional program's board or funding agency, or the next step in the process.

Box 1 Reduced budgets for juvenile corrections in Florida

The budgetary crises that many states have confronted in the past several years have led some states to reduce their budgets for corrections and other services (Florida Department of Juvenile Justice 2013; Lauth 2003). A case in point is the budgets for the Florida juvenile justice system for fiscal year 2005 through 2013 (www.djj.state.fl.us). According to the Florida Department of Juvenile Justice (legislative update) in 2005, a total of $7 million was cut from juvenile facilities and community corrections. These cuts included detention, probation and community corrections, residential and correctional facilities, and more. Across these areas, the cuts affected jobs for staff and administrators, programs, placements, and secure and nonsecure beds for juveniles. Fast forward to the present and we find that the department is still being cut. In a press release from the Florida Department of Juvenile Justice dated January 2013, the department touts the fact that its proposed budget of $513.6 million for 2013–2014 will be $9.7 million less than its current budget. Moreover, the department claims they have shifted their focus from residential beds to "investing in health and front-end services," or prevention over incarceration.

The next stage in the budgeting process, after preparation, is adoption of the budget. This is usually a process that is dominated by politics, economics, and the perceived and real performance of the program. If the current political actors, such as state legislators and the governor in the case of our transitional program, support such programs for youth, think there is enough money in the state budget to continue funding it at the requested level, and believe it fills an important need in juvenile corrections, the budget proposed by our transitional program director will be approved. But if these important people think such programs are unnecessary, or disagree with them philosophically, then the funding request will be slashed or denied. If there is a recession, or if tax collections have decreased or are projected to decrease in the upcoming year, our transitional program's budget request is also likely to suffer. Or if there is little evidence to indicate that our transitional program is successful in reducing the criminal engagement of troubled youth, or if it is perceived to have failed in some capacity, the budget request will not be approved, as submitted, by either the governor or the state legislators.

Should our transitional program's budget remain somewhat intact for the next year, it will enter the third stage of the budgeting process, which is the execution or policy implementation stage. Note that this stage takes the whole year, as the budget is intended to fund a year's worth of operation. Many states, cities, and counties count their fiscal year from July 1 through June 30. The federal government's fiscal year runs from October 1 through September 30. The vast majority of operations in criminal justice continue from year to year, and so the implementation of the budget for these organizations holds few surprises. New staff might be hired or computers purchased in our transitional house for juvenile boys, but normal operations are not disrupted much by the implementation of the budget. It is when new programs are funded or initiatives pursued that the agency feels the jolt and then the urgency that an infusion of, or reduction in, money brings. If, for instance, our transition program was funded to add more treatment space and programming, staff would need to undertake a number of tasks to ensure that expansion is accomplished. For instance, implementation of the budget will possibly require the construction of the space, and hiring and scheduling of new staff (for examples, see also Winkler and Smith 2006). The development of a curriculum or curriculums may also be necessary. Usually all this activity will happen within the span of that budget year, if so specified in the budget plan.

The final stage in the budget process is the audit or evaluation. Typically, organizations of any size will employ internal or external financial auditors to go over their books to ensure that money budgeted for certain programs and activities was spent as intended. Even small organizations, if they are wise, will subject themselves to this kind of review. Some criminal justice organizations will also employ program auditors who, after examining the operation of a program, will make an assessment of its relative success. Both financial and program auditing are very important for at least the following reasons: They can help catch, reduce, or prevent corruption; they can improve financial and program records; they give successful programs some leverage in making their budgeting case to their funding agency; and they provide the organization with the information it needs to make valid budgeting decisions.

SOME THINGS TO REMEMBER ABOUT PUBLIC SECTOR BUDGETING

According to several authors of articles and books on budgeting, there are at least four central facts to remember about all budgets in the public sector that have remained true for some time (Blomquist *et al.* 2004; Ebdon and Franklin 2004; Graham and Hays 1986; Key 1940; Lauth 2003; Nice 2002; Padovani and Young 2012; Poulson 2001; Pyhrr 1977; Schick 1966; Whisenand and Ferguson 1996, 2002):

1. As budgets are created in a political and economic environment, they are products of that environment.
2. Budgets are a mix of science and art.
3. Budgets, as political documents, reflect to some extent public priorities.
4. There is always more demand for public resources than there are resources.

Item 1 means that decisions about the funding of criminal justice agencies are always taken by political actors (Nice 2002). For instance, budgets for sheriff's departments are typically determined and appropriated by elected county commissioners (usually based in large part on agency head proposals). Likewise, budgets at the county and city level for police, city and county courts, jails, detention centers, and juvenile probation and parole organizations (often through the county courts) are mulled over and funded by county commissions and city councils/city managers who are either elected or politically appointed.

For much of the twentieth century, funding criminal justice agencies was not always seen as politically popular, and some agencies were underfunded. As a result, inmates languished in overcrowded facilities, people received little meaningful supervision by community corrections officers, police were unable to investigate all serious crimes, court dockets were overflowing, there were few programs or staff in juvenile or adult institutions, pay was poor, and facilities were nonexistent or falling down. Not surprisingly, these factors led to infamous abuses in any number of agencies and allowed serious offenders to remain on the streets to wreak additional havoc and pain. In the 1980s, as political priorities shifted and lawsuits forced funding, a building and hiring boom in many agencies began, and continues today (Austin and Irwin 2001; Campbell 2003; Wallace *et al.* 1995).

Relatedly, as mentioned in item 2, budgets are a mix of science and art (Nice 2002). The science these days lies in basing the budget on some definable, and even measurable, public good. If a jail is double- or triple-bunked with serious and repeat offenders, then some public good, such as continued public safety, would be achieved by floating a bond to fund construction of a new jail or expansion of the current one. The science comes in when the jail and those who oversee and set its budget (often county commissioners) study its practices, and those of related entities such as the courts and the police, to determine whether that need for space (population forecasting) and funding is real or whether some changes could be made to avert putting more money into the jail (for examples, see also Surette *et al.* 2006). Similarly, if that jail is interested in adding a drug and alcohol program for its long-term residents, it might seek funding at the local level or a grant from the state or the federal government, which in turn may allocate such money based on reigning political priorities (balancing treatment and security concerns, for instance). The "art" in all this is related to negotiating in the political realm to get the funding that is needed for current programs and priorities, while not neglecting to garner funds for any initiatives on the horizon.

Which means, as was noted in item 3, that budgets reflect public priorities (Blomquist *et al.* 2004; Ebdon and Franklin 2004; Nice 2002). Politicians, though often beholden to powerful political interests that are not aligned with everyday citizens, still have to be elected. When jockeying for votes, political actors will tend to shape their message to fit what they believe the public views as important. If the public is concerned about crime, as many polls indicated in the 1980s and 1990s (Merlo and Benekos 2000), the politicians will respond by funding criminal justice agencies more. It is not a coincidence that a building boom in corrections and increased hiring in police and prosecutor's offices in the 1980s and 1990s (and continuing in some jurisdictions) tracked public support and concern about crime control (Austin and Irwin 2001; Wallace *et al.* 1995).

Lipsky (1980) made a point similar to our item 4: There is always more demand for resources in the public sector than there are resources. This is a point that particularly applies to public sector criminal justice agencies, as the clients of these agencies tend to be poor, to have less education than is the norm, and to be "nonvoluntary": That is, they usually did not ask for contact with a criminal justice actor, though the actions of offenders have dictated their entrance into the system. In other words, putting aside what the clients of criminal justice agencies did, this population is relatively powerless and sometimes cannot vote, even when released from incarceration. The clients' relatives and friends may be able to vote, but often they do not. So with a public good like safety prominently on voters' and politicians' minds, coupled with more recent concerns about the costs, criminal justice funding and practice can be affected.

For example, according to data provided by the Judicial Council of California, the number of court filings in Superior or trial courts in California involving criminal and civil cases increased by 14 percent and 6 percent, respectively, from 2002 to 2011 (Judicial Council of California 2012: 73, 76). During this same time period the number of filings per judicial position increased by about 6 percent, which means that not enough judges were hired to keep up with the increased caseloads (Judicial Council of California 2012: 72). Though a distinctive state in many ways, what is happening in California courts is representative of what is occurring in courts across the nation. The use of courts, particularly when involving criminal matters, continues to rise, but not enough judges or other court personnel are being hired to handle those increases.

Large caseloads appear to be a theme not just for the courts, but also for other sectors of the system. According to a study done by the American Probation and Parole Association

(2007: 44), 68 percent of the respondents thought their caseload was too large for community corrections officers. In fact, the average caseload they reported for officers was 106 offenders, whereas the optimal caseload they identified was seventy-seven offenders (APPA 2007: 44). The authors of the study and the respondents acknowledged that in reality what this means is that most offenders on these caseloads are not being supervised with any regularity. As some of these offenders will never commit another crime, or may do something that is a less serious threat to public safety, their lack of supervision is not of much consequence. It is these officers' need to focus on the more serious and violent offenders which concerned the respondents to the APPA survey, as high caseloads make it more difficult to respond to such offenders. In other words, public safety is compromised by the politically, and economically, determined decision to increase the number of crimes that require a prison sentence (drug crimes come to mind), but also by decisions to release people from overcrowded prisons, not to build more prisons, and then to release offenders out onto the streets with virtually no supervision. Based on all these complicated reasons, the status of clients, the politics of crime, the tightness of budgets, the input of a public both concerned for public safety and balking at higher taxes, there is always more demand for resources than there are resources.

RECENT HISTORY OF BUDGETING AND PLANNING

Given the foregoing budgeting maxims, let us consider some recent history on the topic. Recall that before the reform of public agencies, contracts, and hiring ushered in by the civil service reforms, public sector agencies were openly ruled by the politics of the day (see the discussion of this matter in Chapter 2). Political ideology and connections, before the twentieth century, had a much greater impact on the operation of public sector agencies than is true today, though—as mentioned earlier—that political influence is still quite apparent in budget determinations. Corruption and misspending of public funds made the need to control budgets and prevent their abuse a major concern for those in the policymaking and management spheres (Schick 1966). An adherence to Taylorism in management, with its emphasis on control, also influenced the reformation of budgeting determinations. Budgeting was to be done by rote, in a dry and objective fashion. This approach is known as **line item budgeting**, which we will discuss shortly. Tradition has some influence in determining what was funded: If it was funded last year, then it should be funded this year, with perhaps a bit more thrown in to cover inflation. In other words, formally, budgeting was very controlled and was regarded as a very staid and predictable process; the political and economic influences that inevitably intruded were little recognized in the literature on budgeting.

Key (1940), writing over sixty years ago, lamented what he regarded as "a lack of budgetary theory" in his article by the same name. He noted that the prevailing thought about budgeting at the time was consumed with a concern over technique (i.e., forms and their structure), with little attention or recognition of the influence of politics and economics. In contrast, he defined the budgetary process and document as "[a] judgement upon how scarce means should be allocated to bring the maximum return in social utility" (Key 1940: 117). He argued that determining the "social utility" of a given public program was not that difficult, but that budget analysts and managers needed more standardized ways to evaluate and guide choices. He urged such folks to consider the merits or return in social utility of a program and to not be afraid to decrease or end programs that do not yield such benefits.

Schick built on the work of Key when he wrote more than twenty years later that budgeting should be a systematic process that is related to planned objectives: "In this important sense there is a bit of PPB (planning, programming, budgeting) in every budget system" (Schick 1966: 300). He thought that budgeting should involve strategic planning, which considers the objectives and resources of the organization in tandem, as well as the policies that govern the resources. He also believed in management and operational control to ensure task efficiency in operation, to monitor resource acquisition, and to avoid the misuse or abuse of resources. He thought the "watchdog" approach taken by managers married to line item budgeting was an understandable reaction to the graft and corruption that prevailed in the public sector in the nineteenth century. Because the potential for abuse still exists, Schick did not advocate that public sector agencies abandon the controls and oversight of budgets, hence his emphasis on operational and management control; he did, however, think the agencies should lighten up a bit. He thought the line item analysis and work-cost assessments were appropriate tasks for the mid managers, but that top-level managers in the organizations should take a "big-picture" approach to planning and budgeting. Keep in mind that the big-picture approach is analogous of the systems perspective we discussed in Chapter 4, in that top-level managers must be able to understand and react to environmental, external, and internal demands or processes, output, and feedback, and then make adjustments according to such information.

Schick (1966) notes that as we became more sophisticated in economic analysis and informational acquisition in the 1960s, long-range planning for organizations became more doable. His central message was that managers needed to plan and analyze more, or pay attention to the forest as well as the trees.

In the 1970s an innovation in budgeting, perhaps reflective of the fiscal crisis looming at the national level, became popular and was premised on the ability to effectively analyze budgetary and program data. That innovation, which was wildly popular at first, was **zero-based budgeting**. Two questions are addressed under zero-based budgeting (Pyhrr 1977: 496):

1. Are the current activities efficient and effective?

2. Should current activities be eliminated or reduced to fund higher priority new programs or to reduce the current budget?

The appeal of this approach to budgeting was its fiscal conservatism and its related emphasis on limiting governmental growth. Every program would be examined for its social utility (as Key would have defined it) and for its performance as that related to cost. Programs that did not pass muster or produce results would be eliminated or have their funding reduced. Zero-based budgeting requires that program managers defend their entire budgetary appropriation for each year.

Zero-based budgeting became a true budgeting fad, in that it was first adopted by Texas Instruments in 1969 and then by Governor Jimmy Carter for the state of Georgia (Pyhrr 1977). After Carter was elected president in 1976, the use of zero-based budgeting spread to the federal government, and several other states and localities eventually adopted its principles (see Box 2).

Then reality set in. Despite its appeal, zero-based budgeting has a number of problems, the most damning of which is the lack of an easy way to know whether a program is "working." There are problems in defining performance (what is good, what is bad, what is mediocre) and appropriate costs for public sector or public sanctioned programs, such as the courts. Moreover, though part of the appeal of zero-based budgeting was its promised limits on government, carrying out thorough evaluations of program performance is ironically very costly. Moreover, an outcome evaluation requires good solid data on every program, and such information does not always exist in the real world. Finally, some pieces of programs are not measurable. How does one define and measure "justice" in the courtroom, for instance? How about rehabilitation? Is the true measure of rehabilitation only absence of recidivism? What about new programs? Are they likely to produce outcomes in the span of months or a year that would justify their continued existence?

Imagine a court administrator or a judge who could avoid budget cuts only by defending all her programs, every year, for funding (see Box 2). Imagine the funding bodies having to review every little program to determine its value. Imagine the redundancy and tedium in this whole process. Simply put, zero-based budgeting was great in theory, but in practice it was unintentionally costly and time-consuming. Not surprisingly, it was quickly abandoned by most organizations once these realities set in, although it is still used, at least to some extent, in some communities.

In the 1980s and 1990s budgeting continued to emphasize controls, as represented by line item budgets and audits, but with planning. Thus around this time **planning, programming, budgeting systems (PPBS) budgeting** came into vogue (Graham and Hays 1986; Whisenand and Ferguson 2002). **Budgeting by objective** (BBO) **budgeting** also became popular as the sister of the managing-by-objective (MBO) movement during this time period. As with MBO, BBO involves greater input from organizational members into a central part of organizational operation: developing, implementing, and evaluating the budget.

Box 2 Zero-Based Budgeting is Enjoying a Resurgence in Popularity

Due to the work involved in justifying each program, zero-based budgeting for the most part fell into disfavor and disuse for a large part of two decades. Increasingly, however, there is a movement by some lawmakers in states and counties to use zero-based budgeting as a means of cutting government programs. The city of Phoenix, the state of Georgia, and Montgomery County, Pennsylvania, have all incorporated zero-based budgeting in the review of at least some of their programs in the last few years (Bonner 2012; Bui 2011; DeHuff 2012; Jones 2011). Usually the adoption of such budgeting, if utilized widely, can be quite controversial, because the decision about whether to fund or not fund certain programs is a political decision as much as a cost-cutting one (Jones 2011).

One County Commissioner in Ada County, Idaho, argued that zero-based budgeting did not yield the predicted savings when his county tried it. The county commissioners of Ada County, Idaho, used both zero-based and expenditure control (aka mission-driven) budgeting systems in the 1980s and early 1990s. According to a former county commissioner, Roger Simmons, it didn't work very well (Simmons 2001: 8):

> Zero-based budgeting sounds great in theory. But theory is not reality. There are several reasons why zero-base hasn't worked in government budgeting. Zero-based requires department supervisors to start at zero each year and justify every expenditure to the county commissioners. The reality is that any qualified supervisor knows their department's needs far better than the commissioners. Meanwhile, each supervisor, in hopes of funding what they consider to be legitimate needs, argues furiously for every expenditure. That, unfortunately, puts them in an untenable position when it comes to saving. As they approach the end of the fiscal year, they start looking for ways to spend their entire budget. They do that, not because they are bad people, but they are stuck in a system that encourages it.

This is because, as Commissioner Simmons argues, if they don't spend that money then they won't be believed when they ask for the money again next year. Moreover, should they save money, it is pooled and may be given to departments that are less frugal. Commissioner Simmons (2001: 8) concludes by saying, "In all the years Ada County used zero-base, we saved nothing—nothing."

In contrast, he notes that after the county moved to an expenditure control budgeting system, it did save money. "Under expenditure-control budgeting, each department is allowed to roll over 75 percent of its savings into the next budget year, thus eliminating the 'spend it or lose it' philosophy that prevails in zero-base. In Ada County, under expenditure control, we have been rolling over on average of about $3 million in savings each year" (Simmons 2001: 8).

Both initiatives, PPBS and BBO, represent an attempt to rationalize budgets and to tie them to the strategic plan and identifiable and measurable objectives (BBO). As such, both represent an attempt to insert more science and less art into the budgeting process.

Another initiative, **mission-driven budgeting** (aka expenditure control budgeting), is touted as a way of combining some of the science of the PPBS and MBO approaches with the input of workers, while rewarding frugality and keeping the realities of taxpayer revolts and worker calculations in mind (Whisenand and Ferguson 1996). Under a mission-driven budget, each unit and its actors engage in developing a budget that is submitted to a department head. The budget for the organization will be allowed to grow only by the amount of inflation and the amount of community growth. Units that save money from year to year are allowed to keep all or a portion of those savings to reinvest in program activities. As funding is allocated in a lump sum, not line item, determination of how the money is to be spent rests with each unit, or those closest to the program delivery.

The beauty of this approach is that it averts the well-known problem of federal or state managers and workers trying to spend all of their allocation by the end of the budget year to ensure that their budget request for next year can be at the same or a higher level. One cannot blame these workers. They know that they might well need the extra funds next year, even if they did not spend their whole allocation this year. But they will not be able to justify a budget request in the same amount if they had money left over this year. Mission-driven budgeting allows these workers to hoard their funds for next year, thus rewarding frugality, and allowing them to use the funds where they were most needed.

Whisenand and Ferguson (2002), in their book on police management, nicely summarize six budgeting approaches used by both public and private agencies.

1. Line item budgets: These are budgets that are largely based on previous budgets. Each unit of an organization may have input about a given line item. This budget approach is focused on keeping costs down, or at least stable. There is not much attention paid to performance or to public need, and ongoing program costs are allowed to continue.

2. Performance budgets: This approach is focused on measuring the performance of a program. Unfortunately, the output of some organizations is not easily quantifiable, though output for some programs may be.

3. Planning, programming, budgeting systems: This approach ties all parts of the organization, its present and future plans, together with its budget proposal, funding, and implementation. The difficulty with this system, as with performance budgets, is that it requires the generation and review of so much data on programs that it can become overwhelming to use a full-scale PPBS approach for an organization. Also, good data may not be available. This process tends to put budgeting in the hands of technically oriented people who collect and analyze data (i.e., those who can generate and examine statistics).

4. Program or outcome budgets and/or budgeting by objectives: This approach allows for much more input by each unit in the development of the budget or that pesky human element again (recall this discussion as part of the management theories reviewed in Chapter 4). Activities are related to outcomes, but decision making is also allowed at the unit level.

5. Zero-based budgeting: This approach requires that you start with a clean budgetary slate every year. Much data must be collected every year to justify the continued funding of each program. The approach is time-consuming and costly, hence very difficult to implement.

6. Mission-driven budgeting or expenditure control budgeting: This approach, suggested by Whisenand and Ferguson (1996), focuses on limiting expenditure growth to inflation and community growth, retaining year-end savings in organizations to encourage frugality, and basing funding on lump sums, not line items, to allow program employees some decision-making autonomy. These authors like it because they believe it "[p]romotes sound management, simplifies the budget process, focuses on the big picture, restores trust in the budget process and promotes savings" (Whisenand and Ferguson 1996: 314–315). The problem with mission-driven budgeting is that there appears to be no formal approach to performance or outcome evaluation. Despite the difficulty of these activities, the truth is that in an environment of tight budgeting, program performance cannot be ignored, even as one acknowledges that it can't always be assessed effectively, either. But the problems in evaluation of effectiveness do not justify the skirting of the issue altogether.

In reality, most budgeting processes include a mix of these approaches. Because of accounting principles, it is difficult to believe that the basis for most budgets should be anything but line item. Indeed, line item budgets can be the rampart for other budgets that are more focused on performance, planning, and outcomes and that allow for more employee input (Blomquist et al. 2004: Ebdon and Franklin 2004). Many governmental agencies use a form of zero-based budgeting for some limited types of programming, however, despite the problems (Simmons 2001).

BUDGET STRATEGIES

At the beginning of his book *Public Budgeting*, Nice (2002: 10–13) outlines ten different strategies that organizations and interested stakeholders adopt to increase their success in influencing budgetary decisions. These strategies, which may come in handy for managers and/or for those who study criminal justice organizations, are briefly discussed next.

CULTIVATING CLIENT SUPPORT

The first strategy mentioned by Nice (2002) is cultivating client support. As a democratically operated organization presupposes some client input, some organizational scholars believe that both support and input by clients are just a given in the development of a healthy budget (Blomquist *et al.* 2004; Ebdon and Franklin 2004). The clients of criminal justice enterprises in this case, and as defined by Nice, might be conceived broadly. They could include community members, suspects, clients, inmates, and supervisees; in budgetary matters, however, they are more likely to include employees and administrators, the pertinent elected representatives in both the legislative and executive branches of government, and the general public. For instance, if the Department of Corrections in a given state were interested in building a work release facility in a community, it would behoove the administrators to solicit the support, and input, of those most affected by it. At a minimum the DOC would need to garner support from the larger community, but particularly prospective neighbors, local leaders such as the mayor and/or county commissioners, state legislators in that district, and the governor's office—not necessarily in this order.

GAINING THE TRUST OF OTHERS AND DOCUMENTING A NEED

It should be a given in public service that one acts with honesty and integrity in all interactions (see the discussion of ethics in Chapter 3). Unfortunately, experience teaches us that this expectation of the "honest broker" is not always realized in either public or private sector work. Ideally and over the long term, however, being honest and upfront about factual matters usually pays off in a number of ways. In our work release example, the DOC should bring together all the affected persons and discuss with them the need for, costs of, and likely consequences of building and maintaining the work release. After all the facts are on the table, and the DOC has brought all the arguments and evidence to bear, the department may well fail to convince the appropriate parties that a work release is necessary at this time. But in subsequent discussions on the need for a work release, and other topics, the DOC is more likely to be believed and supported because its representatives are thought to operate with integrity.

LOOKING FOR SYMPATHETIC DECISION MAKERS

That said there is nothing wrong with approaching the decision makers who are most inclined to be receptive and who are willing to advocate for your organization's budgetary initiative. As Nice indicates, if one branch of government is not likely to be supportive, the other branches and/or public support can be solicited. Nice (2002: 11) points out that "[w]ith many decision-making arenas and many decision makers, people may shop around for the decision they want."

COPING WITH PAINFUL ACTIONS AND MINIMIZING THE RISK OF FUTURE CUTS

In tight budgetary times, when all levels of government are forced to consider and reconsider funding options, Nice (2002) argues that agencies tend to develop strategies to avoid or reduce cuts. When painful cuts are threatened, he notes that agencies may tend to blame others for the budget crisis. They may also cut less visible positions or programs, and/or do the opposite and cut those that are popular to raise the ire of the program supporters. Another strategy which organizations sometimes employ to minimize the risk or threat of cuts at such times is to quickly spend the monies they have, to avoid having to return them to the state. Another tactic is to pad the original budget proposal with the understanding that less essential items may have to be cut later.

THE CAMEL'S NOSE

A different budgetary strategy might be employed when an organization is starting or enhancing a program. Nice (2002) observes that in such instances, some organizations may tend to de-emphasize the eventual cost of a program by asking for a small amount in the first couple of years and escalating the amount of their requests later as the program becomes more popular. This tactic is premised on the belief that a small allotment is less likely to alarm decision makers and that incremental increases in funding will be the norm.

MAKING THE PROGRAM APPEAR TO BE SELF-SUPPORTING

Funding for a program/policy or agency may be justified if it is partly self-funded. For instance, adding state patrol officers might appear more palatable to decision makers budgetwise if the director can argue that the new hires' salaries will be partly supported by increased tickets paid by traffic violators.

CAPITALIZING ON TEMPORARY CIRCUMSTANCES

Some programs and organizations can effectively argue for more money in their budgets in the immediate aftermath of a crisis (Nice 2002). This phenomenon has occurred in corrections on many occasions in reaction to such events as riots and court orders to remedy conditions of confinement and practices. Correctional managers are quite cognizant of the advantages that such events can produce. For instance, one of the authors attended a conference organized by the National Institute of Corrections for progressive jail managers in 1992. Some of the participating managers wondered aloud how they could get the staff, training, capital inflow for buildings, and programs for inmates from their county budgets if the ability of inmates to sue the jail was decreased. This is not to say that they liked being sued per se, but the prospect of lawsuits gave them leverage to argue for the funds they needed to properly run their jails.

DECEPTION AND CONFUSION

Though he does not recommend such strategies for garnering more resources, Nice (2002) recognizes that some organizations will engage in deception and confusion to increase or maintain their budget. To that end, agency representatives may hide information in their budget, provide misinformation, or engage in doublespeak by telling decision makers that the money will be used for something other than what they intend it for. In this sense, the ignorance about the agency or organization of those in the public and among the decision makers can be used to advantage to conceal budget priorities unlikely to meet with general approval.

AN ADDITIONAL STRATEGY: AGENCY CONSOLIDATION

It is an accepted truism about criminal justice practice that most things are local. We have city/ county/state policing, corrections, and courts (as well as federal, but that is not local!) that vary widely from jurisdiction to jurisdiction and so reflect, to some extent, the local character and culture of each area. The problem is that there is a great deal of duplication of costs when we have each a separate administrative staff for every little city and county criminal justice agency (not to mention state). We also have overlapping services, and thus duplicated costs, when jurisdictions overlap geographically, as they commonly do when cities grow big enough to occupy most of counties. In Box 3 Scott Sotebeer discusses why consolidation of some of these agencies and services makes real fiscal sense for some of these localities.

CONCLUSIONS

Those unfamiliar with organizational operations often regard strategic planning and budgeting as dry and irrelevant exercises. If you have ever gotten a raise, or not gotten one, because of the political or economic environment, or if your program funding was cut or increased for the same reason, you quickly begin to appreciate the relevancy of these organizational functions. How does one, as a political leader or a policymaker, make a bureaucracy more responsive? The answer is cut, or threaten to cut, the agency's budget, forcing a change in plans. Bureaucrats, or wannabe bureaucrats, are also positively influenced (read: Motivated!) by budget increases. Planning and budgeting really are at the center of all things organizational.

The types of budgeting discussed in this chapter reflect the various approaches and techniques that have been attempted over time. The attempts to both control and evaluate budgeting decisions in the twentieth century were a laudable improvement over public sector operation of the 1800s. Criminal justice organizations interested in twenty-first-century practice and with improved access to information will likely be increasingly called upon to evaluate and assess their programs' success, and to tie each budget to a strategic plan that outlines the organization's future.

Part of that plan, if even at the informal level, involves strategies to maintain or increase the organization's budget and/or to make that budget stretch through the consolidation of agencies and services at the local level. Some of these strategies, as outlined by Nice (2002) and Sotebeer (in Box 3), reflect real-world efforts to secure funding for criminal justice agencies.

Box 3 Government Consolidation 101

Changing the business model of local government

M. Scott Sotebeer, PhD, CEO

USA Strategics, www.usastrategics.com

The extended recession is accelerating a serious problem with local governments: Budget cuts, layoffs, wage and benefit freezes or reductions, and outright city (town, borough, or village) bankruptcies are happening everywhere. The costs associated with operating local government are outstripping the amounts coming in—and taxpayers have made it clear that they will not continue to pay more and more for government. As a result, some states and a growing number of local governments have begun to aggressively merge operations and create regional partnerships as a way to save money and sustain basic services. The practice is often referred to as shared services or consolidation.

Actions by the federal government indicate that resources flowing to states are most likely to be severely reduced this year and in the foreseeable future. That impacts the flow of money to local governments. In other words, it is likely to get worse at the state and local level as nationally, most states get as much as 30 percent of their general budget from the federal government in a variety of forms (from Medicaid reimbursement to highway, parks, and other types of grant money). The problem is not going away and will not fix itself on its own.

The immediate problem with our local government setup is primarily driven by redundant administrative infrastructures. It is easy to understand by doing simple math: In my county, we have thirty-nine individual cities with separate police, fire, EMS, parks, library, roads, and other departments—all duplicated to some degree by the county and, in many cases, federal agencies as well. We most likely do not need fewer police officers or parks maintenance workers for the same geographic region because most governments have already significantly cut these types of department workers in the past several years. But in the twenty-first century, there is neither an arguable need nor financial justification for duplicated administrative structures. Our current small government structure is a post-WWII growth and expansion model that has been in place for over sixty years.

The other problem is that in many states, there are too many independent taxing districts that function as separate units of government. Fire, cemetery, PSAP (911 and emergency call centers), library, sewer, school, and many others all get funding from individual households through various taxing structures. Most have some sort of governing board or commission, and the ability to extract increasing amounts of revenue from the public. The various layers are evident when looking at a cable TV, cell phone, public utility, energy, or property tax assessment.

As one example, we have over 6,000 emergency 911 call centers in the US. They all have independent taxing authority. Most have separate governance boards and complete managerial infrastructures and the real estate and operational/administrative overhead to go with it. Communications experts will argue that there should be no more than one to five 911 call centers per individual state. We need the call receivers to take the calls—but not the redundant infrastructures.

Law enforcement and the criminal justice system are generally the single biggest drain on local budgets. Contracting police services between a county and a city, or between cities, as one of several models, has shown to save from 20 to 34 percent annually. Other strategies in use nationally in a variety of service areas also work.

Consolidation has been around for a long time—but it is the "renewed" strategy that might be the answer for some communities to cut costs, protect services, and stabilize community budgets for the long haul. Consolidation has several forms:

1. Merger: Two or more departments combine under a single banner to form a single department serving a larger area and population.

2. Shared services: Two or more departments in a region collaborate on any number of operations.

3. Contracting: One department contracts to provide services for another unit of government. Usually from a county to a city—but not always. Types of government units (townships, villages, towns, cities, boroughs, etc.) vary from state to state.

4. Regionalization or metropolitan arrangements: Several agencies reconstruct themselves legally into one new, regional organization (Las Vegas, Louisville, Indianapolis, Salt Lake City, and Northern York County, PA have done this in policing. Other examples exist in fire, courts, watershed, sewer, library districts, and others).

The most common areas of opportunity for consolidation

- Criminal justice, including police, courts, EMS, and related services
- 911 call centers*
- Roads*
- Parks and recreation*
- Solid waste
- Public works
- Libraries*
- Health/human services*
- Non-criminal prosecutorial/legal services
- Finance
- Human resources
- IT management/records
- School districts*
- Assessor

- Fire departments & fire districts*
- Cemetery and other specialty purpose districts
- Cooperative purchasing.

*may include taxing authority that could be reprogrammed, redistributed, or eliminated

Common concerns—the things that most often surface as objections to consolidation

- Loss of local control (someone else is running my show and making my decisions).
- Loss of identity (this is no longer OUR city's police department).
- Personality and quality of citizen contact (Officer Friendly has left the building).
- Unions/complex contracts (how are all workers affected by change?).
- Lack of political cooperation- (no one [politicians] wants to "give up the kingdom").
- Potential for complex legislative hurdles (does state law and county/city code allow for this?).
- Loss of services (what are we giving up to save money?).
- Cost of change and threat of "buyer's remorse"—there may be no turning back.

Universal advantages—where consolidation works well, there are some common themes and outcomes

- Economies of scale—if all the math works, the idea is that the same number of resources (people/things) can provide a given level of service over a larger geographic area at a lower per-unit cost.
- Lower cost per capita—total per household cost is possible across a broader population base when the right model is used. It should be a measure and goal of a consolidation.
- Risk is spread—this is a major issue for small cities/communities. Insurance and other liability expenses (employee lawsuits, for example) can be spread out in most service partnership deals.
- Improved uniformity, consistency, and coordination of services—the research supports that a region of partners can have a better level of service through uniform policies and management.
- Improvement in personnel (more job competition).

- Improved management and supervision (more job competition).
- Improved training and expanded personnel opportunities (specific to police, fire, and most high-cost, skilled service workers).

Consolidation, when it works, provides for important options to local communities:

1. It can act as a stop-gap to serious financial decline or (local government) bankruptcy;
2. It can simply stop the decline of critical services (parks closed, police officers cut, libraries closed, school programs cut, roads maintenance deferred, etc.);
3. It can provide for better services, depending on the model;
4. It can provide communities the opportunity to "repurpose" financial resources found through savings.

Consolidation is not a magic fix. It is not a guarantee. It is a decision-making and analytical process designed to help communities survive.

Exercise: develop a criminal justice budget

The goal of this group exercise is to acquaint participants with the likely costs of doing business in criminal justice. Here is one thing to remember: It almost always costs more than you think—unless, of course, you happen to be familiar with police, courts, or corrections budgets! The following steps will allow folks to reconcile their projections with reality.

1. Divide the participants into manageable groups of four or five. These always seem to work best if people in each group choose specific tasks (there can be more than one person assigned to each task) and are held responsible for them. In this exercise, specific tasks might include doing the web research, writing the report, and presenting the report. Ask the groups to do the following.
2. Choose a type of criminal justice agency, institution, or program in a city or state, and devise a budget for it. (The group may need to choose more than one city or state, as not all have their budgets available on the web). Hint: States and large cities and counties are more likely to post their budgets on the web.

3. Make an extensive and detailed list of likely expenses for the chosen agency, institution, or program (there should be 20–40 items listed).

4. Assign yearly costs to each of these budget items. To do this for some items on their list, it may be necessary to figure out the daily costs and then project the amount for the year. For instance, a group could calculate the costs of supervising one client on probation, multiply that by 365, and then multiply the product by the number of clients supervised in that community. Costs of buildings, and so on, can more easily be estimated by year. It is okay to make a reasonable guess. That is part of the fun!

5. Search the website chosen for the state or locality, and locate the posted budget. Again, not all states and localities post this material, so the group may have to use more than one resource. Also remember that some agencies and facilities are managed only by a certain level of government. Usually cities do not manage prisons and, with a few exceptions, states do not manage jails. Cities, counties, states, and the federal government all have some form of law enforcement. Adult probation and parole usually are handled at the state or federal level, and juvenile probation/parole and detention at the county or city level. Courts are funded at the local, state, or federal level, depending on type.

6. Examine the most recent posted budget and compare the items to the preliminary budget. Make changes in item categories of the preliminary budget so that they are comparable with the "real" budget, but do not change the figures.

7. Write a brief report (3–5 pages) on the "budget development process" that your group engaged in and include an analysis of the preliminary and real budgets. Be sure to note the differences and similarities between the budgets and try to explain them. Also report on whether there were any surprises for the group upon examining the two budgets in tandem.

8. Present the report to the larger group and discuss.

DISCUSSION QUESTIONS

1. What are the four stages of the budgeting process, and how might politics intrude in each? Give an example for each one.

2. Why is budgeting regarded as both a science and an art? Explain your answer.

3. Where is planning likely to falter and why? Explain your answer and offer some examples.

4. What are the four things to remember about budgeting, and how are they related to the four stages of budgeting and the budgeting approaches discussed in this chapter?

5. What do you think are the most important matters to consider in the development of a plan and a budget for a criminal justice organization? Why?

6. What groups do you think are most represented in the development of criminal justice plans and budgets? Why? Explain your answer.

7. What groups do you think are least represented in the development of criminal justice plans and budgets? Why? Explain your answer.

8. Which budgeting approach appeals to you? Why?

9. Why are auditing and/or evaluation important in the operation of public and private sector criminal justice? Explain your answer.

KEY TERMS

budget: a summary of expenses for a given program or organization.

inflation: "the overall general upward price movement of goods and services in an economy" (US Department of Labor (2007: www.dol.gov/dol/topic/statistics/inflation.htm).

line item budgets: budgets largely based on previous budgets. Each unit of an organization may have input about a given line item. This budget approach is focused on keeping costs down, or at least stable. There is not much attention paid to performance or to public need, and ongoing program costs are allowed to continue.

mission-driven budgeting or expenditure control budgeting: an approach suggested by Whisenand and Ferguson (1996) that focuses on limiting expenditure growth to inflation and community growth, retaining year-end savings in organizations to encourage frugality, and funding on the basis of lump sums, not line item, to allow program employees some decision-making autonomy.

performance budgets: budgetary approach focused on measuring the performance of a program. Unfortunately, the output of some organizations is not easily quantifiable, though that of some programs might be.

planning, programming, budgeting systems: an approach that ties all parts of the organization, its present, and its future plans together with its budget proposal, funding, and implementation.

program or outcome budgets and/or budgeting by objectives: this approach allows for much more input by each unit in the development of the budget or that pesky human element again. Activities are related to outcomes, but decision making is also allowed at the unit level.

strategic planning: "[a] disciplined effort to produce fundamental decisions and actions that shape and guide what an organization is, what it does, and why it does it" (Bryson 1995: 4–5).

zero-based budgeting: the approach that requires starting with a clean slate every year. Much data must be collected every year to justify the continued funding of each program. This time-consuming and costly approach is very difficult to implement.

REFERENCES

American Probation and Parole Association (APPA) (2007) Probation and parole's growing caseloads and workload allocation: Strategies for managerial decision making. Available at www.appa-net.org/eweb/docs/appa/pubs/SMDM.pdf (last accessed January 31, 2013).

Austin, J. and Irwin, J. (2001) *It's about time: America's imprisonment binge*, 3rd edn. Belmont, CA: Wadsworth/Thomson Learning.

Blomquist, G. C., Newsome, M. A. and Stone, D. B. (2004) Public preferences for program tradeoffs: Community values for budget priorities. *Public Budgeting and Finance*, 24(1): 50–71.

Bonner, J. (2012) Zero-based budgeting resurfaces. Georgia Public Broadcasting. Available at www.gpb.org/news/2012/01/17/zero-based-budgeting resurfaces (last accessed January 31, 2013).

Bryson, J. M. (1995) *Strategic planning for public and nonprofit organizations*. San Francisco, CA: Jossey-Bass.

Bui, L. (2011) Phoenix lays plans for zero-based budgeting: Spending controversies mark transparency push. *The Arizona Republic*. Available at www.azcentral.com/news/articles/2011/06/25/20110625phoenix-budget-plan zero-based-budgeting.html (last accessed January 31, 2013).

Campbell, R. (2003) Dollars and sentences: Legislators' views on prisons, punishment, and the budget crisis. The Vera Institute of Justice. Available at www.vera.org/publications (last accessed January 31, 2013).

DeHuff, J. (2012) Montco commissioners unveil 2013 "zero-based budget." *Montgomery News*. Available at www.montgomerynews.com/articles/2012/11/18/montgomery_life/news/doc50a38d9a0baf999028939.txt?viewmode=2 (last accessed January 31, 2013).

Ebdon, C. and Franklin, A. (2004) Searching for a role for citizens in the budget process. *Public Budgeting and Finance*, 24(1): 32–49.

Florida Department of Juvenile Justice. (2013) Governor Scott's 2013–14 juvenile justice budget promotes reform, public safety. Available at www.djj.state.fl.us/news/press-releases/press-release-detail/2013/01/31/governor-scott-s-2013-14-juvenile-justice-budget-promotes-reform-public-safety (last accessed January 31, 2013).

Gaines, L. K., Worrall, J. L., Southerland, M. D. and Angell, J. E. (2003) *Police administration*, 2nd edn. New York, NY: McGraw-Hill.

Graham, C. B. and Hays, S. W. (1986) *Managing the public organization*. Washington, DC: Congressional Quarterly Press.

Hrebiniak, L. G. (2005) *Making strategy work: Leading effective execution and change*. Upper Saddle River, NJ: Wharton School Publishing.

Hudzik, J. K. and Cordner, G. W. (1983) *Planning in criminal justice organizations and systems*. New York, NY: Macmillan.

Jones, W. C. (2011) State's zero-based budgeting program to focus on education. *Athens Banner-Herald*. Available at http://onlineathens.com/local-news/2012-06-11/states-zerobased-budgeting-program-focus-education (last accessed January 31, 2013).

Judicial Council of California. (2012) 2012 Court statistics report: Statewide caseload trends 2001–2002 through 2010–2011. Available at http://www.courts.ca.gov/documents/2012-Court-Statistics-Report.pdf (last accessed January 31, 2013).

Key, V. O. (1940) The lack of budgetary theory. In J. M. Shafritz and A. C. Hyde (eds), *Classics of public administration*. Chicago, IL: Dorsey Press, pp. 116–122.

Lauth, T. P. (2003) Budgeting during a recession phase of the business cycle: The Georgia experience. *Public Budgeting and Finance*, 23(2): 26–38.

Lipsky, M. (1980) *Street-level bureaucracy: Dilemmas of the individual in public services*. New York, NY: Russell Sage Foundation.

Merlo, A. V. and Benekos, P. J. (2000) *What's wrong with the criminal justice system: Ideology, politics and the media*. Cincinnati, OH: Anderson Publishing.

Nice, D. (2002) *Public budgeting*. Belmont, CA: Wadsworth/Thomson Learning.

Padovani, E. and Young, D. W. (2012) *Managing local governments: Designing management control systems that deliver value.* London: Routledge.

Poulson, B. W. (2001) Surplus expenditures: A case study of Colorado. *Public Budgeting and Finance,* 21(4): 18–43.

Pressman, J. L. and Wildavsky, A. (1973) *Implementation,* 2nd edn. Berkeley, CA: University of California Press.

Pyhrr, P. A. (1977) The zero-base approach to government budgeting. In J. M. Shafritz and A.C. Hyde (eds), *Classics of public administration.* Chicago, IL: Dorsey Press, 495–505.

Rothman, D. J. (1980) *Conscience and convenience: The asylum and its alternatives in progressive America.* Glenview, IL: Scott, Foresman.

Royce, D. (2003) State prisons lock up 3,000 new inmates. *The Miami Herald,* August 19. Available at www.MiamiHerald.com (last accessed January 31, 2013).

Schick, A. (1966) The road to PPB: The stages of budget reform. In J. M. Shafritz and A. C. Hyde (eds), *Classics of public administration.* Chicago, IL: Dorsey Press, pp. 299–318.

Simmons, R. (2001) Zero-based budgeting hasn't worked well for Ada County. *The Idaho Statesman,* June 8. Local: p. 8.

Smith, C. E. (1997) *Courts, politics, and the judicial process,* 2nd edn. Chicago, IL: Nelson-Hall.

Surette, R., Applegate, B., McCarthy, B. and Jablonski, P. (2006) Self-destructing prophecies: Long-term forecasting of municipal correctional bed need. *Journal of Criminal Justice,* 34: 57–72.

Swanson, C. R., Territo, L. and Taylor, R. W. (1998) *Police administration: Structures, processes and behavior,* 4th edn. Upper Saddle River, NJ: Prentice Hall.

United States Department of Justice. (2013) No title. Available at http://www.whitehouse.gov/sites/default/files/omb/budget/fy2012/assets/justice.pdf (last accessed January 31, 2013).

Wallace, H., Roberson, C. and Steckler, C. (1995) *Fundamentals of police administration.* Englewood Cliffs, NJ: Prentice Hall.

Welsh, W. N. and Harris, P. W. (1999) *Criminal justice policy and planning.* Cincinnati, OH: Anderson Publishing.

Whisenand, P. M. and Ferguson, R. F. (1996) *The managing of police organizations,* 4th edn. Upper Saddle River, NJ: Prentice Hall.

Whisenand, P. M. and Ferguson, R. F. (2002) *The managing of police organizations,* 5th edn. Upper Saddle River, NJ: Prentice Hall.

Winkler, G. and Smith, J. (2006) Long-term budgeting for operations in construction and design planning for jails. *American Jails,* 20(4): 53–55.

DISCUSSION QUESTIONS

1   Some policymakers consider a budget the ultimate policy document. What do you think they mean by that? Explain how budget and policy are connected.

2   Some management consultants claim that the fatal flaws of strategic planning are that it tends to be an annual process and that it focuses on individual work units instead of the work of the organization as a whole (Mankins and Steele 2006). They recommend replacing strategic plans with ongoing issue-focused blueprints to drive decision making. If you were the head of an agency, what would your strategic blueprint look like? How would you account for unforeseen events and changes in the external environment?

SECTION III CONCLUSION

From working in criminal justice or studying it from an academic perspective, we know the system is complex and the problems of crime and justice are profound. It is for this very reason that criminal justice managers need to seek out and become comfortable with collaborations. With collaborations, such as task forces, partnerships, and other problem-oriented strategic alliances, each entity risks losing some control. However, gaining access to shared resources and expertise should inspire law and justice leaders to prioritize problem-solving over winning turf battles. To stay focused and committed to collaboration, administrators need to remember that the only winners in a law enforcement turf battle are the criminals.

Lastly, some resistance to strategic planning occurs because many of us in the field feel that criminal justice is always changing. It responds to the latest shooting of an unarmed suspect, terrorist attack, scandal, or presidential election. How could we possibly keep to a strategic plan when the walls are crumbling around us? Damage control is a fact of life in the criminal justice arena and something that we can actually plan for. For instance, the book *Masters of Disasters* (Lehane, Fabiani, and Guttentag 2012) outlines several strategies for damage control, such as full disclosure and not feeding the fire. The key is to realize that just because a plan might not get executed exactly as originally designed, planning and budgeting are exercises in discipline and forethought that will serve you well.

IV

ORGANIZATIONAL SOCIALIZATION, EMPLOYEE MOTIVATION

INTRODUCTION

The first reading in this section asks the question, What is my job and how do I do it? This gets to the heart of organizational socialization, but the topic is far more multifaceted than the answers to these two simple questions. A broader, more complete view of socialization includes answers to additional questions, such as How will I be evaluated in my job? How will I get promoted in my job? How should I interact with others in my job? From a personal point of view, each of these questions is instrumental to a successful career. From an organizational perspective, these questions are linked to the mission of the organization. This is the reason why agency leaders should understand the role that socialization plays. The role of a leader is to articulate a clear mission and rally the troops to action in support of the mission. If these efforts fail, an agency will at best be ineffective in carrying out its goals and at worst descend into chaos. When leaders are brought in as change agents to turn around unproductive, dysfunctional agencies, we often hear that the way to handle such a massive undertaking is to produce culture change within the organization. Culture change begins with socialization. Before we even entertain the idea of culture change we first need to know what culture is. From a sociological perspective, culture is a way of life. It includes elements such as beliefs, rules, values, and customs, each of which is deeply ingrained in a community's or society's social fabric. Clearly, organizations have cultures as well. So if culture is the collection of beliefs, etc., socialization is the way beliefs are transmitted to others (Rettig 2017). If leaders want to change an organization's culture, the first step is to examine the process of organizational socialization.

Section IV also introduces the topic of employee motivation. This is an essential aspect of work life, but sadly, it is largely ignored by managers and supervisors (Hlupic 2014). This reading veers away from the theoretical literature on motivation (which is voluminous, abstract, and sometimes contradictory) and instead shine a light on five common workplace views that corrode worker enthusiasm. I recommend that you read the article from two vantage points. First, as an employee, what motivates you in the short and long term? Are there different kinds of incentives for short- and long-term motivation? Does your employer understand the keys to your workplace satisfaction? Does your employer even care about them? Second, if you manage a team of workers, assess your own strategies. Do you attempt to motivate your employees? What works and what doesn't? Do you even care? These are difficult questions to ask oneself and if you strive to become a strong leader, you cannot expect that all workers will be internally motivated to work hard because that's their job. Motivation begins with leaders having a deep appreciation for the fact that humans are complex beings tasked with incredibly demanding duties

SOCIALIZATION, ROLES, AND POWER ISSUES

MARY K. STOHR AND PETER A. COLLINS

> Power corrupts and absolute power corrupts absolutely.
>
> (Lord Acton 1887, in a letter to Bishop Creighton)

> This analysis argues that, instead of being a simple matter of putting on a uniform and learning about schedules, becoming and being a prison officer is a complex process. Behind the walls, through constant interaction that is typically informal and subtle, yet sometimes frighteningly bold and sudden, the recruit learns the contours of the prison world and his place in it…
>
> (Crouch and Marquart 1994: 327)

> Not only does justice require the prosecutor to "weed out" cases where the evidence is weak, but the practical need to conserve scarce legal resources for only the most serious cases demands this…
>
> (Meyer and Grant 2003: 116)

> Cops are selecting modes of adaptation that they prefer, that they sometimes, to use a term uncommon to scholarly studies, simply like … they make choices that are pleasing to them, that make them feel good, or that at appropriate times make them angry.
>
> (Crank 1998: 21)

INTRODUCTION: WHAT IS MY JOB AND HOW DO I DO IT?

The topics of socialization, roles, and power issues in criminal justice organizations are really concerned with what the job of the professional is (roles), how people learn about it (socialization), and how they exercise one of the most important tools at hand (power). In the multicontextual environment of criminal justice organizations, where politics, economics, crime levels, and stakeholder expectations all affect the operation of the multilayered agency, the answers to our questions (what is my job and how do I do it?) may not be as clear in practice as they are in the formal job announcement.

In this chapter we discuss the criminal justice workers at the base of the management chart. They, like managers and others within their larger organizations, are professionals who are often asked to do too much with too little. Recall that these types of workers, such as police and correctional officers, counselors, probation and parole officers, prosecutors, and defense attorneys, fit the description given of street-level bureaucrats (SLBs; Lipsky 1980). Again, these are public service workers who have more demands on their time and agency resources than they can meet, and who also have the discretion to make choices about their work.

This chapter is framed with a focus on SLBs because how they are socialized into the role they adopt essentially defines criminal justice policy in practice. As all who are likely to read this book know, work in the criminal justice field is fascinating because of the human element that defines it. The roles of detention officers, prosecutors, and counselors are diverse, but bound by the nature of the socialization into those roles, including the presence of power. How socialization is accomplished and the choice of roles adopted really defines criminal justice agencies, and the dispersion of "justice" in the United States.

SOCIALIZATION

Occupational socialization, like any form of socialization, involves learning and teaching. A child in school is taught what and how to learn by teachers and fellow classmates. A new member of a book club is initiated into the ways of the club operation and focus by the other members. Likewise, the new police recruit learns from organizational members and others who teach her or him the job, including how to do it. But recruits don't just learn the particulars of the job itself; they learn what the organization's prevailing and conflicting values and beliefs are. This learning curve is steepest at the beginning and will likely begin to level, but as each officer gains more knowledge and experience, they often relearn their role, likely many times over the course of their career.

Therefore, according to Klofas *et al.* (1990: 150), **occupational socialization** is "[t]he process by which a person acquires the values, attitudes, and behaviors of an ongoing occupational social system." Socialization is a process and it is ongoing. What is not said here, but is implied, is that socialization is not done by organizational members only; rather, as we will discuss later in the chapter, clients and other stakeholders also teach the criminal justice worker about the job (Collins *et al.* 2012; Stohr *et al.* 2012; Crank 1998; Lipsky 1980; Lombardo 1989). The socialization process may also vary based on individual personal characteristics; for instance, the gender and race/ethnicity of the jobholder have been shown to influence how criminal justice staff view and perform their jobs (Griffin *et al.* 2012; Camp *et al.* 2001; Haarr 1997; Jenne and Kersting 1998; Morash and Haarr 2012, 1995).

This socialization process is believed to take place in three stages: *anticipatory, formal,* and *informal*. Each stage entails learning, but the first and the third particularly involve some socialization by others outside the organization.

ANTICIPATORY SOCIALIZATION

The **anticipatory socialization** stage begins before the criminal justice worker even starts the job. It occurs as the person *anticipates* perhaps someday working in law, police, or corrections. Those involved in anticipatory socialization for this prospective criminal justice recruit could include family, friends, teachers, and the media. In fact, this process may begin in childhood as a person is influenced by friends and family who are employed by or in contact with the relevant agencies, or by popular media depictions of that kind of work. Although family and friends who work in corrections may be able to supply important and relevant information about work in corrections, depictions of such work in the popular media are usually grossly inaccurate and almost uniformly misleading (e.g. *Dexter*, the "*CSI* effect," *Law and Order SVU*, etc.).

The same holds true, of course, for policing and legal work. Though many of us might be aficionados of the various *Law and Order* series, the reruns of the *NYPD Blue* drama, or even the comical *Reno 911*, someone unacquainted with actual police or legal work may be led to believe by these shows that detectives and prosecutors have the luxury to pursue every lead and to prosecute every case to the fullest extent of the law—or in contrast, as is depicted on *Reno 911*, that the police are hilariously incompetent. Moreover, the defense of cases in such programs is usually vigorous even if the defendant is poor and socially powerless. Although, of course, police, prosecutors, and defense attorneys do at times behave in accordance with the TV dramas, these descriptors hardly represent every case (but see *The Wire* as an example of a more realistic portrayal of work in the CJ system). As Ford (2003: 87) writes regarding the "media tales" told about policing: "Gleaned from the epic stories recounted in police lore, media tales take rare events and magnify and describe heroic stories as the everyday grist of police work." But once on the job, those new recruits "[s]ense that what they will be doing is a far cry from the media's promise" (Ford 2003: 87).

Just as misleading, if not more so, are the depictions of corrections in the movies and on television. The inmates, most of whom are murderers and rapists, are invariably housed in dirty large city jails or in maximum security prisons overseen by guards who are uncaring and sarcastic in their demeanor.

A related problem with anticipatory socialization and the criminal justice system is that much of the work is done outside the view of the public. This heightens the (in)credibility of justice-related media depictions, since those are often the only intimate exposure people have to criminal justice agencies. It is somewhat rare to find a community member who has taken a tour of the local jail, has sat through a trial, or knows how the parole office supervises parolees. Because of this general lack of knowledge and because many people do not know anyone who works in the criminal justice system and have not taken related classes in college, those who anticipate working in criminal justice-related positions tend to be most influenced by inaccurate media depictions, which do not give a complete or true picture of the work.

College students considering a career in criminal justice are also socialized into the nature of the work when they take courses or are assigned coursework related to the criminal justice system. An introductory survey class on the system (police, courts, and corrections) and a research methods class (Southerland 2002) are included by 40 percent (if not more) of criminal justice or criminology programs and departments. Fewer, but still a significant number, require law, juvenile justice/delinquency, and policing courses. Not as many programs, however, require a corrections class. These classes may or may not include much discussion of the actual work done in the field, but to the extent that they do, anticipatory socialization occurs through classroom lectures, readings, criminal justice professionals who give guest lectures, or visits to local work sites. Inevitably, many students note that they find guest speakers and on-site visits to be the most enlivening parts of our criminal justice classes.

Perhaps because of the media depictions, a lack of knowledge, and some notable abuses of power that tend to make the headlines, some types of criminal justice work today (e.g., that of correctional officers) have not achieved the professional status enjoyed by police, lawyers, teachers, and firefighters. Criminal justice will have arrived as a profession when a little boy or girl responds to the ubiquitous adult question, "What do you want to be when you grow up?", with "I want to work in a prison" or "I want to work with kids at the detention center." When children begin to provide such responses, the popular image of corrections will have changed to reflect an understanding of the work and recognition of its professional status. At this point anticipatory socialization may more accurately reflect the positive side of work in corrections. Because of generally higher educational and training requirements, not to mention pay for policing and law, workers in those organizations are more likely to be regarded as "professionals."

FORMAL SOCIALIZATION

Formal socialization occurs when a worker is exposed to the legal or officially sanctioned requirements of a job. Formal socialization can begin in the job interview and, in criminal justice agencies, usually occurs in the initial on-the-job training conducted by a designated official, during the academy training (for corrections and policing), and in ongoing training sessions throughout the career of those workers.

The amount of academy training received by corrections and police workers varies widely across job types, between the states, and between positions at the federal, state, county, and city levels. The average length of a police recruit training program is 640 hours (Thibault *et al*. 2004), although a number of agencies provide far less. For instance, according to their respective websites (accessed spring 2013), the Michigan State Police Training Division provides 594 hours for law enforcement basic training and the Georgia State University Police Department provides only 335 hours. On the other hand, the websites of the police departments of Tulsa, Oklahoma, and Mobile, Alabama (accessed spring 2013), indicate that new recruits receive up to twenty-five weeks, or between 600 and 920 hours, of training.

Required recruit training for corrections jobs is usually far less. Unfortunately, there is no easily accessible national compilation of training requirements for corrections work, as there is for policing in the *Criminal Justice Statistics 2002* Sourcebook (Maguire and Pastore 2004). However, individual states and organizations do publish their entry-level training requirements.

For instance, the private Corrections Corporation of America (CCA) provides all staff with forty hours of training; correctional officers get an additional 120 hours of training during their first year (CCA website 2013). Those first forty hours of training include such topics as corporate history and practice, facility and personnel policies and procedures, employee standards of conduct, communicable diseases, institutional safety, special management of offenders, suicide prevention, unit management, use of force, emergency procedures, and sexual harassment. The 120-hour specialized training course for correctional officers includes such topics as count procedures, cultural diversity, defensive tactics, direct supervision, emergency procedures, facility policy and procedures, firearms training, hostage situations, first aid/CPR, and inmate disciplinary, grievance, and classification procedures.

Though they do not indicate what the training topics are, the Maine Criminal Justice Academy (MCJA) website notes that eighty hours of academy training in a two-week period are provided for correctional officers (MCJA 2013). The Maine officials also do not indicate on their website what training is required for probation and parole or juvenile justice workers. In Delaware, a nine- or twelve-week basic training program is required for either correctional officers (nine) or probation and parole officers (twelve). The state website includes the general training topics, but does not indicate whether the training is at forty hours per week; but if so, then Delaware requires 360–480 hours of entry-level training for these officers (Delaware Department of Correction 2004).

In contrast, in California, probation officers and parole agents are treated somewhat differently. Counties in California hire the probation officers and the state hires the parole agents, who work for either the Department of Corrections or the Youth Authority (California Employment Development Department 2004). Both positions, as is often true for adult and juvenile probation and parole officers, require a four-year degree. Probation officers in California must also complete 200 hours of basic training within their first year, and parole agents must complete four weeks (possibly 160 hours) of training in the same time period. In Nevada, the probation and parole officers are afforded 480 hours of training in their first year of employment, but that includes both classroom and field training hours (Nevada Department of Public Safety 2004).

Attorneys laboring in the criminal courts usually get on-the-job mentoring by more experienced colleagues, much like those in policing and corrections who participate in training in the field, through a field training officer (FTO). Of course, three years of law school, particularly if a clinic (or clerking) is required, might be regarded as providing some formal training, in addition to education. Smith (1997) notes that law school students often do not enroll in clinical programs, though such programs might help them become better lawyers, because they are not tested on bar exams. The stark truth is law students feel the need to focus on those courses that will help them pass the bar exam and the bar exam is not based on clinical practice. In fact, the bar exam tends to be preoccupied with business law (Smith 1997). Therefore, some might argue that ironically, the profession with perhaps the highest regard in the criminal justice system, and which arguably exerts the most power, has the least practical training.

Reddington and Kreisel (2003) found in their research on training requirements for juvenile probation officers that thirty-six states mandate some form of training, which varies widely in amount and type. They noted that one to two weeks of fundamental skills training was typical for most of these states. They note that "[t]his average amount of training for juvenile probation officers is somewhat lower than the average for adult probation officers, which is 125 hours, or for law enforcement officers" (Reddington and Kreisel 2003: 45).

Needless to say, the amount of training for entry-level positions varies widely by position and organization. But generally correctional workers get less formal socialization via training at the beginning of their career than do police officers, and much less anticipatory socialization via education than attorneys (particularly those who take a criminal law clinic) working in the criminal court system.

Ongoing training offered by criminal justice agencies also varies widely by jurisdictions and jobs. Some workers are required to take 10–20 hours per year to remain current in their field, while others may be offered little or no training, or participation is viewed as entirely optional. We will discuss training more in subsequent chapters, but clearly the extent to which training is provided and required for criminal justice workers is a measure of the professional stature that a field has acquired.

In addition to the academy and ongoing training that police and corrections workers are exposed to, they, and new prosecuting and defense attorneys, are often also formally socialized by an on-the-job trainer/mentor or a field training officer, either before or after their initial training. The FTOs, who often have years of tenure in the job, are tasked with teaching the relatively new employee how things are "officially" done in the organization. If selected correctly, the trainer/mentor/FTO can impart valuable knowledge about how to translate formal education and training to actual job practice. They can both model professional work and allow the new employee the opportunity to learn and practice skills while gradually transitioning into full practice on the job (Sun 2003).

The policing field first adopted FTO programs in the 1970s (Thibault *et al.* 2004). Critics of these early programs noted that instead of being the water walkers of the organization, too often FTOs are those who get stuck with the extra task of on-the-job training without instruction in how to do it, without the necessary time to do it right, and without any particular predilection to teach on the part of the officers. Hence, recommendations for current programs hinge on training for the trainers or FTOs and adherence to official policies, procedures, review, and evaluation requirements (Thibault *et al.* 2004). Bradford and Pynes (2000) also note that police academy training has not kept up with changing focuses in police work. Specifically, they note that few academies provide training in problem solving or interpersonal and decision making skills, though such knowledge is key to working in an organization that is focused on community policing.

INFORMAL SOCIALIZATION

Informal socialization is teaching and learning that takes place on the job. It is outside the official strictures of law and procedure and away from the officially recognized instructors. It is learning how the job is actually done, and many times that means learning the official and the unofficial versions. The divide that sometimes separates the official and unofficial versions of how the job is done is represented by the experience of many correctional and police practitioners upon finishing the academy: They were taken aside by an old-timer and told something like "Okay, now forget that bullshit you heard at the academy, I'll show you how we REALLY do things around here." This happened to one of the authors after a week with an FTO when she first started as a correctional officer, and she saw it happen to correctional officers returning from academy training. Our students report having had the same experience when they began work in corrections and policing after academy training.

The means of transmitting this informal socialization can take many forms. In his study of community corrections, Crank (1996) noted that it may happen under the guise of "official" training when stories or "tropes" are told to illustrate how "real" work is done. In Crank's observation of training for probation and parole officers in Nevada, commonsense advice about how to do the job was transmitted to new hires via a linguistic device he termed a *trope*, which he defines as a "[s]tory, an irony, a metaphor, or some combination of these, constituted from everyday experience" (Crank 1996: 271). For example, one instructor was trying to illustrate the importance of body searches and the inherent danger if they are not done correctly:

> This is the place [the groin area] where people hide all kinds of stuff. There was a case in California where a guy was up for parole. He went before the board, and they turned him down. He bent over and pulled a stabbing tool out of his anal cavity. He jumped over the desk and stabbed a parole board member that he didn't like in the shoulder a couple of times.
>
> (Crank 1996: 227)

A different instructor uses a trope to illustrate the understandable sympathy probation and parole officers have when their clients cannot meet their P and P conditions because they are too poor:

> We have a bad situation in our country. A lot of times it is impossible to find work for an unemployed mother. There's no way minimum wage can provide the support she can get from unemployment and ADC. However, a condition of parole is employment. You may have to talk to your supervisor. A low-skill offender with three children, her children will literally starve if she has to take a minimum-wage job. They can't afford childcare. You can write it up so that they have to work, but you can write it up so that they can take care of their children at home.
>
> (Crank 1996: 282)

In both instances the academy instructors for probation and parole are informally socializing the new recruits to the nature of the work. In the second trope, the instructor is even advocating that the officer ignore a formal condition out of compassion for the circumstances some clients face.

Greenhorn criminal justice workers are also informally socialized by their colleagues. They observe what common practice is within given situations/contexts and they sometimes model that (Pollock 2004). If juveniles in the detention center are treated with respect in speech and deed by the majority of the other counselors, then the new counselor understands that this is the norm for behavior. If, however, the kids are referred to as "little criminals" or worse by staff, if their requests for assistance and information are ignored and their privacy is repeatedly violated for no purpose, then new counselors will detect a conflict between the official version of their job and the informal socialization being provided on the job.

In addition to the stories or tropes and observations of common practice, informal socialization may occur when clients train workers. Lipsky (1980) noted that clients will tell SLBs what behavior they expect either directly or indirectly. They might do this with intent or inadvertently.

It is possible that the more prolonged and intense the contact with clients, the more likely they are to be able to "shape" the behavior of the workers. If this is true, those who work in corrections are probably more likely to experience the influence of the client than are police officers or criminal attorneys, whose exposure is likely to be short-term and more remote. For instance, an inmate in a prison or jail might shape the behavior of the correctional officer by refusing to follow an order, by following the order, or by just ignoring it. If the same person refused an order by a police officer, the officer would handle it as she does all such circumstances, without the constraint of knowing that she will have to deal with the person over and over again over a span of days, months, or years.

Even so, repeated exposure to the same victims and offenders, or persons in similar circumstances, surely shapes the reactions of both the police and criminal attorneys. It is often noted in the police literature, for instance, that officers can become cynical about domestic violence because they are called to the same house to mediate the same disputes again and again. Likewise the literature on sentencing indicates that criminal attorneys and judges will develop "norms" for sentencing, or alike sentences for similar offenders and offenses even when the law allows a wide range of sentencing options. In both the domestic violence and sentencing examples just given, it is possible that coworkers and supervisors are also shaping the behavior of the police and attorneys; but we must not forget that the clients in these circumstances may also be exerting some influence (Lipsky 1980).

In corrections, a counselor is subtly reminded to hurry up with the current client by the line of inmates waiting outside the office. Repetitive requests from a juvenile's parents for an alcohol or drug program placement may persuade a probation officer to be a particular advocate for that child's case. A defense attorney may be persuaded by a client's fervent claims of innocence to allocate more time for that case. The point is that clients, and their friends and family, can also serve in a socialization capacity *vis-à-vis* the criminal justice worker.

Crouch and Marquart (1994: 303), in their classic article "On Becoming a Prison Guard," note that the decision to work in institutional corrections comes later in life for many, and it "[o]ften appears to be somewhat accidental, a rather unplanned response to a fortuitous opportunity or a need for immediate employment." Once on the job, the authors found that the inmates and the "guard" subculture were central components to the socialization of the new recruit.

The new officer reacts to and is shaped to some degree by the inmate subculture, which may be foreign to him, as the inmates react to his official status and authority (Crouch and Marquart 1994). Some officers are tested by inmates and some who fail the test are then corrupted in ways that Sykes (1958) identified a half-century ago: officers become too friendly with inmates, they engage in reciprocity with inmates (such as ignoring enforcement of one rule to secure inmate obedience in another matter); officers concede some tasks to inmates (such as mail delivery), and inmates use the officer's transgressions to blackmail them.

In the prison at which one of the authors worked in the 1980s, a sergeant she admired told her to ignore the bulldogging by one powerful inmate. This inmate, whom we'll call Jim, coercively collected soda and potato chips and other store items from inmates in a dorm room one Saturday. The sergeant wanted his younger colleague to ignore the bulldogging because the inmate was an important ally for staff in keeping younger and rowdier inmates in line. Greatly influenced by the wisdom of this sergeant, the new officer did not infract Jim for the prohibited behavior; it was a decision she later came to regret. Eventually, the bulldogging inmate was infracted and transferred out, but only when he went too far in his collection and enforcement efforts—he was involved in a serious assault on an inmate that could not be officially ignored.

Crouch and Marquart also note the influence of the correctional subculture in informally socializing the new officer: "The recruit learns how to be a guard most directly by observing, listening to and imitating the veterans with whom he works" (1994: 312). This subculture teaches the officer how to perceive and manage inmates and how to anticipate and handle trouble. Old-time officers tell the newer officers that if they heed such advice they are less likely to find themselves in a bad spot with inmates and more likely to garner the respect of other officers.

In addition to the circumstances of the job and the socialization that criminal justice workers receive from clients and coworkers, there is evidence that other factors influence socialization. For instance, the personal characteristics and framework that criminal justice workers bring to their jobs have been found to influence how they feel about the work and how they behave in their role. Martin (1990) was one of the first to note that men and women police officers experienced their jobs differently. Jurik and Halemba (1984) and Jurik (1985) also noted this difference between the genders in their research on job perceptions and performance of correctional officers in Arizona in the 1980s. Notably, since that time, and building on Jurik and Halemba's research, others have found both similarities and differences between the genders in how they experience and perform corrections and police work (Daniello 2011; Farkas 1999; Lutze and Murphy 1999; Lawrence and Mahan 1998; Pogrebin and Poole 1997; Belknap 1995; Martin 1990; Zupan 1986). Research has also documented that people of diverse races and ethnicities and/or with diverse backgrounds (e.g., military service) may differ in their views of the work and how they perform it (Stohr et al. 2012; Hemmens et al. 2002; Van Voorhis et al. 1991). When there are differences between groups, however, it is not always clear whether they are the result of a framework people bring to the job or the result of socialization on the job (Ford 2003): Is it nature or nurture? The perennial question indeed—which has no clear answer yet!

THE CRIMINAL JUSTICE ROLE

Anticipatory, formal, and informal socialization in the workplace are geared toward defining what the job is for the criminal justice worker or what his or her role is. According to Katz and Kahn (1978), role behavior is essentially what people do over and over on the job. What you do on the job is your role, be that officially outlined by statutorily defined tasks, position descriptions and policies, and procedural requirements, or unofficially defined by the actual work that is done and required. As we have seen from our discussion of socialization, the criminal justice role is both officially and unofficially defined in the organization (Purkiss *et al.* 2003). But oftentimes those official requirements for the role are in conflict with unofficial requirements.

ROLE CONFLICT: THE SERVICE VS. SECURITY/SERVE VS. PROTECT DICHOTOMIES

Role conflict occurs when there are competing expectations for the role that are difficult to fulfill. A related concept is **role ambiguity**, which occurs when expectations for the role are not clear or are confusing. In corrections and policing there is a classic dichotomy of roles for workers between the informal and formal demands of service work and rehabilitative tasks and the competing requirement that they always be attentive to security, protection, incapacitative, and even punitive requirements (Buerger *et al.* 1999; Cullen and Gilbert 1982; Johnson 1996; Lombardo 1989; Maahs and Pratt 2001).

Prosecutors and defense attorneys have clearer roles, formally speaking, than their sisters and brothers in policing and corrections. Nevertheless it can be said of them, as is true of the police and corrections, that organizational demands on their time, such as caseloads, can serve to informally reduce their ability to perform their defense or prosecutorial roles adequately (Hemmens *et al.* 2010; Smith 1997). According to Smith, lawyers must both defend the rights and interests of the client (in the case of prosecutors this would be the state) and serve as gatekeepers to the court system, keeping out complaints that do not merit prosecution and pursuing those that do. Their role also includes the ability to transform grievances into legal claims, develop new legal theories and arguments, serve as decision makers, exert influence over public policy, and control entry into the legal profession (Hemmens *et al.* 2010; Smith 1997). In the larger sense lawyering includes these grander activities, but down in the trenches of the criminal court the role of the defense or prosecuting attorney is primarily to advocate for the client or case and to get through the caseload.

Lombardo (1989) found in his research on officers working in the state prison in Auburn, New York, in the 1970s and 1980s that institutional rules sometimes prohibited an informal role that was weighted toward rehabilitative services. The roles for corrections workers are often in conflict and at times ambiguous. Similarly, Buerger *et al.* (1999: 125) note the difficulties that arise when police officers who are more traditional in their expectations for law enforcement (e.g. "favoring confrontation, command, and coercion") are suddenly working in a community policing-based organization where interactions with citizens might be expected to include more "participation, promotion, and persuasion."

Role conflict occurs because of the differing expectations for corrections and policing work. Past research shows that the general public and many system actors strongly supported punishment as the primary goal of corrections, which was reflected in how inmates were dealt with within the system, as well as how they were treated once released back into their communities (Norman and Burbridge 1991; Zimmerman *et al.* 1988). More recently, however, several studies indicate a shift to support for rehabilitation among the general public and correctional actors (Collins *et al.* 2012; Cullen *et al.* 1988; Flanagan and Caulfield 1984; Gordon 1999; Kifer *et al.* 2003; McCorkle 1993; Moak and Wallace 2000; Moon *et al.* 2000). The result is that in correctional settings, role conflict is more common because of slow systemic change and the bifurcated interests in rehabilitation and punishment that have resulted.

In an analysis of the statutorily defined role for probation officers, Purkiss *et al.* (2003) found that state legislatures required officers to perform twenty-three tasks in 2002. These tasks included a mix of law enforcement, rehabilitative, and other requirements. The authors note that a comparison of 1992 through 2002 statutes in the states clearly shows that the law enforcement role for probation officers gained primacy in the early 1990s, whereas rehabilitation and a restorative justice focus became more popular as the decade ended and the new century began.

The service or rehabilitative role, also known as the human service role, requires a trust relationship between correctional worker and client and a willingness of the worker to advocate for the client. On the other hand a security or punitive role, also known as the custodial role, requires for the correctional worker distrust and suspicion of clients and the need to maintain distance from them. Johnson, in his important book *Hard Time: Understanding and Reforming the Prison*, starkly defines these two roles, first describing the custodial officer working in prisons as follows (see also Box 1):

> "Smug hacks" … typically account for about a quarter of the guard force. They are custodial officers in the pejorative sense of the term. They seek order at any price, and violence—their own or that of inmate allies—is one of the tools of their trade. Their stance of toughness is exalted in the guard subculture, and is the public image (though not the private reality) adopted by most officers. Smug hacks find their counterparts in the convicts of the prison yard. The combative relations that ensue between these groups account for much of the abuse and even brutality that occurs in the prison.
>
> (Johnson 197: 1996)

In contrast, Johnson defines human service officers as those who:

> Use their authority to help inmates cope with prison life; they provide human service rather than custodial repression. They do the best they can with the resources at their disposal to make the prison a better place in which to live and work. In contrast to their merely custodial colleagues,

these officers cope maturely with their own problems as well as with the problems experienced by prisoners. They serve, by their helping activities and by example, as true correctional officers.

(Johnson 223: 1996)

Clearly, there cannot always be an obvious demarcation in these roles. Police and correctional staff often adopt one role or the other depending on the situation. Sometimes police officers need to exercise a law enforcement role to maintain the safety of the community. Sometimes a human service role might be misinterpreted by inmates and/or might compromise the ability of the correctional officer to objectively supervise. Certainly mindless brutality is never called for in policing or corrections, but an emphasis on protection, security, and order often is. It is the degree to which criminal justice staff fall on one or the other end of this continuum of roles, and how they respond to a given situation, that should be of interest.

Box 1 The Human Service and Custodial Roles for Corrections

Johnson in *Hard Time* (1996) and Lombardo in *Guards Imprisoned: Correctional Officers at Work* (1989), both following in the footsteps of Toch (1978), discuss the human service and custodial roles for correctional officers. The primary attributes of each are as follows: Custodial officer

- mindless
- brutal
- custodian
- emphasis on order maintenance

Human service officer

- provider of goods and services
- referral agent or an advocate
- assistance with institutional adjustment

Both men thought that human service work was common practice for most correctional officers and that the custodial officer role was the exception rather than the rule.

Whereas Johnson (1996) and Lombardo (1989) each developed an understanding of these roles from studies of adult prisons, similar distinctions have been made officially and unofficially for other sectors of criminal justice. Juvenile justice has traditionally had the greatest focus on a service or rehabilitative role for its staff (Rothman 1980). As the juvenile court, juvenile probation and parole programs, and detention and prison facilities were established to function formally in "the best interest of the child," there has naturally been a greater focus on rehabilitation.

In research on the attitudes of juvenile correctional facility directors, Caeti et al. (2003) administered a questionnaire measuring role orientation, job satisfaction, and stress to the 406 facility directors across the nation. They had a 63.5 percent response rate and found that most directors (61.2 percent) ranked rehabilitation as the number-one goal of juvenile corrections, with deterrence (25.6 percent), incapacitation (12.0 percent), and retribution (0.4 percent) following. In that same publication, Caeti and his colleagues compared these responses to those by prison wardens (to a questionnaire administered in the early 1990s). The wardens' ranking was in the following order: retribution, deterrence, rehabilitation, and incapacitation.

Not surprisingly, then, there tends to be a more formal orientation toward a rehabilitative role for criminal justice workers who have juvenile clients or who work in that system. Informally, however, the actual role that the police, attorneys for juveniles, and their probation and parole officers or detention workers or prison counselors adopt is shaped by their roles as SLBs (with too many clients and not enough resources) and by the clients themselves, the ambient subculture, and the political winds. In his book describing the work of juvenile probation officers, Jacobs (1990) notes that because of the crushing pressure of young clients on the caseload, the officer often has to make a King Solomon-like choice—whether to focus their energies on those who need them most, or on those who show the most promise.

As with criminal justice workers who labor in the juvenile justice system the traditional role of probation and parole officers who work with adults has also differed somewhat from that of adult correctional institution workers. Probation and parole departments were established based on the belief that clients were in need of a helping hand to settle into a job and put a roof over their heads (Rothman 1980). Probation and parole officers were expected to help and counsel their clients. In reality, probation and parole officers, termed community corrections officers now in some states, also function as SLBs, with too many demands on their time and too many clients. Their role is also shaped by their clients, by the subculture, and by the politics of the day (Lipsky 1980).

For both the juvenile justice system and adult probation and parole, there has been a move toward a more custodial role. This is due in large part to a shift in the political winds toward a more conservative approach to criminal justice in general (Benekos and Merlo 2001; Seiter 2002). Crowded correctional institutions and crowded caseloads for court personnel and probation and parole officers at both the adult and juvenile levels are a direct consequence of the greater willingness to punish by putting more and more people under some kind of correctional supervision in the past thirty years (e.g., King Davis et al. 2004). Until recently this also meant that the dollars available to fund correctional programming were scarce in most states and communities. In the late 1990s, as governments were flush in terms of tax dollars and as there was a dawning realization that the cost of locking so many people up would eventually claim any extra revenue, there was renewed interest in rehabilitation programming in many states and at the federal level. Unfortunately, funding was uneven and sometimes inadequate at all levels in the first decade of the 2000s.

Moreover, and relatedly, juvenile and adult probation and parole officers lament their client overload and the lack of programming options for the indigent clients they supervise (Jacobs 1990; Seiter 2002). What this means is that even if they were inclined to perform a more reha- bilitative or service-oriented role, their efforts would be stymied by the nature of the work and the lack of funding in their communities.

Seiter (2002), in a survey and interviews of adult parole officers in Missouri, found that despite the crowding and despite political pressures to focus on the security/surveillance and control role, many officers thought that the most important aspects of their job involved help- ing and assisting parolees. When officers were asked to identify the most important aspects of reentry programs for parolees they listed employment, treatment, and support from loved ones first, second, and third, and supervision/monitoring and controlling and holding offend- ers accountable fourth and fifth. Likewise, when parole officers were asked to identify the most important aspect of their job that leads to successful completion of parole, they provided similar responses. Specifically, they listed the supervision/monitoring and controlling activities first, but the assessment of needs and referral to agencies and the support for employment second and third, with accountability fourth.

Criminal justice workers at both the juvenile and adult levels are faced with similar lim- itations on their ability to adopt a service or rehabilitative role. There is little rehabilitative programming in adult corrections in many states and facilities. What does exist is too often delivered in a non-structured way, by volunteers or by staff who have received little training to conduct it. Moreover, the programming is rarely subjected to rigorous evaluation. The "best practices" research provides some hope for improvement in this area, but funding, delivery, and evaluation of programming in correctional institutions and in the communities is prob- lematic, though not hopeless. In policing, and as indicated earlier, the training for officers has not kept up with the move to a more service and problem-solving role for officers working in community policing-oriented organizations.

Not surprisingly, role conflict and ambiguity have been tied to several negative (and in some ways interrelated) outcomes for workers in the criminal justice system, including alienation from their work, cynicism, lowered job satisfaction and commitment, a less favorable attitude toward service and treatment, and stress and turnover (Bennett and Schmitt 2002; Brody *et al.* 2002; Crouch and Marquart 1994; Lombardo 1989; Maahs and Pratt 2001). For the criminal justice manager interested in minimizing role conflict, the answer may lie in greater clarification of the role and reinforcement of the appropriate role both officially and unofficially. Personnel practices such as selection, training, performance evaluation, and promotions should reinforce the expectations for the role. Bennett and Schmitt (2002) find that cynicism among police officers is intimately tied to job satisfaction. In turn, in the other studies just mentioned, levels of job satisfaction have varied depending on role conflict and ambiguity. Johnson (1996) argues that officers who adopt a more human services role in corrections have a more enlarged and enriched job, and are more likely to gain satisfaction from it. Also Lombardo (1989) argues that human service work in corrections reduces the alienation that officers feel from their work. Relatedly, Brody and colleagues (2002) found that police officers report more job satisfaction when they work in agencies most supportive of a community policing role.

An alternative perspective is that criminal justice workers *integrate* the roles of security/law enforcement and service/rehabilitation/treatment, rather than experiencing role conflict as a result of the existence of different sets of requirements. In a study of two probation-intensive supervision sites, one in Ohio and the other in Georgia, Clear and Latessa (1993) found that individual officers' behavior was influenced by the policy of each person's organization. They also found that within the same organization some officers may display an interest in one role over the other, but that the roles were not incompatible, as "[a]n officer's preference for one attitude will not cause avoidance of tasks consistent with the other" (Clear and Latessa 1993: 457).

Our colleague Craig Hemmens and one of the present authors (Stohr) developed the "correctional role instrument" as a means of diagnosing role preference in jails and prisons (see Box 2 and Section 2 of the chapter appendix). This instrument, or a version of it, might be used by correctional managers to research which role preference tends to predominate in their facility. We think that most of these instrument items could be reworded to fit the work of those in probation and parole and the juvenile justice system.

Box 2 A Discussion of the Correctional Role Instrument
By Mary K. Stohr

We developed the thirty-six-item "correctional role instrument" for several reasons (Stohr *et al.* 2012; Hemmens and Stohr 2000; 2001; Hemmens *et al.* 2002). First, we wanted to measure the extent to which correctional staff in jails and prisons identified with either a human services or a custodial role for corrections. We were also interested in perceptions of the use of force by staff and perceptions of male and female staff of the work of women as correctional officers. We were measuring perceptions, not actual behavior.

The instrument items were developed based on a review of the relevant literature and prior work experience (by Stohr), and on comments provided by a correctional role scholar (Robert Johnson). After face validity analysis by a warden and a deputy warden in a medium security prison (Barrier *et al.* 1999; Stohr *et al.* 2000), the items were rewritten and the instrument was pretested at a medium security prison in fall

1997, then refined in 1998 in response to those findings, and used once again in 2007 (Stohr *et al.* 2012; Hemmens and Stohr 2000, 2001). The questionnaire and the research process were subjected to Human Subjects Review before the instrument was pretested and administered.

Respondents were asked to indicate their level of agreement or disagreement with each given statement. Responses could range from 1 (strongly disagree) to 7 (strongly agree). Respondents also had the options of answering "don't know" or leaving a particular item blank. A number of items were reverse coded. This was done to ensure that staff completing the questionnaire were truly reading the questions and responding with some degree of consistency. As recoded, for all items, the higher the mean, the greater the agreement with the human service role.

The studies were conducted in 1998, 1999, and 2007. At each institution, including male minimum and male maximum security prisons, a female prison (combined minimum, medium, and maximum security), two mixed-gender jails, and a jail training academy, the research teams administered and collected the questionnaires. Facility administrators scheduled training or meetings at different times of the day, so that all shifts were given the opportunity to complete the questionnaires. Attendance at the meeting was mandatory, but completion of the survey was entirely voluntary. For most of the facilities, the research team returned on different days and at different times to complete administration of the questionnaire.

The findings are more fully summarized in the publications cited earlier, but here are the basics: Most correctional staff tended to favor a human service role orientation; women were less likely to value the use of force in their work; men and women tended to positively perceive the work of women in corrections, but women had a higher regard for their ability to do corrections work than men; military service tended to have a negative effect on the perception of abilities of female staff; and, as other research has determined regarding cynicism and alienation (see Toch and Klofas 1982), those in midcareer (6–10 years) tend to be less human service-oriented than those at the beginning and end of their careers.

The jail version of the instrument is provided in the appendix at the end of this chapter. Readers may use it, the cover page (without our names!), and the demographics sheet. We would caution anyone who uses the instrument to closely follow the data collection procedures outlined in the cited publications and to secure human subject approval by an accredited university or institution prior to administration of this questionnaire. We would also urge users to abide by accepted methodological practices in terms of questionnaire administration and data analysis. Item means might be compared with those in the publications, though we made slight changes in a few items over the course of the instrument development and testing. Please notify Hemmens and Stohr if you intend to use the instrument, and share your methodology and findings with us afterward.

The popular perception of criminal justice employees is that their role is heavily invested with power, and to some extent this is true. Such employees do have the ability to limit the liberty and freedoms of those they are entrusted to investigate, hold, try, sentence, watch, supervise, treat, and care for. These are awesome powers when situated in a democracy such as ours, where regular citizens are guaranteed a certain level of protection from their government via the Constitution and the Bill of Rights. Given how important power is to the role of criminal justice workers, especially in a democracy, some discussion of its nature is warranted.

Power *is the ability to get others to do what they otherwise wouldn't* (which is very close to Dahl's 1957 definition). This definition works at the individual level, but it does not encompass the power that organizations wield in their environments. In other words, power is exerted at the individual level and at the organizational level in criminal justice agencies and of course within the organization. There is power that attaches to individuals because of their charm, charisma, or other personal abilities. There is power that attaches to a given job or project or team, and supervisors and staff have the power to wield raw coercion over suspects, accused persons, inmates, and clients.

Weber (1947) noted that there were three types of **authority**, a term formally defined as "[t]he right and power to enforce laws, exact obedience, command, determine, or judge," which he equated with *legitimized power* (American Heritage Dictionary 1992: 56). The first type of authority he identified is **traditional**, or the power held by royalty or a head of state, or power that is vested with a sense of tradition and history. The second type is **charismatic**, or based on the personal charm and leadership qualities of the individual. The third type of authority is **legal**, or that based in laws and rules that are generally accepted. These three types of authority give those who wield them the legitimized power to operate without resort to the other types of power.

Relatedly, French and Raven (1959) identified the following five types or bases of power (along with legitimized power):

- *Reward* (or the perception that the power holder can give some kind of reward). In criminal justice agencies actors have the power to decline to arrest, investigate, or prosecute; they can prefer charges or grant sentence reductions; they can secure better housing or job placement, direct that someone receive a positive write-up, or decline to infract or violate a person's probation or parole.

- *Coercive* (or the perception that the power holder can use force to get what he or she wants). In criminal justice agencies this can range from the threat of force if the power recipient does not comply with commands to the actual use of force.

- *Legitimate* (or the perception that the power holder has legal or official status). In criminal justice agencies this means a position as an attorney or officer or counselor or work supervisor or health care provider is recognized as empowering the holder.

- *Referent* (or the perception that the power holder is a reference for the power recipient). In criminal justice agencies this means that the worker is looked upon as a model for the power recipient, which in turn empowers the worker.

- *Expert* (or the perception that the power holder has qualifications that confer this status). In criminal justice agencies this means that the power holder is recognized as possessing experience or knowledge that makes him or her qualified to exert power.

Hepburn (1985) studied each of these bases of power in the correctional environment in the 1980s. He administered questionnaires that included five items related to each type of power. Officers in five prisons in four different states were asked to indicate, by ranking these items, why inmates obey the correctional staff. In the same study, Hepburn collected background information on the officers, as well as their attitudes toward work and toward inmates. What he found was that the officers thought that inmates did what they otherwise would not do because of the legitimate and expert power of the officers. "Legitimate power was ranked first by over one-third of the guards, and three of every five guards ranked legitimate power as either the first or second most important reason why prisoners did what they were told" (Hepburn 1985: 291). The types of power were ranked as follows: legitimate, expert, referent, coercive, and reward. This ranking was relatively stable across the different institutions and states. Hepburn notes that Lombardo (1981) also found that 44 percent of the prison officers he interviewed attributed their base of power to legitimacy.

Hepburn did find that the more experience an officer had, the more likely he or she was to rank expert power as more important and coercion and legitimacy as less so. He found little effect for education, formal contact with inmates, or attitudes toward work. He also found that the higher the custody orientation of the officer, the more likely the officer was to see coercion as an important power base.

Hepburn (1985) explains these findings by drawing attention to the regular duties of correctional staff. On a day-to-day basis and in the context of the normal operation of the institution, officers give direction to inmates based on their legitimate role. Rarely do they need to give orders that are starkly coercive. Rare too are the rewards they can give for ordinary compliance with rules and requirements. Hence, there is little need for reliance on coercion or rewards as bases for power in the usual operation of institutions.

Moreover, the use of coercion on a day-to-day basis would be highly inefficient and disruptive in corrections work. If a correctional officer was continually having to use force or its threat, it would be very difficult to get through the day and hard feelings and resistance would accumulate among the inmates (experiment with the role exercise at the end of the chapter to see how this dynamic might play out). As an officer is usually outnumbered by at least 30 to 1 when out and about with inmates, he could easily be overpowered if the inmates were to choose to cooperate in such a maneuver. Calling for backup continually to get inmates to comply with basic rules would throw the whole institution into disarray and would not be positively viewed by coworkers or administration. The ability to supervise of an officer who makes frequent calls for backup will very quickly be called into question.

On the other hand, corrections work is inherently coercive inasmuch as those who are supervised or incarcerated rarely volunteered for this status. Instead, the state in the form of criminal justice actors like the police, prosecuting attorneys, and correctional workers uses the threat of or actual force to gain compliance (Hemmens and Atherton 1999). Yet it is curious that in the day-to-day relations with inmates, the officers do not perceive coercion as the reason for inmates' general compliance with institutional rules and directives. One wonders whether inmates would respond in a similar manner to the ranking of power bases by Hepburn. Would they mark "legitimacy" as the primary power base for correctional officers?

In policing, the use of force or coercive power has been the subject of much scholarly discussion and study (Alpert and Smith 1999; Crank 1998; Griffin and Bernard 2003; Kaminski et al. 2004; Terrill et al. 2003). In their discussion of the police use of extra-legal force, Griffin and Bernard (2003) argue for the salience of the angry aggression theory. They posit that officers who do not learn coping mechanisms to handle the multiple sources of stress that are inherent in police work (e.g., citizen hostility, danger) are physiologically aroused by this stress, which tends to lead to more fear of threats and eventual aggression. A feedback loop develops (as in systems theory) whereby this chronic physiological arousal leads to the perception of more threats, then to aggression and the development of an "authoritarian" personality, back to still more perceived threats and more aggression. Other related negative outcomes, which only serve to reinforce the perception of threats and the concomitant aggression, are social isolation and displaced aggression (Griffin and Bernard 2003).

Another angle to the discussion of power is the fact that some criminal justice employees feel relatively powerless in their jobs. For instance, in his research on prisons Lombardo (1989: 145) noted frequent job dissatisfaction among correctional staff because officers had a perceived "[i]nability to influence [their] work environment in an effective manner." He found that the most mentioned reason for this feeling was a "lack of support" by administrators, supervisors, and coworkers, who not only were not always helpful but also sometimes worked at cross-purposes with the officer. The officers thought that they were too often obliged to work short-handed; that administrators tended to resolve problems by focusing on short-term rather than on long-term solutions; that officers were not always backed up regarding inmate discipline; and that the behavior of other officers was at times "lax and non-cooperative." Griffin and Bernard (2003) also mention the helplessness that police officers feel vis-à-vis their inability to change aspects of their job, a condition that adds to their stress and ultimately, for some, leads to the abuse of coercive power.

Sometimes it is not just the criminal justice actor who feels powerless in the system. Smith (1997) notes that though 13 percent of the American population falls below the poverty line, less than 2 percent of lawyers do legal work for agencies representing the poor. Clearly this highly skewed distribution of legal resources has led to an imbalance of advantages when the poor are drawn into the criminal courts.

For workers however this sense of powerlessness is to some degree attached to the type of management theory practiced in particular institutions. If criminal justice workers had the opportunity to participate to a greater degree in decisions affecting their workplace, it is unlikely that they would feel so powerless.

CONCLUSIONS

Criminal justice work is composed of complex tasks requiring multiple skills and favoring those with certain propensities. The criminal justice organization has the opportunity to shape the outlook and habits of workers through both informal and formal socialization. The role such workers adopt is determined to a large extent by the emphasis that managers place on it. People generally will do what they are rewarded for. To the extent that a service or security or advocacy role for staff is acceptable to, and supported by, management, organizational members will recognize this fact and respond accordingly.

How criminal justice workers wield power is also shaped by the socialization process and the role the workers have adopted. Officers in Hepburn's study were quite clear in their belief that legitimacy, followed by expertise, constituted their main bases of power. The bureaucratic nature of the job and the inefficiency of force usage preclude the regular use of force to gain compliance. Thus almost by default, criminal justice workers are more likely to need human service role skills to maintain the daily routines of their work. Studies of power in police organization confirm that the organizational culture, along with stressors inherent to the job, can lead to the routinized abuse of power by officers.

KEY TERMS

anticipatory socialization: begins before the criminal justice worker starts the job. It occurs as the person anticipates someday working in law, police, or corrections.
authority: "[t]he right and power to enforce laws, exact obedience, command, determine, or judge" (American Heritage Dictionary 1992: 56).
charismatic authority: based on the personal charm and leadership qualities of the individual.
formal socialization: occurs when the worker is exposed to the legal or officially sanctioned requirements of the job.
informal socialization: the teaching and learning that take place on the job. It is outside the official strictures of law and procedure and occurs away from the officially recognized instructors.
legal authority: based in laws and rules that are generally accepted.
occupational socialization: "[t]he process by which a person acquires the values, attitudes, and behaviors of an ongoing occupational social system" (Klofas *et al.* 1990: 150).
power: the ability to get others to do what they otherwise wouldn't (Dahl 1957).

role: what you do on the job, be it officially outlined by statutorily defined tasks, position descriptions, and policies and procedural requirements, or unofficially defined by the actual work that is done and required.

role ambiguity: occurs when expectations for a role are not clear or are confusing.

role conflict: occurs when there are competing expectations for a role that are difficult to fulfill.

traditional authority: the power one holds in a position (e.g., as royalty or an elected head of state) or which is vested with a sense of tradition and history.

APPENDIX

Feel free to contact Mary Stohr to inquire about acquiring a digital version of this survey for research purposes:

THE CORRECTIONAL ROLE INSTRUMENT: JAIL RESEARCH DESCRIPTION SHEET

Dear Jail Staff Person:

This questionnaire was developed by Mary K. Stohr and Craig Hemmens, professors in the Department of Criminal Justice at Washington State University. WSU students are also assisting in this research. Information obtained from responses to the questionnaire will be kept COMPLETELY CONFIDENTIAL and PARTICIPATION IS COMPLETELY VOLUNTARY. No names should be mentioned on this questionnaire, and all responses will be combined by the research team so that it will be impossible to identify specific persons. We developed this questionnaire so that staff perceptions of jail roles might be better understood by people working in the field and by researchers. In essence, we are trying to determine what people think about their work in jails and why. We would really appreciate it if you would take the time to complete this questionnaire (it should take about 15 minutes).

You may keep this sheet for reference if you like. All responses to this questionnaire will be kept completely confidential and participation is voluntary. There is no reason to provide your name. Questionnaires should be returned directly to: _____. All responses will be grouped together in any report or publication produced using these data. Thanks so much for your participation.

SECTION ONE: Demographics

Please provide us with some general information about yourself.

1. Position:

2. Years of service:

3. Military service:
   Yes   No

4. Age:

5. Education (circle one)
    Less than GED
    GED
    High school graduate
    Some college
    BA or BS degree
    Master's degree or more

6. What is your current shift? (i.e., night, day, swing, other)

7. Did you choose your current shift?
    Yes   No

8. Gender:
    Male   Female

9. Race:
    White
    Black or African American
    Asian
    Other
    Multiracial

10. Ethnicity:
    Hispanic   Non-Hispanic

SECTION TWO: Jail Role Instrument

The role of jail staff presents many challenges and opportunities. This instrument was developed so that the various parts of that role might be identified by staff. Please read each question and using the agreement scale below, place the number that best reflects your level of agreement with the statement in the space provided in front of that question.

Scale (format for survey):

Strongly Disagree = 1
Disagree Slightly = 2
Slightly Disagree = 3
Neutral = 4
Slightly Agree = 5
Agree = 6
Strongly Agree = 7
Don't Know = 8

_____1. Jail staff should make an effort to answer the questions of inmates.

_____2. Jail staff should do what they can to make sure inmates have reasonable access to counselors.

_____3. Jail staff should ignore most inmate complaints.

_____4. Inmates should receive their store/commissary goods on time.

_____5. When an inmate doesn't get the correct medication, a staff member should contact medical staff.

_____6. Anyone who would visit an inmate is likely to be engaged in illegal activity.

_____7. Staff should ensure that inmates have the appropriate access to legal material they have a right to.

_____8. Ensuring that inmates have reasonable access to visitors is a responsibility of jail staff.

_____9. Using force is usually the best method to get inmates to follow orders.

_____10. Most inmates are trying to manipulate staff.

_____11. Explaining the reason for an order will usually gain inmate cooperation.

_____12. Inmate access to medical personnel should be limited to emergency situations.

_____13. When staff members make a mistake, they should admit it.

_____14. Promises made to inmates by staff are promises made to be broken.

_____15. Mail service should be regularly provided to inmates by staff.

_____16. Sometimes a little extra physical force is needed to let inmates know they can't get away with things.

_____17. Providing a set of written rules (dos and don'ts) to inmates at the beginning helps to avoid problems and misunderstandings later.

_____18. An inmate who fails at one task is likely to fail at another.

_____19. Helping inmates to find a suitable work situation is a responsibility of jail staff.

_____20. Inmate complaints are often just whining about nothing in particular.

_____21. Inmates usually choose to attend religious services, not because they have any faith, but so that they can appear to have changed.

_____22. Staff should assist inmates in gaining access to educational, drug/alcohol, and other programming.

_____23. It is part of the jail staff's job responsibilities to provide important information to inmates.

_____24. Staff should rarely have friendly conversations with inmates.

_____25. Use of physical force is not the easiest way to get an inmate to obey an order.

_____26. Staff should act how they want inmates to act.

_____27. It is okay if staff bend the rules every now and then, given that they have to supervise criminals.

_____28. Inmates often claim they are sick just to get out of school or work details.

_____29. When inmates succeed in jail, staff should be happy for them.

_____30. Jail staff should not guide or mentor inmates during their incarceration.

_____31. Staff are in part responsible for whether inmates "succeed" while incarcerated.

_____32. Female staff are as capable in working with inmates as male staff.

_____33. Inmates who complain about their medication are usually trying to get access to more drugs than they need.

_____34. Jail staff should have a voice in determining how their workplace operates.

_____35. Problem inmates can be more effectively handled when staff communicate and work as a team.

_____36. Female jail officers can carry out their duties just as well as male officers.

SECTION THREE: Additional Comments

Please feel free to provide additional information or to comment on all or part of this questionnaire in the space provided below or on the back of this sheet (or contact the researchers):

REFERENCES

Alpert, G. P. and Smith, M. R. (1999) Police use-of-force data: Where we are and where we should be going. *Police Quarterly*, 2: 57–78.

American Heritage Dictionary (1992) *American heritage dictionary*. New York, NY: Houghton Mifflin.

Barrier, G., Stohr, M. K., Hemmens, C. and Marsh, R. (1999) A practical user's guide to ethical practices: Idaho's method for implementing ethical behavior in a correctional setting. *Corrections Compendium*, 24: 1–12.

Belknap, J. (1995) Women in conflict: An analysis of women correctional officers. In B. R. Price and N. J. Sokoloff (eds), *The criminal justice system and women: Offenders, victims and workers*. New York, NY: McGraw Hill, pp. 195–227.

Benekos, P. and Merlo, A. V. (2001) Three strikes and you're out: The political sentencing game. In E. J. Latessa, A. Holsinger, J. W. Marquart and J. R. Sorensen (eds), *Correctional contexts: Contemporary and classical readings*. Los Angeles, LA: Roxbury, pp. 454–463.

Bennett, R. R. and Schmitt, E. L. (2002) The effect of work environment on levels of police cynicism: A comparative study. *Police Quarterly*, 5: 493–522.

Bradford, D. and Pynes, J. E. (2000) Police academy training: Why hasn't it kept up with practice? *Police Quarterly*, 2, 283–301.

Brody, D. C., DeMarco, C. and Lovrich, N. P. (2002) Community policing and job satisfaction: Suggestive evidence of positive workforce effects from a multijurisdictional comparison in Washington State. *Police Quarterly*, 5, 181–205.

Buerger, M. E., Petrosino, A. J. and Petrosino, C. (1999) Extending the police role: Implications of police mediation as a problem-solving tool. *Police Quarterly*, 2: 125–149.

Caeti, T., Hemmens, C., Cullen, F. T. and Burton, V. S., Jr. (2003) Management of juvenile correctional facilities. *The Prison Journal*, 83(4): 1–23.

California Employment Development Department. (2004) *Probation officers and parole agents*. Employment development department: Labor market information. Available at www.calmis.cahwnet.gov (last accessed January 31, 2013).

Camp, S. D., Saylor, W. G. and Wright, K. N. (2001) Research note, racial diversity of correctional workers and inmates: Organizational commitment, teamwork and workers' efficacy in prisons. *Justice Quarterly*, 18(2): 411–427.

CCA. (2013) Careers. Corrections Corporation of America website. Available at www.correctionscorp.com/training (last accessed January 31, 2013).

Clear, T. R. and Latessa, E. J. (1993) Probation officers' roles in intensive supervision: Surveillance versus treatment. *Justice Quarterly*, 10(3): 441–462.

Collins, P. A., Iannacchione, B. Hudson, M. Stohr, M. K. and Hemmens, C. (2012) A comparison of jail inmate and staff correctional goal orientations: Results from across the line. *Journal of Crime and Justice*, 36(1): 100–115.

Crank, J. P. (1996) The construction of meaning during training for probation and parole. *Justice Quarterly*, 13(2): 265–290.

Crank, J. P. (1998) *Understanding police culture*. Cincinnati, OH: Anderson Publishing.

Crouch, B. and Marquart, J. (1994) On becoming a prison guard. In S. Stojkovic, J. Klofas and D. Kalinich (eds), *The administration and management of criminal justice organizations: A book of readings*. Prospect Heights, IL: Waveland Press, pp. 301–331.

Cullen, F., Cullen, J. and Wozniak, J. (1988) Is rehabilitation dead? The myth of the punitive public. *Journal of Criminal Justice*, 16: 303–317.

Cullen, F. T. and Gilbert, K. E. (1982) *Reaffirming rehabilitation*. Cincinnati, OH: Anderson Publishing.

Dahl, R. (1957) The concept of power. *Behavioral Science*, 2(3): 201–215.

Daniello, R. J. (2011) *Police officer stress awareness and management: A handbook for practitioners*. Lanham, MD: Hamilton Books.

Delaware Department of Correction (2013) Probation and parole officer 1. Available at www.doc.delaware.gov/EDC/InitialTraining.shtml (last accessed January 31, 2013).

Farkas, M. A. (1999) Inmate supervisory style: Does gender make a difference? *Women and Criminal Justice*, 10: 25–46.

Flanagan, T. and Caulfield, S. (1984) Public opinion and prison policy: A review. *The Prison Journal*, 64: 31–46.

Ford, R. E. (2003) Saying one thing, meaning another: The role of parables in police training. *Police Quarterly*, 6, 84–110.

French, J. and Raven, B. (1959) The bases of social power. In D. Cartwright (ed.), *Studies in social power*. Ann Arbor, MI: University of Michigan, pp. 150–167.

Gordon, J. (1999) Do staff attitudes vary by position? A look at one juvenile correctional center. *American Journal of Criminal Justice*, 24(1): 81–93.

Griffin, M. L., Hogan, N. L. and Lambert, E. G. (2012) Doing "people work" in the prison setting: An examination of the job characteristics model and correctional staff burnout. *Criminal Justice & Behavior*, 39(9): 1131–1147.

Griffin, S. P. and Bernard, T. J. (2003) Angry aggression among police officers. *Police Quarterly*, 6: 3–21.

Haarr, R. (1997) Patterns of interaction in a police patrol bureau: Race and gender barriers to integration. *Justice Quarterly*, 14(1): 53–85.

Hemmens, C. and Atherton, E. (1999) *Use of force: Current practice and policy*. Lanham, MD: American Correctional Association.

Hemmens, C., Brody, D. C. and Spohn, C. (2010) *Criminal courts: A contemporary perspective*. Thousand Oaks, CA: Sage Publications.

Hemmens, C. and Stohr, M. K. (2000) The two faces of the correctional role: An exploration of the value of the correctional role instrument. *International Journal of Offender Therapy and Comparative Criminology*, 44(3): 326–349.

Hemmens, C. and Stohr, M. K. (2001) Correctional staff attitudes regarding the use of force in corrections. *Corrections Management Quarterly*, 5: 26–39.

Hemmens, C., Stohr, M. K., Schoeler, M. and Miller, B. (2002) One step up, two steps back: The progression of perceptions of women's work in prisons and jails. *Journal of Criminal Justice*, 30(6): 473–489.

Hepburn, J. R. (1985) The exercise of power in coercive organizations. In S. Stojkovic, J. Klofas and D. Kalinich (eds) (1990), *The administration and management of criminal justice organizations*. Prospect Heights, IL: Waveland Press, pp. 249–265.

Jacobs, M. D. (1990) *Screwing the system and making it work: Juvenile justice in the no-fault society*. Chicago, IL: University of Chicago Press.

Jenne, D. L. and Kersting, R. C. (1998) Gender, power, and reciprocity in the correctional setting. *The Prison Journal*, 78(2): 166–186.

Johnson, R. (1996) *Hard time: Understanding and reforming the prison*, 2nd edn. Belmont, CA: Wadsworth.

Jurik, N. (1985) Individual and organizational determinants of correctional officer attitudes toward inmates. *Criminology*, 23: 523–539.

Jurik, N. and Halemba, G. (1984) Gender, working conditions and the job satisfaction of women in a non-traditional occupation: Female correctional officers in men's prisons. *Sociological Quarterly*, 25: 551–566.

Kaminski, R. J., DiGiovanni, C. and Downs, R. (2004) The use of force between the police and persons with impaired judgment. *Police Quarterly*, 7: 311–338.

Katz, D. and Kahn, D. (1978) *The social psychology of organizations*, 2nd edn. New York, NY: Wiley.

Kifer, M., Hemmens, C. and Stohr, M. K. (2003) The goals of corrections: Perspectives from the line. *Criminal Justice Review*, 28(1): 47–69.

King Davis, R., Applegate, B., Otto, C., Surette, R. and McCarthy, B. (2004) Roles and responsibilities: Analyzing local leaders' views on jail crowding from a systems perspective. *Crime and Delinquency*, 50(3): 458–482.

Klofas, J., Stojkovic, S. and Kalinich, D. (1990) *Criminal justice organizations administration and management*. Pacific Grove, CA: Brooks/Cole.

Lawrence, R. and Mahan, S. (1998) Women correctional officers in men's prisons: Acceptance and perceived job performance. *Women and Criminal Justice*, 9: 63–86.

Lipsky, M. (1980) *Street-level bureaucracy: Dilemmas of the individual in public services*. New York, NY: Russell Sage Foundation.

Lombardo, L. X. (1981) *Guards imprisoned: Correctional officers at work*. New York, NY: Elsevier.

Lombardo, L. X. (1989) *Guards imprisoned: Correctional officers at work*, 2nd edn. Cincinnati, OH: Anderson Publishing.

Lutze, F. E. and Murphy, D. W. (1999) Ultramasculine prison environments and inmates' adjustment: It's time to move beyond the 'boys will be boys' paradigm. *Justice Quarterly*, 16: 709–734.

Maahs, J. and Pratt, T. (2001) Uncovering the predictors of correctional officers' attitudes and behaviors: A meta-analysis. *Correctional Management Quarterly*, 5(2), 13–19.

Maguire, K. and Pastore, A. L. (eds) (2004) *Sourcebook of criminal justice statistics*. Available at www.albany.edu/sourcebook.

Martin, S. E. (1990) *On the move: The status of women in policing*. Washington DC: Police Foundation.

McCorkle, R. (1993) Research note: Punish and rehabilitate? Public attitudes toward six common crimes. *Crime and Delinquency*, 39: 240–252.

MCJA. (2013) Basic corrections training program. Maine Criminal Justice Academy website. Available at www.state.me.us/dps/mcja/training (last accessed January 31, 2013).

Meyer, J. and Grant, D. R. (2003) *The courts in our criminal justice system*. Upper Saddle River, NJ: Prentice Hall.

Moak, S. and Wallace, L. (2000) Attitudes of Louisiana practitioners toward rehabilitation of juvenile offenders. *American Journal of Criminal Justice*, 24(2): 272–284.

Mobile Alabama Police Department. Training information. Available at http://www.mobilepd.org/training.php (last accessed January 31, 2013).

Moon, M., Sundt, J., Cullen, F. and Wright, J. P. (2000) Is child saving dead? Public support for juvenile rehabilitation. *Crime and Delinquency*, 46(1): 38–60.

Morash, M. and Haarr, R. N. (2012) Doing, redoing, and undoing gender variation in gender identities of women working as police officers. *Feminist Criminology*, 7(1), 2–23.

Morash, M. and Haarr, R. N. (1995) Gender, workplace problems, and stress in policing. *Justice Quarterly*, 12: 113–140.

Nevada Department of Public Safety. (2004) Officer training. Available at http://dps.gov/pandp/training. htm (last accessed January 31, 2013).

Norman, M. and Burbridge, G. (1991) Attitudes of youth corrections professionals toward juvenile justice reform and policy alternatives—A Utah survey. *Journal of Criminal Justice*, 19: 81–91.

Pogrebin, M. R. and Poole, E. D. (1997) Women deputies and jail work. *Journal of Contemporary Criminal Justice*, 14: 117–134.

Pollock, J. M. (2004) *Prisons and prison life: Costs and consequences.* Los Angeles, CA: Roxbury.

Purkiss, M., Kifer, M., Hemmens, C. and Burton, V. S. (2003) Probation officer functions—A statutory analysis. *Federal Probation*, 67(1): 12–33.

Reddington, F. P. and Kreisel, B. W. (2003) The basic fundamental skills training for juvenile probation officers—Results of a nationwide survey of curriculum content. *Federal Probation*, 67(1): 41–46.

Rothman, D. J. (1980) *Conscience and convenience: The asylum and its alternatives in progressive America.* Boston, MA: Little, Brown.

Seiter, R. P. (2002) Prisoner reentry and the role of parole officers. *Federal Probation*, 66(3): 50–55.

Smith, C. E. (1997) *Courts, politics, and the judicial process*, 2nd edn. Chicago, IL: Nelson-Hall.

Southerland, M. D. (2002) Presidential address: Criminal justice curricula in the United States: A decade of change. *Justice Quarterly*, 19(4): 589–601.

Stohr, M. K., Hemmens, C., Marsh, R. L., Barrier, G. and Palhegyi, D. (2000) Can't scale this: The ethical parameters of correctional work. *The Prison Journal*, 80(1): 40–56.

Stohr, M. K., Hemmens, C., Collins, P. A., Iannacchione, B. and Hudson, M. (2012) Assessing the organizational culture in a jail setting. *The Prison Journal*, 92(3): 358–387.

Sun, I. Y. (2003) A comparison of police field training officers' and non-training officers' conflict resolution styles: Controlling versus supportive strategies. *Police Quarterly*, 6: 22–50.

Sykes, G. (1958) *The society of captives.* Princeton, NJ: Princeton University Press.

Terrill, W., Alpert, G. P., Dunham, R. G. and Smith, M. R. (2003) A management tool for evaluating police use of force: An application of the force factor. *Police Quarterly*, 6: 150–171.

Thibault, E. A., Lynch, L. M. and McBride, R. B. (2004) *Proactive police management*, 6th edn. Upper Saddle River, NJ: Prentice Hall.

Toch, H. (1978) Is a correctional officer, by any other name, a screw? *Criminal Justice Review*, 2: 19–35.

Toch, H. and Klofas, J. (1982) Alienation and desire for job enrichment among correctional officers. *Federal Probation*, 46: 35–44.

Tulsa Oklahoma Police Department. Training information. Available at https://www.tulsapolice.org/ join-tpd/faq-recruiting.aspx#How long academy (last accessed January 31, 2013).

Van Voorhis, P., Cullen, F. T., Link, B. G. and Wolfe, N. T. (1991) The impact of race and gender on correctional officers' orientation to the integrated environment. *Journal of Research in Crime and Delinquency*, 28: 472–500.

Weber, M. (1947) The theory of social and economic organization. New York, NY: The Free Press.

Zimmerman, S., Van Alstyne, D. and Dunn, C. (1988) The national punishment survey and public policy consequences. *Journal of Research in Crime and Delinquency*, 25: 120–149.

Zupan, L. L. (1986) Gender-related differences in correctional officers' perceptions and attitudes. *Journal of Criminal Justice*, 14: 349–361.

DISCUSSION QUESTIONS

1   Do you believe that criminal justice employees with college degrees are less likely to experience role conflict?

2   Sometimes troubled criminal justice organizations need a culture change to conform to professional standards and expectations. Can organizational socialization be a catalyst for culture change?

RETHINKING FIVE BELIEFS THAT ERODE WORKPLACE MOTIVATION

SUSAN FOWLER

Motivation is one of the most vital and essential aspects of leadership and one of the most confused and misunderstood. The result of this confusion and misunderstanding is leaders who have become blind to what does and doesn't work. They engage in counterproductive behaviors believing they are doing the right thing. Leaders are so immersed in five motivation-eroding beliefs that they find it difficult to hear, see, or do something different.

Research over the past sixty years continues to prove the point. Individuals' rankings of workplace motivators are compared to rankings of what their managers think motivates them. The results reflect how most individuals feel: managers simply do not know what motivates their people. Managers tend to attribute external motivation to employees (actions not within the employees' control)—such as good wages, promotions, and job security. On the other hand, employees prefer more internal motivation (actions within the employees' control)—such as interesting work, growth, and learning.[1]

Why the big disconnect? One reason is that leaders do not have access to someone else's internal state of motivation, only their own. That probably explains why managers tend to attribute internal motivations to themselves at the same time they judge others to be externally motivated. However, when it comes to their employees, leaders depend on their observations of external behaviors and conditions to evaluate their employees' motivation. Unfortunately, many leaders are not perceptive observers, nor are they wise interpreters of what they see. It is nearly impossible for a leader to understand others' internal state of motivation by observing their external behavior. (This is another good reason why conducting motivational outlook conversations is so important.)

To make it more confounding, different people can internalize the same conditions differently. For example, in a team meeting where all the members are asked to share personal information, you will find all six motivational outlooks being played out. The leader needs to find ways of shaping the request and the environment so that people might choose an optimal, rather than a suboptimal, motivational outlook.

Research suggests that another reason for the disconnect in the ranking of motivators between employees and their managers is that employees don't understand the true nature of their own motivation. For example, an employee who feels trapped in her job, feels she is being taken advantage of, or feels overwhelmed by what is being asked of her may ask for more money. Under her breath, she is saying, "They don't pay me enough to put up with this." What she doesn't understand is that there will never be enough money to make up for the void created when her psychological needs for autonomy, relatedness, and competence are not satisfied. People can't ask for what they don't know they need.

When leaders and their employees attribute their workplace dissatisfaction to money or external factors, it sets up a series of erroneous assumptions and detrimental actions. First, even though people need and want money and external rewards, believing those will make them happy distracts them from what actually does make them happy. Second, it lets leaders, who typically don't have direct control over pay raises and rewards, off the motivational hook. They throw their arms up in a leadership mea culpa and declare there's nothing they can do. Leaders may also use their lack of control over salaries and benefits as an excuse to avoid dealing with people's emotionally charged discontent. Third, when people use external motivators as the reason for their dissatisfaction in the workplace, it perpetuates outdated beliefs that lead to ineffective motivational leadership.

The primary purpose of this chapter is to explore the third phenomenon—how your unexplored leadership beliefs could be influencing, and maybe even sabotaging, your approach to motivation.

Dr. David Facer began researching leaders' beliefs about what motivates employees because he sees motivation as not only an employee well-being issue but also a strategic one. "The innovation that leaders, especially senior leaders, ask from employees to make the firm more competitive and valuable is the result of a delicate creative process. I am endlessly curious how leaders explain the mixed outcomes that their pressure and the standard incentive programs generate. Go listen to employees talking at Starbucks. As plain as day they're telling us they want a different approach."

A different, long-term approach will require a belief change, David says, but leaders are seldom asked to examine their beliefs. To make that examination easier, he created and validated the Motivation Beliefs Inventory, a short survey that consultants and executive coaches can use to help leaders consciously examine their motivation beliefs—and try on new ones. David is convinced that too many leaders do not understand how their underlying motivational beliefs shape the problems they face. He says, "The negative evidence is too compelling to ignore.

Employees are craving fresh approaches to motivation that make it much easier for them to rise to the innovation challenge."[2]

Consider these unfinished belief statements. How would you fill in the blanks?

1. It's not personal; it's just _____.

2. The purpose of business is to _____.

3. Leaders are in a position of _____.

4. The only thing that really matters is _____.

5. If you cannot measure it, it _____.

These are particularly sticky beliefs that erode workplace motivation. Have you thought about where these common beliefs come from? They are so entrenched in organizational consciousness that we accept them without question. I have yet to find a leader who couldn't complete most, if not all, of the belief statements. This poses a potential problem. Unexplored beliefs become the foundation for programmed values. Then these programmed values become the basis for rules, processes, procedures, actions, and your leadership behaviors.

Your mission, should you choose to accept it, is to explore these workplace beliefs and examine how they tend to undermine your people's optimal motivation and then consider alternative beliefs and best practices. I encourage you to shine a light on potentially unexamined values in the spirit of developing more meaningful motivational leadership values.

RETHINK THE FIRST ERODING BELIEF: IT'S NOT PERSONAL; IT'S JUST BUSINESS

Employees probably spend more of their waking hours connected to work and interacting with their coworkers than with family members. Yet managers believe their actions are not personal and just business.

Every day you deliver information, feedback, or news to those you lead that affects their work, livelihood, opportunities, status, income, mood, health, or well-being. How is this not personal?

Whatever your beliefs, one thing is true: what you say and do *feels* personal to the people you lead! Therein lies the issue: *feelings*. Earlier in this book we explored the issue of the f-word in organizations. Do you believe that ex pressing feelings does not belong in the workplace? If so, challenge yourself by asking, How did this belief become so commonly held? Where did *my* belief come from?

One possibility why feelings are discouraged in the workplace is that managers do not have the skill to effectively deal with them. True, some employees do not self-regulate well and may let their emotions get the best of them from time to time. But the fear of unruly emotions is disproportionate to the occurrence and severity of emotional outbreaks.

What if you changed the belief that it's not personal, it's just business to one more likely to activate optimal motivation? *If it is business, it is personal.*

Try embracing the idea that all emotions are acceptable but not all behavior is acceptable. Notice, acknowledge, and deal with a person's emotions. Practice self-regulation by listening to your heart and acknowledging the crucial role that feelings play in your work and life.

Consider letting go of leadership practices that undermine people's psychological needs and adopt best practices that encourage them. As your beliefs change, watch how your leadership practices change—and how your people respond.[3]

WHAT DOESN'T WORK	WHAT DOES WORK
Think to yourself or tell a person directly, "You shouldn't feel that way."	Acknowledge and validate people's feelings and emotions.
Be judgmental and make approval conditional.	Offer pure or descriptive feedback rather than evaluative feedback or personalized praising.
Tolerate sabotaging actions or unacceptable patterns of behavior.	Facilitate the Generation of options and ask open-ended questions to promote mindfulness.

RETHINK THE SECOND ERODING BELIEF: THE PURPOSE OF BUSINESS IS TO MAKE MONEY

When you hold the belief that making money is the purpose of business, you are likely to focus on dashboard metrics instead of focusing on the people responsible for providing quality service to your customers and clients. You are apt to overemphasize results and resort to pressuring people to get those results. You may be tempted to employ questionable ethical practices. When given a choice, you might choose quantity over quality, short-term results over long-term results, and profits over people.

Consider how an alternative belief would generate a different approach to your leadership. How would your decisions and actions be different if they were based on the following belief: *The purpose of business is to serve.*

Think how this reframed belief might alter your organization's dashboard metrics—or at least the content and quality of the goals. How might reframing the goals so they focus on internal as well as external service, the quality of people's efforts as well as the results of their efforts, or learning and growth in addition to accomplishments change the way you lead day to day?

Hard-nosed businesspeople will push back on these ideas with a traditional argument: "You can serve all you want, but this soft stuff doesn't make you money, and if you don't make a profit, you will go out of business. Then you won't be serving anyone."

Yes, a business must make a profit to sustain itself. But it is an illogical leap to conclude that profit is therefore the purpose of business. You need air to live, plus water and food. But the purpose of your life is not to just breathe, drink, and eat. Your purpose is richer and more profound than basic survival. The more noble your purpose and developed your values are, the more they influence *how* you live day to day.

> *The nature of human motivation is not about making money. The nature of human motivation is in making meaning.*

Making a profit or serving your people who serve your customers is never an either-or decision. It is always both. But service comes before profit. To paraphrase what I have often heard Ken Blanchard proclaim, "Profit is the applause you get from creating an optimally motivating environment for your people so they want to take care of your customers." Definitive evidence shows that organizational vitality measured by return on investment, earnings by share, access to venture capital, stock price, debt load, and other financial indicators is dependent on two factors: employee work passion and customer devotion. It does not work the other way around—organizational vitality is *not* what determines customer devotion or employee work passion.[4]

When you focus on satisfying your employees' psychological needs so they can serve customers' needs, your organization prospers. An old sports analogy works equally well in business: focusing on profit is like playing the game with your eye on the scoreboard instead of the ball.

Challenge the belief that the purpose of business is to make money, and consider an optimal motivation belief: *the purpose of business is to serve—both your people and your customers. Profit is a by-product of doing both of these well.*

Watch how your people respond to your changed belief. When you believe that the purpose of business is to *serve*, you lead differently. Your decisions and actions are more likely to cultivate a workplace that supports people's optimal motivation. Then notice the results and accept the well-earned applause in the form of organizational vitality. Keep that in mind as you avoid practices that undermine people's psychological needs and adopt best practices to encourage them.[5]

WHAT DOESN'T WORK	WHAT DOES WORK
Drive profit at the expense of people.	Help individuals align to work-related values and a sense of purpose. Frame actions in terms of the welfare of the whole.
Delay skill-related feedback or punish lack of competence.	Provide an honest assessment of skills and training needs.
See people as tireless machines.	Clear time for inherently motivating projects.

RETHINK THE THIRD ERODING BELIEF: LEADERS ARE IN A POSITION OF POWER

Imagine you work for a large organization. You catch the elevator to another floor and notice someone is already in it—the company's CEO. You have never met him, but you recognize him from company-wide meetings. Your heart might race a bit. You might think twice before you speak. You might feel excited at the opportunity to make his acquaintance, or you might feel worried about making a bad impression. Suffice it to say, if he was someone of lesser stature or if you hadn't recognized him as the CEO, the dynamic would be different.

"Managers need to be incredibly mindful and clear about the types of power they have and use. Most leaders will be surprised by the potentially negative emotional impact that results from having and using their power, in almost all its forms." These are the words of Dr. Drea Zigarmi, who found himself surprised by the strength of his own research on how a leader's power affects people's motivational outlooks.[6] Even when you don't have intentions to use your power, just having it creates a dynamic that requires your awareness and sensitivity.

Drea and his colleagues studied the use of power by leaders in the workplace. You might find it helpful to consider the most commonly used types of power described below and the potential effect each one has on your people's emotional well-being, intentions, and motivational outlooks. What you discover might surprise you.

- *Reward power* is your power to promise monetary or non-monetary compensation. There are two types of reward power:

    - *Impersonal reward power* is the power to grant special benefits, promotions, or favorable considerations.

    - *Personal reward power* is the power you have when your employees' feelings depend on being accepted, valued, and liked by you.

Employees report that when they perceive either form of reward power at work, they experience a suboptimal motivational outlook.

- *Coercive power* is your power to use threats and punishment if people fail to conform to desired outcomes. Understandably, the use of coercive power usually results in a negative relationship between leader and follower—and a suboptimal motivational outlook. Leaders often see coercive power as the easiest, most expedient, and most justifiable form of power. Truly the junk food of power, coercive power creates a workplace where people need to consciously exercise high-quality self-regulation to avoid a suboptimal motivational outlook.

- *Referent power* is based on how your employees identify with you. Ironically, you may enjoy certain work relationships because your employees' self-identity is enhanced through interaction with you, their actions are based on their desire to be similar to and associated with you, or they think so highly of you that they are afraid to disagree with you. It might surprise you to discover that when employees report that their managers have referent power, they also report experiencing a suboptimal motivational outlook.

Their dependence on you for their internal state of well-being tends to undermine their autonomy, relatedness, and competence.

- *Legitimate power* is bestowed through a position or title that gives a leader the justifiable right to request compliance from another individual. Having legitimate power is a blessing and a curse. With it, you can do more good, but, as Spider-Man will tell you, "With great power comes great responsibility." You must be sensitive to how others perceive and integrate your legitimate power, lest, despite your good intentions, people interpret your power as diminishing their experience of ARC. Often referred to as *position power*, legitimate power is manifest in a variety of forms.

  - *Reciprocity* is the power stemming from your employees feeling obligated to comply with your requests because you have done something positive for them.

  - *Equity power*, thought of as quid pro quo, is the power you have when an employee senses that you expect some type of compensation for the work or the effort you have put into the relationship.

  - *Dependence power* is the power you have when your employees feel obliged to assist you because you're in need—not out of a sense of relatedness but from an imposed sense of social responsibility.

- *Expert power* is power that comes through your depth and breadth of knowledge. Expert power relies on the perceptions your employees hold regarding your superior knowledge.

- *Information power* relies on your employees' perception on how you present persuasive material or logic.

Even these last two types of power can result in employees reporting a suboptimal motivational outlook when they feel manipulated, threatened, or overwhelmed by your expertise or use of information (knowledge or power).

The bottom line is that power undermines people's psychological needs. It's not just your use of the power; it's people's perception that you *have it* and *could use it*. Your power demands that people need to exert more energy self-regulating to internalize a workplace where they experience autonomy, relatedness, and competence. As Drea puts it, "Power is very precious stuff. It entices the leader into flights of self-delusion and separateness from those they lead."[7]

If you are the CEO riding the elevator, by virtue of your title and assumed power, you are not wielding power, but *having* power changes the dynamic between you and the people you lead. So what is a leader to do?

When Dr. Ken Blanchard was elected class president in the seventh grade, his father congratulated him and then told him, "Now that you have power, don't ever use it. Great leaders are great because people trust and respect them, not because they have power." Theodore Blanchard was an admiral in the navy who told Ken that anyone who thinks that military-style leadership is my-way-or-the-highway leadership has never gone to battle. According to Admiral Blanchard, "If leaders acted like that, your men would shoot you before the enemy could."

You can use all your power attempting to motivate people, but it won't work if you want them to experience an optimal motivational outlook. Shifting to an optimal motivational outlook is something people can do only for themselves. But the workplace you create has an enormous influence on how likely—or challenging—it is for people to self-regulate, satisfy their psychological needs for ARC, and experience optimal motivation.

We need to change the belief that leaders are in a position of power. Consider the difference with an optimal motivation belief. *Leaders are in a position of creating a workplace where people are more likely to satisfy their psychological needs for ARC.*

When you avoid undermining practices and adopt best practices, you focus your power on cultivating a workplace where your people, your organization, and you are reaping the rewards of optimal motivation.[8]

WHAT DOESN'T WORK	WHAT DOES WORK
Apply pressure and demand accountability.	Invite choice. Explore options within boundaries.
Rely on your position or coercive power.	Explore individuals' natural interest in and enthusiasm for the goal.
Withhold or hide your reasoning behind decisions.	Provide a rationale and share information. Discuss your intentions openly.

RETHINK THE FOURTH ERODING BELIEF: THE ONLY THING THAT REALLY MATTERS IS RESULTS

At a recent speaking engagement, I asked, "How would you finish this statement: The only thing that really matters in business is *blank*?" The answer was so obvious that over three hundred people spontaneously filled in the blank by yelling in unison, "Results!"

I then asked them to consider the effect this tyranny of results has on the workplace. It was not easy. Leaders tend to tune out as soon as you mess with results. Executives cannot imagine what matters at the end of the day besides results measured by dashboard metrics. I'm asking you what I asked of them—to consider three alternatives to the traditional results focus.

OPTION 1: REDEFINE AND REFRAME RESULTS

People want to achieve organizational metrics and assigned goals (when they are fair and agreed upon), but often internalize them as external or imposed. You can help people shift to an aligned motivational outlook by clarifying the underlying values behind your dashboard metrics. People may even shift to an integrated motivational outlook when metrics are authentically positioned as a means to fulfilling a noble purpose.

When Express Employment Professionals announced sales goals at a recent conference of franchise owners, the leaders reminded the attendees that the purpose of their business is to put a million people to work. The energy generated was electric! When Berrett-Koehler, my publisher, puts out its catalog of offerings to buyers, the cover's primary message is "A community dedicated to creating a world that works for all." My experience has been that every goal, metric, and decision pursued at Berrett-Koehler has that purpose at heart. When I received a detailed production schedule, I no longer perceived deadlines as imposed "dreadlines" but rather as helpful guidelines enabling each of us to do our part. This is my sixth book but my first with Berrett-Koehler. I have never been as optimally motivated to meet deadlines!

Framing results differently and trusting that individuals will still achieve necessary metrics will help people shift their motivational outlook.

OPTION 2: SET HIGH-QUALITY GOALS

Research shows that leaders need to help their people avoid potentially external goals such as

- Social recognition, such as increasing the number of friends or contacts to improve social or professional status
- Image and appearance, such as losing weight to look good at a reunion or to be more attractive
- Material success, such as earning more money, buying a luxury car, or moving to a prestigious neighborhood[9]

Instead, leaders need to help individuals set goals that promote more optimal motivational outlooks, including

- Personal growth, such as improving listening skills or practicing mindfulness
- Affiliation, such as nurturing a mentoring relationship or enhancing working relationships with others
- Community, such as contributing to something bigger than yourself, or making a difference
- Physical health, such as losing weight as a means for increasing energy or changing your eating habits as a way of lowering blood pressure[10]

There is a real and meaningful difference between these two goals:

- If you eat well, you are more likely to be physically appealing and look younger at a later age.
- If you eat well, you are more likely to be fit and remain healthy at a later age.

Applied to a business setting, consider the real and meaningful difference in the expression of these two goals:

- If you make your numbers, you are more likely to be in the President's Club and qualify for the reward trip.
- If you make your numbers, you are more likely to be solving your clients' problems and making a difference.

Individuals will benefit from higher-quality goals. Setting such goals is also a way to shift from results to meaningful results.

The quality of goals your people set determines the quality of their experience. The values behind the goal determine the value of the goal.

OPTION 3: DO NOT IMPLY THAT ENDS JUSTIFY THE MEANS

If you believe results are what really matter without considering *why* those results are meaningful and *how* people go about achieving them, you are in essence saying the ends justify the means. What a sorry picture this paints. We do not need the science of motivation to prove that means matter. We witness the scandals and horror stories of people, organizations, industries, and countries who prize ends over means every day in the news.

A graphic illustration is captured in the Academy Award–nominated 2005 documentary *Enron: The Smartest Guys in the Room*. You could read the book upon which it is based, but then you wouldn't hear the unnerving taped conversations between giddy energy brokers celebrating as California is ravaged by fires and people are losing everything they own—and their lives. The brokers knew the fires would spark higher energy demands and prices, ensuring the results for which they were being held accountable.

Enron is considered one of the ugliest business scandals in American history. But it is more disturbing as an example of what happens when people prize results more than the means to achieve them. You ache for those who suffered at the hands of the energy brokers but also for the brokers themselves who were addicted to motivational junk food so unhealthy it poisoned their morals. The brokers have responsibility for their own actions, which is why I think every individual should learn the skill of optimal motivation. However, the leaders were also responsible for creating a culture based on beliefs that eroded autonomy, relatedness, and competence—and led to inhumane behavior.

A focus on results may yield short-term gains. However, those gains are at risk and compromised when people feel pressure instead of autonomy, disconnection instead of relatedness, and a sense of being used without a sense of the competence they have gained.

The evidence is clear: people *can* achieve the results you want, even if their psychological needs are thwarted in the process. But their negative energy and lack of well-being make it rare for them to sustain or repeat those results—let alone exceed them.

Reframe the belief that the only thing that matters is results. Consider an optimal motivation belief instead. *In the end, what really matters is not just the results people achieve but why and how people achieve them.*

Observe the shift in people's energy—and your own—when you focus on what really matters in the workplace. Focus on *meaningful* results that satisfy people's psychological needs for optimal motivation. Then trust that the numbers will add up.[11]

WHAT DOESN'T WORK	WHAT DOES WORK
Impose goals and deadlines.	Present goals and timelines as valuable information necessary for accomplishing agreed-upon outcomes. Help individuals reframe goals so they are meaningful to them while still achieving the outcomes required.
Focus on the needs of the organization without equal attention to the needs of the individuals you lead.	Provide individuals the appropriate direction and support needed for their level of development.
Evaluate output while ignoring effort.	Explore alternatives for stimulating implementation strategies.

RETHINK THE FIFTH ERODING BELIEF: IF YOU CANNOT MEASURE IT, IT DOESN'T MATTER

I was a longtime aficionado of SMART goal setting when the *M* stood for *Measurable*. However, over time, I found that a specific, measurable, attainable, relevant, and time-bound goal simply was not SMART enough. I changed the *M* to *Motivating* and moved *measurable* into the *S* (*Specific*). Adding another dimension to make my goals more emotionally compelling worked for me. It seemed to work for others, too. Now the science of motivation explains why.

THE NATURE OF THINGS THAT CANNOT BE MEASURED

Setting measurable goals and outcomes is important. Having a defined finish line in front of you can be positively compelling. Previously, I encouraged leaders and individuals to ensure a higher level of results by reframing *measurable* goals into *meaningful* goals. However, we need to move beyond SMART goal setting and embrace aspects of work that are not easily measured.

Case in point: if you are a parent, you probably have SMART goals for your child's education and acquisition of skills. But how would you answer this question: What do you most hope for your child? Most parents tell me they hope their children experience meaningful relationships, enjoy a profound connection to the world, contribute to society, give and receive love, fulfill a noble purpose, are passionate about their work, discover what makes them happy, feel safe and secure, perceive they have choices, and are able to navigate and master the world around them.

The dreams parents most hope for their children cannot be easily measured. I find the same phenomenon happens when I ask leaders what they most hope for their people at work. They may use different terms, but what they want for their people is a positive sense of well-being. At the heart of what leaders hope for their people is the satisfaction of their psychological needs for autonomy, relatedness, and competence. Despite the deep knowledge that what they really want for people are the benefits that come through these emotionally compelling aspects of work, leaders still continue to focus attention on what they can easily measure.

> As in life, the most rewarding aspects of work are those most difficult to measure.

If you believe the statement "If you cannot measure it, it does not matter," ask yourself why. Is dealing with the emotional nature of things not easily measured outside your comfort zone? Do you believe your job is to control circumstances and it is difficult to control something that's not easily measured?

SOME THINGS ARE BEST LEFT UNMEASURED

One of life's great joys is eating in Italy. Ask anyone who has traveled there—food tastes better in Italy. I had the profound experience of attending a weeklong cooking course in Tuscany. I say "profound" because it literally changed the quality of my life—not just my cooking but also my perspective on day-to-day living. The chef refused to provide exact measurements for anything he made. "How can I tell you how much water to put in the pasta dough? It depends on the quality of your flour and the kind of day—the temperature, the humidity. You must add some water and oil until it feels right." He was also hesitant to commit to a menu or plan for the week. If the zucchini flowers were blossoming, we would have fried squash blossoms; if not, then the ripe tomatoes would become the center-piece of a Caprese salad. The chef was really teaching us mindfulness—to be present in the moment, to notice the world around us and be aware of our many options and choices. The food becomes a possibility for something profound. And people can taste the difference.

Reframe the belief that if you cannot measure it, it is not important. Put an optimal motivation belief into practice instead. *If you cannot measure it, it is probably really, really important.*

Of course, we need to measure many things in life and work. Pastries are a science where measuring makes the difference between a fluffy cupcake and a hockey puck. But a true growth step for leaders is to become more mindful of promoting dreams, ideals, and experiences that cannot be easily measured. That includes becoming more comfortable with feelings. If leaders rule out people's emotional nature at work—including their own—because they are not mindful or skilled enough to cope, we all lose what it means to be fully human. That is too high a price to pay for being comfortable. Observe the shift in energy when you focus your leadership on promoting what cannot be easily measured—such as love, joy, and gratitude. Your people will eat it up.

Challenge your own comfort zone as you lead with best practices that encourage people's psychological needs.[12]

WHAT DOESN'T WORK	WHAT DOES WORK
Overemphasize metrics and competition.	Explore individuals' natural interest in and enthusiasm for the goal.
Underestimate learning. Continually delay or cancel learning and development opportunities and training programs.	Emphasize learning goals, not just performance goals.
Make mistakes a mistake.	Encourage self-reflection and growth. Legitimize mistakes as part of the learning process.

RECAPPING "RETHINKING FIVE BELIEFS THAT ERODE WORKPLACE MOTIVATION"

What has become clear to you about why motivating people doesn't work and what does? My hope is that you are willing to challenge your beliefs, and the values built upon those beliefs, when it comes to motivation.

Do your underlying beliefs and values promote or erode optimal motivation in the workplace?

Not all beliefs are values, but all values are beliefs. The quality of your beliefs determines the quality of your leadership values. Your leadership values ultimately determine how you lead and the quality of the workplace you create.

NOTES

1 Kovach, "Why Motivational Theories Don't Work"; and Facer et al. "Motivation Beliefs Inventory."

2 Facer et al., "Motivation Beliefs Inventory."

3 Optimal Motivation by Susan Fowler, David Facer, and Drea Zigarmi.

4 Zigarmi et al., *Leadership-Profit Chain*.

5 Optimal Motivation by Susan Fowler, David Facer, and Drea Zigarmi.

6 Interview with Dr. Drea Zigarm, February 2014.

7 Ibid.

8 Optimal Motivation by Susan Fowler, David Facer, and Drea Zigarmi.

9 Sheldon et al. "Effects of Goal Contents and Motives."

10 Ibid.

11 Optimal Motivation by Susan Fowler, David Facer, and Drea Zigarmi.

12 Ibid.

BIBLIOGRAPHY

Facer, D. C., Jr., F. Galloway, N. Inoue, and D. Zigarmi. "Creation and Initial Validation of the Motivation Beliefs Inventory: Measuring Leaders' Beliefs about Employee Motivation Using Four Motivation Theories." *Journal of Business Administration Research* 3, no. 1 (2014): 1–18. http://www.sciedu.ca/journal/index.php/jbar/article/view/3905.

Kovach, Kenneth. A. "Why Motivational Theories Don't Work." *Society for Advancement of Management* 45, no. 2 (Spring 1980): 54–59.

Sheldon, Kennon, Richard M. Ryan, Edward L. Deci, and Tim Kasser. "The Independent Effects of Goal Contents and Motives on Well-Being: It's Both What You Pursue and Why You Pursue It." *Personality and Social Psychology Bulletin* 30, no. 4 (April 2004): 475–486.

DISCUSSION QUESTIONS

1. Though the author discusses the idea of "motivational junk food," she does so without an explicit definition of it. How would you define the term and explain why it can be harmful to an employee's motivation?

2. ARC refers to autonomy, relatedness, and competence. Discuss how each one of these concepts can be applied as a motivational tool in a criminal justice setting.

SECTION IV CONCLUSION

Organizational culture and socialization are different yet related concepts. They differ in that culture refers to what employees need to learn, and socialization pertains to how they learn it. As you progress in your career and advance to positions of leadership, you might be tasked with changing the culture of a troubled organization. Why is this important? Renowned management consultant, author, and professor Peter Drucker once said, "Culture eats strategy for breakfast." In other words, you could have the best business plan in the world, but if you do not have employees who identify with it, believe in it, and value it, then it will go nowhere. Think of culture as rigid and tenacious. This beast must be tamed first, because strategic plans come and go. Understanding the interplay between organizational culture and socialization is a necessary first step to reform.

Here are some final thoughts on employee *motivation*. Try this trick: replace the word motivation with *enthusiasm*. The word *motivation* itself sounds somewhat dry, clinical, and dull. But *enthusiasm* evokes eagerness, passion, and excitement. Next, think about the last time you were at work and felt enthusiastic—not just ready and willing to do your job, but carrying it out with gusto, curiosity, and attention. Ask yourself what made you feel that way. What was the context? Do you still possess enthusiasm for your work? If so, why? If not, why not? What changed? These are some of the questions and ideas that effective leaders need to consider when pondering employee motivation and enthusiasm. We know that extrinsic motivators, like a pay raise, inspire us only briefly. Long-lasting enthusiasm comes from a sense of equity in the workplace, knowing that we are respected by our supervisors and coworkers, having some measure of autonomy because superiors trust us, following clear and logical policies, and getting direction and support instead of orders. To the extent leaders can influence these factors, they will have an enthusiastic workforce.

SECTION

V

OCCUPATIONAL STRESS, LEADERSHIP

INTRODUCTION

In this section, we turn our gaze first to occupational stress and burnout and then to leadership. The topics of occupational stress and burnout are particularly challenging in the criminal justice field for several reasons. First, stress and burnout can have devastating effects on employees, including emotional distress that leads to behaviors ranging from divorce to suicide, and physical health problems such as high blood pressure and insomnia. Second, the paramilitary nature of the profession inhibits employees from asking for help or engaging in self-care practices. The quality of toughness is highly valued, much to the detriment of criminal justice workers. The meaning of toughness is so extremely skewed that toughness offers little room for individuals to take the necessary steps to function normally. Subscribing to unrealistic behavioral expectations is unhealthy for individuals, their loved ones, and the organization. This brings us to the last point: managers who ignore occupational stress and burnout harm their agencies in costly ways. Organizational research shows that high turnover, excessive absenteeism, low morale, and problematic employee conduct can sometimes be attributed to workplace stress and burnout (Finney et al. 2013).

Unfortunately, stress and burnout are not rare phenomena. Every workplace, whether public or private, has its fair share of occupational stress, What is rare is agency leadership that acknowledges this occupational hazard and does something about it. The assigned articles discuss general approaches to dealing with employee stress and acknowledges the strain associated with trauma. Dealing with traumatic events is where criminal justice employees are at an increased risk. And as the risk increases, organizations must increase their responses to help employees manage the risk. Our business demands that we be rule compliant, tough in the face of danger, and in control of our emotions. But toughness and control can backfire when we witness or hear about horrific events. Sometimes it is therapeutic and an act of strength to acknowledge our emotions and cry.

A police deputy superintendent told me that in the weeks following the Boston Marathon bombing, she ordered several of the responding police officers to attend a stress reduction and debriefing session after they initially declined her suggestion to do so. One might think that ordering personnel to do something they don't want to do just adds more stress to an already difficult situation. Yet after completing the session, the officers thanked the deputy for making them go. They found the session extremely beneficial and it went a long way toward helping their state of mind.

The third reading in this section concerns leadership—its theories, how it differs from the concept of management, and the interplay between leadership and power. Even though the examples discussed in the reading are taken from the business world and not the field of criminal justice, try not to feel cheated. The concept of leadership spans all organizational domains and there are many facets that you will easily identify with. As you read, think about your own leadership strengths and weaknesses. There are many different styles to choose from to lead effectively. Pick one that matches your personality. Note that certain behaviors and traits (such as arrogance and incompetence) should be avoided at all costs. None of us wants to work for a toxic leader, nor do we want to become one.

MANAGING EMPLOYEES' OCCUPATIONAL STRESS

KIMBERLY E. O'BRIEN AND TERRY A. BEEHR

ABSTRACT

Occupational stress can result when workplace demands or stressors lead to declines in employees' health and well-being, and stress can be costly for the organization itself in the form of sick leave, insurance costs, and lowered productivity. Fortunately there are several ways to prevent and/or alleviate the stressful situations. Some occupational stress treatments involve changing the environment in order either to reduce the strength of unnecessary stressors or to create resources to help employees cope with them. Others involve teaching the employees themselves to cope with the stressors without experiencing too much strain. Challenges to the implementation of stress treatment interventions are discussed, and best practices are outlined.

Occupational stress occurs when an employee's work environment, such as the nature of job demands or physical or social situations, results in reactions that are detrimental to the person's well-being (physical or mental health). The elements of the work environment are stressors, and the employee's harmful reactions are strains (e.g., Jex & Yankelevich, 2008). Estimates of the prevalence of occupational stress cannot be precise because there is no widely accepted measure that has a cutoff to indicate that a job either has stress or does not. Furthermore, stress is a continuous construct, making it difficult to argue that a cutoff even makes sense. With that caveat, we note that estimates of the prevalence of occupational stress have often been in the range of 30–40% of the U.S. jobs being stressful (e.g., Centers for Disease Control, 2011).

In addition to harm to employees in the form of strain, work-related stress can affect the well-being or effectiveness of the organization, in the form of heightened use of sick leave, absenteeism, turnover, and effects on productivity. A recent estimate is that stress costs the UK about 6.5 billion pounds per year (Shearer, 2013), mainly due to lost work hours. By any estimates, studies of work stress show it is related to important employee behaviors, and the cost is likely to be substantial. The focus of this chapter is managing occupational stress, which encompasses actions that go under labels such as interventions or treatments. Employees often find their own ways of adapting to or coping with work stressors, just as we all tend to do with the stressors in our nonwork lives; there are situations, however, in which the work stressors are too many or too strong, so that the employee does not cope effectively with them without help or direction.

Some stressors are related to required changes in an employee's work. That is, jobs can be stable for a long period of time but then undergo changes, after which they become relatively stable and routine again. During a time of change, the job can be stressful for the employees. In addition, some jobs are "routinely" changing. For example, a hospital nurse in an emergency ward might receive a wide variety of patient problems such as broken bones, infectious diseases, heart attacks, and shooting victims, such that the tasks, expertise, and urgency could change several times over the course of a shift. Such variety or frequent change in tasks can be stressful if it requires constant vigilance (Warm, Parasuraman, & Matthews, 2008) and readjustment to new job situations. We must note that for busy employees, even a well-intentioned stress intervention might require another change and take time from the employees' hectic schedules, causing stress. Nevertheless, if the stressors already existing in an employee's job are having detrimental effects, then it is worthwhile to try to improve the situation.

Of course some employees will be affected more than others by job stressors (Beehr & Bowling, 2005). A variety of terms are used to designate employees who are less affected under stressful circumstances, including stress-resistance, resilience, hardiness, and effective copers. An organization could try to select people who are effective copers, but they are difficult to identify. Aside from attempting to select stress-resistant applicants, the alternative is to help the people already employed by the organization. This includes actions to alleviate either strains directly or stressors that lead to them, in order to improve the employees' well-being (Figure 1).

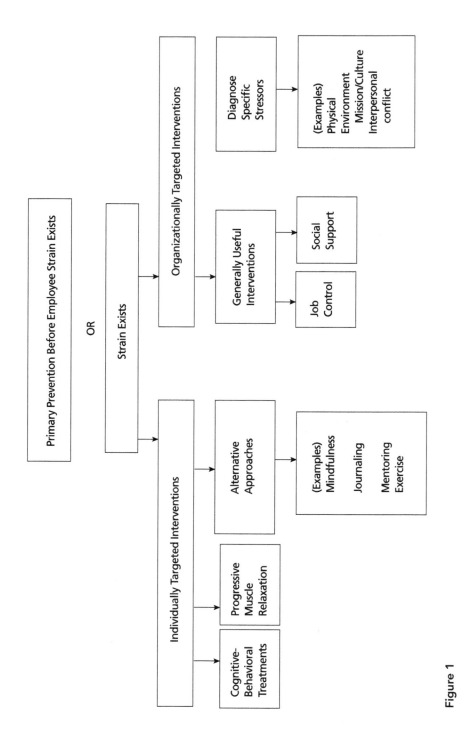

Figure 1

Flow chart illustrating potentially appropriate stress inervention methods.

PRIMARY, SECONDARY, AND TERTIARY STRESS INTERVENTIONS

A major consideration when undertaking a stress management program is the timing of the intervention. Primary interventions target people who are not yet at risk by making changes to their work environment to prevent problems from arising in the future. Although this sounds like a potential waste of resources, it is often more cost-effective to make small changes that affect more people, and to do it early (Brannon & Feist, 2010). For example, previous research shows that smoke-free workplaces reduce the number of cigarettes smoked and encourage quitting (Fichtenberg & Glantz, 2002). In comparison, a secondary intervention targets people at risk for stress or stress-induced disease. Many people do not know that they are at risk, as many health indicators have no visible symptoms (e.g., high blood pressure, restricted blood flow). As such, companies might choose to incentivize testing (such as providing access to empirically validated health questionnaires and providing referrals for, or do, onsite blood screening). Finally, in a tertiary intervention, people who have already been negatively affected by stress are given tools to help them recover; that is, the employee has already begun to experience physical or psychological strains. The tertiary interventions typically include employee assistance programs (EAPs) but might also comprise smoking cessation programs or weight management meetings.

Although alleviating the stressors is a logical approach to dealing with occupational stress, in some cases it may be impossible to reduce the stressors. Certain healthcare workers or law enforcement officers, for example, might be exposed to workplace trauma that is not preventable because it is a necessary part of their jobs. In these cases, it might be useful to prepare buffers against stress-related disease. One of the most effective ways to do this is to provide coping skills. For example, one study showed a video with industrial accidents to three groups of participants. The first group was not prepared beforehand and had the highest stress response. The second group was told to view the video like a movie and pretend that the accidents weren't real. The third group was told to remain emotionally detached (intellectualize), as medical personnel often need to do (Lazarus, 1966). When people are given specific preparation for viewing traumatic scenes, they are better able to cope. This research has been extrapolated to propose that people who are mentally prepared for stress fare better than those who are unprepared.

Aside from preparation, perceived control is very important in stress reactions. This concept includes both the employees' personal beliefs that they can take charge of their own work and the degree to which the job actually allows control over the environment. A large, multinational study found that employees who felt they had more control over their work environment were less likely to report cardiovascular disease and pain symptoms (Spector, 2002). Similarly, predictability helps for short-term stressors (Abbott, Schoen, & Badia, 1984). For example, people who have had time to prepare on their own for the loss of a loved one fare better than when a death is unexpected (Schulz et al., 2001). Overall, perceived control and predictability are important factors that can help to mitigate stress. Organizations may choose to empower employees through suggestion boxes or survey-feedback type organizational development programs, which may give some sense of control, especially if an agent of the organization responds to the suggestions or surveys. We encourage interventions to develop employee health-related self-efficacy by providing small goals that become gradually more challenging (e.g., start by walking five minutes a day or taking the stairs), rather than asking people to make large lifestyle changes quickly (e.g., run a 5k by the end of the quarter). The smaller changes can be seen as more controllable by the employees and help build confidence to achieve more difficult goals.

Finally, if work stressors are not preventable, it still might be beneficial to try to recruit employees with disease-resistant abilities and personalities (e.g., optimistic, non-hostile; Nelson & Simmons, 2011) when appropriate, given other selection criteria and concerns. Besides selection, which we discussed earlier, it is also possible to train some of these resistances. For example, cognitive behavioral training can be used to reduce stressful thoughts such as catastrophizing or rumination, or hostile employees might engage in an anger management or interpersonal negotiation training. Other programs generally can be used to provide people with specific coping skills (relaxation or breathing techniques, time management skills, assertiveness training). Likewise, some people would benefit from primary prevention actions to enhance disease resistance (Selye, 1956), such as influenza vaccines or blood pressure screening with referrals for cardiovascular care (Robles, Glaser, Kiecolt-Glaser, 2005).

CHANGING THE ENVIRONMENT

Research is mixed regarding whether interventions should target the organization versus its members, but a strong stress-treatment program would do both (note both in Figure 1). On one hand, it is sometimes easier to change a person, and organizational changes can have unintended consequences (Semmer, 2011). Likewise, stress is extremely perceptual, and employees might disagree about whether there is work overload, noisy working conditions, or other assumed stressful aspects of the work environment. Adding a flextime component to jobs may help employees with families but might also cause more stress for managers who will have to supervise over a longer day (or allow employees to work unsupervised during certain hours) and juggle schedules, and for employees who do not use it (because they might have to adjust their schedules to coordinate with coworkers who use flextime), for example. On the other hand, Lewin's (1951) law states that it is easier to change individuals formed into groups than to change individuals separately. For example, research on exercise shows that people going through an exercise program are more successful when their friends and family also take up an exercise regimen (Gorin, Phelan, Tate, Sherwood, Jeffery, & Wing, 2005).

Overall, you might choose to target objective problems if they are stressful to a broad portion of your constituents, but in other cases you might be better off targeting individual perceptions. For example, research shows that employees can sometimes define increased workload as a challenge that will allow them to show themselves and others how ingenious they are and how they can succeed in challenging situations. Interpreting stressors as challenges may be better than labeling them as burdens. The challenges sometimes still result in strains, but usually not as much as more negatively appraised stressors (Podsakoff, LePine, & LePine, 2007), and in addition, employees often get to feel they are successful and accomplished people by meeting challenges and succeeding. As such, we encourage always taking this approach when discussing potential changes to the environment. Consulting with the workers themselves about the nature of the work and determining what they would see as challenging is a good start. The combination of work that is both challenging and over which employees have some control is likely to result in less harmful stress responses for the employees. Allowing flexible options for stress management and work in general is beneficial to the most employees.

EXISTING STRESS MANAGEMENT INTERVENTIONS

Although stress management interventions are relatively common, few have been systematically evaluated, leading to many questions regarding the efficacy of any given type of intervention. However, it is known that the average stress management intervention does benefit the psychological well-being of employees (Richardson & Rothstein, 2008). In order to perform a stress management intervention, the first decision point is to determine whether you want to more directly change the environment versus the people within it, based on a thorough needs assessment. It is sometimes appropriate to change the organization rather than its constituents by altering the sources of stress (e.g., primary intervention). However, there are many cases in which it is not possible or practical, and so as noted earlier, it may be best to try selecting people whose knowledge, skills, and abilities match the job (stress-resilient personalities for police officers) or to train employees in some stress management skills. Depending on the situation, it may be appropriate to combine organizational change, selection, and training approaches. Previous research has categorized stress management interventions into five groups: cognitive-behavioral, relaxation, alternative, combined or multimodal, and organizational (see Figure 1; van der Klink, Blonk, Schene, & van Dijk, 2001).

COGNITIVE-BEHAVIORAL INTERVENTIONS

Some stress treatments help employees identify the role that their thoughts and feelings have in the stress that they experience. Employees are then encouraged to target their negative and irrational thoughts and replace them with more adaptive ones. To engage in a cognitive-behavioral intervention, the organization could hire a professional to give a workshop that addresses the specific needs of the organization members. For example, if interpersonal stress seems to be problematic, the trainer could discuss communication skills (e.g., "when my coworker says *a*, it makes me feel *b*, so let's try saying *c*"), practicing making alternative attributions ("if a coworker doesn't greet me in the morning, it might be because she is preoccupied, rather than because she is ignoring me"), and avoiding provocative situations (if you know that you get upset because a coworker frequently leaves a breakroom in a mess, use a different breakroom even if it is out of the way). Ultimately, many employees would benefit from understanding that they cannot change other people, only the way they respond to other people's behaviors. According to a meta-analysis, cognitive-behavioral interventions have the best outcomes (Richardson & Rothstein, 2008).

RELAXATION INTERVENTIONS

Relaxation is the most common form of organizational stress management intervention, probably because it requires the fewest resources (Richardson & Rothstein, 2008). A common type of relaxation training is progressive muscle relaxation (PMR), which is consistently found to be effective at reducing stress (e.g., Jacobs, 2001) and is rated by the National Institutes of Health Technology as one of the best methods for managing pain (Lebovits, 2007). PMR is a technique in which people tense and then relax each muscle group in order, starting from the head and working towards the toes, with special attention paid to the specific difference in feeling between the tense and relaxed states. Many people report feeling less stressed after even a brief PMR session, and more importantly, PMR may give people an opportunity to emotionally detach from a stressful situation and have time to process it rationally instead of having a spontaneous, potentially irrational reaction.

ALTERNATIVE METHODS

In addition, there are a wide variety of other interventions, such as mindfulness, journaling, mentoring, and exercise. Mindfulness (Michel, Bosch, & Rexroth, 2014) can be considered as a newer version of cognitive behavioral therapy, but instead of changing the cognitions to change the behavior, mindfulness is about being in the moment and savoring the pleasant aspects. People often do things without thinking, such as driving somewhere and not remembering all of the turns and landmarks along the way. In mindfulness interventions and meditations, people are asked to pay attention to and evaluate everything as if this is their first time experiencing it. For example, if you are under stress, how would you explain that feeling to someone who has never experienced stress before? People might be asked to describe in detail how different parts of their body feel ("my head hurts, my chest feels tight, I feel like I can't eat"). Doing so tends to take the focus off of the stressor and allow people to think rationally about what they are experiencing, and sometimes even determine if they are overreacting. Mindfulness interventions are also successful in mitigating pain and overeating, which can both be caused by stress.

Journaling is another effective method of dampening stress and preventing stress-related disease. Research has shown that translating thoughts into clear, calm language allows people to become more aware of their stress levels, recurrent causes of stress, and their reactions to stressful situations. Journaling is helpful in a variety of applications, such as resolving interpersonal conflicts (Pettigrove, 2007) and preventing burnout (Medland, Howard-Ruben, & Whitaker, 2004), and it is even related to fewer doctor visits (Burton & King, 2004).

Another alternative that might be useful is mentoring. Mentoring has been shown to alleviate some problems with work–family interference (Nielson, Carlson, & Lankau, 2001), stress felt by organizational newcomers (Allen, McManus, & Russell, 1999), stress during organizational change (Eby, 1997; Kram & Hall, 1989), and overall job-related stress (Sosik & Goshalk, 2000). However, mentoring programs require their own needs assessments and careful planning (O'Brien, Rodopman, & Allen, 2007).

Finally, exercise has been shown to relieve chronic stress and prevent stress-related disease for those who experience chronic stress. However, it is not beneficial for acute stress. Thus, organizations may want to incentivize joining a gym but allowing flexibility such that people who are having trouble meeting all their responsibilities can take time off from exercise without facing repercussions, such as losing benefits of exercising (e.g., paid gym membership, reduction of insurance premiums) during other periods of time.

ORGANIZATION-TARGETED APPROACHES

Logically, dealing with occupational stress by changing the nature of the employees' workplace would require a diagnosis of stressors. For example, change the furniture if furniture is diagnosed as the problem, but change the department's mission or culture if that is the problem. When there is role ambiguity for example, then role clarification is needed. If there is role conflict, resolving the role messages specific to the conflicting expectations makes sense. If there are constraints or lack of resources, then more resources are needed, or constraining situations need to be removed.

Diagnosis can take place in two phases (Beehr & O'Driscoll, 2002). The first is to identify strains to determine if there is actually any potential stress problem for employees in your organization. Some specific physical illnesses are expected to be related to stress, and the number of instances of employees reporting illnesses (e.g., taking days off for sick leave) can be an indicator. Some illnesses are more likely to be stress-related than others, however, with cardiovascular illnesses being among the prime candidates. A high rate or increase in employees experiencing such illnesses can be an initial indicator of stress in the organization, especially if they are concentrated in certain types of jobs, departments, locations, or times of year. Employers may not know about these illnesses if the employee does not report them and they do not require employees to take sick days off work, however. Regarding psychological strains, the simplest way to diagnose them is through employee questionnaires. There are many well-used questionnaire items that can be employed as indicators of strains, including psychological burnout, negative moods like depression or anxiety, frustration, and even an accumulation of minor physical complaints such as aches and pains (e.g., headaches or other body aches), and exhaustion. If these seem high or are increasing, the next step is to determine how likely it is that the strains are linked to any stressors in the work environment that can be changed. One way to do this is to include items (in the same questionnaire with the strain items) that ask about the existence of typical stressors such as overload, ambiguity, conflicting goals, lack of resources, or interpersonal conflict. If those do exist and are part of the cause of the strains, they should be statistically related to the strains. Simple statistics such as correlations are enough to establish a possibility that the stressors could be a cause of the strains. If there is a relationship (e.g., a correlation) between specific stressors and strains, the implication is that finding ways to reduce those specific stressors would help to relieve the strains, which is the ultimate goal.

The method described above requires some experience in psychological measurement and statistics, but it can be kept fairly simple. Fortunately, there are other, more general approaches to stressor reduction in the workplace that are likely to be easier to implement and yet widely useful. There is a great deal of sound research and theory showing that the introduction of two changes (control and support) in the work environment can be generally useful for reducing employee strains due to occupational stress. Control and support are two of the most important job characteristics, both for purposes of combatting harmful stress (Thoits, 2011) and for helping to achieve organization-relevant goals (Semmer & Beehr, 2014). Job control, which involves allowing employees to participate in some decisions about their work situation, can be motivating and satisfying, and the provision of social support to employees can have similarly positive effects.

Employee participation is related to many positive job characteristics going under different labels, such as job autonomy, empowerment, and control. Recommendations are often made to provide such participation for employees in order to motivate them, but the control inherent in participation can also be helpful for reducing employees' strains. Most employees appreciate control over their work because it typically can provide positive experiences of optimism and respect. In general, control can act for many employees as a resource to be used in solving their own problems (e.g., by reducing their own stressors). In addition, attempts to reduce any specific stressors in an employee's work are likely to be more successful if the employee participates in or has control over deciding how to do it. There are two reasons for this. First, a veteran employee who has done the job for a long time knows the details about the job better than anyone else. If there are better ways to do the job, including better ways to change it to reduce the stressors, the employee is most likely to understand that; and even if someone else recommends an idea, the employee is likely to know how well it will work and how to implement the idea. Second, if the employees participate meaningfully in redesigning their jobs to reduce stressors, they are more motivated to make the new system (i.e., new way of doing the work) be effective in the future. In summary, participation or control is useful for reducing stressors and strains because it is generally appreciated feature of jobs for most employees, because employees often will come up with some of the best solutions for problems on their own jobs, and because they will be more motivated to make the new job design be effective if they helped to develop it (Semmer & Beehr 2014).

Social support can take many forms, but most forms can help stressed employees feel better by reducing their strains, especially if they "feel" supported. Two major categories of support are instrumental and emotional support (Semmer, Elfering, Jacobshagen, Perrot, Beehr, & Boos, 2008). Instrumental support is tangible in the sense of helping the employee to overcome the stressors in the work environment. Related to problem solving, examples can be helping the employee to meet a tight deadline by joining in the work, providing information or other resources (e.g., tools) to aid in completing a task, and intervening to solve a conflict or dispute with a another coworker. Like all organizational interventions, which instrumental supportive intervention will help most depends on what the problem or potential stressor is (e.g., overload, ambiguity, or conflict). Emotional support, on the other hand, focuses directly on employees' negative emotions or psychological strains. It can include behaviors like expressing sympathy, positive thinking, or almost any form of comforting the stressed employee, and it can be provided by anyone (coworkers, supervisors, family, and friends). Overall, emotional social support is generally helpful in many situations, and so to some extent it can be provided regardless of what the stressors are in the workplace.

Overall, if work can be challenging but not overwhelming, many employees react better to the job. In addition, some variability is usually good, as are clear expectations and security. Many of these work characteristics are subject to the Goldilocks effect; that is, there can be too much or too little of them, and the difficulty is to find just the right level for each employee. Allowing employees to have control can help, however, by allowing them to adjust the job to fit themselves a little better.

In contrast to the generally favorable effects of control and support, some interventions are especially aimed at specific stressors. Interpersonal conflict is one such commonly cited stressor (Bruk-Lee & Spector, 2012; Spector & Jex, 1998). In fact, interpersonal conflict is detrimental to more than just the people directly involved. For example, employees who observe rude behavior of one coworker to another might feel uncomfortable, angry, or offended (Fisher, 2001). There are a number of observer interventions (Fisher, 2001) available. For example, conciliation occurs when a trusted third party is used as an informal communication link (such as a departmental administrative assistant acting as a gatekeeper when an executive is under stress, to protect the executive or to protect the coworkers from the executive when he or she is being difficult) or as a mediator in which a third party offers binding negotiated settlements. In a consultation, a third party can provide skills training for people who often experience conflict.

Finally, aside from changing the nature of the job, an obvious way for stressed employees to recover is to take time off. During time off, the employee is in a different location doing different activities, and thus this is another form of changing the environment. Employers normally provide vacation and sick leave time for their employees, but potential stress-related problems come with employees who do not use these times for recovery (for example, *presenteeism* is a term used to denote employees coming to work while they are ill; e.g., Johns, 2011). Besides the official policies of the organization, the culture needs to be sure to encourage employees to use their available vacation time—that is, to make clear that vacations are expected, deserved, and needed. Time off from work in the form of vacations can help to relieve the strains due to occupational stress (de Bloom, Geurts, Sonnentag, de Weerth, & Kompier, 2011; de Bloom, Geurts, Taris, Sonnentag, de Weerth, & Kompier, 2010; Etzion, 2003; Fritz, Ellis, Demsky, Lin, & Guros, 2013; Westman & Eden, 1997; Westman & Etzion, 2001). A problem, however, is that such recovery from work-related stress is often short-lived after some time back at work (Fritz et al., 2013). Nevertheless, the relief from stress during the vacation time itself and a maybe few more weeks after returning may be valuable stress-reducing times.

CHALLENGES

There are some major gaps in what we know about implementing stress interventions, and there are several reasons for this. Perhaps unexpectedly, one of the applied problems is directly related to traditional research methods. Programs are often implemented with the implicit assumption that it will be obvious whether it works or not, but it usually does not turn out that way. Some planning needs to go into evaluating the success of practical approaches to deal with employee stress. Keeping in mind the goals of a particular program, at a minimum some measurement of the scope of the problem before and after the intervention is necessary. Much more effective, however, is to also measure the same stress indicators (stressors or strains) for people who are not subject to the intervention (before and after the target people experience their intervention). Then you can compare the two groups to determine whether the group receiving the treatment actually improved more than somebody who did not receive it. This is a crude version of the classic control group research strategy, and it is important because stressors and strains can get better (or worse) for many reasons, such as people learning to cope on their own, the time of the year (e.g., maybe stress indicators get better at certain times of year even if no effort is made to improve the situation), or coworkers seeing that problems exist and deciding to help out. Regarding measurement, remember that if something is important in the workplace, the organization usually keeps track of it (e.g., production, attendance, and sales). If stress is important, then some periodic measures of stressors and strains need to be taken.

A second challenge is getting buy-in from the necessary people. Obviously, in most cases, the stressed employee might need to agree the program is worthwhile. If some unit in the organization is displaying stress symptoms but the employees in the unit do not believe any stress-coping intervention is worthwhile, efforts to help might be futile. Employees might sometimes feel that it is nobody else's business and they just need to "gut it out" and be tough enough to stand any stressful job pressures, or they might simply believe the issue is unsolvable and do not want to "waste their time." In addition, buy-in from higher-level management is usually necessary. If they think stress-reduction efforts are unneeded, disruptive, expensive, or ineffective, their lack of support might make it difficult even to get the program started, especially if some resources are needed (e.g., time, money, or possibly equipment).

Finally, a third challenge is inherent in some stress treatments and can be even more relevant to future stress treatments than to the original one. It makes sense to use as many treatments as feasible (e.g., participation through focus groups plus relaxation training) if you really want to resolve the stressful situation, and the multiple-pronged approach might give the best chance for success. If there are improvements in stress levels after such "mixed" interventions, however, we do not know whether all the interventions were really necessary or if only one accounted for the improvement. If it is the former, then in the next stress situation all of the interventions in the mix need to be repeated, but if only one of the intervention approaches was the reason for success, only that one needs to be repeated, which might be easier, more palatable, and even less costly. But in the case of multiple or mixed interventions, we do not have information on the effectiveness of each separate treatment to guide our next attempt.

BEST PRACTICES FOR WORKPLACE STRESS MANAGEMENT INTERVENTIONS

Like any other organizational change, there are a variety of conditions that allow for better expected results. We choose to describe only a few in the following section, but others are also important.

The first step in any successful organizational intervention is a needs assessment. Specifically, in order to use organizational resources to their fullest, interventions need to target the unique type and amount of stressors within the organization and identify how much the constituents exhibit strain due to these stressors. This process refers to diagnosis, which was described earlier. In other words, where is there a mismatch between employee stress management skill and environmental needs? For example, some people respond positively to time pressure or negative feedback, whereas other people do not. A needs assessment using focus groups or survey feedback, for example, can help identify whether specific people are unable to cope and would benefit from participating in an individual-targeted intervention, or if something in the environment needs to be changed via an organizationally targeted intervention. Only 27% of (training) interventions are based on a needs assessment, which means that a great deal of resources may be wasted.

The needs assessment will help complete the next step in the intervention: setting objectives. Once the type of stressors to be addressed is decided, as well as the targeted population of employees, the intervention needs to be created to meet these needs. Part of this is setting expectations from participants and other organizational members—that is, identifying what the participants and management expect to get out of the program and communicating clearly in order to set those expectations. It is necessary to address any discrepancies up front, as the main reason for the failure of some programs is unmet expectations (O'Brien et al., 2007).

In a similar vein, it is helpful to achieve top-level buy-in. People are very much affected by their peers. Many safety interventions, for example, will not work if people feel like they are a curve breaker, or otherwise do not fit what is normal for their organization. For example, people are resistant to being the only employee wearing safety goggles. As such, interventions work best when they are part of a global change, including top-down buy-in followed by multiple people participating. Relatedly, it helps to incentivize the group rather than the individual. People are hesitant to be the sole person making a change (especially a norm-violating one for personal gain), but if a coworker's benefit is at stake and if other people also participate, they are more likely to follow the program. For example, an incentive might be that all members of teams that complete the workshop can receive a pedometer or gift certificate for a health food store.

Once the objectives are set, the next step is to design the training program itself. Many characteristics to consider depend on the specific program goals and resources. For example, spaced training (intervention that takes place over time) leads to better transfer from the learning situation to the job than massed (all at once) training; however, massed training requires fewer resources. It is important to provide feedback during the training so that participants understand if they are using the skills correctly. Similarly, the training should be as similar as possible to the actual scenarios in which the skills will be used. Finally, it is important to teach the principles regarding why the skills should be used, to best help participants understand when to apply the skills. Using multiple delivery methods (e.g., lecture, self-paced computer workshop, video, role playing, and discussion groups) can balance the individual strengths and weaknesses of each approach. A description of training program components can be found in Spector (2011).

In terms of delivering the intervention, it is typical to hire an expert on the topic. For example, it might be worthwhile to bring in a licensed clinician to teach about mindfulness or an experienced professional coach to teach about interpersonal skills. Relaxation interventions tend to be more popular, however—probably because there are easily available "off-the-shelf" programs that managers can deliver or employees can learn themselves, often via computer.

Finally, a successful intervention must have a program evaluation in order to determine if needs are being met, to see if stress levels are improving, and to inform changes to later iterations of stress interventions. As described earlier, planning for program evaluations is best done before the intervention begins. The evaluations are formal comparisons of outcomes of interventions via pretest and posttest scores on related variables (as determined by the needs assessment, such as amount of interpersonal conflict experiences) or by comparing the group receiving the intervention to a similar (control) group. Without formal comparisons, it is difficult to know if the program was successful and how to improve the intervention in the future.

CONCLUSION

In conclusion, many organizations and their employees would benefit from stress management programs. Certain stress management interventions have at least 300% return on investment (Baicker, Cutler, & Song, 2010; Chapman, 2012) and can increase the organization's reputation among the organization's employees and the larger community (which leads to good reputation for corporate social responsibility and increasing the number and quality of people who would like to work there). Although many decisions need to be made about whom to target, when, and how, most of these questions can be answered by engaging in a comprehensive *needs assessment*. The needs assessment should also determine what resources are available, in terms of time, funding, and buy-in. Next, the *program is designed* to address goals established in the needs assessment, and *expectations are set* from the perspective of HR as well as the participants. Finally, a *program evaluation* will allow practitioners to determine the value of the program and increase the quality of future interventions.

REFERENCES

Abbott, B., Schoen, L. S., & Badia, P. (1984). Predictable and unpredictable shock: Behavioral measures of aversion and physiological measures of stress. *Psychological Bulletin, 96,* 45–71.

Allen, T. D., McManus, S. E., & Russell, J. E. A., (1999). Newcomer socialization and stress: Formal peer relationships as a source of support. *Journal of Vocational Behavior, 54,* 453–470.

Baicker, K., Cutler, D., & Song, Z. (2010). Workplace wellness programs can generate savings. *Health Affairs 29,* 304–311.

Beehr, T. A., & Bowling, N. A. (2005). Hardy personality, stress, and health. In C. L. Cooper (Ed.), *Handbook of stress medicine and health second edition* (pp. 193–211). London, UK: CRC Press.

Beehr, T. A., & O'Driscoll, M. P. (2002). Organizationally targeted interventions aimed at reducing workplace stress. In J. C. Thomas & M. Hersen (Eds.), *Handbook of mental health in the workplace* (pp. 103–119). Thousand Oaks, CA: Sage.

Brannon, L., & Feist, J. (2010). *Health psychology* (7th ed.). Los Angeles, CA: Wadsworth.

Bruk-Lee, V., & Spector, P. E. (2012). Interpersonal conflict and stress at work: Implications for employee health and well-being. In A. M. Rossi, P. L. Perrewé, & J. A. Meurs (Eds.), *Coping and prevention* (pp. 3–22). Charlotte, NC: Information Age Publishing.

Burton, C. M., & King, L.A. (2004). The health benefits of writing about intensely positive experiences. *Journal of Research in Personality, 38*, 150–163.

Centers for Disease Control. (2011, May 23). Work organization and stress-related disorders. *NIOSH Program Portfolio.* Retrieved from http://www.cdc.gov/niosh/programs/workorg/risks.html

Chapman, L. S. (2012). Meta-evaluation of worksite health promotion economic return studies: 2012 update. *Journal of Health Promotion 6*, 1–12.

de Bloom, J., Geurts, S. A. E., Sonnentag, S., Taris, T., de Weerth, C., & Kompier, M. A. J. (2011). How does a vacation from work affect employee health and well-being? *Psychology and Health, 26*, 1606–1622.

de Bloom, J., Geurts, S. A., Taris, T. W., Sonnentag, S., Weerth, C. D. & Kompier, M. A. (2010). Effects of vacation from work on health and well-being: Lots of fun, quickly gone. *Work & Stress: An International Journal of Work, Health & Organizations, 24*, 196–216.

Eby, L. T. (1997). Alternative forms of mentoring in changing organizational environments: A conceptual extension of the mentoring literature. *Journal of Vocational Behavior, 51*, 125–144.

Etzion, D. (2003). Annual vacation: Duration of relief from job stressors and burnout. *Anxiety, Stress & Coping: An International Journal, 16*, 213–226.

Fichtenberg, C. M., & Glantz, S. A. (2002). Effect of smoke-free workplaces on smoking behavior. *Systematic review, 325*, 188–195.

Fisher, R. J. (2001). Methods of Third-Party Intervention. In N. Ropers, M. Fischer & E. Manton (Eds.), *Berghof handbook for conflict transformation* (pp. 1–25). Berlin, Germany: Berghof Center for Conflict Management.

Fritz, C., Ellis, A. M., Demsky, C. A., Lin, B. C., & Guros, F. (2013). Embracing work breaks: Recovering from work stress. *Organizational Dynamics, 42*, 274–280.

Gorin, A., Phelan, S., Tate, D., Sherwood, N., Jeffery, R., & Wing, R. (2005). Involving support partners in obesity treatment. *Journal of Consulting and Clinical Psychology, 73*, 341.

Jacobs, G. D. (2001). Clinical applications of the relaxation response and mind-body interventions. *Journal of Alternative and Complementary Medicine, 7*, 93–101.

Jex, S. M., & Yankelevich, M. (2008). Work stress. In J. Barling & C. L. Cooper (Eds.), *The Sage handbook of organizational behavior* (Vol. 1, pp. 498–518). Los Angeles CA: Sage.

Johns, G. (2011). Attendance dynamics at work: The antecedents and correlates of presenteeism, absenteeism, and productivity loss. *Journal of Occupational Health Psychology, 16*, 483–500.

Kram, K. E., & Hall, D. T., (1989). Mentoring as an antidote to stress during corporate trauma. *Human Resource Management, 28*(4), 493–511.

Lazarus, R. S. (1966). *Psychological stress and the coping process.* New York, NY: McGraw-Hill.

Lebovits, A. (2007). Cognitive-behavioral approaches to chronic pain. *Primary Psychiatry, 14*, 48–54.

Lewin, K. (1951). *Field theory in social science.* London, UK: Tavistock Publications.

Medland, J., Howard-Ruben, J., & Whitaker, E. (2004, January). Fostering psychosocial wellness in oncology nurses: Addressing burnout and social support in the workplace. *Oncology Nursing Forum, 31*(1), 47–54.

Michel, A., Bosch, C., & Rexroth, M. (2014). Mindfulness as a cognitive-emotional segmentation strategy: An intervention promoting work-life balance. *Journal of Occupational and Organizational Psychology, 87*, 733–754.

Nelson, D. L., & Simmons, B. L (2011). Savoring eustress while coping with distress: The holistic model of stress. In J. C. Quick & L. E. Tetrick (Eds.), *Handbook of occupational health psychology* (pp. 299–318). Washington, DC: American Psychological Association.

Nielson, T. R., Carlson, D. S., & Lankau, M. J. (2001). The supportive mentor as a means of reducing work-family conflict. *Journal of Vocational Behavior, 59*, 364–381.

O'Brien, K. E., Rodopman, O. B., & Allen, T. D. (2007). Reflections on best practices for formal mentoring programs. In T. D. Allen & L. T. Eby (Eds.), *The Blackwell handbook of mentoring: A multiple perspectives approach* (pp. 369–372). Malden, MA: Blackwell Publishing.

Pettigrove, G. (2007). Forgiveness and interpretation. *Journal of Religious Ethics, 35,* 429–452.

Podsakoff, N. P., LePine, J. A., & LePine, M. A. (2007). Differential challenge stress-or-hindrance stressor relationships with job attitudes, turnover intentions, turnover, and withdrawal behavior: A meta-analysis. *Journal of Applied Psychology 92,* 438–454.

Richardson, K. M., & Rothstein, H. R. (2008). Effects of occupational stress management intervention programs: A meta-analysis. *Journal of Occupational Health Psychology, 13,* 69–93.

Robles, T. F., Glaser, R., & Kiecolt-Glaser, J. K. (2005). Out of balance: A new look at chronic stress, depression, and immunity. *Current Directions in Psychological Science, 14,* 111–115.

Schulz, R., Beach, S. R., Lind, B., Martire, L. M., Zdaniuk, B., Hirsch, C., Jackson, S., & Burton, L. (2001). Involvement in caregiving and adjustment to death of a spouse. *Journal of the American Medical Association, 285,* 3123–3129.

Selye, H. (1956). *The stress of life.* New York, NY: McGraw-Hill.

Semmer, N. K. (2011). Job stress interventions and organization of work. In J. C. Quick & L. E. Tetrick (Eds.), *Handbook of occupational health psychology* (pp. 299–318). Washington, DC: American Psychological Association.

Semmer, N. K., & Beehr, T. A. (2014). Job control and social aspects of work. In M. C. W. Peeters, J. de Jong, & T. W. Taris (Eds.), *An introduction to contemporary work psychology* (pp. 171–195). Chichester, UK: Wiley.

Semmer, N. K., Elfering, A., Jacobshagen, N., Perrot, T., Beehr, T. A., & Boos, N. (2008). The emotional meaning of instrumental support. *International Journal of Stress management, 15,* 235–251.

Shearer, N. (2013, March 9). As work related stress costs the U. K. economy nearly L6.5 billion each year, what steps should businesses and employees be taking? *The Huffington Post.* Retrieved from http://www.huffingtonpost.co.uk/natasha-shearer/work-related-stress-business_b_3545476.html

Sosik, J. J., & Godshalk, V. M. (2000). Leadership styles, mentoring functions received, and job-related stress: A conceptual model and preliminary study. *Journal of Organizational Behavior, 21,* 365–390.

Spector, P. E. (2002). Employee control and occupational stress. *Current Directions in Psychological Science, 11,* 133–136.

Spector, P. E. (2012). *Industrial and organizational psychology: Research and practice* (6th ed.). Hoboken, NJ: John Wiley & Sons.

Spector, P. E., & Jex, S. M. (1998). Development of four self-report measures of job stressors and strain: Interpersonal conflict at work scale, organizational constraints scale, quantitative workload inventory, and physical symptoms inventory. *Journal of Occupational Health Psychology, 3,* 356–367.

Thoits, P. A. (2011). Stress and health: Major findings and policy implications. *Journal of Health and Social Behavior, 51,* S42–S53.

Van der Klink, J. V. L., Blonk, R. W. B., Shene, A. H., & van Dijk, F. J. H. (2001). The benefits of interventions for work related stress. *American Journal of Public Health, 91,* 270–276.

Warm, J. S., Parasuraman, R., & Matthews, G. (2008). Vigilance requires hard mental work and is stressful. *Human Factors: The Journal of the Human Factors and Ergonomics Society, 50,* 433–441.

Westman, M., & Eden, D. (1997). Effect of a respite from work on burnout: Vacation relief and fade-out. *Journal of Applied Psychology, 82,* 516–527.

Westman, M., & Etzion, D. (2001). The impact of vacation and job stress on burnout and absenteeism. *Psychology and Health, 16,* 595–606.

LAW and ORDER **SPECIAL REPORT** Solutions to Stress from Traumatic Incidents

▶ **SUMMARY**
Law enforcement generates a higher rate of stress because of the frequency and severity of exposure to traumatic events. Most officers have likely experienced a distressing or traumatic event within the past year. Just becoming a police officer does not provide a way for managing the stress of the job or avoiding any emotional reactions to it.

◀ Be proactive. Don't say, It will not happen here. Don't say, We will cross that bridge when we come to it.

SOLUTIONS TO STRESS FROM TRAUMATIC INCIDENTS
WE MUST BE PROACTIVE.
> By Rodney Steams

While officers and the public rarely question physical injuries sustained while on duty, the disabling effects of job-related trauma are not always readily visible. Having a traumatic reaction, or the fear of even acknowledging a traumatic reaction, is somehow seen as a weakness. We need to accept that a reaction may occur. Preparing for it is a fundamental duty.

Typically, law enforcement supervisors are at a loss for words following a traumatic event involving their personnel and simply choose to say nothing. This act alone may be a defining point for managers and can be easily conceptualized as lacking empathy and understanding. Most new officers cannot truly understand the magnitude of the impact of exposure to critical events, and even veteran officers can succumb to cumulative effects of prolonged exposure to tragedy and loss over time.

POST-TRAUMATIC STRESS

Post-Traumatic Stress Disorder is defined by the Diagnostic and Statistical Manual of Mental Disorders as the development of specific characteristics after being exposed to a traumatic stressor. It occurs from direct exposure to an event that involves actual or threatened death or serious injury, or witnessing such an event with another. Symptoms develop due to an inability to adapt to the event and the event, regardless of the type or severity, overwhelms an individual's ability to cope.

Not every incident will result in post-traumatic stress. Not every officer has a propensity for developing a stress-related disorder. There are factors within the law enforcement profession as well as individual officer characteristics that make them more susceptible. Without proper preventative measures and post-incident intervention and support, that risk increases exponentially.

Following a traumatic incident, an officer may experience many of the common trauma symptoms, including sleep difficulties, disturbing memories that create anxiety, inability to concentrate, and emotional numbing. Though the officer experiences the symptoms, they directly affect family members as well. Officers may be easily aroused and have difficulty calming down.

In addition, they may be more irritable or show frustration with even minor issues. Police officers may not always have positive support and commonly turn to maladaptive coping mechanisms such as alcohol or drugs to disengage from reality. The concern is that law enforcement also has a very high rate of suicide, which is related to job stress, though not yet accepted as such.

PRIMARY SOURCE OF SUPPORT

Law enforcement personnel experiencing these life-altering events will likely use, or try to use their primary source of support—their family. Although family may be the first choice for support, they can inadvertently exacerbate the problem through misunderstanding and unknowingly incorrect approaches. During these highly emotional periods, officers are vulnerable and give their friends and family members a sort of unwritten authority for helping.

Family, co-workers, and close friends will seemingly provide comfort and recommendations similar to counseling, but lacking in any foundation beyond the typical intuitive conviction. Even with the best of intentions, laypersons tend to provide opinions and extemporaneously

▲ Just becoming a police officer does not insulate you from the effects of experiencing trauma or of being exposed to trauma.

relay a similar experience in their life as a means of lessening the traumatic shock. Although they may feel they are trying to lessen the burden of the pain by sharing their own experience, it is not always interpreted as intended.

Positive social support is a very prevalent means for coping with the stress of trauma. Law enforcement co-workers can be a detrimental part of the social support system, providing advice is given sparingly with proper empathy. Fellow officers typically want to show their support to their troubled comrade and continuously offer guidance, words of encouragement, and their willingness to help.

Again, though admirable, they may overwhelm the officer and create additional stressors particularly if they have to explain or repeat details of the traumatic event. Those who indulge their own curiosity by questioning them about the event, even supervisors, may further compound the trauma response. It is also not appropriate to assume just because a person may have experienced a similar past traumatic event, they can fully appreciate the other's experience or their feelings are even similar.

CRITICAL STRESS DEBRIEFING

Many of the emergency professions utilize Critical Incident Stress Debriefing (CISD), which is a semi-structured method for managing critical incidents through group sessions designed to normalize the emotions that follow a critical event. CISD is a great tool for educating and keeping the work family together and validating each of their feelings and concerns.

One of the known factors that can contribute to an officer externalizing distressing events is their perception of a traumatic event coupled with their previous experience. The CISD can be beneficial in validating their feelings as well as correcting any misperceptions they may have about the event.

While the family bond within law enforcement does serve as a very important emotional support, the close bonds an officer develops with co-workers during this emotional period may inadvertently force a disconnection and withdrawal from using their family for support. Officers commonly tend to feel those outside of the law enforcement community cannot understand their work or what they have been through.

SHARE VERSUS ALIENATE

Furthermore, officers make a conscious choice to not share things with their family in an attempt to "shield" them from exposure to their work-related trauma. The exclusion of the victim's natural support network is one drawback of CISD and can inadvertently further alienate family at a time when it may be at its highest need.

Another drawback to CISD is that information shared during the group process is not always protected information that can prevent officers from sharing openly. Often times, facilitators are from outside agencies and while conducting the debriefings, they are fully aware of the grieving process. Unfortunately, the facilitator may lack a full understanding of acute trauma as well as stressors specific to law enforcement including the jaded and at times, distrustful environments in which they work.

CISD is one of many different treatment modalities. However, it is not a stop-gap mechanism that once completed, allows administration to "wash their hands" of any further obligation to their officers. Nor should they be utilized as the sole means of intervention. Debriefings can be a starting point for early trauma intervention and can also be utilized to prevent the development of long-term stress disorders. Unfortunately, studies suggest that those attending a CISD may not be any better off than not attending at all.

PROCESS OF EARLY INTERVENTION

Police agencies need to set goals and practices to deploy in the event officers are exposed to trauma. First and foremost, police administrators cannot assume their past is an accurate way of measuring what officers are experiencing. If a CISD is used, it should be voluntary and not the mission end for assisting the officers in the agency.

The agency should have a process for early intervention by having field

▲ A voluntary Critical Incident Stress Debriefing following an especially bad incident is one option. But it is not a cure-all.

▲ Supervisors should make a conscious effort to regularly contact the officers involved in an especially severe traumatic event.

supervisors better trained to identify some of the stressors accompanying a traumatic incident. Supervisors and managers should not only be able to discern with the issues of stress, but make a conscious effort to contact the officers regularly after an incident.

It is not only a matter of saying something wrong, but saying nothing may carry a far greater danger for your role as a leader. It is not uncommon for officers to say they are doing fine and that they do not need additional assistance; however, that does not mean they are providing an accurate account of their feelings or level of functioning.

Field supervisors who know their officers well are in a position where they can discuss their observations with officers rather than having it appear as though they are badgering their subordinates with a barrage of questions about the incident. Supervisors who are trauma-informed and know their officers can have unrelated conversations while drawing conclusions in reference to the traumatic incident.

BENEFIT FROM OTHERS' STORIES?

Some key points to remember when confronting officers are that they are not necessarily emotionally able to hear or benefit from the personal stories of others. Comments made that frequently focus on "how it could have been worse" or "I know how you feel," while perhaps genuine and made with the best of intentions, can make the victim feel worse. Comments of that nature can feel like attempts to minimize the event and can be perceived as more of an insult than supportive.

Supervisors should be able to see some of the most common symptoms associated with trauma such as social isolation and wanting to spend more time alone; lack of self care or change in uniform appearance; poor concentration or memory; agitation or irritation over simple issues; or change in communication pattern (less talkative).

The long-term effects of allowing stress to continue unmitigated may ultimately create problems even with outstanding officers. An initial untreated or mismanaged traumatic incident can easily spill over into other problem areas within the agency and can create unpredictable liability issues.

Operating under the auspice of "It will not happen here" or even, "We will cross that bridge when we get to it," will only exasperate the problem and could result in the officer leaving the agency, the career, or developing full-blown stress disorder. If agencies do not properly and continually support their officers involved in traumatic incidents, they are not absolved from responsibility for future difficulties. Officers may have other unrelated issues that arise as they unsuccessfully attempt to cope with ongoing stressors in isolation.

SEEK PROFESSIONAL HELP

The next crucial component to managing officers involved in a traumatic incident is providing them with a professional mental-health care worker. Agencies should consider having a mental health official on the payroll but not under their control. The counselor should not be required to report any of the results of a session with victims unless it may be deleterious to the agency or the person.

The mental health counselor could ride with officers and spend time with the agency to have a better understanding of those personnel within the agency. This would also help employees build a rapport with the counselor. However, following a traumatic event, employees should be encouraged to speak with the counselor and not forced unless no other option exists.

POSITIVE PREVENTATIVE STEPS

Essentially, we not only have a duty to ensure our officers are cared for following their exposure to a critical incident, but our responsibility starts even before a critical incident occurs. With the proper choice of a mental health counselor, they could be required to provide annual education on the normal reactions to stressful situations.

We must be proactive and implement preventative techniques to minimize the potential for long-term stress disorders, which includes having solid policies and procedures in place that are utilized consistently for every traumatic incident as well as policies specific for repeated traumatic incidents involving the same officer.

Continual supervisory training will allow for more accurate assessments before seeking outside help from a clinical professional. To have the greatest impact, we need to develop and implement an integrated approach that includes preventative techniques, appropriate screening, and evaluation practices as well as ongoing follow-up and services.

It is imperative that administrators provide full support and commitment throughout the entire process. Treatment should include interventions as well as an educational component and should be both flexible and responsive to the individual officer's needs. We must assure that intervention occurs immediately following the event and before any symptoms emerge.

Family, as well as the officer's natural supports should be included, as they may need advice and guidance in their vital role in the officer's healing process. It is even more imperative that we implement better prevention techniques to ward off the effects of prolonged exposure to trauma as well as to prevent long-term stress disorders.

We never seem to have issues with responding to, and correcting, the physical trauma our officers receive. It is the invisible scars of trauma that we seem to mismanage. Doing nothing has never been an option, especially under circumstances that may affect the lives of our officers. If you have had traumatic events in your agency, and meet the officer in the hallway, you should at least know what to say.

Rodney Stearns is a Lieutenant with the Field Services Division at the Eau Claire County, Wisc. Sheriff's Office. As a crash reconstructionist, he responded to many fatal crashes. He is an instructor for various colleges in criminal justice. He has a Master's Degree in Human Development—Family Studies, concentrating in mental health. He can be contacted at rod.stearns@co.eau-claire.wi.us. Photos by Mark C. Ide.

DISCUSSION QUESTIONS

1   Do a web search and find current statistics on the suicide rates of correction officers and police officers. Are they higher than the rates of other professions? Are there gender, race, and age differences among those who work in the criminal justice field and commit suicide? If so, how do you understand the differences?

2   The Stearns article "Solutions to Stress from Traumatic Incidents" discusses how family members of a law enforcement officer can be adversely affected when a loved one experiences symptoms of post-traumatic stress disorder. However, the family can also be a source of support for the officer. Do you think criminal justice agencies should consider the needs and strengths of families when dealing with officer stress from traumatic incidents? If so, what would such an approach look like? If not, why not?

EFFECTIVE LEADERSHIP IN THE ORGANIZATION

LEONARD BIERMAN, O. C. FERRELL, AND LINDA FERRELL

CHAPTER OUTLINE

Introduction
The Nature of Leadership
Trait Approach to Leadership
Behavioral Models of Leadership
Contingency Theories of Leadership
Current Trends in the Study and Practice of Leadership

INTRODUCTION

Leadership is one of the most fascinating and widely discussed aspects of management. Because of its intangible, elusive nature, writers and practitioners have been interested in what makes good or bad leaders for centuries: scientists have been studying it for around 100 years. The number of approaches to and definitions of good leadership are nearly as numerous as the writers who have studied it. In this chapter, we define leadership and distinguish it from management, and then examine different sources of leadership power. Next, we explore several theories that attempt to determine what makes an effective leader. We conclude with a discussion of some of the approaches in the study and practice of leadership.

INSIDE MANAGEMENT

Employees Feel at Home at SAS

According to founder Charles Goodnight, "95 percent of [his] assets drive out the gate every evening." When Goodnight and his partners founded Statistical Analysis Software (SAS) in 1976, they knew they wanted to create a desirable workplace for employees. Shortly after the firm was founded, SAS began to offer health care, profit sharing, and child care. Today, the perks at SAS facilities also include recreation and fitness centers (where employees often get massages), aquatic centers, racquetball courts, an organic farm for SAS's four cafeterias, and more. When developing its campus, Google reportedly used SAS for inspiration. As the largest privately-held software company, SAS has seen its revenues grow for 35 consecutive years.

At SAS managers are encouraged not only to manage, but to do the same tasks as those they manage. This type of management has created a unified organization with little bureaucracy. It has earned respect among employees, with one employee fondly describing the organizational culture as "creative anarchy." Goodnight and all managers have set an example for employees by encouraging them to communicate with one another to accomplish all tasks and projects effectively. Managers are able to create unity among their teams, resulting in a fluid organizational structure that motivates employees to produce exceptional work in every facet of the organization.

Although the recession caused problems for SAS, Goodnight didn't lay off employees. Rather, he encouraged them to develop ideas to help SAS reduce costs. The resulting solutions enabled SAS to cut expenses by 6 to 7 percent. As a result of its employee-friendly atmosphere, SAS was number one on *Fortune's* "100 Best Places to Work For" list for two consecutive years. And these employee benefits not only contribute to a happy workplace; its low turnover rate of 4 percent versus the industry average of 20 percent also saves the company between $60 and $80 million in annual costs. The average rate of employee retention is about 10 years, although many employees have been with the company for at least 25 years.[1]

THE NATURE OF LEADERSHIP

Leadership is the process of influencing the activities of an individual or a group toward the achievement of a goal. This definition reflects three elements: the leader, the followers, and the process of influencing goal-directed behavior. Sam Walton, the late founder of Walmart stores, Mahatmas Gandhi, and President John F. Kennedy are examples of strong leaders who influenced different kinds of groups of followers to accomplish goals.

LEADERSHIP VERSUS MANAGEMENT

Management is a broad concept that encompasses activities such as planning, organizing, staffing, and controlling, as well as leading—as we have seen throughout this book. Leadership, on the other hand, focuses almost exclusively on the "people" aspects of getting a job done—inspiring, motivating, directing, and gaining commitment to organizational activities and goals. Leadership accompanies and complements the management functions, but it has more to do with coping with the dynamic, ever-changing marketplace, with rapid technological innovation, increased foreign competition, and other fluctuating market forces. In short, management influences the brain, while leadership encourages the heart and the spirit.[2]

Organizations need both management and leadership, and some leaders can provide both. Others manage but cannot lead, while still others seem born to lead, but cannot manage. Managers provide and maintain stability and predictability within the organization by setting goals, implementing appropriate action steps to achieve those goals, and allocating resources accordingly. Leaders are less reactive. They formulate and develop the vision and strategies that guide the company into the future. Additionally, managers take care of the more pragmatic matters related to employees such as job structuring, training, and delegating, whereas leaders appeal to the emotions of the employees. Leaders will connect with different employees with the organization to reinforce the company's vision, incite motivation, and encourage learning and risk taking. In this way, one can see that managers and leaders complement each other and provide a healthy balance between reason and emotion and rational behavior and risk-taking. Unfortunately, most U.S. companies today appear to be over-managed and under-led.

When Fred Smith founded the Federal Express Co., he was acting as a leader. His vision of overnight package delivery represented a quantum leap forward in the industry, and he had to inspire acceptance of and commitment to that vision by all employees, customers, and investors. Now FedEx has grown into a gigantic organization, with hundreds of complex systems. Smith and the company's executives spend much of their time managing these systems in order to provide stability and avoid chaos. Smith still spends time communicating his vision to his workers by emphasizing the need for quality and service to meet the competition.

SOURCES OF POWER

Understanding leadership requires insight into the possession and use of power. **Power** refers to a person's capacity to influence the behavior and attitudes of others. We can think of it as potential ability attributed to a person. Bosses can fire employees but seldom do on a regular basis. We can also think of power as actively attempting to influence someone to do what you want. A boss actively directing an employee's behavior represents the use of power.

In either case, power is inherent in a relationship between two people and is based on one's ability to satisfy or deny satisfaction of some need of the other. That ability may be based on a formal contractual relationship between an organization and an individual, called **organizational power**, or it can be based on an interpersonal relationship between individuals or on one's personal characteristics, called **personal power**.[3] There are eight major sources of power: legitimate, reward, coercive, expert, referent, charisma, information, and affiliative.[4]

LEGITIMATE POWER

Legitimate power comes from a person's formal position in an organization and the authority that accompanies that position. The contractual relationship between employees and managers, for example, grants managers legitimate power to influence certain kinds of behavior. However, this kind of power may be limited by the formal contract—for example, when an employee refuses to do anything more than what the specific job description dictates. Thus, using a "do it because I'm the boss" approach may limit a manager's capacity to lead.

REWARD POWER

Reward power stems from a person's ability to bestow rewards. This, too, is an organizationally based source of power because companies generally grant managers the right to assign formal rewards, such as bonuses, days off, and promotions. Managers can also use social rewards, such as praise and recognition. Effective leaders learn that the creative use of informal rewards along with formal ones enhances their ability to lead. For example, one company gives a ticket to employees who get their projects done well ahead of the deadline. The employees can then "cash in" their ticket for a paid day off during designated times of the year. Such rewards can serve to increase both productivity and employee morale.

COERCIVE POWER

Coercive power, another organizationally based source of power, is derived from a leader's control over punishments or the capacity to deny rewards. Leaders who demote, berate, withhold an expected pay increase, or threaten someone with a poor job assignment are using coercive power. Physical coercion was common in many businesses prior to the 21st century, and regulations were passed against it. Psychological and emotional coercion are more commonly used forms of negative influence today. Although regulations and laws limit a leader's ability to use coercive power, it is still all too common in many business settings. For instance, it is estimated that one in three workers have been a victim of bullying sometime during their careers. The use of punishment to gain compliance has the negative side effect of creating hostility and resentment toward the punisher and possibly reduced dedication to an organization. For instance, Enron had adopted what was termed a "rank and yank" system in which employees in the lowest 20 percent of performance levels were systematically fired. This led employees to compete against one another rather than work together, which served to create a highly competitive culture where success and profitability surpassed a concern for ethical conduct. While some still cling to the model of the hard-nosed executive boss, many CEOs see the use of coercion diminishing in favor of more positive sources of power.[5]

EXPERT POWER

Expert power is derived from a person's special knowledge or expertise in a particular area. The mechanic fixing a piece of equipment would probably have more expert power in that technical area than would a CEO. Professors and researchers rely mostly on expert power. Managers who wish also to be leaders learn to develop and use this personal source of power more than the formal sources. Bill Gates had tremendous expert power because of his computer knowledge, in addition to the formal, legitimate power that he had as founder and former CEO of Microsoft.

REFERENT POWER

Referent power results when one person identifies with and admires another. Referent power cannot be granted by organizations; it is a personal source of power you develop on your own. Through friendly communication, sharing of information, and mutually rewarding and close interpersonal relations, even friendships may develop. In such relationships, the employee may want to please the manager or some other person simply because it gives both of them pleasure or satisfaction. We do things for our friends that we will not do for others, simply because we like them.

CHARISMA

People with **charisma**, another personal source of power, inspire admiration, respect, and loyalty. People desire to emulate them based on some intangible set of personality traits. Charismatic leaders are often distinguished by two characteristics: They are usually excellent communicators, the proverbial "silver-tongued devils," and they make people feel more secure and more powerful in themselves. Martin Luther King, Jr. and Malcolm X made their followers feel strong enough to resist racism and segregation. John F. Kennedy beseeched U.S. citizens to "ask not what your country can do for you, ask what you can do for your country." More recently, President Barack Obama has inspired similar loyalty and excitement around the world. These charismatic leaders empowered their followers to serve their causes. Like referent power, charisma cannot be granted by an organization. See Table 1 for more examples of leaders who use these sources of power.

INFORMATION POWER

Information power requires having access to important information that is not common knowledge, or having the ability to control the flow of information to and from others. The information may come from formal organizational sources or informal reciprocal relationships. People at all levels of an organization can have this source of power; indeed, it is not uncommon for a CEO's secretary to be one of the most influential and powerful employees in the company. Information power may be organizational or personal.

AFFILIATIVE POWER

Affiliative power comes by virtue of a person's association with someone else who has power. It works only when those being influenced are aware of the association and recognize the power of the person from whom the power is being "borrowed." A substitute teacher, for instance, is essentially "borrowing" the power of the teacher for a day.

TABLE 1 Different Power Sources and Examples of Leaders

SOURCE	EXAMPLE
Legitimate	Jeff Bezos, CEO of Amazon, has become respected as a result of his revolutionary business savvy
Reward	James Dimon, CEO of J.P. Morgan, offers several types of rewards to employees
Coercive	Charlie Ergen, Chairman of Dish Network Corporation, is known for influencing employees' behavior aggressively
Expert/Information	Jack Welch, former CEO of General Electric, is widely followed for his precise knowledge of business management
Referent	Warren Buffett, CEO of Berkshire Hathaway, is admired by many for his integrity and decision making skills
Charisma/Affiliative	Richard Branson, CEO of Virgin Group, is authentic and inspirational to the people around him

THE USE OF POWER

Managers and leaders exercise power to garner an appropriate response from subordinates. Indra Nooyi, CEO of PepsiCo., ranks as the tenth most powerful woman in the world because of her high position within the company, which is legitimate power, but also because of the personal power she possesses in the form of expert power and charisma.[6] Responses to power from subordinates fall into three major categories: commitment, compliance, or resistance. Commitment means the subordinate does what the leader wants because he or she really wants to and is dedicated to successfully fulfilling the request. Commitment comes about because of a desire to please the other person (referent power), respect for the leader's knowledge and the belief that the desired action is the best thing to do (expert power), or the inspiration or empowerment to engage in what might be perceived as a noble behavior (charisma power). Compliance means the subordinate does only what is required and nothing more. Compliance is the likely response when a manager exercises the formal authority of his or her position (legitimate power), offers special inducements contingent on fulfilling the request (reward power), or threatens punishment (coercive power). Resistance can take many forms, from the subtle (such as working slowly) to the obvious and extreme (such as destroying products or personal belongings and systematic employee theft). Although resistance is possible with any of the sources of power, it is least likely with the personal power sources and very likely when coercion is used. Information and affiliative power may have various effects, depending on how they are exercised.

If managers want to foster employee commitment to tasks, they should develop and use personal sources of power as the primary means of influencing their employees' behavior. Organizational power sources—particularly legitimate and coercive—should be used selectively, such as when there is little time to explain rationally or encourage commitment or when the dangers of noncompliance are severe. Personal sources of power are essential when extra effort is required, when close surveillance is impossible, and when the manager has no legitimate authority or control over rewards and punishments.

EMPOWERMENT

While power is an essential component to leadership, employee empowerment has been used to encourage an innovative and productive organization. **Empowerment** is the process of providing employees with the ability to contribute input and take on responsibilities for organizational decisions. Some leaders adopt an employee-centered approach to empower employees to take on more leadership responsibilities. Although it is up to leaders to make the final decisions, they realize that involving employees in the decision making process is beneficial to the firm. For instance, research suggests that employee empowerment and effective communication from managers leads to greater employee satisfaction.[7] Other benefits of employee empowerment include increased productivity by encouraging employees to contribute their unique ideas and accept responsibilities; better customer service because employees are empowered to adjust their customer relationship strategies to different situations; and a greater ability to embrace change because empowered employees are encouraged to challenge the status quo.[8] Employee empowerment also takes some of the burden off of leaders, allowing other employees to take on greater roles in the decision making process within the organization.

To create employee empowerment, leaders must establish a transparent workplace where employees feel encouraged in contributing ideas and communicating with managers. However, this requires leaders of the organization to allow for dissent. Some managers find that they have a difficult time sharing power and permitting employees to challenge the status quo. Employees themselves often feel uncomfortable taking on additional roles due to worries about failure or getting on the wrong side of company leaders. As a result, many organizations are instituting leadership programs to help train employees to become more effective leaders. Such programs are important for both managers and employees. Managers can be trained in employee empowerment and empathy, while employees can learn leadership skills such as teamwork, conflict resolution, and communication.[9]

TRAIT APPROACH TO LEADERSHIP

The earliest approaches to the study of leadership focused, not on the process of influencing others, but on the personal characteristics of the leaders themselves. Psychologists and researchers alike tried to determine what traits—physical, intellectual, and personal—distinguish leaders from followers. Early studies revealed a perplexingly large number of traits related to leadership success. Researchers have analyzed over 300 of these studies and found a few traits to be fairly consistent characteristics of leaders.[10] However, because researchers found no definable set of traits that consistently predicts leadership success in a variety of situations, the trait approach lost credibility by the 1950s and 1960s. Experts now recognize that certain traits increase the likelihood that a person will be an effective leader, but they do not guarantee effectiveness, and the relative importance of different traits depends on the nature of the leadership situation.[11] The trait approach has not fully died out, but the focus has shifted more to what leaders do to be successful, rather than on what kinds of personalities or physiques they might have. Table 2 highlights some skills that leaders need to be effective.

TABLE 2 Skills for Successful Leaders

Empathy	Sense of humor
Truthfulness	Attracts and motivates strong employees
Poise and confidence	Commitment
Communication	Competency
Delegation	

A published analysis of leadership traits condensed the important primary ones into six core-trait categories:

Drive: Leaders desire to achieve and are ambitious about their work; they take initiatives and show energy and tenacity in accomplishing chosen goals.

Motivation: Leaders want to lead; they possess a socialized or positive need for power and are willing to take charge.

Honesty and Integrity: The best leaders are honest and truthful, and they do what they say they will do.

Self-Confidence: Leaders project their confidence by being assertive and decisive and taking risks. They admit mistakes and foster trust and commitment to a vision. They are emotionally stable, rather than recklessly adventurous.

Cognitive Ability: Leaders tend to be intelligent, perceptive, and conceptually skilled, but are not necessarily geniuses. They show analytical ability, good judgment, and the capacity to think strategically.

Business Knowledge: Leaders tend to have technical expertise in their businesses.[12]

EMOTIONAL INTELLIGENCE

Although researchers have found no definable set of traits that consistently predicts leadership success, many agree that emotional intelligence is important to being a good leader. **Emotional intelligence** involves being able to manage oneself as well as form relationships with others. Emotionally intelligent leaders such as Warren Buffett are self-aware and are able to control their emotions, enabling them to handle conflicts and challenging situations. Emotionally intelligent leaders are also able to empathize with employee concerns and make employees feel like they are important contributors to the organization.[13] Because emotional intelligence impacts how one relates to others in the organization, some employers consider it to be a better predictor of success than IQ.[14]

Psychologist Daniel Goleman classified leadership styles based upon emotional intelligence. He developed six categories for leaders: coercive, authoritative, affiliative, democratic, pace-setting, and coaching. The coercive style generally uses threats and punishments to control people, whereas the authoritative style incites followers' confidence in the leader. Leaders who employ the affiliative style hold relationships in high regard as a way to connect with others. The democratic style allows everyone to take part in important decisions. Pacesetters may intimidate their followers with their high standards, while coaches have the opposite effect by helping others achieve their goals.[15] Richard Boyatzis and Annie McKee used Goleman's categories as a jumping off point to come up with the idea of a resonant leader. Resonant leaders are aware of themselves and their emotions, have a strong passion and belief in the outcome of company objectives, and adopt a caring attitude toward employees.[16] These types of leaders also have the ability to change their leadership styles to adapt to different situations. Resonant leaders inspire employees to believe in the firm and take ownership of the company goals and mission.

BEHAVIORAL MODELS OF LEADERSHIP

As the trait approach waned, researchers began trying to identify the behaviors that distinguish effective from less effective leaders. Two major dimensions of leader behavior emerged from this body of research: One deals with how leaders get the job done, and the other deals with how leaders treat and interact with their subordinates. In this section, we will discuss three models that developed from this research: the Ohio State model, the University of Michigan model, and the leadership grid model.

THE OHIO STATE STUDIES

In an effort to describe what leaders actually do, researchers at Ohio State University analyzed the results of questionnaires they administered to a sample of leaders and followers. From this, they concluded that leadership behavior consists of two broadly defined dimensions they labeled "consideration" and "initiating structure."[17] **Consideration behaviors** involve being friendly and supportive by listening to employees' problems, supporting their actions, "going to bat" for them, and getting their input on a variety of issues. **Initiating-structure behaviors** involve defining and structuring leader-subordinate roles through activities such as scheduling, defining work tasks, setting deadlines, criticizing poor work, getting employees to accept work standards, and resolving problems. The dimensions seem to be relatively independent of each other, so leaders may rank high on one dimension and low on another at the same time.[18]

Early studies found that "Hi-Hi leaders," those ranking high in both dimensions, are most effective, although results were inconsistent. Subsequent research found that there may not be a simple relationship between the two dimensions and effectiveness. The only reliable finding has been that leaders exhibiting consideration behaviors tend to have more satisfied subordinates. Relationships between the two dimensions and effectiveness appear to depend on the situation. That "Hi-Hi" leaders are always the best leaders appears to be myth.[19]

THE UNIVERSITY OF MICHIGAN STUDIES

At about the same time the Ohio State studies were being conducted, researchers at the University of Michigan were also studying leadership effectiveness from a behavioral perspective. They too compared effective leaders to less effective leaders and came up with two dimensions of leadership behavior, which they labeled "task-oriented behaviors" and "relationship-oriented" behaviors.[20] The researchers found that effective managers engage in **task-oriented behaviors** such as planning and scheduling work, coordinating employee activities, and providing necessary supplies, equipment, and technical assistance—all designed primarily and specifically to get tasks completed and goals met. This task-oriented behavior appears to correspond to the initiating-structure dimension identified in the Ohio State studies. Martha Stewart could be considered a task-oriented leader. A self-proclaimed "control freak," Martha Stewart's ability to plan, coordinate, and provide her expertise created a media empire.[21]

The researchers also found that effective managers employ **relationship-oriented behaviors**, such as being considerate, supportive, and helpful to subordinates by showing trust and confidence, listening to employees' problems and suggestions, showing appreciation for contributions, and supporting employees' careers. Tony Hsieh at Zappos has developed a corporate culture focused on relationships and employee well-being. Employees at Zappos are encouraged to hang out together even outside of the workplace. These relationship-oriented behaviors correspond to the consideration behaviors of the Ohio State research.

Rensis Likert, a management theorist and leader of the Michigan Institute for Social Research, summarized the research by concluding that the most effective managers engage in both dimensions of leadership behavior by getting employees involved in the operation of their departments or divisions in a positive and constructive manner, setting general goals, providing fairly loose supervision, and recognizing their contributions. He called these managers **employee-centered leaders**.

Less effective managers are mostly directive in their approaches and more concerned with closely directing employees, explaining work procedures, and monitoring progress in task accomplishment; these he called **job-centered leaders**.[22]

Figure 1

Continuum of People vs. Operations

ADAPTATION OF THE LEADERSHIP GRID

The leadership grid grew out of the two-dimensional behavioral approach to leadership. Developed originally as a managerial network by consultants Robert Blake and Jane Mouton, this model builds on the Ohio State and Michigan studies and describes a leader's style as a position on a continuum between concern for operations and concern for people.[23] We have adapted the original model into a continuum shown in Figure 1. Concern for operations, which parallels task-oriented behavior and initiating structure, is on one end of the continuum, while concern for people is at the opposite end of the continuum.

There are three major styles in the continuum reflected by differing levels of the two leadership behaviors. Each extreme of the continuum represents a disproportionate management style. For example, the high touch management style represents a concern for people but little concern for operations. Google, while not completely fitting into this extreme, has some practices that cater to employees while not necessarily contributing to overall goals. The low touch management style reflects concern for operations at the expense of concern for people. For example, Charlie Ergen, former CEO of Dish Network Corporation, was known for his harsh leadership. In order to address employee tardiness, he instituted fingerprint scanners to replace employee badge scanners to enter the building. If they were even one minute late, employees were reprimanded and not allowed to offer an explanation for their tardiness. Despite the fact that this practice left employees feeling dispirited, Ergen appeared to care more about employees being to work on time than their morale. It is rare for any company, however, to fit into these two extremes because neither type usually lasts very long. A concern for people at the expense of operations will result in goals not being met, which impacts the bottom line. A concern for operations at the expense of people will lead to a dissatisfied workplace with high turnover and low productivity.

The trick for managers is to balance these two extremes to consider both people and operations. This balance is often considered the ultimate style. Those that are able to balance these two styles will achieve both efficiency and effectiveness in their operations and management. Goals are accomplished through the joint efforts of managers and employees working closely together for the good of the company and all employees. Evernote functions at a level similar to this. Employees work in teams, and while there is a team manager, hierarchic ranks are not emphasized. Additionally, the company takes steps to take care of employees with benefits such as unlimited vacation time, $1,000 spending money for vacation, and paid housecleaning two times per month for each employee.[24]

Two additional styles of leadership, not considered on the continuum, are paternalism and opportunism. *Paternalistic*, or "father knows best," management raises a high level of concern for people to reward for compliance, or punish for rejection. The paternalist strives for high results. The *opportunistic*, or "what's in it for me?" management style describes a leader who uses whatever grid style needed to obtain selfish interests and for self-promotion. These managers adapt to situations to gain maximum advantage. Performance by the manager occurs according to a system of exchanges, and effort is given only for an equivalent measure of effort from employees.

The continuum approach has as an underlying assumption that one approach—balancing between operations and people—is best. The contradictory results of the research into this style, however, suggest that some flexibility is needed in the application of this and other models.

CONTINGENCY THEORIES OF LEADERSHIP

Neither the trait nor the early behavioral approaches to leadership were able to identify conclusively a single best style of leadership. In fact, the most effective leadership style depends on the situation a leader faces. Whether to be task- or people-oriented, or job- or employee-centered, or even how much employees should be allowed to participate in decision making is contingent on certain situational characteristics. In this section, we will examine several leadership models that address contingency factors, including situational leadership theory, Fiedler's contingency theory, and path-goal theory.

SITUATIONAL LEADERSHIP THEORY

Probably the most popular leadership model, and the one most frequently applied in leadership development and training, was originally developed by Paul Hersey and Ken Blanchard as the "life cycle theory of leadership."[25] It evolved through several versions into the **situational leadership theory**, the premise of which is that a leader's style should be contingent on subordinates' skills and dedication.[26]

To understand situational leadership theory, we must define several concepts. *Directive behaviors* involve telling a subordinate the how, what, when, and where of a task and closely supervising task accomplishment. *Supportive behaviors* entail listening to subordinates, supporting and encouraging their progress, and involving them in decision making. Levels of directive and supportive behaviors are shown in Figure 2, with a leader's style falling into one of the four areas. Hersey and Blanchard suggest that the levels of directive behavior (akin to task-oriented or initiating structure behaviors) and supportive behavior (akin to people-oriented or consideration behaviors) that a leader uses should depend on the development level of the subordinates. *Development level* refers to a subordinate's skills or ability in setting and attaining goals related to a specific task and his or her dedication toward accepting responsibility for those goals.

According to this theory, managers assess an employee's development level and ascertain the appropriate levels of directive and supportive behaviors based upon how much support and oversight is needed. A directive leadership style involves high oversight with low support. Managers assuming this style tell the employee what to do and when, where, and how to do it, to guide the employee in properly carrying out the task. This style may be appropriate with new employees unfamiliar with how to perform. A coaching leadership style involves both high oversight and high support. Employees at this level have gained some, but not full knowledge of their tasks and have low dedication because they have not figured out a strategy for the long-term. Managers can coach employees with fairly high levels of direction as well as a high level of support to deal with their waning dedication.

Employees that require a mainly supportive management style require high support but not much oversight. The manager may listen to complaints, show support, and help talk through personal issues, but seldom needs to provide direction in task areas. This occurs when employees have been around the organization a while and have the skills, motivation, and desire to perform their job duties. Finally, the most highly competent employees are both competent and committed. For these employees a delegating style of leadership characterized by low support and low oversight is appropriate. It provides subordinates full rein to determine how to perform their tasks.

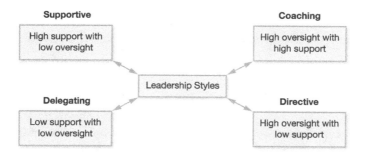

Figure 2

Alternative Situational Leadership Styles

The biggest takeaway of this theory is that management styles depend on the situation of where employees are at in their development. Therefore, a manager might assume a delegating leadership style to an employee that has been at the organization for a long time while assuming a directive leadership style with new hires.

For example, in a football team of eleven players, only one or two might be superstars like Tom Brady, Peyton Manning, or Brett Favre, who need little coaching because they have both high skills and high dedication. Six or seven players might have varying levels of skills or dedication; they perform well but require the appropriate motivation and direction to do so. One or two players may not show much ability and have little dedication to the team. In order to be successful, coaches need to focus on the middle six or seven who make up the bulk of the team and should probably avoid those without strong skills or dedication.[27]

Application of the situational leadership model is not easy. Managers must first observe and communicate with employees to determine their level of development. Managers must also be flexible in applying direction and support because employees vary from one to another, as well as within themselves, over time and from task to task. Some managers are inflexible in their leadership style. Moreover, employees may not initially agree with a manager's assessment of their development level, thus requiring a leader's skill in arriving at an assessment consensus and an agreed-upon leadership style, a process called **contracting for leadership style**. It is also important for a leader to be constantly aware of the need to develop team members by gradually moving ahead of them on the leadership curve and pulling them along the development continuum. Yet another difficulty with the model is that it deals with only one aspect of a situation, the subordinates, and ignores other possibly important factors.

FIEDLER'S CONTINGENCY THEORY

While Blanchard's theory calls for leaders to adjust their behaviors to meet the situational needs of subordinates, Professor Fred Fiedler took a different approach in his earlier **contingency theory**, suggesting that successful leadership requires matching leaders with primarily stable leadership styles to the demands of the situation.[28] If a leader's style does not match the situation, then either the situation should be changed or another leader should be found who does match the situation.

LEADERSHIP STYLE

A major, often controversial aspect of Fiedler's theory is how he characterizes and measures leadership style. Fiedler asserts that a leader tends to be either relationship-oriented (similar to the consideration or employee-centered styles) or task-oriented (comparable to the initiating structure and directive styles). He considers a leader's style, like a trait, to be rooted in his or her personality and to be stable, regardless of the situation. Task-oriented leaders consistently emphasize getting the job done without much concern for their subordinates' feelings; relationship-oriented leaders are most concerned about their people across all kinds of tasks. However, Fiedler's critics counter that people are capable of learning and changing their behaviors, even leadership behavior.[29]

To measure a leader's style, Fiedler devised a **Least Preferred Coworker (LPC) Scale** consisting of a series of adjective continuums. Low-LPC leaders view and describe their least preferred coworkers negatively and are thought to be task-oriented. High-LPC leaders view even their least preferred coworker in a relatively favorable light and are thought to be relationship-oriented. Fiedler's LPC scale to measure leadership style is also controversial, with some researchers questioning the scale's validity.[30]

SITUATIONAL CONTINGENCIES

Whether a relationship-oriented or task-oriented leader will be successful depends on the favorability of the situation—that is, the extent to which the situation gives the leader control over subordinate behavior. Favorability is defined by three aspects of the situation:

Leader-member relations—The extent to which the leader is accepted by group members and has their support, respect, and goodwill is the most important determinant of favorability.

Task structure—The degree to which a task is well-defined or has standard procedures for goal accomplishment. Creative or ambiguous tasks would be less structured.

Position power—The extent to which a leader has formal authority over employees to evaluate their work, assign tasks, and administer rewards and punishment.

By combining these three situational variables, Fiedler's Contingency Model derives eight different situations, called octants. The most favorable situation (octant 1) is one in which leader-member relations are good, the task is structured, and the leader has strong position power. The least favorable situation (octant 8) is one where a leader has poor relations with subordinates, an unstructured task, and little formal power.

STYLE EFFECTIVENESS

In his research, Fiedler found that task-oriented leaders tended to be most effective (have higher group productivity) in the three most favorable and the very least favorable situations (octants 1, 2, 3, 8), while relationship-oriented leaders were most effective in the situations of moderate favorableness. If the leader's style does not match the situational demands, Fiedler would advise the leader to alter the situation, perhaps by restructuring the task or seeking more position power.

There has been considerable research on Fiedler's model, generating both support and criticism for his ideas. Criticisms of the model include its neglect of leaders who score in the middle on the LPC scale, the use of the LPC scale itself, the fact that many leaders can and do change their behaviors, and the relative lack of consideration of other situational characteristics related to the followers.[31] Nonetheless, Fiedler's contingency theory was one of the first to recognize the importance of the situation to leadership effectiveness, and it sensitized managers and researchers alike to the ineffectiveness of the one-best-way approach to leadership.

PATH-GOAL THEORY

Another contingency model of leadership was developed by Robert House as an outgrowth of the expectancy theory of motivation. **Path-goal theory** is so named because it is concerned with how leaders affect subordinates' perceptions of their personal and work goals and the paths to goal attainment. It considers leaders effective to the degree that their behavior increases employees' attainment of goals and clarifies paths to these goals. What behaviors will help to accomplish these positive results depend on two aspects: leader behavior and situational factors.[32]

LEADER BEHAVIOR

Path-goal theory recognizes four major types of behavior:

> *Directive Leadership:* As with situational leadership theory, directive behaviors include giving task guidance, scheduling work, maintaining standards, and clarifying expectations.
> *Supportive Leadership:* Leaders concentrate on being approachable, showing concern for employees' well-being, doing little things to make the work environment more pleasant, and helping to satisfy employees' personal needs.
> *Participative Leadership:* Leaders consult with subordinates, solicit suggestions, and seriously consider their input when making decisions.
> *Achievement-Oriented Leadership:* Leaders set challenging goals, expect high performance, constantly seek improved performance, and show confidence in employees' ability to accomplish goals.

At different times and under different conditions, any of these leader behaviors may be most effective. Unlike Fiedler's model, path-goal theory assumes that leaders can adapt their styles to meet the demands of the situation or needs of subordinates to gain favorable outcomes. See Table 3 for examples of these four types of leader behavior.

TABLE 3 Examples of Path-Goal Theory Behaviors

BEHAVIOR	EXAMPLE
Directive	Anne Mulcahy, former CEO of Xerox, successfully guided the company through the 2008 recession by setting new standards and reorienting employees
Supportive	Mark Zuckerberg, CEO of Facebook, sits among his employees, who see him as approachable and concerned for them
Participative	Marissa Mayer, CEO of Yahoo!, holds regular office hours for employees to give feedback or offer new ideas
Achievement-Oriented	Wendy Kopp, Founder of Teach for America, wanted to create educational equality and has been successful by setting goals and inspiring others

SITUATIONAL FACTORS

Path-goal theory proposes that two classes of situational factors affect what leadership behaviors are appropriate: (1) employees' personal characteristics, and (2) environmental pressures and demands with which the employee must cope to accomplish the goal.

One important personal characteristic is an individual's locus of control (LOC), the extent to which a person believes he or she has control over what happens to him or her in life. Individuals who have an internal LOC believe they largely control what happens to them; those with an external LOC believe that their lives are more controlled by fate, luck, chance, or significant other people. Consider Sarah, who has done poorly on a management test. If Sarah has an internal LOC, she will probably say that her poor grade is due to not studying hard enough, but if she has an external LOC, she may attribute the poor grade to bad luck or an excessively difficult test. An individual with an internal locus of control may require less directive behavior than one with an external LOC. Another personal factor is an employee's belief in his or her own ability to perform the task at hand. People with low confidence in their ability will likely respond better to directive behavior.

Environmental characteristics include (1) the nature of the task structure, (2) the formal authority of the situation, and (3) the nature of primary work groups. Although there are many propositions concerning how situational characteristics, personal characteristics, and leader behaviors interact to influence employees, the general premise of the path-goal theory is that the leader should apply whatever behavior helps to provide more positive rewards for employees, to strengthen employees' beliefs that their efforts will lead to goal accomplishment and positive rewards, or to make rewards more contingent on goal accomplishment.

Path-goal theory has been very beneficial by pointing out a number of important situational contingency variables not covered in other theories; it also points out the important motivational consequences of leader style on subordinate attitudes, beliefs, and behaviors.

CURRENT TRENDS IN THE STUDY AND PRACTICE OF LEADERSHIP

Although the contingency approach is still used, a number of other approaches to the study of leadership have been introduced in recent years. In this section, we will discuss the leader substitute approach, the leader-member exchange theory, charismatic leadership, authentic leadership, servant leadership, transactional and transformational leadership, gender and leadership, and leadership challenges, none of which totally abandons the contingency approach.

LEADERSHIP SUBSTITUTES THEORY

The contingency models discuss conditions that call for certain leadership behaviors. Some situational aspects have an even greater effect by severely limiting the ability of a leader to influence outcomes. Two such situational factors have been identified as substitutes and neutralizers.[33] Some other situational aspects actually have a positive impact on the leader behaviors; hence, they are called enhancers.

Leadership substitutes are aspects of the task, subordinates, or organization that act in place of leader behavior and thus render it unnecessary. For example, unambiguous, routine tasks or employees' knowledge, ability, and experience can substitute for task-oriented or directive behaviors. For example, Whole Foods allows service employees to form teams and make independent decisions.

In other situations, leaders may not even be necessary. If a cohesive work team of trained professionals performs structured tasks in a highly formalized environment, then little direct supervision and involvement by a leader may be warranted. Indeed, the understanding and creative use of leadership substitutes may be integral to the success of self-managed work teams.

Leadership neutralizers are aspects of the task, subordinates, or organization that either paralyze, destroy, or counteract the effect of a leadership behavior. For example, if employees, such as those at FedEx and UPS, are indifferent to organizational rewards, then a supervisor engaging in the supportive leadership behavior of praising and rewarding would likely have little positive effect on employee satisfaction or motivation. In such a situation, the supervisor may have to stick to task-oriented behaviors, try other supportive (but non-reward-oriented) behaviors, or replace these employees with ones who will work within the system.

In some situations, other changes might be made that enhance the effectiveness of a leader's behavior. **Leadership enhancers** are aspects of the task, subordinates, or organization that amplify a leader's impact on employees. For example, if a nonperformance-based reward system is neutralizing a leader's impact, then changing the system to give the leader more power to influence rewards can make the same leadership behavior more effective. FedEx has an award that can be given on the spot for doing something outstanding. Likewise, having team-building exercises as part of a training program may aid in fostering positive group norms and values that help employees accept the task-oriented behaviors of a fairly directive leader. Dig This is a company offering team-building and motivational leadership exercises. The company uses heavy equipment, such as tractors and bulldozers, as tools to teach groups of employees how to work together. The company has been successful because it combines training with elements of fun. The creation of leadership enhancers can work very well when a leader has the necessary skill and appropriate organizational goals but is prevented by one or more neutralizers from being effective.[34]

In general, understanding how substitutes, neutralizers, and enhancers influence the effectiveness of leadership behavior can help an organization when a leader cannot be changed for political, financial, ethical, or other practical reasons. It can also play an important role when leadership is in transition.

LEADER-MEMBER EXCHANGE THEORY

The **Leader-Member Exchange (LMX) Theory** describes how leaders develop "unique" working relationships with each of their subordinates, based on the nature of their social exchanges.[35] Each leader-subordinate relationship differs in terms of both the feelings present and the behaviors demonstrated. Higher-quality relationships are reflected by more positive attitudinal statements, closer emotional ties, and stronger mutual commitment and loyalty, as well as more employee influence and autonomy.[36] Based on these relationships, leaders tend to develop *in-groups*—those subordinates who are part of their "team"—and *out-groups*—those who are not.

Research has found that in-group members perform better, have higher levels of satisfaction, are promoted more quickly, and have lower turnover rates. This implies that employees should try to be in the in-group if they desire more rewards. Managers need to be aware that these two distinct groups can develop, with both positive and negative consequences. If the in-group includes virtually every employee, then all workers will be more likely to receive these positive outcomes. Out-group members, though, will often feel disenchanted and resentful and lose their team identification and commitment.

Although the theory is somewhat vague on how leader-member exchange relationships develop, some recent research suggests that friendship and the process of forming friendships may parallel the LMX relationship development process and have similar effects. Simply becoming and remaining friends on the job may be the essential element of positive LMX relationships and may assist the leader in motivating employees.[37]

CHARISMATIC LEADERSHIP

Much has been written about charismatic leaders in nearly all phases of public life. The founder of Walmart Sam Walton; Michael Dell of Dell Inc.; Payton Manning, the quarterback of the Denver Broncos; and George Steinbrenner the shipbuilder turned Yankees baseball team owner—all are examples of charismatic leaders. Charisma has become even more important as competition has grown; today's companies need to inspire employees to higher levels of performance in order to meet stiff competition. If we can find out what makes a leader charismatic, then we may be able to advance our organizations and motivate employees like never before. Thus, a closer look at charisma is warranted.

Charismatic leaders inspire followers to a higher level of performance, instill confidence in themselves and other leaders, empower employees and subordinates, and generate tremendous devotion and obedience.[38] This devotion can sometimes rise to the level of cult leaders. Charismatic leaders have a strong sense of dominance, self-confidence, a need to influence, and a belief in the value and righteousness of their causes.[39] They are typically eloquent speakers who can clearly express a vision or ideology, and convince people of its value no matter how extreme.[40] Howard Schultz of Starbucks had to return as CEO to lead the coffee chain after the company declined under new leadership. The first thing he did was to re-communicate the vision and values of Starbucks.

For our purposes, it is more important to know what charismatic leaders actually do, especially in the business world. They tend to promote causes that deviate greatly from the status quo, yet still fall within the realm of acceptance by followers. They take personal risks that often appear heroic and engage in unconventional behavior to achieve the changes they desire. They assess the environment realistically and implement innovative strategies when the environment appears favorable. Finally, they engage in self-promotion to inspire employees or followers, often by presenting the status quo as negative and their vision and themselves as the solution. They exert personal power (expert and referent) that may involve elitist, entrepreneurial, and exemplary behaviors that position them as reformers, rather than administrators or managers.[41] Finally, charismatic leaders maintain intensely personal relationships with their followers, based on emotional rather than rational grounds.

Contrary to traditional beliefs, not only can many of these behaviors be learned, but they represent a separate dimension of leadership behavior, distinct from consideration or initiating structure, that enhances employees' task performance and satisfaction. Charismatic leadership may help convey the importance of a given task, while initiating structure conveys the orderliness of the task, and consideration expresses the shared responsibility (supportiveness) for the task.[42] Table 4 provides some steps for successful leadership.

TABLE 4 Steps for Effective Leadership

1. Act as a role model for employees.
2. Clearly communicate company expectations and mission.
3. Encourage employee participation and creativity.
4. Communicate core values.
5. Listen as much as you speak and encourage feedback.
6. Empower employees to make decisions.
7. Identify and guard against ethical risks.
8. Build sincere relationships.
9. Evaluate employee successes and failures.
10. Engage the workforce in continuous improvement.

AUTHENTIC LEADERSHIP

Another form of leadership that is gaining acceptance is authentic leadership. **Authentic leaders** are passionate about company objectives, model corporate values in the workplace, and form strong relationships with stakeholders.[43] In other words, authentic leaders "practice what they preach." Other characteristics of authentic leaders include self-awareness, a drive to achieve the company's mission, strong connections with stakeholders, and the ability to adopt a long-term perspective.[44] Kim Jordan, CEO of New Belgium Brewing, is an example of an authentic leader. When she co-founded the company, she collaborated on a set of values that would direct the company's corporate culture. Among these values was a strong emphasis on employee involvement and sustainability. As a leader, she tries to ensure that every activity performed by New Belgium Brewing aligns with its core values. Today NBB engages in numerous sustainability initiatives. It purchases wind credits to offset its energy use, investigates ways to recycle packaging and other materials, and even provides employees with a bicycle after one year of employment to reduce gas emissions from driving. It is also 100 percent employee-owned, and employees actively participate in company operations.

SERVANT LEADERSHIP

Servant leadership is not mutually exclusive of authentic leadership, as servant leaders also lead by example and form strong relationships with employees. Servant leadership was first coined by Robert K. Greenleaf in his 1970 essay "The Servant as Leader." According to Greenleaf, servant leaders try to ensure that the highest priorities of their followers are met. Effective servant leaders help followers to grow.[45] In an organization, a servant leader would not measure success solely by productivity but also by how employees are growing in their skills, well-being, and career opportunities.

Servant leaders model servant leadership for their followers, are people-centric, treat others with respect and integrity, demonstrate humility, and remain vigilant and disciplined.[46] Former CEO of ServiceMaster William Pollard modeled this type of leadership. During one particular board meeting, when Pollard spilled a cup of coffee, he got down on his hands and knees to clean the spill himself rather than letting someone else do it.[47] TD Industries and Synovus Financial Corporation have adopted servant leadership as the foundation and philosophy of their companies. Employees at TD Industries are considered to be partners rather than subordinates and own most of the stock, while Synovus has instituted family-friendly policies to encourage employees to have a healthy work-life balance.[48]

TRANSACTIONAL VERSUS TRANSFORMATIONAL LEADERSHIP

The discussions of leader-member exchanges and charismatic leadership highlight the contrast between two major leadership styles currently being discussed by leadership experts: transactional and transformational leadership.[50] Although these two leadership styles differ, studies have shown that both forms of leadership can have positive outcomes. One study, for instance, found that transactional and transformational leadership decreased the likelihood for unethical communication (bullying) in the workplace.[51]

Transactional leadership is more traditional, with managers engaging in both task-and consideration-oriented behaviors in an exchange manner—you do things for me, and I'll do things for you. Transactional leaders get things done by promising and providing recognition, praise, pay increases, and advancements in return for higher performance. They also impose punishments on workers who perform poorly. Some managers actively engage in these types of transactions by seeking out opportunities to take action to improve performance and thus reward employees. Other less effective managers use a more passive management-by-exception approach and often concentrate on punishing non-standard performance.[52] Although the active-reward approach has shown better results than the passive-punishment approach, both can result in mediocre performance. In a path-goal fashion, these two approaches require the manager to clarify subordinate roles, define subordinate needs, and clarify how those needs will be met in exchange for valued outcomes. The leaders' effectiveness is limited in many cases by lack of control over organizational rewards and punishments as well as the inability to excite, inspire, or foster commitment in employees.[53]

Transformational leadership goes beyond mere exchange relationships by inspiring employees to look beyond their own self-interests and by generating awareness and acceptance of the group's purposes and mission. Transformational leaders often appeal to higher ideals and ethical values such as truthfulness, transparency, fairness, and diversity. Transformational leaders have tremendous power to do good things, however. In business, they can excite employees to perform beyond what they thought they were capable of doing. Employees in these organizations work in order to satisfy the higher-order needs identified in Maslow's hierarchy. Research has shown that transformational leadership is even more effective than servant leadership in organizational learning.[54] Examples of transformational leaders would be Ursula Burns, who led Xerox out of a major crisis; Michael Dell, whose vision and inventory strategies caused his company to rapidly grow into a multi-billion dollar firm; and Steve Jobs, who transformed a struggling Apple into the world's most valuable brand. Table 5 compares transformational leadership with transactional leadership.

TABLE 5 Transactional versus Transformational Leadership

TRANSACTIONAL LEADERSHIP CHARACTERISTICS	EXAMPLES	TRANSFORMATIONAL LEADERSHIP CHARACTERISTICS	EXAMPLES
▪ Use of reward power ▪ Negotiates for performance ▪ Emphasis on required conduct ▪ Good for rapidly changing situations	▪ U.S. Army ▪ General Motors ▪ New Orleans Saints ▪ Delta Airlines ▪ Bank of America	▪ Uses charisma to inspire employees ▪ Communicates a shared vision ▪ Promotes change ▪ Strong support for an ethical culture	▪ Whole Foods ▪ Amazon ▪ Apple ▪ Berkshire Hathaway ▪ 3M

A number of characteristics seem to distinguish transformational leaders from the more traditional transactional leaders:

Charisma: Transformational leaders provide a vision and mission, instilling a sense of trust and respect in followers. Charisma is a necessary condition for transformational leadership, but it is insufficient without the remaining traits. Tony Hsieh of Zappos is charismatic with his emphasis on WOW customer service and his ability to motivate employees.

Inspiration: Transformational leaders communicate through images, conveying a simple yet powerful message that inspires followers to a higher purpose. Google's corporate motto, "Don't be evil," is a result of this aspect of transformational leadership.

Intellectual Stimulation and Empowerment: Transformational leaders stimulate their followers' intellectual process by promoting rationality and problem solving. They are willing to take risks and get their followers thoroughly involved in their purpose. Steve Jobs of Apple, Inc. led his company with these characteristics.

Individual Consideration: They give individualized and personal attention to followers. They act as coaches, developers, and supporters, admonishing when necessary, but emphasizing the positive. John Mackey, CEO of Whole Foods, embodies individual consideration by making sure his employees and their families are taken care of.

Change Facilitation: They recognize the need for and promote change. They see themselves as agents of change who are willing to commit themselves and their subordinates' involvement to the future they envision. Jeff Bezos is a change facilitator. He left his job to start an online book store company and refused to stop there. Today Amazon sells everything from media to electronics.

Integrity: They promote the higher-order values noted above and model honesty and integrity with their own behavior.[55] Warren Buffet tries to hire managers with integrity and a concern for ethics.

Transformational leadership, although not common in business and government, is certainly not restricted to a few "born" charismatics. Moreover, research has found that transformational leadership exists at all levels of organizational hierarchies and is positively related to a number of different performance criteria in an extremely broad range of organizations: senior U. S. Navy officers, business and industry leaders in many countries, educational administrators, and religious leaders.[56] Perhaps the most exciting aspect of transformational leadership is that there is increasing evidence that it can be learned.

GENDER AND LEADERSHIP

With more and more women advancing to higher managerial positions, it is natural to examine the relationship between leadership and gender. Numerous studies over the years have shown that while male and female leaders may have different leadership styles, overall both are equally effective in leading others.[57] However, there continues to be a gap between female top managers and male top managers in business. Female CEOs such as Marillyn Hewson of Lockheed Martin, Indra Nooyi of PepsiCo, and Virginia Rometty from IBM make up a much smaller percentage than their male counterparts. Approximately 4 percent of CEOs at Fortune 500 companies are women.

However, recent studies are showing that female leaders actually score higher on many leadership dimensions.[58] For instance, women leaders tend to score higher on interpersonal skills, teamwork, empathy, and mentoring.[59] As collaboration becomes increasingly important in organizations, demand for these types of leadership skills is rising. More attention is being paid to "soft" leadership skills including self-awareness, empathy, motivation, and social skills.[60] Many of these skills have traditionally been thought of as feminine and therefore less useful to management. Yet in recent years the business landscape has begun to shift from a hierarchal leadership style to one built upon relationships and collaboration. The more masculine qualities of assertiveness, vision, and ambition continue to remain important,[61] and both genders should try to incorporate both "soft" and "hard" skills into their management styles.

Despite the equal leadership effectiveness of the two genders, women remain underrepresented in leadership roles. Due to popular stereotypes, women tend to be characterized as nurturers and selfless, traits that have not been traditionally looked upon with favor in terms of leadership qualities. Even female leaders who adopt more "masculine" traits of aggressiveness, ambition, and dominance may be looked down upon for acting "too masculine."[62] However, as the business environment continues to evolve, more women are being recognized for their leadership abilities. Evidence also suggests that women might have advantages in transformational leadership due to their ability to connect with followers.

Sheryl Sandberg, the corporate operations officer at Facebook, has exemplified the woman as a leader. Named as one of the "50 Most Powerful Women in Business," Sandberg is in charge of maintaining positive relationships with stakeholders, expanding Facebook into other markets, and anticipating threats to the company such as new regulation. Her previous job as vice president of online sales at Google helped hone her leadership abilities, enabling her to take on a major managerial role when she arrived at Facebook. Sandberg also appears to possess the people skills that CEO Mark Zuckerberg sometimes appears to lack.[63] Sandberg demonstrates how ambition, interpersonal skills, and collaboration can successfully lead a firm to greater opportunities. In the next section, we present a set of behavioral practices that leaders of all kinds in all types of situations can develop in themselves and help to develop in others.

THE LEADERSHIP CHALLENGE

James Kouzes and Barry Posner list five major leadership practices—each with two behavioral subcategories—that they found present in successful leaders.[64] These five practices are quite similar to the characteristics of transformational leadership and, moreover, are behaviors that nearly any manager (or aspiring manager) can learn. Kouzes and Posner challenge managers to become true leaders by:

CHALLENGING THE PROCESS

Leaders act as pioneers by changing the status quo. They do this by searching out opportunities to change, grow, and improve, as well as experiment, take risks, and learn from their mistakes. They actively look for things to change, and they encourage subordinates not to fear taking a calculated risk with them. Former Target CEO Bob Ulrich began a process of reinventing Target to be perceived as hipper and more stylish, as well as affordable enough to compete directly with Walmart. Current CEO Gregg Steinhafel has continued this mission to provide low-cost yet stylish items.

INSPIRING A SHARED VISION

Leaders begin to inspire by envisioning the future—perhaps a new facility, a major process innovation, or a new product or market. They then enlist others in the common vision by appealing to their values, interests, hopes, and dreams. They paint a picture with language, using metaphors and symbols to give life to their vision and attract others to it. Steve Jobs and Michael Dell epitomize the visionary leader.

ENABLING OTHERS TO ACT

Leaders build successful teams and make others feel like owners of the vision by fostering collaboration and strengthening others. They encourage collaboration by emphasizing cooperative, instead of competitive, goals, by seeking integrative solutions, and by building relationships based on trust, mutual respect, and individual dignity. They empower others by involving them in planning and decision making, along with granting autonomy and discretion.

MODELING THE WAY

Leaders epitomize what they want others to do, and they encourage them to do it. First, they set the example by developing a set of values. They then reflect those values in decisions they make and actions they take. They also plan small wins by dividing tasks into smaller chunks and experimenting frequently, giving people a sense of choice and accomplishment along the way. They build commitment to the goal and the process. Bill Gates modeled the work ethic of Microsoft by working long hours when he led the company.

ENCOURAGING THE HEART

Leaders make people feel good about what they are doing by recognizing contributions and celebrating accomplishments. Effective leaders use a variety of rewards and strive to link them to performance. Leaders who encourage the heart also cheerlead, have public ceremonies and rituals, stay personally involved, and build caring social networks. They give heart to others. Vince Lombardi said that love—which he defined as loyalty and teamwork—was at the core of his success as a coach.

Additionally, leaders must be able to influence others to follow them. Good interpersonal skills and the ability to persuade others are therefore important components of leadership. Figure 3 shows some of the ways that leaders can build influence within an organization. Managers who engage in these leadership practices are more likely to be perceived as leaders and gain the personal sense of achievement that accompanies the accomplishment of important goals through people.

Figure 3

Steps for Building Persuasion

KEY TERMS AND CONCEPTS

affiliative power 322
authentic leader 335
charisma 321
coercive power 320
consideration behaviors 325
contingency theory 329
contracting for leadership style 329
emotional intelligence 324
employee-centered leaders 326
empowerment 323
expert power 320
information power 321
initiating-structure behaviors 325
job-centered leaders 326
Leader-Member Exchange (LMX)
Theory 334
leadership 318
leadership enhancers 333

leadership neutralizers 332
leadership substitutes 332
Least Preferred Coworker (LPC)
Scale 330
legitimate power 319
organizational power 319
path-goal theory 331
personal power 319
power 319
referent power 321
relationship-oriented behaviors 326
reward power 320
servant leader 336
situational leadership theory 328
task-oriented behaviors 325
transactional leadership 337
transformational leadership 338

• • •

NOTES

1 "No Doubt About It," *Inc.*, September 2011, pp. 104–10; Michael Lee Stallard, "Has SAS Chairman Jim Goodnight Cracked the Code of Corporate Culture?" *The Economic Times*, June 18, 2010, http://economictimes.indiatimes.com/features/corporate-dossier/has-sas-chairmanjim-goodnight-cracked-the-code-ofcorporate-culture/articleshow/6060110.cms (accessed September 6, 2013); "100 Best Companies to Work For: SAS," *CNNMoney*, http://money.cnn.com/magazines/fortune/bestcompanies/2011/snapshots/1.html (accessed September 6, 2013); "100 Best Companies to Work For," *CNN Money*, http://money.cnn.com/magazines/fortune/best-companies/ (accessed September 6, 2013); "SAS: A new no. one best employer," *CNN Money*, January 22, 2010, http://money.cnn.com/2010/01/21/technology/sas_best_companies.fortune/ (accessed September 6, 2013).

2 James M. Kouzes and Barry Z. Posner, *The Leadership Challenge: How to Get Extraordinary Things Done in Organizations* (San Francisco: Jossey-Bass Publishers, 1987).

3 See Gary Yukl, *Leadership in Organizations*, 2nd ed. (Engle-wood Cliffs, NJ: Prentice Hall, 1989) for a thorough discussion of the subtleties surrounding the definitions and approaches to the study of power.

4 Adapted from Gary Yukl, *Leadership in Organizations*; and Robert C. Benfari, Harry E. Wilkinson, and Charles D. Orth, "The Effective Use of Power," *Business Horizons* 29(May-June 1986): 12–16.

5 Thomas A. Stewart, "New Ways to Exercise Power,' *Fortune*, November 6, 1989, 52–64; and Benfari, Wilkinson, and Orth, "The Effective Use of Power."

6 "The World's 100 Most Powerful Women," *Forbes*, 2013, http://www.forbes.com/power-women/list/ (accessed September 6, 2013).

7 Soonhee Kim, "Participative Management and Job Satisfaction: Lessons for Management Leadership," *Public Administration Review* 62 (March/April 2002): 231–241.

8 Leigh Richards, "What Are the Benefits of Employee Empowerment?" *Small Business Chronicle*, http://smallbusiness.chron.com/benefits-employee-empowerment-1177.html (accessed September 12, 2013).

9 Craig L. Pearce and Charles C. Manz, "*The New Silver Bullets of Leadership:* The Importance of Self- and Shared Leadership in Knowledge Work," *Organizational Dynamics, 34* (2005):, 130–140; S. Holt and J. Marques, "Empathy in Leadership: Appropriate or Misplaced? An Empirical Study on a Topic that is Asking for Attention," *Journal of Business Ethics, 105* (2012): 95–105.

10 Ralph M. Stogdill, *Handbook of Leadership: A Survey of the Literature* (New York: Free Press, 1974).

11 Bernard Bass, *Handbook of Leadership: A Survey of Theory and Research* (New York: Free Press, 1981) as summarized in Yukl's *Leadership in Organizations.*

12 Shelley A. Kirkpatrick and Edwin A. Locke, "Leadership: Do Traits Matter?" *The Academy of Management Executive* 5 (May 1991): 48–60.

13 Robert Kerr, John Garvin, Norma Heaton, and Emily Boyle, "Emotional intelligence and leadership effectiveness," *Leadership & Organizational Development Journal* 27 (2006): 265–279.

14 "Seventy-One Percent of Employers Say They Value Emotional Intelligence over IQ, According to CareerBuilderSurvey," CareerBuilder, August18, 2011, http://www.careerbuilder.com/share/aboutus/pressreleasesdetail.aspx?id=pr652&sd =8/18/2011&ed=8/18/2099 (accessed March 21, 2013).

15 Daniel Goleman, "Leadership That Gets Results," Harvard Business Review, March-April 2000, pp. 82–83.

16 Richard Boyatzis and Annie McKee, *Resonant Leadership: Renewing Yourself and Connecting with Others Through Mindfulness, Hope and Compassion* (Boston: Harvard Business Review Press, 2005); Bruce Rosenstein, "Resonant leader is one in tune with himself, others," USA Today, November 27, 2005, http://usatoday30.usatoday.com/money/books/reviews/2005-11-27-resonant-book-usat_x.htm (accessed March 21, 2013).

17 Chester A. Schriesheim and Barbara J. Bird, "Contributions of the Ohio State Studies to the Field of Leadership,' *Journal of Management* 5 (Fall 1979): 135–145; Carroll L. Shartle, "Early Years of the Ohio State University Leadership Studies," *Journal of Management* 5 (Fall 1979): 126–134.

18 Steven Kerr, Chester A. Schriesheim, Charles J. Murphy, and Ralph M. Stogdill, "Toward a Contingency Theory of Leadership Based Upon the Consideration and Initiating Structure Literature," *Organizational Behavior and Human Performance* 12 (August 1974): 62–82; L. L. Larson, J. G. Hunt, and R. N. Osburn, "The Great Hi-Hi Leader Behavior Myth: A Lesson from Occam's Razor," *Academy of Management Journal* 19 (December 1976): 628–641.

19 Paul C. Nystrom, "Managers and the Hi-Hi Leader Myth," *Academy of Management Journal* 21 (June 1978): 325–331.

20 Bass, *Handbook of Leadership.*

21 Patty LaNoue Stearns, "Martha Stewart consorts with fans," *Herald-Journal*, July 12, 1995, E3.

22 Rensis Likert, "From Production—and Employee—Centeredness to Systems 1–4," *Journal of Management* 5 (Fall 1979): 147–156; and Rensis Likert, *The Human Organization* (New York: McGraw-Hill Book Company, 1967).

23 Robert R. Blake and Anne Adams McCanse, *Leadership Dilemmas-Grid Solutions* (Houston: Gulf Publishing Co., 1991).

24 Adam Bryant, "Phones Are Out, But the Robot Is In," *The New York Times*, April 7, 2012, http://www.nytimes.com/2012/04/08/business/phil-libin-of-evernote-on-its-unusual-corporate-culture.html?pagewanted=all&_r=0 (accessed September 16, 2013).

25 Paul Hersey and Kenneth Blanchard, "Life Cycle Theory of Leadership," *Training and Development Journal* 2 (May 1969): 4–6.

26 Kenneth Blanchard, Patricia Zigarmi, and Drea Zigarmi, *Leadership and the One Minute Manager* (New York: William Morrow & Company, 1985).

27 Richard Rapaport, "To Build a Winning Team: An Interview with Head Coach Bill Walsh," *Harvard Business Review* 71 (January-February 1993): 110–120.

28 Fred E. Fiedler, "Engineer the Job to Fit the Man," *Harvard Business Review* 53 (September-October 1965): 115–122.

29 Yukl, *Leadership in Organizations*.

30 Ramadhar Singh, "Leadership Style and Reward Allocation: Does Least Preferred Co-Worker Scale Measure Task and Relation Orientation?" *Organizational Behavior and Human Performance* 33 (October 1983): 178–197; and Chester A. Schriesheim and Steven Kerr, "Theories and Measures of Leadership: A Critical Appraisal of Current and Future Directions," in *Leadership: The Cutting Edge*, eds. J.G. Hunt and L.L. Larson (Carbondale, IL: Southern Illinois University Press, 1977).

31 Yukl.

32 Robert J. House and Terence R. Mitchell, "Path-Goal Theory of Leadership," *Journal of Contemporary Business* 3 (Autumn 1974): 81–97.

33 Steven Kerr and John M. Jermier, "Substitutes for Leadership: Their Meaning and Measurement," *Organizational Behavior and Human Performance* 22 (December 1978): 375–403.

34 Jon F. Howell, David E. Bowen, Peter W. Dorfman, Steven Kerr, and Phillip M. Podsokoff, "Substitutes for Leadership: Effective Alternatives to Ineffective Leadership," *Organizational Dynamics* 19 (Summer 1990): 21–38.

35 Fred Dansereau, Jr., George Graen, and William J. Haga, "A Vertical Dyad Linkage Approach to Leadership Within Formal Organizations: A Longitudinal Investigation of the Role Making Process," *Organizational Behavior and Human Performance* 13 (February 1975): 46–78.

36 Gary Yukl, "Managerial Leadership: A Review of Theory and Research," *Journal of Management* 15 (June 1989): 251–289.

37 Nancy G. Boyd and Robert R. Taylor, "The Influence of Leader-Subordinate Friendship on the Evaluation of Subordinate Performance," *1992 Southern Management Association Proceedings*, 164–166.

38 Jay A. Conger and Rabindra N. Kanungo, "Toward a Behavioral Theory of Charismatic Leadership in Organizational Settings," *Academy of Management Review* 12 (October 1987): 637–647.

39 M. Potts and P. Behr, *The Leading Edge* (New York: McGraw-Hill, 1987).

40 Conger and Kanungo, "Toward a Behavioral Theory of Charismatic Leadership."

41 Conger and Kanungo.

42 Jane M. Howell and Peter J. Frost, "A Laboratory Study of Charismatic Leadership," *Organizational Behavior and Human Decision Processes* 43 (April 1989): 243–269.

43 Bill George, Peter Sims, Andrew M. McLean, and Diana Mayer, "Discovering Your Authentic Leadership," *Harvard Business Review*, February 2007, http://hbr.org/2007/02/discovering-your-authentic-leadership/ar/1 (accessed September 6, 2013).

44 Kevin Kruse, "What Is Authentic Leadership?" *Forbes*, May 12, 2013, http://www.forbes.com/sites/kevinkruse/2013/05/12/what-is-authentic-leadership/ (accessed September 6, 2013). http://www.forbes.com/sites/kevinkruse/2013/05/12/what-is-authentic-leadership/ (accessed September 6, 2013).

45 Robert K. Greenleaf, *The Servant as Leader* (Westfield, IN: Robert K. Greenleaf Center, 1982).

46 Edward D. Hess, "Servant leadership: a path to high performance," *The Washington Post*, April 28, 2013, http://articles.washingtonpost.com/2013-04-28/business/38885511_1_leaders-organizations-employee (accessed September 13, 2013).

47 Jim Heskett, "Why Isn't 'Servant Leadership' More Prevalent?" *Harvard Business School Working Knowledge*, May 1, 2013, http://hbswk.hbs.edu/item/7207.html (accessed September 13, 2013).

48 Sen Sendjaya and James C. Sarros, "Servant Leadership: Its Origins, Development, and Application in Organizations," *Journal of Leadership & Organizational Studies* 9 (Fall 2002): 57–64; Clay Brewer, "Servant Leadership: A Review of Literature," *Online Journal of Workforce Education and Development* 4 (Spring 2010): 1–8, http://opensiuc.lib.siu.edu/cgi/viewcontent.cgi?article=1008&context=ojwed (accessed September 13, 2013).

49 Bo Burlingham, "Lessons From a Blue-Collar Millionaire," Inc., February 2010, pp. 57–63; www.nickspizzapub.com (accessed March 22, 2011); Bo Burlingham, "Lessons of a Blue-Collar Millionaire—Addendum," Small Giants Community, February 1, 2010, www.smallgiants.org/article.php?article_id=2 (accessed March 22, 2011). "About Nick Sarillo," http://www.nicksarillo.com/about-nick-sarillo/ (accessed July 2, 2013); Carol Roth, "Humble email saves suburban Chicago pizza pub," *Chicago Business*, March 15, 2012, http://www.chicagobusiness.com/article/20120315/BLOGS06/120319853/humble-email-saves-suburban-chicago-pizza-pub (accessed July 2, 2013).

50 James M. Burns, *Leadership* (New York: Harper and Row, 1978).

51 Aysegul Ertureten, Zeynep Cemalcilar, Zeynep Aycan, "The Relationship of Downward Mobbing with Leadership Style and Organizational Attitudes," *Journal of Business Ethics* 116 (2013): 205–216.

52 Bernard M. Bass, "From Transactional to Transformational Leadership: Learning to Share the Vision," *Organizational Dynamics* 18 (Winter 1990): 19–31.

53 Bernard M. Bass, "Leadership: Good, Better, Best," *Organizational Dynamics* 13 (Winter 1985): 26–40.

54 "Impact of Transformational and Servant Leadership on Organizational Performance: A Comparative Analysis," *Journal of Business Ethics* Vol. 116, No. 2 (2013): 433–440.

55 Bass, "From Transactional to Transformational Leadership."

56 Bass, "From Transactional to Transformational Leadership."

57 Alice H. Eagly, S. J. Karau, and M. G. Makhijani, "Gender and the effectiveness of leaders: a meta-analysis," *Psychological Bulletin* 177 (January 1995): 125–145.

58 Herminia Ibarra and Otilia Obodaru, "Women and the Vision Thing," *Harvard Business Review*, January 2009, http://hbr.org/2009/01/women-and-the-vision-thing/ar/1 (accessed September 13, 2013).

59 Judy B. Rosener, "Ways Women Lead," *Harvard Business Review*, November 1990, http://hbr.org/1990/11/ways-women-lead/ar/ (accessed September 13, 2013); Rochelle Sharpe, "As Leaders, Women Rule," *Bloomberg Businessweek*, 2000, http://www.businessweek.com/2000/00_47/b3708145.htm (accessed September 13, 2013).

60 Joan Marques, "Understanding the Strength of Gentleness: Soft-Skilled Leadership on the Rise," *Journal of Business Ethics* 116 (2013): 163–171.

61 Leigh Buchanan, "Between Venus and Mars," *Inc.*, June 2013, pp. 64–74.

62 Alice H. Eagly and Linda L. Carli, "The female leadership advantage: An evaluation of the evidence," *The Leadership Quarterly* 14 (2003): 807–834.

63 Brad Stone, "Everybody Needs a Sheryl Sandberg," *Bloomberg Businessweek*, May 16–22, 2011, pp. 50–58; Ken Auletta, "A Woman's Place," *The New Yorker*, July 11, 2011, www.newyorker.com/reporting/2011/07/11/110711fa_fact_auletta?currentPage 5 1 (accessed August 3, 2011); "Mark E. Zuckerberg," *The New York Times*, updated January 3, 2011, http://topics.nytimes.com/topics/reference/timestopics/people/z/mark_e_zuckerberg/index.html (accessed August 4, 2011); Jefferson Graham, "Facebook Wants to Be Big among Small Businesses," *USA Today*, September 16, 2011, p. 3B.

64 Kouzes and Posner, *The Leadership Challenge*.

65 "2010 Most Ethical Companies in the World," Barrett-Jackson website, http://www.barrett-jackson.com/articles/most-ethical-auction-company.asp (accessed June 9, 2011); "2010 World's Most Ethical Companies," *Ethisphere*, http://ethisphere.com/wme2010 (accessed June 8, 2011); Barrett-Jackson, "Barrett-Jackson Proudly Raises Nearly $5.9 Million For Local And National Charities," January 25, 2012, http://news.barrett-jackson.com/barrett-jackson-proudly-raises-nearly-5-9-million-for-local-and-national-charities/ (accessed July 30, 2013); "Barrett-Jackson Cancer Research Fund and TGen," TGen website, https://www.tgenfoundation.org/NetCommunity/Page.aspx?pid=828 (accessed June 9, 2011); "The Barrett-Jackson Legacy," Barrett-Jackson website, http://www.barrett-jackson.com/about (accessed June 8, 2011); Barrett-Jackson News, "Barrett-Jackson Celebrates Four Decades Of Charitable Work At 40th Annual Scottsdale Auction," Barrett-Jackson website, January 18, 2011, http://news.barrett-jackson.com/barrett-jackson-celebrates-four-decades-of-charitable-work-at-40th-annual-scottsdale-auction (accessed June 9, 2011); Paul M. Barrett, "Barrett-Jackson Auction: Dude, There's My Car!" *Bloomberg Businessweek*, January 28, 2011, http://www.businessweek.com/magazine/content/11_06/b4214071705361.htm (accessed June 7, 2011); Larry Edsall, "Real Buyers. Real Sellers. Real Auctions," Barrett-Jackson website, http://www.barrett-jackson.com/articles/real-auctions.asp (accessed June 9, 2011); Hannah Elliot, "Inside the Million-Dollar Garage of the Man Behind the Barrett-Jackson Auctions," *Forbes*, December 24, 2012, http://www.forbes.com/sites/hannahelliott/2012/12/06/pick-of-the-litter-inside-the-million-dollar-garage-of-the-man-behind-barrett-jackson/ (accessed July 30, 2013); "Reserve Consignments at Barrett-Jackson Palm Beach Auction," *Sports Car Digest*, February 16, 2011, http://www.sportscardigest.com/reserve-consignments-at-barrett-jackson-palm-beach-auction (accessed June 9, 2011); Beth Schwartz, "Dream Chasers, *Luxury Las Vegas*, November 2009, http://luxurylv.com/2009/11/features/3495 (accessed June 9, 2011).

KEY TERMS

affiliative power: Power that is derived by virtue of a person's association with someone else who has some source of power.

authentic leader: A leader who is passionate about company objectives, models corporate values in the workplace, and forms strong relationships with stakeholders.

charisma: The ability to inspire admiration, respect, loyalty, and a desire to emulate, based on some intangible set of personality traits; a personal source of power.

coercive power: An organizationally based source of power derived from a leader's control over punishments or the capacity to deny rewards.

consideration behaviors: Patterns of being friendly and supportive by listening to employees' problems, supporting their actions, "going to bat" for them, and getting their input on a variety of issues.

contingency theory: The suggestion that successful leadership requires matching leaders with primarily stable leadership styles to the demands of the situation.

contracting for leadership style: A process whereby employees may not initially agree with a manager's assessment of their developmental level, thus requiring a leader's skill in arriving at an assessment consensus and an agreed-upon leadership style.

emotional intelligence: The capacity to be aware of, control, and express one's emotions, and to handle interpersonal relationships judiciously and empathetically.

employee-centered leaders: The most effective managers, who engage in both dimensions of leadership behaviors by getting employees involved in the operation of their departments or divisions in a positive and constructive manner, setting general goals, providing fairly loose supervision, and recognizing employees' contributions.

empowerment: The process of providing employees with the ability to contribute input and take on responsibilities for organizational decisions.

expert power: Power or influence derived from a person's special knowledge or expertise in a particular area.

information power: Power that is a result of having access to important information that is not common knowledge, or of having the ability to control the flow of information to and from others.

initiating-structure behaviors: Defining and structuring leader-employee roles through activities such as scheduling, defining work tasks, setting deadlines, criticizing poor work, getting employees to accept work standards, and resolving problems.

job-centered leaders: Less-effective managers, who are mostly directive in their approaches and more concerned with closely supervising employees, explaining work procedures, and monitoring progress in task accomplishment.

Leader-Member Exchange (LMX) Theory: A description of how leaders develop "unique" working relationships with each of their employees, based on the nature of their social exchanges.

leadership substitutes: Aspects of the task, subordinates, or organization that act in place of leader behavior and thus render it unnecessary.

leadership enhancers: Aspects of the task, subordinates, or organization that amplify a leader's impact on employees.

leadership neutralizers: Aspects of the task, subordinates, or organization that have the effect of paralyzing, destroying, or counteracting the effect of a leadership behavior.

leadership: The process of influencing the activities of an individual or a group toward the achievement of a goal.

Least Preferred Coworker (LPC) Scale: A measurement of a leader's style consisting of a series of adjective continuums.

legitimate power: The influence that comes from a person's formal position in an organization and the authority that accompanies that position.

organizational power: A person's ability to satisfy or deny satisfaction of another's need, based on a formal contractual relationship between an organization and the individual.

path-goal theory: A model concerned with how a leader affects employees' perceptions of their personal and work goals and the paths to goal attainment.

personal power: A person's ability to satisfy or deny satisfaction of another's need, based on an interpersonal relationship between individuals or on his or her personal characteristics.

power: A person's capacity to influence the behavior and attitudes of others.

referent power: Personal power that results when one person identifies with and admires another.

relationship-oriented behaviors: Behaviors such as being considerate, supportive, and helpful to employees by showing trust and confidence, listening to employees' problems and suggestions, showing appreciation for contributions, and supporting employees' concerns.

reward power: Organizational power that stems from a person's ability to bestow rewards.

servant leader: A leader who leads by example and forms strong relationships with employees.

situational leadership theory: A leadership model whose premise is that a leader's style should be contingent on subordinates' competence and commitment.

task-oriented behaviors: Behaviors—such as planning and scheduling work, coordinating employee activities, and providing necessary supplies, equipment, and technical assistance—designed primarily and specifically to get tasks completed.

transactional leadership: A more traditional approach in which managers engage in both task- and consideration-oriented behaviors in an exchange manner.

transformational leadership: A style that goes beyond mere exchange relationships by inspiring employees to look beyond their own self-interests and by generating awareness and acceptance of the group's purposes and mission.

DISCUSSION QUESTIONS

1   Would you describe leadership in a criminal justice organization as mostly transactional or transformational? Provide at least two reasons to support your answer.

2   Describe the qualities of two leaders you have worked for: one who you thought was effective and the other who you thought was not. In what key ways did they differ? How have they informed your own style of leadership?

SECTION V
CONCLUSION

From the readings and discussion questions in Section V, you should have a clearer sense of how important it is to deal affirmatively with workplace stress and trauma and what it means to be a true leader. Preventing burnout and dealing with occupational stress isn't just a feel-good exercise. It is smart management that leads to reduced absenteeism and increased productivity.

Regarding your own experiences with leadership, it is probably fair to say that most leaders you have encountered were average. While average leaders do little harm to an organization's mission or its people, superior leaders can produce everlasting effects in terms of agency productivity and employee morale. Consider this sobering fact: the average American spends approximately 110,000 hours at work over the course of a lifetime. That's about 47 hours a week for 44 years (Reference.com, n.d.). Our work lives have a tremendous impact on the overall quality of our lives. Even though some bosses are naturally gifted leaders, leadership skills can also be learned. In this section, we have come full circle. Poor leaders, not just workplace conditions, contribute to stress and burnout, while effective leaders mitigate it.

ORGANIZATIONAL POWER, ORGANIZATIONAL CHANGE

INTRODUCTION

Section VI explores the world of office politics, organizational power, and leadership development. Let us first discuss a topic that everyone complains about: office politics. Despite an almost universal distaste for office politics, they are a workplace reality. When someone consults me about how to avoid the gossip, power struggles, and kissing up that they witness on the job, I tell them to figure out how best to handle those behaviors rather than how to escape or eliminate them. We have all heard the saying from Benjamin Franklin, "but in this world nothing can be said to be certain, except death and taxes." I would like to add a third certainty: office politics. The beauty of the first reading is that it tackles the topic head-on. It does not sugarcoat this unsavory feature of work life. Rather, it provides useful tips on how we can make office politics work for us in an ethical way. When we accept our reality we suffer less and are in a better position to identify the things we can control. All too often, workers become cynical when they see office politics playing out around them. This cynicism can cause them to become unmotivated, dissatisfied, and unproductive. We want to show up at work happy to be there and work hard to promote our agency's mission. A surefire way to do this consistently is to understand the dynamics of office politics and practice strategies that promote positive political tactics.

The second reading in Section VI addresses how to alter a work environment through leadership development. The Brough et al. article reminds us that transforming a negative workplace culture requires an investment in leadership development at all levels of the organization. Managerial and executive employees often fail to appreciate the value of leadership development, considering it a luxury rather than a necessity. I challenge you to think hard about that for a moment. For better or worse, leaders leave their fingerprints all over an organization. Should an executive just leave to chance that a high-ranking employee is skilled enough to manage crises, motivate employees, influence collaborators, engage in long-term and short-term planning, and prepare realistic budgets? These are just a few things leaders are expected to do well. Given those formidable tasks, it logically follows that agencies investing in their current and future leaders is a necessary and a sound business strategy.

POWER, POLITICS, AND INFLUENCE

ANDREW J. DUBRIN

CHAPTER OUTLINE

The Meaning of Power, Politics, and Influence
Sources of Individual and Subunit Power
Empowerment of Group Members
Organizational Politics
Organizational Influence Tactics
The Control of Dysfunctional Politics and Ethical Considerations
Implications for Managerial Practice

michaeljung/Shutterstock.com

David Novak is the Chairman and CEO of Yum! Brands, a company that consists of 40,000 KFC, Pizza Hut, and Taco Bell locations in 120 countries around the world, making it the largest restaurant chain in terms of units. The company's restaurants are now the leader in the chicken, pizza, and Mexican-style food categories. (KFC was previously called "Kentucky Fried Chicken.") In the United States, Yum! has 60 restaurants per million people.

Novak has become a powerful executive by creating an organizational culture that emphasizes employee recognition and the empowerment of his team members and restaurant managers. The affable executive sees himself as the chief teaching officer of Yum! Brands and believes ardently that recognition is the foundation of motivation. His attitude toward empowerment is expressed in these words: "When you think about what you need to get done in your company, you know you can't get it done by yourself. There is no way you can get it done without taking people with you." Taking People With You has become the name of the company leadership development program.

Novak's first approach to employee recognition became legendary. Each time he was informed that an employee deserved recognition, Novak would give that worker a signed, numbered, rubber chicken, along with a $100 on-the-spot bonus. The Yum! Award now takes the form of a set of smiling plastic teeth with legs that denotes "walking the talk" of leadership. The wall and ceiling in Novak's office is crammed with hundreds of photos depicting him with restaurant managers, office workers, and other employees recognized for noteworthy achievement.

Novak has been referred to as the business world's ultimate team builder. His top-level management team has been exceptionally stable, with an average tenure of 10 years. Among the team members are a "chief people officer," the CEO of Yum Brands–China, the president of Yum Brands–India, and a general counsel and chief franchise policy officer. Novak explains that part of the company's growth can be attributed to the trust team members had in each other, and the belief that they could work together to create something that was bigger than their own individual capabilities. All team members are empowered to manage their vast spheres of influence without micromanagement by Novak. Restaurant general managers are regarded by Novak as the company's No. 1 leaders because they build empowered teams closest to the customers.

Novak believes that the recognition culture he has created, along with the Taking People With You program, is a fulfillment of his life's purpose. "Why am I on earth?" he asks. "I'm on earth to encourage others, lift lives, help create leaders, inspire people, recognize others." Novak graduated from the University of Missouri with a journalism degree with an advertising major.[1]

This story about the CEO of a giant chain of quick-service restaurants illustrates the importance of employee recognition, and also how empowerment of team members can influence them to perform well. Power, politics, and influence are such major parts of the workplace that they have become standard topics of organizational behavior.

In this chapter, we approach power, politics, and influence from multiple perspectives. We describe the meaning of these concepts, how power is obtained, and how it is shared (empowerment). We examine why organizational politics is so prevalent, and then describe the tactics of politics and influence. In addition, we describe the control of dysfunctional politics, and ethical considerations about the use of power, politics, and influence. As you read the chapter, you will learn that some tactics of power, politics, and influence violate ethical codes and therefore should be avoided.

THE MEANING OF POWER, POLITICS, AND INFLUENCE

A challenge in understanding power, politics, and influence in organizations is that the terms appear close in meaning. Here we present meanings of these terms aimed at providing useful distinctions. **Power** is the potential or ability to influence decisions and control resources. The predominant view of power is that it is the influence over others' actions, thoughts, and outcomes.[2] Realize that, like gravity, power cannot be observed directly. Yet you can observe its effects, such as when the corporate name is used as a verb.[3] For example, "Have you 'googled' that job applicant yet?" Or, "Have you 'Scotch Taped' the envelope?"

Many definitions of *power* center on the ability of a person to overcome resistance in achieving a result. Some researchers suggest that power lies in the potential, while others focus on use.[4] As a hedge, our definition includes both potential and use. If you have a powerful battery in your car, isn't it still powerful whether or not it is in use?

Politics is a way of achieving power. As used here, **organizational politics** refers to informal approaches to gaining power through means other than merit or luck. In recent years, scholars have recognized that being skilled in organizational politics is a positive force for individuals and can help the organization. **Political skill** is a combination of social astuteness with the capacity to adjust and adapt behavior to different situational demands. As a result, the person with political skill inspires trust and support, controls and influences the responses of others, and appears genuine and sincere.[5]

Influence is close in meaning to *power*. *Influence* is also the ability to change behavior, but it tends to be more subtle and indirect than *power*. *Power* indicates the ability to affect outcomes with greater facility and ease than *influence*.[6] A person who has political skill is able to use influence behaviors in organizations, such as building strong relationships with key people.

Managers and professionals often need to use political tactics to achieve the power and influence they need to accomplish their work. An example would be a human resources manager cultivating the support of a top executive so he or she can proceed with a program of employee wellness. Cultivating support is a political tactic.

SOURCES OF INDIVIDUAL AND SUBUNIT POWER

An encouraging note about the study of power is that the basic ideas behind power have remained stable over time, no matter how much technological change takes place. Part of the reason, explains Jeffrey Pfeffer, is that the use of power can be linked to survival advantages. For example, most people have a self-enhancement motive, and they have a desire to be identified and associated with success and winners.[7]

The sources or bases of power in organizations can be classified in different ways. A useful starting point is to recognize that power can be used to forward either the interests of the organization or personal interests. **Socialized power** is the use of power to achieve constructive ends. An example would be the manager who attempted to gain power to spearhead a program of employee wellness. **Personalized power** is the use of power primarily for the sake of personal aggrandizement and gain.[8] An example would be a new CEO using his power to insist that company headquarters be moved to a location near his home or that his family members be allowed to use a company jet.

Here we classify the sources (and also the bases and origins) of power that stem from the organization, from the individual, and from providing resources.[9]

POWER GRANTED BY THE ORGANIZATION (POSITION POWER)

Managers and professionals often have power because of the authority, or right, granted by their positions. The power of a manager's position stems from three sources: legitimate power, coercive power, and reward power. **Legitimate power** is based on the manager's formal position within the hierarchy. A government agency head, for example, has much more position power than a unit supervisor in the same agency. Managers can enhance their position power by formulating policies and procedures. For example, a manager might establish a requirement that he or she must approve all new hires, thus exercising authority over hiring.

Your appearance can contribute to your personal power.

Coercive power comes from controlling others through fear or threat of punishment. Typical organizational punishments include bypassing an employee for promotion, terminating employment, and giving damaging performance evaluations to people who do not support initiatives, even if the initiatives are unethical or illegal. The threat of a lawsuit by an employee who is treated unjustly serves as a constraint on legitimate power and is referred to as *subordinate power*. Another source of power for employees stems from being a shareholder, such as an employee who owns company stock criticizing the CEO during a shareholder meeting, and being listened to.[10] **Reward power** involves controlling others through rewards or the promise of rewards. Examples of this include promotions, challenging assignments, and recognition given to employees.

The effectiveness of coercive power and reward power depends on the perceptions and needs of group members. For coercive power to be effective, the employee must fear punishment and care about being a member of the firm. Conversely, an employee who does not care much for recognition or power would not be strongly influenced by the prospect of a promotion.

POWER STEMMING FROM THE INDIVIDUAL (PERSONAL POWER)

Managers and other categories of workers also derive power from two separate personal characteristics: knowledge and personality. **Expert power** is the ability to influence others because of one's specialized knowledge, skills, or abilities. For expertise to be an effective source of power, group members must respect that expertise.

Exercising expert power is the logical starting point for building one's power base. Powerful people in business, government, and education almost invariably launched their careers by developing expertise in a specialty of value to their employers. Furthermore, expert power keeps a person in demand for executive positions. A representative example is Hugo Barra, who was the vice president of Android product management at Google Inc. when he left the company for a Chinese smartphone maker, Xiaomi. Barra began at Google after the company bought the voice-recognition company Nuance Communications Inc. Barra launched his career as a software engineer and has been an in-demand manager since early in his career.[11]

Expert power is a key source of power.

Referent power is the ability to influence others that stems from one's desirable traits and characteristics. It is based on the desire of others to be led by or to identify with an inspiring person. Having referent power contributes to a perception of being charismatic, but expert power also makes a contribution. For example, being perceived as highly creative contributes to a person's charisma.

POWER FROM PROVIDING RESOURCES

Another way of understanding the sources of power is through the **resource dependence perspective**. According to this perspective, the organization requires a continuing flow of human resources, money, customers, technological inputs, and material to continue to function. Subunits or individuals within the organization who can provide these resources derive power from this ability.[12]

A variation on power from providing resources is the derivation of power from gossip, which is an important resource in many organizations. Most people know that an influential member of the grapevine can accrue a small degree of power, and a scientific analysis supports this idea. The authors of the analysis define *gossip* as "informal and evaluative talk in an organization, usually among no more than a few individuals, about another member of that organization who is not present."[13] According to the model developed, a supplier of gossip will develop the sources of power already described, such as reward, expert, and coercive power. However, if the person provides mostly negative gossip, his or her referent power will decrease.

POWER FROM MEETING THE EXPECTATIONS OF GROUP MEMBERS: IMPLICIT LEADERSHIP THEORY

Another perspective on leadership power is that a leader can accrue power by behaving and acting in the way group members expect. For example, a team leader who is intelligent and dedicated when team members want an intelligent and dedicated leader will have some power based on meeting these expectations. According to **implicit leadership theory**, group members develop prototypes specifying the traits and abilities that characterize an ideal business leader. People are characterized as true leaders on the basis of the perceived match between their behavior and character and the leader category they have in their minds. Implicit leadership theories (or expectations) are the benchmarks group members use to form an impression of their leader/manager. Group members have both prototypes and antiprototypes (what they want the leader not to be).

In organizational settings, the leadership prototypes (desirable characteristics and traits) are as follows: sensitivity, intelligence, dedication, charisma, strength, and attractiveness. The antiprototypes are tyranny and masculinity (a sexist term for being cold and nonrelationship oriented). A study of 439 employees indicated that the closer the employees perceived their manager's profile to fit the implicit leadership theory they endorsed, the better the quality of the leader–member exchange.[14] It can be inferred that, as a result of these high-quality exchanges, the leader has a little more power.

The Organizational Behavior in Action box describes an executive who has made intelligent use of a variety of types of power.

EMPOWERMENT OF GROUP MEMBERS

Distributing power throughout the organization has become a major strategy for improving productivity, quality, satisfaction, and motivation. Employees experience a greater sense of self-efficacy (self-confidence for a particular task) and ownership in their jobs when they share power. **Empowerment** is the process of sharing power with group members, thereby enhancing their feelings of self-efficacy.[15] A few basic points about empowerment are shown in Figure 1.

ORGANIZATIONAL BEHAVIOR IN ACTION
Marillyn Hewson Climbs to Power at Lockheed Martin
In early 2013, Marillyn Hewson, a longtime Lockheed Martin Corp. executive, became the company's chairman and CEO after a 31-year steady climb to the top. Lockheed Martin is the biggest defense company in the history of the world. Hewson became the most powerful person at Lockheed Martin and has been named by both *Forbes* and *Fortune* as one of the 100 most powerful women in business. Hewson's previous position was president, chief operating officer, and executive vice president of the Electronic Systems division. She had held 18 leadership roles since joining Lock-heed Martin in 1983 as an engineer, although she was a business administration major. Among these positions were vice president of Global Supply Chain Management and vice president of Corporate Internal Audit.

Hewson combines her knowledge of technology and strategic leadership skills with strong interpersonal skills. When she took over for Robert J. Stevens, the outgoing CEO, he joked with investors, "People seem to like Marillyn more than they like me. She is a genuinely likeable person who understands people and connects with people in this company at an individual level." Another time Stevens said, "Marillyn is an exceptional leader with impeccable credentials She knows our business, our customers, our share-holders, our commitments, and our employees."

A consultant to Lockheed Martin said, "Marillyn will be exactly what Lockheed Martin needed in terms of patching up its relationship with its Pentagon customer. Marillyn manages to combine toughness and knowledge with graciousness and an ability to listen." A Lockheed Martin employee posted, "Great female leader in Marillyn Hewson. She genuinely cares about employees and is very real."

Lockheed Martin has long been led by self-made individuals, with Hewson fitting the pattern. She has gradually risen though the ranks over the years, having succeeded mostly through her self-discipline and determination. Although Hewson has a reputation for being gracious and gregarious, she is an executive ready to make tough choices, such as finding ways to boost earnings per share. Hewson says her management approach is "opportunistic," meaning that her strategy does not change, but her tactics and timing are dictated by market conditions. She is also known to have a deep and unwavering commitment to Lock-heed Martin, considered by some analysts to be one of the greatest centers of technological innovation in the world.

Hewson said during an interview with a journalist that she wants to continue to be a role model for women in business. "But I don't think it's necessarily about being a female in our business. I think it's about my track record, my results."

Born in Junction City, Kansas, Hewson received a Bachelor of Science degree in business administration and a Master of Arts degree from the University of Alabama. She also attended executive development programs at Columbia Business School and Harvard Business School.

Source: Original story created from facts and observations in the following sources: Loren Thompson, "Lockheed Martin Chairman & CEO Marillyn Hewson's Vision: Continuous Innovation, Sustained Profitability," *Forbes* (www.forbes.com), August 6, 2014, pp. 1–5; Marjorie Censer, "After Nearly 30 Years with Lockheed, Hewson Is Named Chief Executive," (www.washingtonpost.com), November 13, 2012, pp. 1–6; Doug Cameron and Joann S. Lublin, "Vaulted to Top at Lockheed, and Ready to Navigate 'Cliff'," *The Wall Street Journal*, November 12, 2012, pp. B1, B2; "Marillyn A. Hewson: Chairman, President, and Chief Executive Officer Lockheed Martin Corporation" (www.lockheedmartin.com), September 26, 2014; "Lockheed Martin" (www. glassdoor.com), September 5, 2013, p. 1; Andrea Shalai-Esa, "Hewson's Long Lockheed Journey Ends at the Top" (www.reuters.com), November 9, 2012, pp. 1–2.

Figure 1

The Basics of Empowerment

Participative management or leadership is the general strategy for empowering workers. The techniques of participative management, such as goal setting, modeling, and job enrichment, have been described in previous chapters. The information about empowering teams presented in Chapter 10 is also relevant here. To link empowerment directly to leadership, empowerment can be regarded as shared leadership as opposed to vertical leadership. Such shared leadership is particularly necessary when the work within the group is interdependent, creative, and complex. The typical work of cross-functional teams and virtual teams calls for shared leadership or empowerment.[16]

A study of 35 sales and service virtual teams showed that team empowerment was related to two measures of team performance—process improvement and customer satisfaction. Empowerment was measured by a questionnaire with statements such as, "My team makes its own choices without being told by management." Empowerment was even more effective for the virtual teams with fewer face-to-face meetings, suggesting that the less virtual team members meet with a manager, the more empowerment they need.[17]

To bring about empowerment, managers must remove conditions that keep employees powerless, such as authoritarian supervision or a job over which they have little control. An example of a person in a low-control job would be a manager who cannot shut off interruptions even to prepare budgets or to plan. Employees must also receive information that increases their feelings of self-efficacy. When employees are empowered, they will take the initiative to solve problems and strive hard to reach objectives.

Empowerment may not proceed smoothly unless certain conditions are met. A major consideration is that the potentially empowered workers must be competent and interested in assuming more responsibility. Otherwise the work will not get accomplished. W. Alan Randolph observed 10 companies that made the transition to empowerment.[18] The first key to effective empowerment is *information sharing*. Lacking information, it is difficult for workers to act with responsibility.

Another critical factor for successful empowerment is for management to *provide more structure* as teams move into self-management. To initiate empowerment, managers must teach people new skills and make the parameters clear. Workers need to know, for example, "What are the limits to my empowerment?" The third critical factor is that *teams must gradually replace the traditional organizational hierarchy.* Empowered teams not only make recommendations, they also make and implement decisions and are held accountable. A major contributing factor to successful empowerment, found in a study of a large food company, was that teams acted as managers. They hired and fired people, appraised performance, scheduled work, and managed a budget.

Empowerment is also more effective when the empowered individuals

An empowered group is often productive and satisfied.

and teams are told what needs to be done but are *free to determine how to achieve the objectives.* Allowing people to determine the most efficient and effective work techniques is the essence of empowerment. A final consideration for successful empowerment is implied in the other conditions. *Unless managers trust employees*, empowerment will not be effective or even take place. For example, when employees are trusted, they are more likely to be given the information they need and be granted the freedom to choose an appropriate method.

Meg Whitman, the former eBay CEO who now holds the same position at Hewlett-Packard, is an example of a prominent business leader who believes that sharing power improves organizational effectiveness. She claims, "I don't actually think of myself as powerful" and endorses the statement, "To have power, you must be willing to not have any of it."[19] In practice, this means that Whitman relies on consensus leadership, and believes that the Hewlett-Packard community is the true source of the company's greatness.

Another way of looking at the contribution of empowerment is that, when the leader has too much power, team performance might decline. This conclusion was reached on the basis of a series of three studies conducted with students participating in simulation exercises, including solving a homicide investigation. Team performance was linked to finding the correct solution to the problems. Among the findings was that leaders who felt they had a high degree of power spent more time talking (or verbally dominating) during the team meetings than did leaders who felt they had less power. High-power leadership also was associated with lower levels of open communication in teams, and consequently led to diminished team performance.[20] The take-away from this study for the workplace is that group leaders who feel they have a lot of power might tend to dominate the discussion during meetings and therefore not make good use of talent within the team.

Now that we have described the sources of power and empowerment, we shift focus to more details about political behavior and influence tactics.

ORGANIZATIONAL POLITICS

Our study of organizational politics includes the reasons behind political behavior in the workplace, ethical and unethical tactics, and gender differences in the use of politics. We emphasize again that the effective use of organizational politics can enhance leader effectiveness and the well-being of subordinates. A relatively new concept, **leader political support** points to the positive effects just mentioned. The concept refers to tactics of organizational politics and influence engaged in by leaders to provide followers with necessary resources to advance individual, group, or organizational objectives.[21] An information technology manager might build into his or her network a good relationship with the vice president of finance. The goal would be to make the vice president more amenable to funding a project that would develop mobile apps for a wide range of the company's services.

FACTORS CONTRIBUTING TO POLITICAL BEHAVIOR

The most fundamental reason for organizational politics is the political nature of organizations. Coalitions of interests and demands arise both within and outside organizations. Similarly, organizations can be viewed as loose structures of interests and demands in competition with one another for attention and resources. The interaction among different coalitions results in an undercurrent of political tactics, such as when one group tries to promote itself and discredit another.

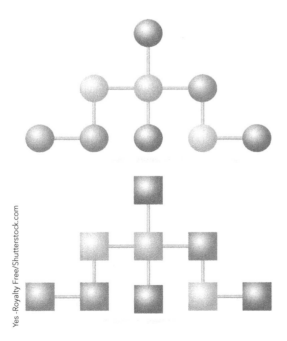

A pyramid-shaped organization is a source of organizational politics.

Another contributor to political activity is the pyramid structure of organizations—a reality despite all the emphasis on shared leadership and empowerment. The people at the top of the organization hold most of the power, while people at each successive level down the hierarchy hold less power. The amount of power that can be distributed in a hierarchy is limited. Power-oriented managers sometimes cope with the limited amount of power available by expanding their sphere of influence sideways. For example, the director of the food-stamp program in a government agency might attempt to gain control over the housing assistance program, which is at the same level.

Yes -Royalty Free/Shutterstock.com

Executive coach Marshall Goldsmith observes what is a major reason for "kissing up" (a form of organizational politics) to people in power. Without meaning to, many managers create an environment in which people learn to reward others with accolades that are not really warranted. People who are kind, courteous, and complimentary toward their managers are most likely to receive the most recognition—assuming their job performance is at least in the acceptable range.[22]

Political behavior by senior management helps establish a climate for such behavior. When C-level executives are highly political, it contributes to a climate of acceptance for organizational politics. One of the most visible aspects of political behavior is favoritism in its many forms. When lower-ranking managers perceive that the practice exists among senior management of placing poorly qualified friends into high-paying positions, the lower-ranking managers are likely to follow suit.

Downsizing and team structures create even less opportunity for climbing the hierarchy, thus intensifying political behavior for the few remaining powerful positions. Worried about layoffs themselves, many workers attempt to discredit others so that the latter would be the first to go. Internal politics generally increase as good jobs, promotions, and bonuses become scarcer. A business columnist made an observation a few years back that continues to be true during economic downturns: "The art of fawning over a boss may be more important now because of the stagnant economy and shortage of well-paying, full-time jobs."[23]

Organizational politics is also fostered by the need for power. Executives have much stronger power needs than others, and thus propel themselves toward frequent episodes of political behavior. Because executives are responsible for controlling resources, their inner desire to do so helps them in their jobs. A personalized power need is more likely to trigger political behavior than a socialized power need.

Finally, a devious reason for the existence of politicking is **Machiavellianism**, a tendency to manipulate others for personal gain. (Niccolo Machiavelli was a 15th-century political philosopher whose book, *The Prince*, describes how leaders may acquire and maintain power by placing expediency above morality.) One analysis suggests that many ambitious and successful corporate executives have strong Machiavellian tendencies, such as acquiring other companies just to give the appearance of true corporate growth.[24]

To make effective use of organizational politics, managerial workers must be aware of specific political strategies and tactics. To identify and explain the majority of political behaviors would require years of study and observation. Managers so frequently need support for their programs that they search for innovative political maneuvers. Furthermore, new tactics continue to emerge as the workplace becomes increasingly competitive.

Self-Assessment 12-1 gives you an opportunity to think through your tendencies to engage in organizational politics. In the two following sections we describe mostly ethical, followed by unethical, political tactics.

MOSTLY ETHICAL AND POSITIVE POLITICAL TACTICS

Here we describe political tactics that many people would consider to be ethical and positive. Nevertheless, some managers and management scholars regard all political tactics as being ethically tainted. The relevance of being able to use political tactics effectively was demonstrated in a study of 408 leaders (headmasters) and 1,429 subordinates (teachers) of state schools in Germany. Political skill was measured by a standard measure somewhat similar to Self-Assessment 12-1, and effectiveness was measured by teachers' evaluations of the headmasters. The study showed that politically skilled leaders were able to attain effectiveness through both transformational and transactional behaviors.[25]

1. *Develop power contacts through networking.* A fundamental principle of success is to identify powerful people and then establish alliances with them. Cultivating friendly, cooperative relationships with powerful organizational members and outsiders can make the managerial worker's cause much easier to advance. These contacts can support a person's ideas and recommend him or her for promotions and visible temporary assignments. A challenge in the era of electronic communications is that face time, or in-person contact, is helpful for building contacts. It is important to converse with powerful people in person in addition to sending them electronic messages. Although still electronic, an occasional telephone call is a useful supplement to e-mail or text messages for purposes of building a network.

2. *Manage your impression.* You will recall that charismatic leaders rely heavily on impression management, and the same technique is important for other success-oriented people. An example of an ethical impression-management tactic would be to contribute outstanding performance and then make sure key people know of your accomplishments. Making others aware of what you accomplish is often referred to as *achieving visibility*. When tactics of impression management appear insincere, they are likely to create a negative impression and thus be self-defeating. A key person to impress is your immediate superior. Many firms send professionals to etiquette training because displaying proper etiquette makes a positive impression on customers and clients.[26]

3. *Make your boss look good.* A bedrock principle of organizational politics is to help your boss perform well, which is one of the reasons you probably were hired. Positioning yourself as a supporting player for your boss will help your performance evaluation and therefore your career. Consultant Karl Bimshas suggests that a good starting point is to ask questions of this nature: "What do you think should be my highest priority right now?" Then turn in a good performance with respect to the priority.[27]

SELF-ASSESSMENT 1

The Positive Organizational Politics Questionnaire

Answer each question "mostly agree" or "mostly disagree," even if it is difficult for you to decide which alternative best describes your opinion.

	MOSTLY AGREE	MOSTLY DISAGREE
1. Pleasing my boss is a major goal of mine.	____	____
2. I go out of my way to flatter important people.	____	____
3. I am most likely to do favors for people who can help me in return.	____	____
4. Given the opportunity, I would cultivate friendships with powerful people.	____	____
5. I will compliment a coworker even if I have to think hard about what might be praiseworthy.	____	____
6. If I thought my boss needed the help, and I had the expertise, I would show him or her how to use an electronic gadget for personal life.	____	____
7. I laugh heartily at my boss's humor, so long as I think he or she is at least a little funny.	____	____
8. I would not be too concerned about following a company dress code, so long as I looked neat.	____	____
9. If a customer sent me a compliment through e-mail, I would forward a copy to my boss and another influential person.	____	____
10. I smile only at people in the workplace whom I genuinely like.	____	____
11. An effective way to impress people is to tell them what they want to hear.	____	____
12. I would never publicly correct mistakes made by the boss.	____	____
13. I would be willing to use my personal contacts to gain a promotion or desirable transfer.	____	____
14. I think it is a good idea to send a congratulatory note to someone in the company who receives a promotion to an executive position.	____	____
15. I think "office politics" is only for losers.	____	____

Scoring and Interpretation: Give yourself a plus 1 for each answer that agrees with the keyed answer. Each question that receives a score of plus 1 shows a tendency toward playing positive organizational politics. The scoring key is as follows:

1. Mostly agree	9. Mostly agree
2. Mostly agree	10. Mostly disagree
3. Mostly agree	11. Mostly agree
4. Mostly agree	12. Mostly agree
5. Mostly agree	13. Mostly agree
6. Mostly agree	14. Mostly agree
7. Mostly agree	15. Mostly disagree
8. Mostly disagree	

1–6, Below-average tendency to play office politics
7–11, Average tendency to play office politics
12 and above, Above-average tendency to play office politics; strong need for power

Thinking about your political tendencies in the workplace is important for your career because most successful leaders are moderately political. The ability to use politics effectively and ethically increases with importance in the executive suite. Most top players are effective office politicians. Yet being overly and blatantly political can lead to distrust, thereby damaging your career.

Managing your impression is a necessary political tactic.

4. *Keep informed.* In addition to controlling vital information, it is politically important to keep informed. Successful managers and professionals develop a pipeline to help them keep abreast, or even ahead, of developments within the firm. For example, a politically astute individual might befriend a major executive's assistant.

5. *Be courteous, pleasant, and positive.* Courteous, pleasant, and positive people are the first to be hired and the last to be fired (assuming they are also technically qualified).[28] A key part of being courteous, pleasant, and positive is to socialize with coworkers, including having meals and drinks with them. Executive coach Leslie Williams observes: "Socialization has everything to do with influence. It's not enough to just be good at your job." In addition to doing a good job, you have to be somebody that people know and know well enough to trust.[29]

6. *Ask satisfied customers to contact your manager.* A favorable comment by a customer receives considerable weight because customer satisfaction is a top corporate priority. If a customer says something nice, the comment will carry more weight than one from a coworker or subordinate. The reason is that insiders might praise you for political reasons, whereas a customer's motivation is thought to be pure.

7. *Avoid political blunders.* A strategy for retaining power is to refrain from making power-eroding blunders. Committing these politically insensitive acts can also prevent you from attaining power. Leading blunders include: strong criticism of a superior in a public forum; going around your manager with a complaint; and making a negative social media post about your employer. Another blunder is burning your bridges by creating ill will with former employees. The Organizational Behavior Checklist will serve as a reminder of the types of political blunders (gaffes) to avoid in order to preserve a positive image.

8. *Sincere flattery.* A powerful tactic for ingratiating yourself to others is to flatter them honestly and sincerely. Although one meaning of the term *flattery* is insincere praise, another meaning refers to a legitimate compliment. Charismatic people use flattery regularly. Skill-Development Exercise 12-1 will help you develop flattery skills.

ORGANIZATIONAL BEHAVIOR CHECKLIST

A Sampling of Political Blunders and Gaffes to Avoid in the Workplace

Insert a checkmark for each of the following blunders and gaffes you have committed in the past, or are likely to commit in the future.

☐ 1. I have criticized my manager or a colleague in an in-person meeting.

☐ 2. I have posted a negative comment about company management or the company on social media.

☐ 3. I make racist, sexist, or ethnically offensive jokes on the job.

☐ 4. When I do not agree with an idea or policy, I will say or write, "It sucks."

☐ 5. During a major election, I place campaign banners for my favorite candidate outside my cubicle, office, or table workspace.

☐ 6. I have done unfavorable imitations of my boss to humor coworkers.

☐ 7. If we have a visitor from another country, I do imitations of that person's speech once he or she leaves.

☐ 8. I brag about using a competitor's products or services.

☐ 9. I openly claim in talk or on social media about how much my organization overpays the top executive.

☐ 10. I am quick to criticize a person's clothing, grooming, or hairstyle if I think it is awful.

Scoring and Interpretation: The closer you are to having checked none or 1 of the 10 blunders, the more skilled you are at organizational politics. If you checked all 10, it is time to study the classic book by Dale Carnegie, *How to Win Friends and Influence People.*

Political skill can be developed through careful observation and experience, coupled with improving one's emotional intelligence. Research with 260 business graduate students showed that mentoring can be an effective way of developing political skill. Ninety percent of the students were employed, and those who had a mentor or mentors responded to a questionnaire about the quality of their mentoring. Results indicated that participants who had a mentor showed significantly better political skill than participants who did not have a mentor.[30]

MOSTLY UNETHICAL AND NEGATIVE POLITICAL TACTICS

In this section we describe tactics of organizational politics that most people would consider to be unethical and negative. The majority of people who use these tactics would not admit to their use.

1. *Backstabbing.* The ubiquitous backstab requires that you pretend to be nice but all the while plan someone's demise. A frequent form of backstabbing is to inform your rival's immediate superior that he or she is faltering under the pressure of job responsibilities. The recommended approach to dealing with a backstabber is to confront the person directly, ask for an explanation of his or her behavior, and demand that he or she stop. Threaten to complain to the person's superior.[31]

2. *Embrace-or-demolish.* The ancient strategy of embrace-or-demolish suggests that you remove from the premises rivals who suffered past hurts through your efforts. (The same tactic is called "take no prisoners.") Otherwise the wounded rivals might retaliate at a vulnerable moment. An illustration of embrace-or-demolish is when, after a hostile takeover, many executives lose their jobs because they opposed the takeover.

3. *Stealing credit.* For many workers, the most detestable form of office politics is for their boss, or other worker, to take credit for their ideas without acknowledging the source of the idea. Paul Lapides estimates that up to 80 percent of workers suffer this indignity at some time in their careers. The credit stealing breeds distrust, damages motivation, and is sometimes misperceived as a perk of power.[32] A good starting point in stopping idea thieves is to hold a one-on-one session with the thief, and confront the issue. If the issue is not resolved, tell key decision makers about the idea theft.[33]

SKILL-DEVELOPMENT EXERCISE 1

A Short Course in Effective Flattery

Flattering others is an effective way of building personal relationships (or engaging in organizational politics), if done properly. Suggestions for effective flattery are presented here. *Flattery* here refers to pleasing others through complimentary remarks or attention; we are not referring to *flattery* in the sense of giving insincere or excessive compliments. To build your skills in flattering others, practice these suggestions as the opportunity presents itself. Rehearse your flattery approaches until they feel natural. If your first attempt at flattery does not work well, analyze what went wrong the best you can.

- *Use sensible flattery.* Effective flattery has at least a spoonful of credibility, implying that you say something positive about the target person that is quite plausible. Credibility is also increased when you point to a person's tangible accomplishment. Technical people in particular expect flattery to be specific and aimed at genuine accomplishment.

- *Compliment what is of major importance to the flattery target.* You might find out what is important to the person by observing what he or she talks about with the most enthusiasm.

- *Flatter others by listening intently.* Listening intently to another person is a powerful form of flattery. Use active listening (see Chapter 8) for best results.

- *Flatter by referring to or quoting the other person.* By referring to or quoting (including paraphrasing) another person, you are paying that person a substantial compliment.

- *Use confirmation behaviors.* Use behaviors that have a positive or therapeutic effect on other people, such as praise and courtesy. Because confirmation behaviors have such a positive effect on others, they are likely to be perceived as a form of flattery.

- *Give positive feedback.* A mild form of flattering others is to give them positive feedback about their statements, actions, and results. The type of feedback referred to here is a straightforward and specific declaration of what the person did right.

- *Remember names.* Remembering the names of people with whom you have infrequent contact makes them feel important. To help remember the person's name, study the name carefully when you first hear it and repeat it immediately.

- *Explain the impact on you.* Tell the person how his or her actions or behavior positively affect you. An example: "I tried your suggestion about avoiding multitasking on important tasks, and my error rate has gone down dramatically."

■ *Avoid flattery that has a built-in insult or barb.* The positive effect of flattery is eradicated when it is accompanied by a hurtful comment, such as "You have good people skills for an engineer" or "You look good. I bet you were really beautiful when you were younger."

To build your skills in flattering others, you must try some of the previous techniques. For starters, within the next few days flatter a classmate, coworker, boss, or friend for something laudable the person accomplished. Or, flatter a customer-contact worker for a service well delivered. Observe carefully the results of your flattery.

Sources: Andrew J. DuBrin, *Political Behavior in Organizations* (Thousand Oaks, CA: Sage, 2009), p. 105; Karen Judson, "The Fine Art of Flattery," *Kiwanis*, March 1998, pp. 34–36, 43; Elizabeth Bernstein, "Why Do Compliments Cause So Much Grief?" *The Wall Street Journal*, May 4, 2010, pp. D, D6; DuBrin, "Self-Perceived Technical Orientation and Attitudes toward Being Flattered," *Psychological Reports*, 96 (2005), pp. 852–854.

4. *Territorial games.* Also referred to as *turf wars*, **territorial games** involve protecting and hoarding resources that give a person power, such as information, relationships, and decision-making authority. The purpose of territorial games is to compete for three kinds of territory in the modern corporate survival game: information, relationships, and authority. A relationship is "hoarded" in such ways as not encouraging others to visit a key customer, or blocking a higher performer from getting a promotion or transfer by informing other managers that he or she is mediocre.[34] Other examples of territorial games include monopolizing time with clients, scheduling meetings so someone cannot attend, and shutting out coworkers on an important assignment.

5. *Good-mouthing an incompetent to make him or her transferable.* A long-entrenched devious political maneuver in large firms is for a manager to give outstanding performance evaluations to an incompetent worker or troublemaker within the group. By good-mouthing the undesired worker, he or she becomes more marketable within the company. Although this technique can sometimes work, most experienced human resource professionals are aware of this tactic. An HR director noted, "We look for a certain pattern when a manager is puffing up a worker for transfer. Typically the problem worker received low evaluations for a long time, then starts getting outstanding evaluations. When this happens, we really grill the manager about the worker who has been offered for transfer."

6. *Placing a weak manager under you to help secure your position.* A negative political tactic practiced mostly in the executive suite is for a high-level manager to recruit a lame person to a managerial position reporting to him or her. The lame person is valued because he or she is unlikely to become a candidate as a successor to the first executive—who would not have pulled this stunt if he or she were highly competent and secure. As a financial executive describes the situation, "Normally a boob has a boob for a boss."[35]

E-mail, including instant messaging and text messaging, has become a major vehicle for conducting both ethical and unethical organizational politics. To help manage their impressions, many people distribute e-mails regarding their positive contribution to a project to many key people. E-networking is a convenient way to maintain minimum contact with many people, until the in-person meeting can be arranged. People flatter their target person via e-mail, and send copies to key people. On the downside, some people reprimand others by e-mail and let others know of the target's mistakes. Sometimes managers who are haggling with each other will send a copy to a common boss, hoping that the boss will intervene in the dispute.[36] A productivity problem with so many people being copied for political purposes is that in-boxes can become overloaded.

GENDER DIFFERENCES IN POLITICAL SKILL

A major message from this section of the chapter is that positive political skills are necessary to succeed in the workplace. Pamela L. Perrewé and Debra L. Nelson argue that, because of barriers hampering their success such as job discrimination, women need to develop even greater political astuteness than men. (Less job discrimination against women appears to exist today, as indicated by so many women holding key positions in major organizations in business, government, and the nonprofit sector.) Political skills will not only enhance the performance of women but will also decrease stress and increase well-being. For example, if a woman fails to network with men in power, she will experience job stress and lower well-being as a result of being excluded from consideration for a promotion or important work assignment.

Perrewé and Nelson contend that women are more reluctant than men to use politics because they are less politically skilled than men, may not see the relevance of politics, and often find politics distasteful. Instead, women are more likely to rely on merit and traditional values to advance their careers. Women tend to be excluded from the inside power group in organizations, so they do not know the informal rules for getting ahead. The authors propose that women in organizations obtain the right coaching and mentoring to obtain the political skills they need to level the playing field in competing with men.[37]

The argument that there are great gender differences in political skill can be challenged. Women leaders are often cited as being more effective at relationship building than are men, and relationship building is a primary political skill. Furthermore, the number of businesswomen playing golf has surged, and golf is important because of its networking potential. Women also tend to score as high as men on the traits within the implicit leadership theory described previously. An example of support for this argument comes from a study conducted by the research firm Caliper. The researchers administered personality tests and conducted interviews with 59 women leaders in 19 different business sectors from major companies in the United Kingdom and the United States. Among the findings were that (a) women leaders are more persuasive than their male counterparts, and (b) women leaders have an inclusive, team-building style of problem solving and decision making. These results suggest strongly that women leaders have good political skills.[38] (Of course, these highly placed women may not be a representative sample of women in organizations.)

Fresh insights into gender differences in political skill come from a study of participants in a leadership seminar who rated themselves on political skills. They were also rated by managers, direct reports, peers, and clients or customers on 13 skillsets related to organizational politics, such as "knows the corporate buzz," "enhances power image," "essential networking," and "ethical lobbying." With respect to "savvy attitudes," females were rated higher by all four rater groups than they rated themselves. Women tended to be rated slightly higher than men in "essential networking." However, two conclusions drawn by the study were that (a) there were no gender differences in self-perceptions of political skill, and (b) few gender differences exist in the level of organizational political skill as perceived by others.[39]

ORGANIZATIONAL INFLUENCE TACTICS

In addition to using power and political tactics to win people over to their way of thinking, managerial workers use a variety of influence tactics. Extensive research has been conducted on social influence tactics aimed at upward, horizontal, and downward relations.[40] The person doing the influencing chooses which tactic seems most appropriate for a given situation. Nine of the most frequently used influence tactics are described here.

1. *Leading by example* means that the manager influences group members by serving as a positive model of desirable behavior. A manager who leads by example shows consistency between actions and words. For example, suppose a firm has a strict policy on punctuality. The manager explains the policy and is always punctual. The manager's words and actions provide a consistent model. Leading by example is also considered quite useful as a way of encouraging ethical behavior.

2. *Assertiveness* refers to being forthright in making demands without violating the rights of others. It involves a person expressing what he or she wants done and how he or she feels about it. A manager might say, for example, "Your report is late, and that makes me angry. I want you to get it done by noon tomorrow." Assertiveness, as this example shows, also refers to making orders clear.

3. *Rationality* means appealing to reason and logic. Strong managers and leaders frequently use this influence tactic. Pointing out the facts of a situation to group members to get them to do something exemplifies rationality. Intelligent people respond the best to rational appeals.

4. *Ingratiation* refers to getting someone else to like you, often through the use of flattery and doing favors. A typical ingratiating tactic would be to act in a friendly manner just before making a demand. Effective managerial workers treat people well consistently to get cooperation when it is needed. Ingratiation, or simply being likable, is an effective way of gaining the cooperation of others. A study of 133 managers found that, if an

auditor is likable and gives a well-organized argument, managers tend to comply with his or her suggestions even when they disagree and the auditor has insufficient supporting evidence.[41]

A theoretical analysis of the subject concluded that humor is an effective type of ingratiatory behavior. One reason humor leads to ingratiation is because it makes the person with the sense of humor more attractive to the target. Humor may also be seen as more acceptable than an ingratiation tactic such as doing a favor for another person.[42]

5. *Projecting warmth before emphasizing competence* is a major workplace influence tactic. Considerable research about human behavior indicates that, by first focusing on displaying warmth and then blending in shows of competence, leaders will be more influential. For example, before presenting facts about the value of using cloud technology, the leader might smile and wave gently. Two specific ways of being perceived as warm are (a) to speak with lower pitch and volume, as if comforting a friend, and (b) to express agreement with something the influence target says.[43] (Projecting warmth might be classified as an ingratiating tactic.)

6. *Exchange* is a method of influencing others by offering to reciprocate if they meet your demands. When asking favors in a busy workplace, it is best to specify the amount of time the task will take, such as by saying "I will need 10 minutes of your time sometime between now and next Wednesday." Be aware of what skills or capabilities you have that you can barter with others. Perhaps you are good at removing a computer virus or explaining the tax code. You can then offer to perform these tasks in exchange for favors granted to you. Skill-Development Exercise 12-2 will help you personalize the use of exchange as an influence tactic.

7. *Inspirational appeal and emotional display* is an influence method centering on the affective (as opposed to the cognitive) domain. Given that leaders are supposed to inspire others, such an influence tactic is important. As Jeffrey Pfeffer observes, "Executives and others seeking to exercise influence in organizations often develop skill in displaying, or not displaying, their feelings in a strategic fashion."[44] An inspirational appeal usually involves an emotional display by the person seeking to influence. It also involves appealing to group members' emotions.

8. *Joking and kidding*, according to one survey, are widely used to influence others on the job.[45] Good-natured ribbing is especially effective when a straightforward statement might be interpreted as harsh criticism. A manager concerned about the number of errors in a group member's report might say, "Now I know what you are up to. You planted all those errors just to see if I really read your reports."

9. *Strategic sexual performance* has recently been recognized by a group of scholars as a positive influence tactic if used properly. The authors of the research refer to sexuality outside the realm of disruptive behavior such as an office romance or sexual harassment. They define *strategic sexual performance* as "behavior that is imbued with sexual intent,

content, or meaning by its performers, observers, or both, and that is intended to influence a target person or persons in some way." Such a behavior would include lightly touching an influence target to capture his or her attention about a work-related suggestion, or simply winking. Other examples include smiling, giving long gazes or intense eye contact, and compliments about the target's physical features. An everyday example would be for a restaurant server to wear provocative clothing in order to receive higher tips.[46] (The strategic use of sexual performance can also be framed as ingratiation.)

Warmth and friendliness are important sources of influence.

Which influence tactic should you choose? Managers are unlikely to use all the influence tactics in a given situation. Instead, they tend to choose an influence tactic that fits the demands of the circumstance. The outcome of a specific influence attempt is also determined by factors such as the target's motivation and organizational culture. For example, strategic sexual performance is likely to be more acceptable in a restaurant or manufacturing plant than in a research laboratory. Also, any influence tactic can trigger target resistance if it is inappropriate for the situation or is applied unskillfully. Tact, diplomacy, and insight are required for effective application of influence (and political) tactics.

THE CONTROL OF DYSFUNCTIONAL POLITICS AND ETHICAL CONSIDERATIONS

Carried to excess, organizational politics and influence tactics can hurt an organization and its members. One consequence is that when political factors far outweigh merit, competent employees may become unhappy and quit. Another problem is that politicking takes time away from tasks that could contribute directly to achieving the firm's goals. Many managers spend more time developing political allies (including "kissing up") than coaching group members or doing analytical work.

The most comprehensive antidote to improper, excessive, and unethical organizational politics is to rely on objective measures of performance. This is true because people have less need to behave politically when their contributions can be measured directly. With a formal system of goal setting and review, the results a person attains should be much more important than the impression the person creates. However, even a goal-setting program is not immune to politics. Sometimes the goals are designed to impress key people in the organization. As such, they may not be the most important goals for getting work accomplished. Another political problem with goal setting is that some people will set relatively easy goals so they can look good by attaining all their goals.

Meshing individual and organizational objectives would be the ideal method of controlling excessive, negative political behavior. If their objectives, needs, and interests can be met through their jobs, employees will tend to engage in behavior that fosters the growth, longevity, and productivity of the firm. L. A. Witt investigated how goal congruence between the individual and the organization affected political behavior. When employees perceived considerable politics in the workplace, their commitment to the organization and job performance both suffered. However, when employees and their superiors shared the same goals, commitment and performance were less negatively affected by politics. Witt concluded that one way to reduce the negative impact of organizational politics is for the manager to ensure that his or her subordinates hold the appropriate goal priorities. In this way, group members will have a greater sense of control over, and understanding of, the workplace and thus be less affected by the presence of organizational politics.[47]

Finally, open communication can also constrain the impact of political behavior. For instance, open communication can let everyone know the basis for allocating resources, thus reducing the amount of politicking. Organizational politics can also be curtailed by threatening to discuss questionable information in a public forum. If one employee engages in backstabbing of another, the manager might ask her or him to repeat the anecdote in a staff meeting. It has been said that sunlight is the best disinfectant to deviousness.

Our discussion of sources of power, political tactics, and influence tactics should not imply an endorsement of all of these methods to gain an advantage in the workplace. Each strategy and tactic must be evaluated on its merit by an ethical test, such as those described in chapter 4. One guiding principle is to turn the strategy or tactic inward. Assume that you believe that a particular tactic (e.g., ingratiation) would be ethical in working against you. It would then be fair and ethical for you to use this tactic in attempting to influence others.

Another guiding principle is that it is generally ethical to use power and influence to help attain organizational goals. In contrast, it is generally unethical to use the same tactics to achieve a personal agenda and goals not sanctioned by the organization. Yet even this guideline involves enough "grayness" to be open for interpretation. Skill-Development Exercise 12-3 provides an opportunity to evaluate the ethics of behavior.

Recognize also that both the means and the ends of political behavior must be considered. A study of the subject cautioned, "Instead of determining whether human rights or standards of justice are violated, we are often content to judge political behavior according to its outcomes."[48] The authors of the study suggest that when it comes to the ethics of organizational politics, respect for justice and human rights should prevail for its own sake.

SKILL-DEVELOPMENT EXERCISE 2

The Ethics of Influence Tactics

You decide if the following manager made ethical use of influence tactics.

Sara is a marketing manager for a finance company that lends money to companies as well as individuals. She comes up with the idea of forming a division in the company that would collect delinquent student loans, strictly on commission. Her company would retain about one-third of the money collected. The clients would be banks having difficulty collecting loans after students graduate. Sara brings her idea to the CEO, and he grants her the opportunity to make a presentation about the new idea to top management within 1 month. The CEO states that he sees some merit in the idea, but that the opinion of the rest of the committee will be given considerable weight.

With 29 days to go before the meeting, Sara invites all five members of the executive committee to join her for lunch or breakfast individually. All five finally agree on a date for the lunch or breakfast meeting. During the meals, Sara makes a strong pitch for her idea, and explains that she will need the person's support to sell the idea to the rest of the committee. She also promises, "If you can help me get this collection division launched, you will have one big IOU to cash." Sara stays in touch with the CEO about the upcoming meeting, but does not mention her "preselling" lunches.

During the new-initiative review meeting, the five members of the committee support Sara's idea, and the CEO says that he is encouraged and will now warmly consider the idea of a student loan collection division.

QUESTIONS

1. Was Sara behaving ethically?

2. Which influence tactic did she use in attempting to achieve her goals?

IMPLICATIONS FOR MANAGERIAL PRACTICE

1. Recognize that a significant portion of the efforts of organizational members will be directed toward gaining power for themselves or their group. At times, some of this behavior will be directed more toward self-interest than organizational interest. It is therefore often necessary to ask, "Is this action being taken to help this person or is it being done to help the organization?" Your answer to this question should influence your willingness to submit to that person's demands.

2. If you want to establish a power base for yourself, a good starting point is to develop expert power. Most powerful people began their climb to power by demonstrating their

expertise in a particular area, such as being outstanding in sales or a niche within information technology. (This tactic is referred to as becoming a subject-matter expert.)

3. In determining if a particular behavior is motivated by political or merit considerations, evaluate the intent of the actor. The same action might be based on self-interest or concern for others. For instance, a team member might praise you because he believed that you accomplished something of merit. On the other hand, that same individual might praise you to attain a favorable work assignment or salary increase.

SUMMARY OF KEY POINTS

1. *Identify sources of power for individuals and subunits within organizations.* Power, politics, and influence are needed by managers to accomplish their work. In the model presented here, managers and professionals use organizational politics to achieve power and influence, thus attaining desired outcomes.

   Socialized power is used to forward organizational interests, whereas personalized power is used to forward personal interests. Power granted by the organization consists of legitimate power, coercive power, and reward power. Power stemming from the individual consists of expert power and referent power (the basis for charisma). According to the resource dependence perspective, subunits or individuals who can provide key resources to the organization accrue power. At times, gossip can be a power-giving source. Power can also be derived from meeting the group members' expectations of how a leader should behave (implicit leadership theory).

2. *Describe the essence of empowerment.* Managers must act in specific ways to empower employees, including removing conditions that keep employees powerless and giving information that enhances employee feelings of self-efficacy. Five critical conditions for empowerment are for an organization to share information with employees, provide them with structure, use teams to replace the traditional hierarchy, grant employees the freedom to determine how to achieve objectives, and trust employees. When the leader has too much power, team performance might decline.

3. *Pinpoint factors contributing to, and examples of, organizational politics.* Contributors to organizational politics include the political nature of organizations, the pyramid structure of organizations, encouragement of unwarranted accolades from subordinates, political behavior by senior management, less opportunity for vertical advancement, the need for power, and Machiavellianism.

   Among the ethical tactics of organizational politics are: developing power contacts; managing your impression; making your boss look good; keeping informed; being courteous, pleasant, and positive; asking satisfied customers to contact your manager; avoiding political blunders; and using sincere flattery. Among the unethical tactics are:

backstabbing, embracing-or-demolishing, stealing credit, playing territorial games, good-mouthing incompetents, and choosing a weak manager as an underling.

According to one analysis, women need to develop greater political skills because of barriers hampering their success. However, it can be argued that many women have exceptional political skills, such as relationship building. Recent research suggests that few gender differences exist in the area of political skill.

4. *Differentiate between the ethical and unethical use of power, politics, and influence.* Political behaviors chosen by an individual or organizational unit must rest on ethical considerations. A guiding principle is to use only those tactics you would consider fair and ethical if used against you. Also recognize that both the means and the ends of political behavior must be considered.

5. *Identify and describe a variety of influence tactics.* Influence tactics frequently used by managerial workers include: leadership by example; assertiveness; rationality; ingratiation; projecting warmth; exchange; inspirational appeal and emotional display; the use of joking and kidding; and strategic sexual performance.

6. *Explain how managers can control dysfunctional politics.* Approaches to controlling dysfunctional politics include relying on objective performance measures, meshing individual and organizational objectives, minimizing political behavior by top management, and implementing open communication, including threatening to discuss politicking publicly.

KEY TERMS AND PHRASES

power, p. 251
organizational politics, p. 251
political skill, p. 251
socialized power, p. 251
personalized power, p. 251
legitimate power, p. 251
coercive power, p. 252
reward power, p. 252

expert power, p. 252
referent power, p. 253
resource dependence perspective, p. 253
implicit leadership theory, p. 253
empowerment, p. 253
leader political support, p. 256
Machiavellianism, p. 257
territorial games, p. 261

ENDNOTES

1. Original story based on facts and observations in the following sources: Barney Wolf, "David Novak's Global Vision," *QSR* (www.qsrmagazine.com), May 2012, pp. 1–3; Kevin Kruse, "Leadership Secrets from Yum! Brands' CEO David Novak" (www.forbes.com), June 25, 2014, pp. 1–4; Geoff Colvin, "Great Job! Or How Yum Brands Uses Recognition to Build Teams and Get Results," *Fortune*, August 12, 2013, pp. 62–66; J. P. Donlin, "CEO of the Year David Novak: The Recognition Leader," *Chief Executive* (http://chiefexecutive.net), June 27, 2012, pp. 1–3.
2. Book review in *Personnel Psychology*, Summer 2002, p. 502.

3. Jerry Useem, "Power," *Fortune*, August 11, 2003, p. 58.

4. Daniel J. Brass and Marlene E. Burkhardt, "Potential Power and Power Use: An Integration of Structure and Behavior," *Academy of Management Journal*, June 1993, pp. 441–442.

5. Christian Ewen et al., ""Further Specification of the Leader Political Skill-Leadership Effectiveness Relationships: Transformational and Transactional Leader Behaviors as Moderators," *The Leadership Quarterly*, August 2013, p. 517.

6. Robert P. Vecchio, *Organizational Behavior: Core Concepts*, 4th ed. (Mason, OH: South-Western/Thomson Learning, 2000), p. 126.

7. Jeffrey Pfeffer, "You're Still the Same: Why Theories of Power Hold over Time and across Countries," *Academy of Management Perspectives*, November 2013, pp. 269–280.

8. Leonard H. Chusmir, "Personalized vs. Socialized Power Needs among Working Men and Women," *Human Relations*, February 1986, p. 149.

9. John R. P. French and Bertram Raven, "The Basis of Social Power," in Dorwin Cartwright and Alvin Zander, eds., *Group Dynamics: Research and Theory* (Evanston, IL: Row, Peterson and Company, 1962), pp. 607–623.

10. Lydia Depillis, "Rank-and-File Workers Have a Lot More Power over Corporations Than They Think," (www.washingtonpost.com), June 13, 2014, pp. 1–5.

11. Paul Mozur and Evelyn M. Rusli, "Google Executive Leaves for Startup," *The Wall Street Journal*, August 30, 2013, p. B3.

12. Jeffrey Pfeffer, *Managing with Power* (Boston: Harvard Business Review Publications, 1990), pp. 100–101.

13. Nancy B. Kurland and Lisa Hope Pelled, "Passing the Word: Toward a Model of Gossip and Power in the Workplace," *Academy of Management Review*, April 2000, p. 429.

14. Olga Epitropaki and Robin Martin, "Implicit Leadership Theories in Applied Settings: Factor Structure, Generalizability, and Stability Over Time," *Journal of Applied Psychology*, April 2004, pp. 293–310; Epitropaki and Martin, "From Ideal to Real: A Longitudinal Study of the Role of Implicit Leadership Theories on Leader-Member Exchanges and Employee Outcomes," *Journal of Applied Psychology*, July 2005, pp. 659–676.

15. Jay A. Conger and Rabindra N. Kanungo, "The Empowerment Process: Integrating Theory and Practice," *Academy of Management Review*, July 1988, pp. 473–474.

16. Craig L. Pearce, "The Future of Leadership: Combining Vertical and Shared Leadership to Transform Knowledge Work," *Academy of Management Executive*, February 2004, pp. 47–57.

17. Braley L. Kirkman, Benson Rosen, Paul E. Tesluk, and Cristina B. Gibson, "The Impact of Team Empowerment on Virtual Team Performance: The Moderating Role of Face-to-Face Interaction, *Academy of Management Journal*, April 2004, pp. 175–192.

18. W. Alan Randolph, "Navigating the Journey to Empowerment," *Organizational Dynamics*, Spring 1995, pp. 19–31.

19. Patricia Sellers, "eBay's Secret," *Fortune*, October 18, 2004, p. 161.

20. Leigh Plunkett Tost, Francesca Gino, and Richard P. Larrick, "When Power Makes Others Speechless: The Negative Impact of Leader Power on Team Performance," *Academy of Management Journal*, October 2013, pp. 1465–1486.

21. B. Parker Ellen III, Gerald R. Ferris, and M. Ronald Buckley, "Leader Political Support: Reconsidering Leader Political Behavior," *The Leadership Quarterly*, December 2013, pp. 842–857.

22. Marshall Goldsmith, "All of Us Are Stuck on Suck-Ups," *Fast Company*, December 2003, p. 117.

23. Chad Graham and Dawn Sagario, "'Good Fawning' Over Boss Can Help in Tough Times," *The Des Moines Register* syndicated story, April 20, 2003.

24. Stanley Bing, *What Would Machiavelli Do?* (New York: HarperCollins, 2000).

25. Ewen et al., "Further Specification of the Leader Political Skill-Leadership Effectiveness Relationships: Transformational and Transactional Leader Behaviors as Moderators," pp. 516–533.

26. Susan Ricker, "Manners Make for Good Business," CareerBuilder.com, April 13, 2014, p. 1; "Etiquette for the Young—with Bite," *The Associated Press*, June 8, 2002.

27. Cited in Susan Ricker, "Make Your Boss, Yourself Look Good," CareerBuilder.com, October 26, 2014, p. 1.
28. "'Career Insurance' Protects DP Professionals from Setbacks, Encourages Growth," *Data Management*, June 1986, p. 33. The same principle is equally valid today.
29. Quoted in Amy Joyce, "Schmoozing on the Job Pays Dividends," *The Washington Post*, November 13, 2005.
30. Suzette M. Chopin, Steven J. Danish, Anson Seers, and Joshua N. Hook, "Effects of Mentoring on the Development of Leadership Self-Efficacy and Political Skill," *Journal of Leadership Studies*, Issue 3, 2013, pp. 17–32.
31. "Face Cowardly Backstabbers in the Workplace," *Knight Ridder* story, February 13, 2000.
32. Jared Sandberg, "Some Bosses Never Meet a Success That Isn't Theirs," *The Wall Street Journal*, April 23, 2003, p. B1.
33. "Stopping Idea Thieves: Strike Back When Rivals Steal Credit," *Executive LeadershipExtra!*, April 2003, p. 3.
34. Annette Simmons, *Territorial Games: Understanding & Ending Turf Wars at Work* (New York: AMACOM, 1998).
35. Quoted in Jared Sandberg, "When Affixing Blame for Inept Managers, Go Over Their Heads," *The Wall Street Journal*, April 20, 2005, p. B1.
36. Jeffrey Zaslow, "The Politics of the 'CC' Line," *The Wall Street Journal*, May 28, 2003, p. D2.
37. Pamela L. Perrewé and Debra L. Nelson, "Gender and Career Success: The Facilitative Role of Political Skill," *Organizational Dynamics*, 4 (2004), p. 366.
38. "Women Leaders Study: The Qualities That Distinguish Women Leaders" (www.calipercorp.com/womenstudy/index.shtml).
39. Thomas S. Westbrook, James R. Veale, and Roger E. Karnes, "Multirater and Gender Differences in the Measurement of Political Skill In Organizations," *Journal of Leadership Studies*, Number 1, 2013, pp. 6–17.
40. Several of the tactics are from Gary Yukl and Cecilia M. Falbe, "Influence Tactics and Objectives in Upward, Downward, and Lateral Influence Attempts," *Journal of Applied Psychology*, April 1990, pp. 132–140. Part of the definitions of assertiveness and ingratiation stem from Perrewé and Nelson, "Gender and Career Success," pp. 372–373.
41. Research reported in Sue Shellenbarger, "Why Likability Matters More Than Ever at Work," *The Wall Street Journal*, March 26, 2014, p. D3.
42. Cecily D. Cooper, "Just Joking Around? Employee Humor Expression as Ingratiatory Behavior," *Academy of Management Review*, October 2005, pp. 765–776.
43. Amy J. C. Cuddy, Matthew Kohut, and John Neffinger, "Connect, Then Lead: To Exert Influence, You Must Balance Competence with Warmth," *Harvard Business Review*, July–August 2013, pp. 54–61.
44. Pfeffer, *Managing with Power*, p. 224.
45. Andrew J. DuBrin, "Sex Differences in the Use and Effectiveness of Tactics of Impression Management," *Psychological Reports*, 74 (1994), pp. 531–544.
46. Marla Baskerville Watkins, Alexis Nicole Smith, and Karl Aquino, "The Use and Consequences of Strategic Sexual Performances," *Academy of Management Perspective*, August 2013, pp. 173–186.
47. L. A. Witt, "Enhancing Organizational Goal Congruence: A Solution to Organizational Politics," *Journal of Applied Psychology*, August 1998, pp. 666–674.
48. Gerald F. Cavanagh, Dennis J. Moberg, and Manuel Velasquez, "The Ethics of Organizational Politics," *Academy of Management Review*, July 1981, p. 372.

KEY TERMS

coercive power Controlling others through fear or threat of punishment.
empowerment The process of sharing power with group members, thereby enhancing their feelings of self-efficacy.

expert power The ability to influence others because of one's specialized knowledge, skills, or abilities.

implicit leadership theory An explanation of leadership contending that group members develop prototypes specifying the traits and abilities that characterize an ideal business leader.

leader political support The concept refers to tactics of organizational politics and influence engaged in by leaders to provide followers with necessary resources to advance individual, group, or organizational objectives.

legitimate power Power based on one's formal position within the hierarchy of the organization.

Machiavellianism A tendency to manipulate others for personal gain.

organizational politics Informal approaches to gaining power through means other than merit or luck.

personalized power The use of power primarily for the sake of personal aggrandizement and gain.

political skill A combination of social astuteness with the capacity to adjust and adapt behavior to different situational demands.

power The potential or ability to influence decisions and control resources.

referent power The ability to influence others that stems from one's desirable traits and characteristics; it is the basis for charisma.

resource dependence perspective The need of the organization for a continuing flow of human resources, money, customers, technological inputs, and material to continue to function.

reward power Controlling others through rewards or the promise of rewards.

socialized power The use of power to achieve constructive ends.

territorial games Also known as turf wars, territorial games refer to behaviors involving the hoarding of information and other resources.

DISCUSSION QUESTIONS

1   Do the self-assessment about the positive organizational politics. Do the results surprise you? Explain your position on workplace politics and discuss what behavioral changes you would consider making.

2   Even though DuBrin's article on office politics isn't specifically related to criminal justice, do you see any overlap between the author's piece and criminal justice organizations? What is it about office politics that spans professions?

TRANSFORMING ENVIRONMENTS

LEADERSHIP DEVELOPMENT

PAULA BROUGH, JENNIFER M. BROWN, AND AMANDA BIGGS

INTRODUCTION

[L]eadership has a profound capacity to shape the culture of an organisation, impacting on employees' well-being and performance, role-modelling appropriate behaviours, and influencing the quality of the service provided by the organisation. Although earlier perspectives considered leadership ability to be innate, most contemporary perspectives consider that effective leadership can be developed, contingent upon appropriate learning opportunities and supportive organisational culture and policies. An ongoing challenge for criminal justice organisations is to support leadership development at all levels throughout the organisation. This chapter will discuss the need for leadership development in criminal justice organisations, in addition to common challenges and barriers to developing effective leaders in these organisational contexts. We then discuss a best-practice approach to conducting leadership development programmes. Finally, the chapter will conclude with an example of a successful leadership development programme conducted in an Australian police service. ... [T]his chapter examines in detail the key issues for the development of effective leaders in criminal justice workplaces.

LEADERSHIP DEVELOPMENT IN CRIMINAL JUSTICE ORGANISATIONS

[I]t is increasingly recognised that in order for criminal justice organisations to provide a high quality of service and successfully meet emerging challenges, a change in culture and practice is required. In order to navigate these changes, strong leadership and management are simultaneously needed. The practice of selecting and developing leaders and managers in criminal justice organisations has been subjected to much criticism, debate, and attempted reform, particularly within police services (Winsor, 2012). Two primary areas of concern will be discussed: (a) strategic investment in leadership development programmes; and (b) alignment of leadership development with Human Resource Management (HRM) strategies, such as talent management and succession planning.

LEADERSHIP DEVELOPMENT PROGRAMMES

There is ample evidence to demonstrate that leadership development programmes successfully improve leadership capabilities of individuals, teams, and organisations (Kelloway and Barling, 2010); stimulate organisational culture change; improve the well-being and motivation of followers; and strengthen the organisation's strategic direction (Biggs *et al.*, 2014a, 2014b, 2014c). Bass (1990), for example, discussed an experiment conducted in prison industrial shops, in which shop supervisors worked with groups of prisoners to produce products for sale outside the prison. Supervisors were allocated to four conditions: (a) transformational training and pre- and post-surveys; (b) transactional training and pre- and post-surveys; (c) pre- and post-surveys only; and (d) post-surveys only (this 'quasi-experimental' research design was discussed in detail in Chapter 7). Bass reported that the performance of both trained groups improved, although the transformational leadership group reported the greatest improvement in productivity, absenteeism, and citizenship behaviours amongst prisoners, and won more respect from prisoners.

Despite the promising effects of leadership development on an array of outcomes, organisations typically fail to commit adequate resources to develop organisational leadership as part of their business strategy (Leskiw and Singh, 2007). According to Bass (1990, p. 25) 'many executives still feel that leadership is like the weather – something to talk about, but about which not much can be done.' This trend is also reflected within criminal justice organisations, where relatively few leadership development programmes exist and barriers to instigating such programmes are common.

First, resourcing for frontline services and mandatory training tends to be prioritised over non-essential training, including leadership development programmes (Stojkovic *et al.*, 2012). For instance, Stojkovic *et al.* (2012) discussed a successful leadership development programme conducted for approximately ten years in a US Corrective Service agency, which was ultimately removed due to cost-cutting measures, rather than issues with quality. The programme in question 'was viewed as a luxury that could be ended when compared to other pressing needs facing the department' (Stojkovic *et al.*, 2012, p. 190). When resources are limited, there is strong pressure on administrators to commit those resources to frontline operations and withdraw from areas such as training. Focus groups conducted with criminal justice employees reflected this sentiment: participants consistently repeated the theme that levels of management and administration within the organisation need to be streamlined in order to commit more human and economic resources to frontline operations (Biggs, 2011).

Second, existing leadership development programmes emphasise managerial skills, with insufficient focus on leadership (Stojkovic *et al.*, 2008; Winsor, 2012). Effective leadership is linked with the ability to: combine authentic transformational and … [C]ontingent reward (transactional) leadership; role-model competent and ethical practices; encourage participation in decision-making; and adapt styles to suit the context (Campbell and Kodz, 2011). It has been recommended that contemporary understandings of leadership effectiveness need to be embraced in leadership development programmes: for example, the UK Police Leadership Development Board have endorsed the need to integrate transformational leadership within learning and development training (Dobby *et al.*, 2004).

Third, a greater focus on ethical behaviour is needed in criminal justice leadership development programmes. … [R]ecent research has demonstrated the importance of authentic and ethical practice amongst leaders (Burgess and Hawkes, 2013; Hannah *et al.*, 2011). Research in criminal justice settings has also emphasised the importance of leaders role-modelling competent and ethical behaviours to set the standard of behaviour required in their subordinates (Neyroud, 2011).

Finally, leadership development programmes need to be supported by the organisation's culture and infrastructure (Leskiw and Singh, 2007). Several aspects of the organisational culture, structure, and policies in criminal justice organisations that represent significant barriers for leadership development, particularly for authentic, transformational leadership, were discussed. These included the existence of strong organisational cultures that are resistant to change, which is problematic as leadership development requires a degree of organisational change in order to support new styles of leadership.

ALIGNING LEADERSHIP DEVELOPMENT WITH HRM STRATEGIES

It is not sufficient to conduct leadership development training programmes; they also need to be aligned with HRM strategies, such as systems that assess leadership capabilities and identify development opportunities for employees at all levels, succession planning, and performance management and promotion processes (Dobby *et al.*, 2004; Neyroud, 2011). Leadership development programmes tend to be reserved for executive leaders located at the top of the organisation's hierarchy, despite the recognised necessity of building leadership capacity at multiple levels throughout the organisation (Bass, 1990; Neyroud, 2011). This is especially relevant for criminal justice employees, such as police officers and correctional officers, who are responsible for managing and/or leading members of the public and using authority to command situations, regardless of their organisational level (Neyroud, 2011; Stojkovic et al., 2012). The challenge for criminal justice organisations, therefore, is to develop the leadership capacity of the entire organisation, rather than focusing on the development of a small number of senior leaders (Neyroud, 2011).

Developing leaders at lower levels of the organisation is also important for succession planning (Leskiw and Singh, 2007; Stojkovic et al., 2012). Leskiw and Singh (2007, p. 449) noted 'best-practice organizations do not necessarily select the same level, position, or type of employee as the target of leadership development,' and emphasised the need to connect succession planning and leadership development to identify and prepare future leaders. This is particularly important, as leadership development in criminal justice organisations tends to be undermined by the high level of change amongst managers and leaders. This is due to turnover, transfers, and a substantial proportion of employees acting in managerial roles for shorter periods of time. The latter is particularly problematic if employees acting in leadership roles are excluded from development opportunities.

An additional point supporting leadership development throughout the organisational hierarchy is research revealing that the effectiveness of leadership development programmes targeting lower-, middle-, and higher-level managers is greater for those programmes aimed at lower leadership levels (Avolio et al., 2009). This is likely due to the greater interaction between followers and their immediate supervisors: this effect further reinforces the need to conduct leadership development at multiple levels in hierarchical organisations. In fact, we recommend a top-down approach, in which senior leaders undergo development first, followed by leaders at lower levels of the organisation's hierarchy. This approach was successfully conducted in an Australian police service (Biggs et al., 2014a; Brough et al., 2012).

Finally, in order to develop leadership and management capability within criminal justice organisations, it may be necessary to modify recruitment, selection, and promotion systems to enable multiple entry points to senior leadership positions (Winsor, 2012). The traditional practice of appointing senior leaders based on experience within the organisation, rather than leadership capability, is still widespread (Stojkovic et al., 2008; Villiers, 2009). However, it has long been evident that such an approach is limited and alternate strategies are needed (Winsor, 2012). A review commissioned by the Home Department (Winsor, 2012), investigating UK police remuneration and conditions, recommended multiple-point entry into senior police leadership in order to:

- expand the pool of future potential leaders;
- diversify the skills and experience of senior leaders, enriching leadership;
- implement positive cultural change; and
- address the under-representation of women and minority group officers in senior ranks.

Drawing on several sources, the Winsor (2012) review also acknowledged several difficulties with multiple-point entry to senior leadership positions:

- Effective leaders in other organisational contexts may not be effective police leaders.

- Effective police management and leadership requires expertise in operational decision-making, which is difficult to attain without on-the-job experience.

- Appointment to senior leadership positions, without frontline experience, may result in a lack credibility and respect from subordinates.

- The authority of leaders may be undermined if they are perceived to have been promoted for diversity reasons rather than on the basis of merit.

Another review, also conducted within the UK police (Neyroud, 2011), acknowledged that despite recommendations for multiple-point entry to senior leadership, there is continuing and overwhelming resistance against the idea. This sentiment was also observed by Biggs (2011) in a sample of correctional officers:

- Generally, there tends to be lower acceptance of senior leaders who did not achieve their position through the culturally accepted route of internal promotion through the ranks.

- Such leaders tend to be viewed as 'out of touch' due to perceptions that they have had no direct experience with frontline operations, have no idea about the issues faced by employees at 'the coal face' of the organisation, and are, therefore, incapable of making effective decisions about how the service is run.

- Finally, these leaders also tend to be perceived as 'career public servants' with little vested interest in the department itself, who wish to initiate unnecessary changes and programmes purely to boost their CV.

Despite acknowledging this resistance, Winsor (2012) still recommended multiple-point entry as a means to progress leadership development, noting 'I do not accept that every officer must start as a constable and work his way through every rank before reaching the highest ranks' (p. 20). To minimise resistance, he recommended that: leadership development programmes include a balance between internal and external recruits; development programmes and advancement opportunities be better aligned; and all external entrants join as constables to attain some experience in the rank prior to promotion:

> This does not need to be a lengthy process, but officers do need experience of what it means to be on the streets. They should have used the powers of a constable, and understand how serious it is to make a decision to arrest a suspect, subject an unwilling person to a search, and to use reasonable force. They should have faced danger.
>
> (Winsor, 2012, p. 147)

SUMMARY

This chapter discussed just a few of the challenges for developing leaders in criminal justice organisations. However, to ensure the future success of these organisations, it is critical to overcome these barriers, particularly the idea that leadership development is a non-essential function. As noted by Leskiw and Singh (2007), organisations committed to fostering effective leadership development and adopting strategic plans to align leadership development with HRM strategies will more effectively address emerging challenges. Failing to adequately develop leadership capabilities throughout the hierarchies within criminal justice organisations has an adverse effect on every aspect of organisational functioning, including the capacity to perform frontline duties adequately (Stojkovic et al., 2012). Inadequate resourcing and focus on leadership development results in 'the quality of leader who will make decisions that do not reflect the best possible practices; communities will ultimately suffer and waste an enormous number of resources' (Stojkovic et al., 2012, p. 190).

REFERENCES

Avolio, B. J., Richard, R. J., Hannah, S. T., Walumbwa, F. O., and Chan, A. (2009) A meta-analytic review of leadership impact research: experimental and quasi-experimental studies. *The Leadership Quarterly*, 20: 764–784. doi:10.1016/j.leaqua.2009.06.006.

Bass, B.M. (1990) From transactional to transformational leadership: learning to share the vision. *Organizational Dynamics*, 18(3): 19–31. doi:10.1016/0090-2616(90)90061-S.

Biggs, A. (2011) *A longitudinal evaluation of strain, work engagement, and intervention strategies to address the health of high-risk employees.* Doctoral Thesis, Griffith University, Brisbane.

Biggs, A., Brough, P., and Barbour, J. P. (2014a) Enhancing work-related attitudes and work engagement: a quasi-experimental study of the impact of a leadership development intervention. *International Journal of Stress Management*, 21(1): 43–68. doi:10.1037/a0034508.

Biggs, A., Brough, P., and Barbour, J. P. (2014b) Relationships of individual and organizational support with engagement: examining various types of causality in a three-wave study. *Work and Stress*, 28(3): 236–254. doi:10.1080/02678373.2014.934316.

Biggs, A., Brough, P., and Barbour, J. P. (2014c) Strategic alignment with organizational priorities and work engagement: a multi-wave analysis. *Journal of Organizational Behavior*, 35(3): 301–317. doi:10.1002/job.1866.

Brough, P., Biggs, A., and Barbour, J. P. (2012) *Healthy Workplace Project: final report.* Brisbane: Griffith University.

Burgess, M., and Hawkes, A. (2013) *Authentic leadership and affective, normative and continuance commitment: the mediating effects of trust in leadership and caring ethical climate.* Paper presented at the Proceedings of the 10th Industrial and Organisational Psychology Conference, Perth.

Campbell, I., and Kodz, J. (2011) *What makes great police leadership? What research can tell us about the effectiveness of different leadership styles, competencies and behaviours: A rapid evidence review.* London: National Policing Improvement Agency.

Dobby, J., Anscombe, J., and Tuffin, R. (2004) *Police leadership: exectations and impact.* London: Research, Development and Statistics Directorate, Home Office.

Hannah, S.T., Walumbwa, F.O., and Fry, L.W. (2011) Leadership in action teams: team leader and members' authenticity, authenticity strength, and team outcomes. *Personnel Psychology*, 64: 771–802. doi:10.1111/j.1744–6570.2011.01225.x.

Kelloway, E. K., and Barling, J. (2010) Leadership development as an intervention in occupational health psychology. *Work and Stress*, 24(3): 260–279. doi:10.1080/02678373.2010.518441.

Leskiw, S., and Singh, P. (2007) Leadership development: learning from best practices. *Leadership and Organization Development Journal*, 28(5): 444–464. doi:http://dx.doi.org/10.1108/01437730710761742.

Neyroud, P. (2011) *Review of police leadership and training*. London: Home Office.

Pollard, F. (2010) *Leadership development program*. Brisbane.

Stojkovic, S., Kalinich, D., and Klofas, J. (2008) *Criminal justice: administration and management*, 4th edn. Belmont, CA: Thompson Wadsworth.

Stojkovic, S., Kalinich, D., and Klofas, J. (2012) *Criminal justice organizations: administration and management*, 5th edn. Belmont, CA: Wadsworth.

Villiers, P. (2009) *Police and policing: an introduction*. Hook, UK: Waterside Press.

Walumbwa, F.O., and Wernsing, T. (2012) From transactional and transformational leadership to authentic leadership. In Rumsey, M.G. (ed.) *The Oxford handbook of leadership*. New York: Oxford University Press. doi:10.1093/oxfordhb/9780195398793.013.0023.

Winsor, T.P. (2012) *Independent review of police officer and staff remuneration and conditions*. London: HMSO.

DISCUSSION QUESTIONS

1   Throughout the article the authors distinguish between management and leadership. Consult a few outside sources and list three differences between management and leadership. Thinking about your own professional experience, have you worked for a stronger manager who was a weak leader or vice versa? If you had to choose which type of supervisor to work for, which would it be and why?

2   The authors cite Winsor (2012), who argues that criminal justice organizations need to be open to multiple-point entry into senior police leadership positions and not rely solely on workers climbing up the ranks. What makes criminal justice organizations resistant to the idea of multiple-point entry? Is frontline experience the most important quality to be a successful leader? Why or why not?

SECTION VI CONCLUSION

We have learned about the nuances and challenges associated with office power, politics, and influence. These workplace realities, when mismanaged, can lead to a level of dysfunction that can bring down a leader and do lasting harm to an organization. Leaders need to be particularly skilled, attentive, and ethical about power and politics.

Competent leadership is a rare skill. According to Steve Tobak (2014), management consultant and contributor to *Entrepreneur Magazine*, it demands "courage, strength, and discipline." He explains that as social beings, we are inclined to be followers, not leaders. To break out of this natural tendency requires determination and fearlessness. Clearly these qualities are important, but a leader needs hands-on skills too. This is precisely the reason that organizations need to invest in their leaders through training and development.

Brough et al. persuasively argue that research supports the notion that leadership development programs improve the leadership competencies of individuals and work teams. Seeing that leadership is a consistent theme in all of the readings and how organizations prosper or languish depending upon the talent and skills of their leaders, one thing is undeniably clear: an investment in leadership development is an investment in success.

REFERENCES

Finney, Caitlin, Stergiopoulos, Erene, Hensel, Jennifer, Bonato, Sarah, and Dewa, Carolyn S. 2013. "Organizational Stressors Associated with Job Stress and Burnout in Correctional Officers: A Systematic Review" *BMC Public Health*, 13: 82.

Forst, Brian. 2014. "Legitimacy." http://www.oxfordbibliographies.com/view/document/obo-9780195396607/obo-9780195396607-0134.xml. Retrieved March 23, 2018.

Hlupic, Vlatka. 2014. "The Management Shift: How to Harness the Power of People and Transform Your Organization for Sustainable Success," London: Palgrave Macmillan.

Lehane, Christopher, Fabiani, Mark, and Guttentag, Bill. 2012. *Masters of Disaster: The Ten Commandments of Damage Control*. New York: St. Martin's Press.

Mankins, Michael, and Steele, Richard 2006. "Stop Making Plans; Start Making Decisions." *Harvard Business Review (January)*. https://hbr.org/2006/01/stop-making-plans-start-making-decisions. Retrieved April 12, 2018.

Reference.com. n.d. "How Much Time Does a Person Spend at Work during His Lifetime." https://www.reference.com/world-view/much-time-person-spend-work-during-his-lifetime-57a76289b54a4ea8. Retrieved June 14, 2018.

Rettig, Tim. 2017. "What Is the Relationship between Socialization and Culture?" https://www.quora.com/What-is-the-relationship-between-socialization-and-culture. Retrieved March 29, 2018.

Tobak, Steve. 2014. "Why True Leaders Are So Rare." *Entrepreneur*. https://www.entrepreneur.com/article/239464. Retrieved April 9, 2018.

CPSIA information can be obtained
at www.ICGtesting.com
Printed in the USA
BVHW081536170720
583818BV00002B/121

9 781516 529926